TO THE LENGTHS OF GOD

To the Lengths of God

TRUTHS AND THE ECUMENICAL AGE

B. R. Brinkman, S.J.

Sheed & Ward

London

ISBN 0–7220–9180–X

Published in Great Britain in 1988 by
Sheed & Ward Limited,
2, Creechurch Lane,
London, EC3A 5AQ

Book production Bill Ireson

Filmset by Waveney Typesetters, Norwich, Norfolk
Printed and bound by Biddles Limited, Guildford, Surrey

Contents

Chapter		Page
	PREFACE	ix
	ACKNOWLEDGEMENT	xv
ONE	Why a Hierarchy of Truths?	1
	Council and Church	3
	'Foundation' and Method	7
	Faith, Love and Order	11
	Existential and Situational	21
	A Genuine Christian Fit	27
	Staying in the Truth	32
	A New Sense of Proportion	37
	And Openness	42
TWO	Suffering and the Creator God	45
	Knowing Evil and Knowing Suffering	46
	Experience and Suffering	59
	Two Figures	69
	That Darkness can Become Light	75
	On the Continuing Scandal	82
THREE	Christ Relevant	87
	Relevance	87
	Our Seasons and Our Project of Self	93
	Grace's Form and Finality	96
	And the World's Seasons	98
	Christ and Modern Docetism	102
	He Was Thus and Thus	104
	His Humanness for Us	110

Chapter		Page
	Like Seeks After Like	115
	Healer Against Anxiety	119
	God in the Anxious Life	127
FOUR	The Cross in Question	131
	The Cross is Primordial Now	135
	The God-shaped Picture	139
	The Live Trinity	145
	Pathos and Consummation	149
	An Existential Way	151
	Comprehensibility	153
	The Cross and Healing Reason	156
	Open-endedness and the Trinity	159
FIVE	Sacramental Intimacy, the Hinge of Salvation	164
	Time and Times	165
	The 'Great Time' and Now	172
	Body and Space	176
	The Consummative Mode	179
	Potent Mediation	186
	Caro Salutis est Cardo	191
SIX	Sacramental Interiorization, the 'Yes' to Communion	193
	The Process	193
	Negativity and Beyond	198
	Binary Opposition	201
	The Relational Setting	205
	Vital Feeling	207
	The Right Régime	212
	Night and Day, Alive	215
SEVEN	Without 'Justification'	219
	In the Ecumenical Context	220
	The Original Certitude	227
	Anthropology Comes In	234
	Fortress Trent	243

Chapter   *Page*

    The Lutheran Blow   255
    A New Horizon   261
    Involvement Beyond   265
    Convergence   270

    NOTES   281

    THEMATIC INDEX   325

    INDEX OF NAMES   329

Preface

The title of this book has fallen out from the things I have tried to say. The writing has not followed the title. The reason lies in the working life of a theologian who also has to be a teacher. The day's programme of work comes to be punctuated, at times overshadowed, by the promise made to give an occasional lecture, to contribute an article to a journal. If the topic of the lecture or of the article is central to one's thinking, then giving the lecture or publishing the article is far from being the end of the matter. When the performance is over and the offprints scanned, the topic soon sprouts an after-life which will not let the begetter alone.

For my part I then come to see better what I have left out, and how I may have distorted the perspective I intended. I become more sensitive about what 'they' should rather have heard or have read. The actuality of the topic renews itself. Personal investment in it becomes more committed. So does the urge to try again.

The Fathers of the Church show us how a surface question, a growing Church movement, or a passionately controverted question may soon enough provoke a writer into genuine talk about God himself. If the talk about God is genuine, then the talk about ourselves has a chance too. The side of the Fathers that bordered on journalism did not obscure the theological challenge. That is especially true of Augustine of Hippo, whom the reader will soon sense is one of my masters. But journalism or no, the passion rises, and the talk goes out to God, the God who can go so far as to be with men just as they are.

That is why there is a chapter in this book, 'Christ Relevant'. It tries to speak of Christ for all seasons, risking imparticularity and its scandal. Yet Christ must be of this season. Again we risk scandal, that of particularity. Hence the reader will find me anti-rationalist, but looking for a reason. He will find me unsystematic, but seeking system. A system with a variable geometry. For there is only one created invariable, the Christ who is God. Only God is the constant outside seasons and ages. We cannot put ourselves outside the variability.

Thus it is a re-reading of my text which has prompted the present title. As may be suspected, it is in any case a borrowed plume. It belongs to Christopher Fry's lines which once heralded the purpose and set perspective of the now very sadly missed John A. T. Robinson's *Exploration into God* (1967). The verses are apt not merely for the single pilgrim's journeying into God, but for the pilgrim Church's exploration. The lines touch both our books:

> The human heart can go to the lengths of God,
> Dark and cold we may be, but this
> Is no winter now. The frozen misery
> Of centuries breaks, cracks, begins to move;
> The thunder is the thunder of the floes,
> The thaw, the flood, the upstart Spring.
> Thank God our time is now when wrong
> Comes up to face us everywhere,
> Never to leave us till we take
> The longest stride of soul men ever took,
> Affairs are now soul size.
> The enterprise
> Is exploration into God.
>   (Christopher Fry, *A Sleep of Prisoners*)

We cannot aim to speak of God without being touched by the season's relativities. We cannot aim to speak of the busy, empirical Church without some awareness that we are trying to tread and explore 'the lengths of God'. It is an old idea that the Church knows winters and springs. Two factors now seem to make formulations and declarations more relative than in other ages, at other seasons. The first is our sluggard reponse to the real imperatives of ecumenism which themselves lie under the absolute imperative of the end-time (Jn 4: 21). The second factor finds perhaps a less clear expression in my text, but in my mind it overshadows the second chapter, 'Suffering and the Creator God'. The religious implications of anxiety in the nuclear age come high in our apprehension of how God deals with man.

But relativities demand focus. A hierarchy of truths calls for a sense of proportion, the beginning of focus. So from the topic of creation focused on suffering, we pass to a consideration, yet again, of the identity of Christ, now focused on sexuality. Then, if we ask what happened to him, we have to focus upon the very godforsakenness. As if in recoil we then close up and in upon ourselves. The cracks in the 'frozen misery' are warmed by sacramental intimacy, by a holy imagination that interiorizes. But I am haunted in the first and last chapters by the need for a thoroughly open-ended ecumenical appeal. When will 'the flood' come? It can only be out of the history of divided experience. So I suggest we must try and learn the real lesson from that old war-horse, justification. The issues are at bottom anthropological. They must be opened up and clarified. This the ecumenics of the common ground will never do.

So I have tried to keep close to experience. Human religious experience is one of unsurpassable complexity. It is confused still, it is tragic. There is no meeting it with logic or abstraction. So I have tried to avoid religious and theological banalities. With Jüngel I think that the basic question about God is 'Where?' As a corollary I think the question about man is 'How?' The question 'What?' can hardly be asked or answered. If it should be thought that I have strayed from theology into spirituality or some form of existential concern, then I can only be glad. With the Church Fathers I see no reason to acknowledge any formal limits or boundaries.

Three of the chapters here published are entirely new. 'Why a Hierarchy of Truths?' (Chapter One) is a much extended and fresh replacement for a previous, impatient exclamation, 'Isn't there a Hierarchy of Truths?' (Part I, II, *The Month*, July 1980, August 1980, pp. 234–40; 267–74). 'Suffering and the Creator God' (Chapter Two) is based upon a paper delivered before the International Academy of Religious Sciences (Brussels) at its Session at Princeton, New Jersey in March–April, 1982. In 'Christ Relevant' (Chapter Three) I have reworked material from *The Clergy Review* and *The Way* ('The Relevant Christ' — review essay — appeared in *The Clergy Review*, LVIII (1973), pp. 598–610). 'The Man for All Seasons'; 'The Humanity of Christ I, Christ and Sexuality'; 'The Humanity of Christ II, Christ and Anxiety'

appeared in *The Way* and have also been drawn upon, cf. vol.
14 (1974), pp. 129–40; vol. 15 (1975), pp. 209–24; vol. 16
(1976), pp. 136–45. 'The Cross in Question' (Chapter Four is
a revision and expansion of two articles with the same title in
The Clergy Review, LX (1975), pp. 277–93; pp. 428–43).
Chapters Five and Six form two excerpts from a series of five
substantial articles published under the title 'On Sacramental
Man' in *The Heythrop Journal* (cf. my 'On Sacramental Man
II, The Way of Intimacy'; 'On Sacramental Man IV, The
Way of Interiorization', XIV (1973), pp. 5–34 and pp. 280–
306).

I am most obliged and grateful to the respective editors of
these journals for their kind permission to use these
materials. It is also a great pleasure to mention the interest
and kindness of Diogenes Allen, Stuart Professor of
Philosophy at Princeton Theological Seminary, for his most
helpful criticisms and suggestions in connexion with Chapter
Two. He has also made available for me some of his own
writings on the subject of Suffering and Theodicy. I only
wish I could live up to the inspiration afforded by his
correspondence and generous help.

Within my College I must offer most cordial thanks to the
Head of the Department of Doctrine, Dr Francis Laishley,
who has given me much personal encouragement, and who
has, I suspect, shielded me from more academic vexations
than I know. I have been privileged to see notes taken at
lectures I once gave under the title, 'On Sacramental Man'.
These were made by my sociologist friend and one-time
colleague, Dr Ralph Tanner. I owe him belated thanks, and
appreciate that there must be traces of his observations in
Chapters Five and Six. Dr Elizabeth Lord must also be
thanked for her generous help and much needed criticisms. I
am indebted to the College Librarian, Mr Michael Walsh,
who with his staff has been most helpful and forbearing.

My gratitude also goes out to Tracy Redfearn of this
College for her help and initiative with proofs. To Miss
Elfriede Isler, assistant to my late and very good friend, Dr
Oscar Forel, I owe thanks for permission to reproduce a
Synchromie on the cover of this volume. As a welcoming
hostess for over sixteen years, she will understand this
memorial gesture to a great friend, in whose private library

overlooking the Lake of Geneva, many a discussion has helped this theologian, always in need of yet another view of what it is to be human.

B. R. Brinkman, S.J.
Heythrop College
(University of London)

Acknowledgement

The author and publishers are grateful to Oxford University Press for their permission to quote the passage from Christopher Fry's *A Sleep of Prisoners* on page x.

CHAPTER ONE

Why a Hierarchy of Truths?

Soon after Vatican II published its Decree on Ecumenism there was no need to ask this question. Once the hierarchy of truths was mentioned, it seemed obvious that in some way or other it had always been there, if unrecognized. The Council text does make a concession to doubters. It prints the term in inverted commas, as though to say 'there is something here we have known all along, but we admit that the expression of it is novel, so we will call it the "hierarchy of truths" '. In some ears no doubt the term does still sound new-fangled.

Let us put the point in better perspective. In practice it was never doubted that, if a baptism were urgent, then anyone might perform the rite. The sacrament was more important, ritual correctness less so. But would the same hold good for a doctrinal preference? Could one take precedence over another? Were not both equal, because equally true? You could not find a truer doctrine than a true doctrine. Are not all revealed truths to be accepted as revealed and therefore demanding the same assent of faith? If, particularly in the Roman system, we say 'Yes', then we appear to leave ourselves no room for ecumenical manoeuvre. If we say 'No', do we not place ourselves in opposition to a revealed religion?

Of course some doctrines might be more relevant than others to our daily living. Or doctrines could be so related among themselves, that some were at a centre of belief and others further out on a periphery.[1] Or again could not doctrines have, as it were, a life of their own, being sometimes at the centre and sometimes away from it? Doctrines must have to do with the future as well as the past.

It would be an understatement to say that we need bigger maps. Indeed we do. Maps from life rather than from Church authority. It is our job to read the map anyway. Too often we have to read it under a 'safety first' motto. Now above all the map must show an inter-Church projection. It must show a widespread hunger for the Word of God, a curiosity to get behind Church façades and boundaries.

Monolithic Church-thinking is cracking, has cracked. Cracks mean gaps, spaces to be filled according as the Spirit calls. There are the charisms in today's Church, and through them the Spirit builds it up. Often the charisms are graces of witness ensuring that the Church is not merely a safe, ritualized, social institution. The cracks, the gaps, the charisms make possible the presence of Christ, the prophet in his Church.

Let us say there are two clear poles of tension. On one side the Church of stability, order and homogeneous even centralized authority. In this perspective obedience, correctness, and service to the *magisterium* must prevail. There is no need to mention the ecclesiastical fate of Küng or Schillebeeckx, or the selection of Rome-minded bishops for the Church in the Netherlands, or even the subsidence of a great moral and religious force once generated by the National Pastoral Congress of Liverpool (1980).[2]

On the other side it is the same Church, feeling that this is a moment of history, which concentrates upon the discovery or re-discovery of its own identity. There are enough forms on offer, from basic communities to the close-structured organization, with unwonted jurisdictional autonomy, like Opus Dei. Authority or liberty. Both find a way of self-discovery in the cracks.

A lurch is given now one way, now another. The Constitution on the Church and the Modern World contained a most serious word on liberty within the Church:

> By no human law can the personal dignity and liberty of man be so aptly safeguarded as by the gospel of Christ which has been entrusted to the Church. For this gospel announces and proclaims the liberty of the sons of God, and repudiates all the bondage which results from sin. The gospel honours as sacred the dignity of conscience and its freedom of choice, unceasingly advises that all human talents be made fruitful in the service of God and the welfare of man, and finally commends all to the charity of all. That corresponds to the fundamental law of the Christian economy (*Gaudium et Spes*, no. 41).

A different lurch is given by the enormous mass success of Pope John Paul II. He holds mass crowds, earns the respect of mass media. Yet such a situation of undoubted strength conceals a weakness, one that may even increase the gaps we have spoken of. On his way to Rome for his non-trial by the ex-Holy Office the suffering Schillebeeckx said: 'People need a father figure. Of any kind. For the moment the Pope provides it. But when the masses "adore" a Pope, this means that the masses themselves are scattered. And so there are big problems over and above the Wojtyla papacy.'[3] One such problem is that of the polarization of Church opinion. So long as conservative opinion holds fast to the idea that, as all truths are intellectually and logically true, then they must all have an equal religious value, the polarization of opinion is an inevitable result. It is always the easiest way out of confusion, if you absolutize on an all or nothing principle.

But truths relate to *something*, and religious truths are professed by *somebody*.[4] That *something* in the case of religious truths is a relational *something*. The reason is that in being religious, somebody is highly interested, and may be struggling to reconcile the certainty of what he or she believes with its inevitable obscurity. In the lived experience of the Christian faith the obscurity is helped not so much by evidence, as by order and context. Recite the Creed, say the Lord's Prayer and there is a certain order even logic in the contents. Then comes an awareness that the Christian truths, besides being in one way related to you, the believer, are in another way related among themselves. Even the Church has had to learn and to discover those relationships, sometimes through its own unfolding history. It is not merely the order that a master teacher imposes on his materials so that they can be learned more easily. It is an order in what we have come to call salvation history, an order in history, logic and reality. That is why we always need bigger maps.

COUNCIL AND CHURCH

We may start with some remarks about the context of what the Council said about the hierarchy of truths. The reason why it said anything was ecumenical. But there are more reasons than that for saying the Council was right. Still, rifts and heresies call for discrimination, a *Yes* here and a *No* there.

And as to what is genuinely Christian, even partially so, it will not be contrary to anything that genuinely belongs to the faith.[5] So to discriminate we must perceive a scale of some kind, a hierarchy, and 'in faith' try to see what lies behind it.

The most positive factor about ecumenism is that it is an option somehow for the Church. Consequently when we accept that there are differences, perhaps grades, and an order or hierarchy between truths, we give expression to our option for the Church. The Council does not forget this. It speaks of a difference between the 'formulations' of Church teaching, and the 'deposit of faith' (n. 6). Then the Council turns from theory to practice and lays down two principles on an ever-burning practical question, that of the famous joint celebration in worship, *communicatio in sacris*. Yet in themselves the principles are not so much practical or liturgical as simply doctrinal. *First*, unity in worship should be a witness to existing unity in church adhesion. That is clearly a consideration on the corporate or public level. *Secondly*, in the sphere of the individual's life before God, the sacraments involve a 'sharing in the means of grace'. The first principle is at bottom a declaration about the worshipping community or communities as such. The second, though it has corporate implications, is obviously meant to apply to the individual with his need for and growth in God's life of grace. In fact the text as it stands allows for a clash between the welfare of the community and that of the individual. May not the community's present condition and needs be at variance with those of the individual? So the Council does not leave things just like that. It adds a negative on the community scale, while not omitting an exception in favour of the individual. 'Witness to the unity of the Church very generally forbids common worship to Christians, but the grace to be had from it *sometimes commends this practice*' (n. 8, author's italics). Thus in a practical dilemma it may be the individual's salvationary need that may prevail. Who then will in practice decide? It will be 'episcopal authority'; and the Council then gives some hints to this authority.

Next, our way of putting the Catholic faith should never become an obstacle to dialogue with the brethren. Does that imply that we may weaken the content of the faith? No, that is impossible. What then? Surely, a *common study* of doctrine between Christians remains possible. That is the passport to genuine ecumenical dialogue. It is at that point that the Council formulates its apparently new principle: 'When comparing doctrines with one another they should remember that in Catholic doctrine there is an order or "hierarchy" (*ordinem seu "hierarchiam"*) of truths, since they vary in their relation to the foundation of Christian faith' (*cum fundamento fidei christianae*, n. 11). By that formulation the Council passes from the practical dilemma about worship in common to the more general dilemma within dialogue itself. The answer it comes up with remains on the plane of the dilemma; but it gives out the classical call for larger and higher horizons.

The Council does not seem to be sure that other Christians will of necessity rejoice in this new perspective. But it does seem to think that they will want it. 'Thus the way will be opened whereby this kind of "fraternal emulation" will incite all to have a clearer awareness and a deeper realisation of the unfathomable riches of Christ' (n. 11, cf. Eph 3: 8). Certainly the Council is vague about the other Christians. That is easily understood. Two things, however, do matter. First in an ecumenical context the Catholic participant as well as his partner, may with Paul, as in Ephesians, consider himself 'the very least of all the saints'. For the emulation is not a matter of ecumenical brilliancè or prowess, but it is the 'emulation' of humility. Now, if the hint from Ephesians is taken, it is the guilty humility which is at stake, namely the humility of one who knows he has in the past persecuted the Church, or the brethren. *Secondly*, it also matters very much that the Council just at this juncture finds it has to reach out for the larger perspective, the bigger map, in fact the hierarchy among truths.

Yet a current dilemma among and for Roman Catholics is not to be concealed. The truths of the faith and its teaching, as they are formulated, do have a binding power. Their acceptance is Catholic. Their rejection, their reformation, their being subsumed one into the other, their being submerged one under the other is not. So the cry goes up, 'the faithful do not know what to believe any more'. On the non-theological scale there are other fears also. Will not institutions crumble? Will not the non-theological Catholic masses 'opt out'?[6] Rome has its own fears. Excessive theological pluralism bringing perplexity to the faithful, parallel theologizing, splinter systems — all this must surely be harmful. On the other side, the theological party (for the sake of some name) also has its fears. The alternative seems to be constraint on free research, the attempt to re-impose a pre-conciliar attitude towards the *magisterium*, infringements upon the expression of free and sincere opinion — all these seem not to be far distant threats. Bare confrontation, however long and skilfully protracted, is not the wished for solution. No one, who is not on the Church fringe in some form of neurotic dissidence, wishes to see a revival of the post-Modernist climate within the Roman Church. The long-lived suspicion and repression was notorious in damaging men and theology itself. It is perhaps very significant of a malaise that many, who at the time of the rumpus disagreed with Küng or Schillebeeckx in theology, nevertheless felt they had to add their names in protest on grounds that the Roman procedures were unacceptable in the post-Conciliar Church.[7] This preoccupation with Rome, however, has to be matched against the fact that there is now a younger generation of Church believers not even indirectly preoccupied with the *magisterium*. For them the figure of Jesus of Nazareth was enough.

The lessons of the partial alienation of the Dutch Church should concern us all. How could the post-conciliar climate have gone so sour in a regional Church never beforehand suspect of disloyalty? Did Rome, as Walter Goddijn has suggested, quite misinterpret the process? The period of analysis is not yet over, but it cannot be denied that there has been polarization both in Rome and in the Netherlands. The special methods, quite extraordinarily applied, of a regional Church Synod being summoned for its meeting to Rome certainly failed to heal the wounds as it was meant to do. The imposition of subsequent control methods by Rome has not succeeded either.[8]

I bring up these Church perplexities in this conviction. If the Church will have faith in its own declaration of the hierarchy of truths, there indeed will lie a way to having 'a clearer awareness and a deeper realisation of the unfathomable riches of Christ'. As proposed by the Council the hierarchy of truths must increasingly come into play. It is more than legitimate to use the principle not only in ecumenism, but also where serious theologizing is at stake. Theology is no longer a domestic affair. It carries its ecumenical responsibilities throughout.

'FOUNDATION' AND METHOD

But the Council's main purpose in adopting the recommendation of the hierarchy of truths did concern partnership in ecumenical dialogue. It was a call for a new method. The hoary old method of 'affirming the truth', as Bishop De Smedt insisted, had resulted in failure. Moreover, Denzinger theology, unhistorical theology, theology without regard 'for the central concern of Christian revelation', is valueless. A distorted picture is often given of the Catholic situation. But the 'hierarchy of truths', if it were not also a truly Catholic perspective, could not genuinely be offered for dialogue on the part of the Council.' So the Vorgrimler Commentary is wholly reasonable when it states: 'the strict enjoining of the basic principle of the "hierarchy of truths" . . . is ultimately addressed . . . to all Catholics'.

As Vorgrimler goes on to spell out, the implication is that without this principle theology would run the risk of glibness and inadequacy. So to that extent the teaching of this principle is in the nature of an answer to a perfectly natural demand. Indeed the demand for it is already on record in the ancient practice of the Church and in its Creeds. For only those truths or articles appeared in the Creeds which 'were the most important'. In addition 'the awareness of a hierarchy of truths, based upon their contents, had always been present in the Church'.[9] It cannot perhaps be said that this awareness was always reflected upon, but the general conclusion cannot be gainsaid.

In addition to the hierarchy principle or factor of the truths of faith, the Decree adds that there will be a differentiation in the relationship between the individual truths on the one hand, and the *foundation* of those truths on the other (*cum diversus sit earum nexus cum fundamento fidei Christianae*, — n. 11). What then is meant there by the 'foundation of the Christian faith'? The Council does not say. But it may have had in mind the often so styled credal materials in the New Testament, or some core materials in the early history of the

Creeds. I doubt whether that answer is on the right lines. It would be difficult if so to give a very precise meaning to the term *foundation*.

Should we not turn rather to 1 Cor 3: 11? 'For no other foundation can any one lay than that which is laid, Jesus Christ.' There Christ is the sole foundation. Round this point St Augustine well elaborated his own theological position. As Congar says, 'There are countless texts in Luther, who uses the "analogy of faith" for the designation of everything to Jesus Christ, dead and risen for us as the centre of revelation.'[10] In *Mortalium animos* (1928) Pius XI sees Catholic doctrine as organized 'rather like a tree, the smallest branches of which are connected to the trunk by others. The trunk is Christ . . .'[11] This insistence in tradition, now a precious ecumenical one, that the centre, or trunk, or foundation is Christ gives us a strong presumption as to how we should interpret the Council's use of the idea.

In passing we should look back with gratitude on the optimistic spirit of Archbishop Pangrazio who had proposed the insertion of the small section on the hierarchy of truths. 'I think the existing unity among all Christians will be seen more clearly, and it will become evident that all Christians are already a family united in the primary truths of the Christian religion.'[12]

From Pangrazio something important may also be gleaned about the intellectual model he had in mind when he introduced the hierarchy of truths precisely as a hierarchy. What he proposed was not new. He used the classical division between Christian truths, *first* the 'truths on the level of our final goal' (Trinity, Incarnation, Redemption), and *secondly* those 'on the level of means towards salvation' (Sacraments, Church structure, Apostolic Succession). The first are 'primary' truths, and the second, which are not called secondary, 'are certainly subordinate to those other primary truths'.[13] These truths are therefore differently graded within an 'order', as the text says, while the rest are 'certainly subordinate'.

We should avoid the temptation to treat the hierarchy of truths as though it were a merely undifferentiated order of precedence among Christian truths. It is of great value for us to know that we do not have to look for a utopia of a uniform hierarchy throughout. That would imply no greater penetration of the truth in the Spirit and would lead us into the temptation of desiring uniformity, which, as Cullmann insists, would be a sin against the Holy Ghost. The search we join in must be a search for unity in pluriformity. This fortunately is consistent with the logic of the Decree.[14]

Insofar as this terminology suggests a spatial metaphor, it is not unreasonable to suppose that the author is thinking along a vertical line in which what is primary is *higher* in the hierarchy than the rest. The rest must include those elements which make up the Church on the *level* of the subordinate truths already mentioned. Later on we shall have occasion to raise again the question of the fairly obvious spatial image raised by the question of 'order' and 'hierarchy'.

We can agree with Vorgrimler that the hierarchy of truths is an ancient reality in the presentation of the faith. The novelty perhaps lies in the adoption of the term 'hierarchy'. The way the term is inserted in the text suggests that the drafting of the phrase uses 'hierarchy' to designate the sort of order of truths which is being referred to. The process of a preferential selection of truths is obviously quite primordial. New Testament hymns and credal materials are a witness to that. Signs of a hierarchy in importance are even clear before the appearance of the Pauline texts. Articles about God and articles about Christ hold a primary position. It may even be true that it was the deliberate exclusion of gnostic tendencies which ensured that those articles should acquire and retain the primacy which they did.[15]

Added importance accrues to this hierarchy when it is realized that such materials must carry the guarantee of apostolicity. It is important that what happened, for example in the Christ event, is guaranteed by apostolic witness (cf. Lk 1: 2). Moreover the sheer process of uttering the right credal doctrine is guaranteed by the Spirit (1 Cor 2: 13). Tertullian will agree that, if Churches without an apostolic founder agree in the same faith with those of apostolic descent, then they happen to rejoice in a 'consanguinity of doctrine'.[16] Right belief, if kept, according to Hermas, will cast off wicked men, clothe one with righteousness and give life unto God. So 'First of all believe that God is One, even He who created all things and set them in order, and brought all things from non-existence into being, who comprehends . . . being alone incomprehensible'. Such belief must be accompanied by fear and continence.[17] Belief in Christ and in his saving work appears repeatedly as a demand in Hebrews, 1 Clement and 2 Clement as well as in similar documents of the third Christian generation. At this point in the Church's career the doctrinal confession becomes so important as almost to overshadow 'tradition about the actions of Jesus'.[18] Now all the documents of Church Law or Order begin with a statement on the profession of faith.

So we find that we are soon launched on the idea that some doctrines are more important than others either because they are guaranteed as in some way authentic or because they are more effective as prayers. What stood on an equal footing with the Church's Bible was the *regula fidei* which gave an explicitation of 'the cardinal truths about God the Father, Jesus Christ and the Holy Spirit'.[19] With an ample number of Creeds in the second and third centuries, J. N. D. Kelly sees several types of Creeds as co-existing. The principal items were on the way to being 'stereotyped', but 'no official declaratory Creed had been in existence'. Scholars would certainly have known it. Orthodox belief is stressed; and there is the conviction that 'there is one, universally accepted system of dogma, or rule of faith in the Catholic Church'.[20] Baptismal interrogations tended to 'acquire verbal fixity', and for our purpose Kelly appositely reminds us that in his day Tertullian thought they were 'rather fuller' than Christ had prescribed in the Gospel.[21]

If we ask ourselves whether credal materials showed evidence of partiality to one type of clause rather than to another, we have with Kelly to remember that the stabilizing influence of liturgy was probably stronger than the motive of rebutting heresy. This does not exclude the fact that a clause may be present in order to satisfy the desire for 'soundness of the catechumen's attitude'.[22] It does not exclude either the possibility that one may rightly look in the Creeds for some practical test as to the presence of a hierarchy of truths among the articles presented. After the Trinity we might expect that the Nicene *homoousios* would automatically find its place. But against conservative tendencies the Nicene *homoousios* did not straightaway make its appearance. East and West remained in temporary independence.[23] In due course Church life would take on the appearance of a mere battle between heresies and Creeds.

FAITH, LOVE AND ORDER

Nevertheless a due sense of the comparative importance of things survived in the demands of practical living. There appeared an area, located somewhere in the life of the Christian between what we now call faith in the intellectual sense and charity or love in the affective sense. One could point·to an area such as de Lubac designates as the *élan de la foi*.[24] This quite primordial Christian attitude to faith shows that a solely intellectual reaction to the invitation to believe is simply not possible. Thus Paul and the Johannine writings are fully aware that our believing is directed to the God who is love, and that we make our response accordingly. This fact alone makes it possible for the existence of degrees or grades or even shades of warmth in the Christian response. There will thus be gradations which themselves will demand preferential attention. To some extent the intellectual difference between ends and means, when we consider the truths of belief, is much more analytical. It is clear that here values and interest are at stake. What is forgotten is that they always are at stake.

In fact the response to God or Christ in faith is one embedded in a movement of the whole believer with his intellect and sensibility. 'What is it to believe in him?', asks Augustine, 'In believing we have our affection (*amamus*), in believing we love (*diligimus*), in believing we go (*imus*) to him . . .'[25] The same very basic idea of faith as part of a movement reappears among the medieval scholastics under the patronage of William of Auxerre for whom 'faith is a perception of divine truth in its tending to that truth (*tendens in ipsam*)'.[26] The reason for bringing out this historically elementary point here is this. It shows quite simply how the idea of a faith which moves, or a faith which has a tendency, is a faith which, as it should, resembles hope and charity in an order of reality. That order is an *order towards the good things awaiting it*. So the mind is in a movement towards a reality, and God is that which determines the order of movement simply because he is its term. So it is not hard to see that all

that has to be known on the way to God must always be
subordinated to that which is known as the term of that
order. The hierarchy of the known is in turn subordinated to
the hierarchy of things that are. Considered from this point
of view there cannot be any relationship between truths of
faith or doctrine or even theology which lie outside the
hierarchical order. To quote Augustine once more, 'it is only
towards God that our mind is directed towards its final
term'.[27]

Nevertheless historical theology can also show that there is
at least a double movement of the mind in faith. There is the
credere in Deum, the believing for example that in the mind's
movement towards God all that is said is both true and of
interest to me. There is also the *credere Deo*, the believing God
as believing on the promised assurance, on the guarantor in
obscurity, on the one to whom commitment goes. These
two lines of thought are well known to St Thomas for whom
faith is the vehicle and recipient not only of truth but also of
love-charity. In faith, he thinks, we react with the intellect
and with the will.[28] Again historically speaking, nothing is
clearer than that those two lines of the double dynamism in
faith are lines of a dynamic impulse demanding the final
submission of all its articulations to its term which is God. In
time the double dynamism became fissured and it is part of
the Reformation tragedy that this was so. The Catholic then
was unable to recognize in Luther and Calvin a strand of
emphasis upon will and affectivity which corresponded to an
already neglected element in tradition.[29] The split in the
dynamism of faith of course made it more difficult to see the
existence of an overriding hierarchy in the order of religious
truths. Catholic certitude and Protestant assurance should
have contributed together to such a perception. Finding itself
opposed to a *soli Deo* Catholic theology was thrown off
balance until the advent of the transcendental Thomism of
this century.

In a more profoundly theological way than that, Catholic
theology had already suffered. Nominalism certainly helped
to obscure the theology of a faith structured in the Spirit.
From Paul, Irenaeus, Gregory of Nyssa and from Augustine
the dynamism of the faith was clearly designated as a
dynamism of God's Spirit. In so being of the Spirit, and for

man's spirit, it drew its order and coherence from its
unfleshly strength. It was no longer milk for babes.[30]

   Though now often neglected, a difficult text (1 Cor 2: 13)
inspired the Fathers as to the preferential wisdom and
structure of what constitutes the Christian faith. We are
being taught, says Paul, of his preaching, not 'by human
nature' but 'by the Spirit'. We interpret spiritual things 'to
people of the spirit' (*pneumatikois pneumatika sugkrinontes*), or
perhaps 'we compare spiritual things with spiritual'. The
main point of this passage must include the idea that
Christian wisdom supposes a deeper understanding than one
that is merely 'fleshly'. In addition, if that understanding is
genuinely 'spiritual', then the preacher cannot be made liable
to human judgment (v. 15). The importance of the text for us
is this. It supposes that the content of faith has a structure,
and it supposes the possibility of a truth or truths to be
preferred above the rest. The Apostle is enabled to do the
necessary interpreting or comparing between truths because
'we have the mind of Christ' (v. 15). At the conclusion of his
remark Paul indulges in a *soli Deo*, again a preferential truth:
only God gives the increase (1 Cor 3: 7), and additionally
preference must be given to Christ, 'the foundation' (v. 12).
So an order in faith is basic. It is in the Spirit that we perceive
the existing primacy of the hierarchy of *pneumatika*, and just
because they are *pneumatika* they depend upon God and upon
nothing else.

   We should also remember that when the *doctrina fidei* of
Christians was looked upon as a *sapientia*, it was looked upon
as a *wisdom for living*. From the beginning of the third century
the ethical philosophy of Christian living persisted in fruitful
symbiosis with the content of Christian teaching. Our
modern separation of faith and morals owes much to the
Nominalists, and to the sterile demands of the Enlightenment. As late as the Council of Trent it could not be said that
'heresy' was looked upon solely as a matter of intellectual
deviance. An older Augustinian tradition had lived on. In it
there was a touchstone of rightness affecting one's attitude to
Scripture as well as to Church authority, and that was
closeness to Christ. Christ is the foundation not only of faith
as belief, but of faith as lived in life. It is the loss of that
proximity which gives rise to heresy. Perseverance in that

proximity implies love and right living. Severance in love and right living implies absence or distance from that foundation of the Christian life, namely Christ. Since Christ is present as the *foundation*, so he is also present as God the ultimate truth in the hierarchy of truths thus submitted to him. And this is the hierarchy that is brought into the life of the believer. He who has Christ in his heart, has Christ also as his *foundation*.[31]

It would be true to say that both in the East and the West just this theology, or 'philosophy' as at first it would more often have been called, served to keep faith and morals united. The distinction between them was known, but they still had to be kept together. Christ the Mediator helped to effect this. In his humanity he was clearly subordinated to God his Father. But it was the same Christ who had called for a supreme priority of love in human attitudes. He had demanded that as much as he had demanded acceptance of himself. In faith and in love there is a scale. The perspective opened up in 1 Cor 13 on love-charity terminates in an unequivocal supremacy of the love-charity in living now and beyond.[32] That piece of *philosophia* is paralleled in Matthew's exposition of the Law, which through the command to love must now be seen as a totality. And there is nothing esoteric about Matthew's teaching. It is part of a teaching ministry for the world. So it is not surprising that in the post-apostolic Church the two great commandments (Matt 22: 37, 39, etc.) retain the priority already given them. In faith being lived through love, faith and morality coalesce. Thus in line with Matthew Justin already speaks 'of the culmination of all divine law in Christ'. To such an extent is Christ both Nomos and Logos, that after him 'there shall be no Law, no precept, no Commandment'.[33] So again it is clear that total priority is present for the sole reason that it belongs to Christ and his commands. At no point is the primacy of a twofold command in love ever challenged.

Our best witnesses to that primacy of love are Basil of Caesarea and Augustine of Hippo. Basil was a man of the hour at a time, 'when the burden of the ecclesiastical situation and advances in theology had begun to weigh heavily on the freedom of research and were forcing theologians to consolidate and contain their energies rather than make fresh advances'.[34] So he at once takes care to give his Moral Rules a New Testament basis. Naturally he begins with the Two Great Commandments. The love of God is the 'first duty', 'the one aim', 'the love of wisdom with the love of God'. Basil's letters also show the love of God as a persistent first priority. 'Man's response to God's infinite love and mercy is in both commandments . . .'[35] Basil, who as much as any other father, never separates morality from faith, places all his moral teaching under the final priority of love.

Augustine in the West will give the same top priority to the command to love. 'We cannot know God unless we know what love truly is. In loving the brethren, loving charity, loving a soul in holiness, one loves God.'[36] In obeying the gospel command there is 'the cult of God, true religion, right-minded piety, the service due to God alone'.[37] The two commandments of the Gospel 'contain within themselves every other divine precept'. Of course there is a rival love, and Augustine compares it. He finds it 'wanting, since it is only the love commanded by God's law which will in fact exclude the vice of pride'.[38]

Such allusions to an ancient and privileged theology enable us to see perhaps more clearly than in our own post-Enlightenment language how the question of an order/hierarchy of truths, whether these are of faith (The Creed, Christ the *foundation*) or of morals (the primacy of charity), is simply no more than a reflection of the way Christian faith *in vivo* came to understand itself. It is an argument for Christian authenticity which can hardly be over-exploited.

It does good to acknowledge that our mental split between faith and morals is to a large extent a nineteenth-century affair, already favoured indeed by the moralism, especially in France, of the seventeenth century. But the situation we live with is basically undiscriminating in a profound sense. In its attempts to make a virtue of an all-or-nothing uniformity of Catholic truths it debases the autonomy and hence the true purpose of *theo*-logical enterprise. Such a mental split was not even present in the mind of the Council of Trent. It is true that *fides* there primarily refers to things revealed, but it could also 'stand for all that a Catholic should in conscience hold . . . also the acceptance of the ways of conduct which the Church

authorities . . . might lay down for the faithful'. At Trent
the opposition between 'dogmata' and 'mores' was not, in
Maurice Bévenot's word, 'absolute'. Whereas partly for
philosophical reasons the disjunction at Vatican I was the
one we now commonly use.[39] Of course I am not saying
that in this Trent was right and Vatican I was wrong. Each
Council was a witness to the philosophical outlook it lived
with. But that fact makes Trent a better witness to the more
historic way of thinking of the Church, namely that of
seeing Christian life as a whole. For where doctrinal issues
and moral ones are together at stake it is still the one living
subject who makes the preferential choice. Vatican II's
revival of a more ancient way of thinking, when it
propounds the hierarchy of truths, enables it to ride above
both Trent and Vatican I.

Indeed it rides higher above Vatican I than it does above
Trent. To assert an order of things in believing and acting
emphasizes the rationality of human existence. It also
emphasizes the intelligibility of any truths and commands
involved. In using, as I think, the metaphor of verticality
Vatican II is bringing us back to the ancient Patristic concept
that all reality in itself is orderly and that it is dependent
upon the ultimate ground of that order. Such is the wide
rationality of Christian *sapientia*. This state of affairs
constitutes an entitlement. We should thus look upon the
hierarchy of truths in Vatican II not merely as something we
have to accept, but as something we have the right to
develop. As Professor Torrance writes: 'We must develop
the concept of order by relating the creation to the
Incarnation as the embodiment of the love of God in the
world, and this, by relating the *actual order* we find in the
world to the *redemptive order* with which the message of the
Gospel has so much to do.' The question of order is not a
case of just one more convenient theological metaphor,
which may or may not be a good fit for all sorts of
argument. Rather 'in the Christian Faith we look for a *new
order* in which the *damaged order*, or the order that
inexplicably arises in the world, will be healed . . .'[40] This
search for a *new order* can take place only within the
overarching order by which the orders we know, actual and
damaged, are inserted. The relative and the contingent can

look or mount towards only one apex, namely that of the absolute and ultimate constant which is God.

Pope John Paul II speaking to theologians in Germany (Altöting, 1980) insisted upon this last point. It is most urgent that we concentrate upon 'The Trinitarian God as the origin and abiding ground of our life'. So the Triune God and his relation with his creation should be underlined. The text continues: 'Concentration upon God and his salvation for man implies (*bedeutet*) an *inner order* of theological truths' (italics mine). The Pope explicitly states that he has the hierarchy of truths in mind, as he does also in his phrase 'demanded' by Vatican II. But the papal text imports a changed metaphor from that simply used by the text of the Council. The Decree on Ecumenism, insofar as a metaphor is at work in its thinking, uses the simple correlative of 'hierarchy', namely that of vertical superiority perhaps that merely of qualitative superiority. At all events this must be insisted upon. The Council distinguishes clearly and emphatically between the truths of ends, those relating to the ultimate term of all things, namely God, and those that belong to the realm of means towards that end. Like St Thomas the Council sees that some things must be believed in for their own sake (God, Christ, the mystery of redemption), while others are believed in as means for attaining the term and purpose which is God. The Council sees greater importance in ends over means. The idea is simple and so far as it is a picture it suggests verticality.

The papal address to the German theologians, however, embarks upon the idea of centrality with a circumference. 'God the Father, Jesus Christ and the Holy Spirit are in the centre. The Word of Scripture, the Church and the Sacraments remain the great historical endowments (*Stiftungen*) of salvation for the world.' Thus the argument from ends and means is omitted and the practical conclusion drawn which was of course not in the mind of the Council:

Nevertheless the 'hierarchy of truths' demanded by Vatican II does not imply a simple-minded reduction of the comprehensive Catholic faith to a few basic truths (*Grundwahrheiten*), as many have thought. The more deeply and the more radically the centre is being grasped, so all the clearer and more convincing should those lines become that connect the centre with those truths which rather appear to be on the circumference.[41]

The shift of the metaphor to that of the circle or sphere showing the relationship between the centre and the circumference has one advantage. It certainly enhances the fact of the inner connexions between different theological truths. But once this emphasis has been made, another advantage has been lost. The idea of the difference between truths expressing the end, and truths expressing the means to the end is much more difficult to bring out. And when the connexions between the various truths are thus inspected as it were on the flat, then their appearance of homogeneity can be misleading. Baptism and Trinitarian faith are connected and arguably too on the score of ends. Apostolic succession and the validity of orders might appear to be on the same level, until one reflects that they can be truths relating only to means. The question of the difference between means and ends, even if the categories seem inappropriate, remains a needle question.

Still we must admit that the image of the circle or sphere brings us back to a more important point yet. The way of Christian belief, as our remarks upon the history, especially the patristic history of the hierarchy of truths and of the living conjunction of faith and morals were meant to suggest — that way of belief is first and foremost the appropriation somehow in the consciousness of the believer of a properly Catholic whole, a humanly believed totality of truths as a *totality phenomenon*. As Rahner points out, the 'Focus is always on the simple totality of truth, and therefore it can understand the individual truth only within the total act of faith'.[42] To have to subscribe to a set of propositions about the faith, as Bautain had to do, is a grotesque caricature of what it is to believe. For this there are several reasons.

First of all it distorts the fact that faith establishes or is the expression of a relationship with the living God. Of course like our first parents we can hide from that personal relationship. 'I was afraid, because I was naked; and I hid myself' (Gen 3: 10). The modern counterpart is: 'What do I have to believe nowadays?' The fact is that normally several propositions expressing the *fides quae* follow, but do not precede, the believer's enlightenment into the personal relationship with God. Of course, I recognize that my assent terminates in this or that assertion. But the real term is beyond. It is not the proposition which is the term of my assent, but as St Thomas says, the *res*, the reality.

Thus in any case the believer goes beyond the proposition. In this going beyond he goes out to an integrality and singleness in all that he believes. What he attains does two things for him. The personal encounter is there, a mysterious personal contact, in which God is perceived as witnessing to himself, and the believer goes out in an apprehension of faith that there is an objective integral reality in which he believes and that it shares in objective rationality as he knows it. Here the beyondness and the rationality of things meet. That is why Rahner can say that the *fides qua* itself participates in the hierarchical structure of the *fides quae*, and 'therefore the proposition that all truths must be adhered to with the same divine faith must be regarded as an exaggeration' ('cum grano salis zu verstehen ist').[43] This must be said, for it gives us the reason why we approve of the faith of the charcoal-burner. In the first outward movement of his faith to the transcendent God, he is at no disadvantage with the most sophisticated analyst of the propositional expressions of the faith.

But what then of the hierarchy of truths? Should the charcoal-burner not be in a position to understand the preference of one proposition before another? It is not the charcoal-burner who falls under the papal disapprobation of a 'simple-minded reduction of the comprehensive Catholic faith to a few basic truths'. No responsible theological judgment can be in favour of such a reduction. To say that would be arbitrary, and such arbitrariness is precisely what the notion of order and hierarchy excludes.[44] But what it does allow for is vital, namely the living '*in the implicit faith of the Church*'. The hierarchy of truths demands the opposite of reductionism. It calls for openness.[45]

Does the vertical picture, so to call it, of the hierarchy have an advantage over the centre-periphery image? I suspect that it does in allowing more easily for the historical reality that faith may both grow and decay. In the vertical image it is easier to see that doctrinal development is not always an improved understanding of the totality. Vertical progress allows for a zig-zag climb as well as for incidental falls. Time comes into it. Theologoumena in one period seem important, at another less so. Then for reasons of acculturation Church authority may one day have to accept a pluriformity of doctrinal expression at present deemed unacceptable. Let us admit that only when we see the hierarchy of truths as a principle shall we be in a position to accept a genuine pluriformity in doctrinal expression. Of course we shall also be surrounded by perplexity. We shall only be in a position to make the necessary rational judgment, if we make the effort to penetrate further into the notion of the hierarchy of truths. The Church may have tried before by a certain instinct. How else do we allow for the historic fact that before the Council of Florence the Trinitarian formulation of belief in God, which did indeed exist, nevertheless had a lower rating within the totality of dogmatic expressions than it did afterwards? The like can be said of the septenary number of sacraments in Catholicism before and after the Council of Trent. Variation and perplexity have been lived with before. There is no reason why in the genuine service of the faith we should not have to live with them again.[46]

Vatican II, it seems, began to foresee this possibility. The text speaks as though it were almost inevitable, if the Church remains faithful to the mission she sees as essential of bringing Christ to the world. The Pastoral Constitution on the Church and the Modern World has no fear of theological adaptation in a culturally pluralist society:

> Furthermore, while adhering to the methods and requirements proper to theology, theologians are invited to seek continually for more suitable ways of communicating doctrine to the men of their times. For the deposit of faith or revealed truths are one thing: the manner in which they are formulated without violence to their meaning signifies another.

Like Pope John Paul II afterwards, the Council was concerned to show that 'the knowledge of God can be better revealed . . . the gospel can become clearer to man's mind and show its relevance to the conditions of human life'.[47]

Without an inner acceptance by the Church of the transcendental order, and therefore of the hierarchy of the truths of faith, there cannot be a way in which the Church of this decree can be faithful to its own insight. Every Church truth is good as a truth, insofar as it helps to show how Christ, our *foundation*, bridges the ontological gap between God and the world, between the rescuing and restoring order of things on one side, and the damaged order on the other.

The Patristic as well as the Biblical stress of Vatican II showed with what entitlement Vatican II broke through to new horizons. So, when the Council sees that the truths of the hierarchy can 'vary in their relation to the "foundation" of the Christian faith' (*Unitatis integratio*, n. 11), it gives us an apt reminiscence once more of St Augustine. As ever of course it is Christ who is meant as *foundation* (cf. 1 Cor 3: 11).[48] Now the location selected for the personal priority of Christ by Augustine is man's heart. He tells us why. For it is desire, thought, taste even, which are to be found together in the heart. Being also Augustinian Pascal summed it up: '*C'est le coeur qui sent Dieu*.'[49] Such language and such an insight is far from being a 'simple-minded reduction' of the truths about God as the believer appropriates them. It is a *glimpse* of the divine inner order of truths offered to humanity in its inmost striving for life.

EXISTENTIAL AND SITUATIONAL

Today a general problem faces theologians across the board. In effect they are being challenged. Can they and will they sustain the position bequeathed to them by Vatican II over pluralism? There are several ways in which pluralism may be conceived. But the burning problem concerns the truths of faith. Is Christian unity in faith a matter of cultural uniformity? Are the simple, the faithful, the people, who belong to the five continents of this planet to be allowed access to the gospel of Jesus Christ and its consequences only through the classicist, or now neo-classicistic culture of the Western Church. As Lonergan, echoing Augustine, powerfully asserts: 'The real root and ground of unity is being in love with God — the fact that God's love has flooded our inmost hearts through the Holy Spirit he has given us' (Rom 5: 5).[50] It is only that unity which can transcend the rival world-views in which the Christian faith has a right to be heard.

A neo-classicist back-lash may gain the upper hand. It cannot show that it will stay. On nationalisms, on oppression as in Latin-America, on nuclear disarmament, even on sexual morality it is not foreseeable that neo-classicist positions will regain authority, for the neo-classicist view-point is no longer an interpretation of concrete human experience. This also must be most firmly said.

The late Fr Cornelius Ernst O.P. saw the issue clearly. We need a 'truly generous recognition of a genuine pluralism within the ecumenical unity of the Church'.[51] We should notice his word 'ecumenical'. It is not at all misplaced. Re-discovering what is within the Church, re-discovering its genuine theological dynamics must be recognized as no longer an essentially Roman enterprise. One lesson of the Vatican II doctrine on the hierarchy of truths would be that thinking theologically upon burning issues, such as we have just mentioned, is both the most ecclesiological and ecumenical thing we could do. If the Congregation for the Doctrine of the Faith had to adjust its sights in the process, then so much the better. As Fr Cornelius saw it, 'while we cannot and need not stop thinking theologically as Europeans, we must stop thinking as though thirteenth-century Europe . . . was the only really important moment in the thought of all mankind'.[52] But we cannot think at all in terms of yesterday's Europe. If we do, then the Church's theology and all its efforts at acculturation of the faith are either doomed to sterility in a 'shabby shell' of its own thinking, or to a fragmentation of the gospel message along the jagged edges of a circle in danger of collapse.

The only way forward, as Karl Rahner has pointed out, is to 'work with them'.[53] Across the grain of plural views of man there is no solution. Nor is there a solution in going it alone. Nor is there in this 'working with them' some possible new synthesis. That cannot now happen from the planet-wide variety of ideas as to what constitutes man. It should be obvious that we have much to learn, and perhaps more to forget, through philosophical contacts with India, China and Japan. Yet there can be no future gospel explicitation through a mere reconciliation of irreconcilables. No returned missionary has ever been able to explain to me how the doctrine of 'two natures' in Christ can become acculturated in the East. Our master in the West (Aristotle) grasped the point more acutely than we do: 'Those who are being initiated are not required to grasp anything with the understanding, but to have a certain inner experience, and so to be put into a particular frame of mind, presuming that they are capable of this frame of mind in the first place.'[54]

Against that, of course, it must be said that the gospel cannot be relativized. Equally, sheer rejection of another's thought-form is sterile. Communication is then cut off. Without thinking of the East–West chasm the plurality of western philosophies remains irremediably plural and until our Marxist subjugation will so remain. Rahner speaks of Existentialism, Marxism, 'modern Philosophy of Language', hermeneutics, philosophies of science, and the philosophies of the East just mentioned, 'in as yet uncomprehended quantities'. Outside the totalitarian empire of Cominthink there is no single mastery to be dreamed of. Ecumenism and pluralism within the Church become ever more imperative.

For Rahner the remedy is not to be found outside theology itself, but within it. Theology can retain its hold. But how? Rahner's direction of thought is worth following. What is it that will help us all in the Church to come 'to a deeper realisation of the riches of Christ'? It must be a method, or perhaps better an experience, as Aristotle would have it, for initiates. It will be an experience not so much of authority, as of witness in dialogue. Here too there must be order. The first question is not so much how we can at once communicate across, let us say, the East–West boundaries. Rather our first effort must centre upon the re-discovery of the gospel within the shifting forms of West–West dialogue.

The older efforts have done their work. It was by contrast with our present predicament a relatively simple problem to combine the Latinization of the African with the process of our bringing him the gospel. It is now we, not so much the African, who have to break through cultural barriers. We have to keep our nerve through a process of de-Latinization, even de-classicization, for something no less basic than the purpose of talking to each other. One example seems to me to show this quite clearly. The history of the Roman priest, as we have known him, has, through his now stereotyped roles, summed up a part of the cultural experience of Western Europe. We have now lived through perhaps the experience of his so-called crisis of identity. There is, however, no sign that that was a problem to be taken in isolation, solved and then dismissed. On the contrary there are strong signs that the problem pointed to another larger one beyond itself. If the state of theological reflection is anything to go by, it points to the basic question we can only answer in outdated bits of symbolism, 'What is Christian man?' It was supposed that we had an answer, but it now hardly looks like an answer acculturated even to ourselves. The classical terms and symbols may still work for the transcendentals of our faith (God's fatherhood, Christ's sacrifice, the Spirit's movements), but where some immediate cash value is demanded ('What is man?') the case is different. Our religious geniuses have given the question itself *their* form. Augustine was traumatic and dominant. Aquinas brilliantly synthetic. Luther and the Reformation, ever-questing and even more traumatic. We are now in competition with Marxism, positivism and Freud's variant inheritors. Pope John Paul II's instinct was right, when in his first encyclical he put before the world the urgency of the problem of man and his dignity, but his Christian offer remains one in competition (*Redemptor Hominis*).

Such are areas of weakness. The strength we may at present have does not come from any ability to provide a cultural or transcultural remedy. It comes, perhaps as never before, from God's Word. That Word of his can in cultural confusion nourish the essential fidelity in thinking. In the long run our hope even for our own self-rediscovery is in his Word. The same is true for any effort at communicating that self-rediscovery. There is beneath our perverse human pluralisms a root that lasts. It is the unanalysable root bedded in God's own transcendence. In the concrete life of faith it is the root through which we draw into ourselves the truth of God's triunity, God's incarnation. In a reflex movement towards that root we can begin to say what in our becoming we are and must be, as well as where we see our destiny.

There too our awareness is hierarchical and dynamic. It is dynamic in our perception of God's dynamism, already moving us. For the Triune God is the God who is on the way to us and draws us to him. The Incarnate God is the God enabling and engracing all at once. That we can see what is of God and what is from us, requires a differentiation in awareness we cannot of ourselves elaborate. In the perplexed experience even of the faith, the life-line of the faith acquires differentiation from a movement of understanding. For the understanding sees itself subject to truths, to order and to hierarchy. The hierarchy of truths is not yet sufficiently recognized, but it must be invoked, else no rational assimilation or reflection on the faith is possible. In addition only that hierarchy can generate the all-important refocusing in our faith.

When the relationship between the mysteries of salvation is deepened, then the mysteries themselves take on a further depth of meaning. In an insufficiently noticed phrase Vatican I enjoined that our method of deepening our faith-knowledge should be drawn 'from the connexion of mysteries among themselves and from their connexion with the end of man'.[55] Thus, if we are to deepen our understanding of God's dealing with man, then we must look to what man is becoming and what his destiny will be. Indeed without this ordering from God himself there would have been no reality principle in our believing process. A sort of perverse theological infantilism would have been the only thing. It is only a theology of believing which can perceive the order in thought which comes from the order or hierarchy of disclosed truths, owing their disclosed order to the disclosing mind-Logos.

What has just been said is an implication of the doctrine of the incarnate Logos. It is nothing less than God's incarnation which gives ground for optimism. If we cannot bring ourselves to think that the truths of the faith are not in danger from cultural pluralism, then we have begun to lose our nerve over the full doctrine of the incarnation. When God in his incarnate Son dealt with his 'rational creatures', as the Greek Fathers well understood, he disclosed the fullness of our likeness to him and his likeness to us. Of course the unlikeness may be greater; but all final arbitrariness about our belief is by the same token removed. Gospel teaching gives us an astonishing guarantee of the intelligibility of God and of his revelation in his Son: 'All things have been delivered to me by my Father; and no one knows the Son except the Father, and no one knows the Father except the Son and any one to whom the Son chooses to reveal him' (Matt 11: 27). The very intelligibility of God is shown in the fact of the relationship between incarnate Son and Father as being a relationship of knowledge, hence of intelligibility. The text at first sight reminds us, fairly enough, of Nicene doctrine. But it concludes by telling us that the Nicene doctrine with its divine intimacy is also knowable by us.

In the life of the believing Church God asks for our belief. Within the ambit of that asking we respond. The effect is, in the classic phrase, that we see with the eye of faith. True that between God and the believer there is a make or break point. The believer can refuse. But in the end the one and only witness who can make an absolute demand upon us is God the uncreated witness and also the *First Truth*. On God's level only God counts. Vatican II's Declaration on Religious Freedom goes straight for the credibility space of man before God. It speaks serenely and optimistically. It takes its stand upon man's dignity within that credibility space before God. 'The truth cannot impose itself except by virtue of its own truth, as it makes its entrance into the mind at once quietly and with power.'[56] So ultimately we come back to Truth's own witness and it is in the light of that that there remains 'the moral duty of men and societies towards the true religion and toward the one Church of Christ' (ibid.).

Thus truth arrives within God's ordering order. We can appropriate it because in grace we can accept the differentiations that order proposes. God's ordering order becomes our ordered order. Faith, destiny, our tending towards the *First Truth* these are all given us. The centre of the universe of thought constituted by the gospel and the mediating Church can be only one thing: it is God who saves. No other emphasis, however motivated, can change that. No apparently peripheral truth can rise to it. To that extent the image of the circle of sphere of truths in illustration of the hierarchy does nothing other than follow this central insight of the Judaeo–Christian faith. In Rahner's language that truth belongs to the *existential and situational hierarchy of truths*. God is our absolute saviour.

A GENUINE CHRISTIAN FIT

But the intellectual and cultural polymorph of today still has to integrate his own faith (*fides quae*) with the Church. It is sometimes said that this believer or any other has a right to a clear representation of the faith from the side of the authority of the Church, let us say the *magisterium*. That the faith should be fed from the teachers of the Church is an obligation that flows clearly from the Lord's command that the flock should be fed. But the teachers themselves are bound by the principle enunciated by St Thomas that nothing falls under faith unless it is ordered by God. It is the abiding task of the Church's teachers always to recur to that principle.

The 'rights' of the faithful to receive clarity of exposition are clearly subjected to restraints. The Church in its faith is not a spiritual variant of a welfare-state-cum-consumer-society. Calvin saw the human race as a perpetual idol-factory. The clarity of representation in mass media religion comes near to falling under Calvin's indictment. Clarity, tangibility, effulgent presence not to mention religious legalisms and taboos are by no means signs of a deeper faith. They may even come to suggest that created things can take the place of God. But God is his own true witness in the heart of the believer. And in the hierarchy of truths God will always be his own true witness as to what is primary and what secondary, what is in the centre or at the top as well as at the periphery or below. In doing that God witnesses to his own supremacy.

The Church is God's secondary witness. But she herself also bears witness to that sovereign witness which is God's alone. The Church's proclamation must not only state that that is true, it must offer the means to its faithful so that they shall with the eye of faith see that it is true. If it is not seen to be true then the Church's teaching and the theology in dialogue with it must collapse. Unless somehow we perceive the divine witness through the secondary witness of the Church, then the Church cannot be recognized as 'the Light of all nations'. Nor in its sacramental aspect can the Church be seen to be primordial, the *Ursakrament*.

In addition, when the Church and the *magisterium* speak about themselves, they must continue always to make it clear that what they say is uttered under God's universal call to repentance. If that particular condition disappears then the apostolic plausibility of the Church disappears. But it must be made clear that the call to repentance is genuinely the divine one and by no means a device to spread a feeling of guilt among the faithful, keeping them in a simply docile submission to the empirical Church as to a power structure. And, let it be said, showing concrete evidence of submission to the testimony of God as unique, demands far more than the repetition of what is good old curial style. It is not only the simple faithful who are in danger of infidelity to grace. Creeping infallibility is also an infidelity to the grace of God's primary witness.

On the other side, when the chips are down, there has to be within the Church a 'binding "Yes" ' and an 'unequivocal "No" '. It is part of sober gospel sincerity that such a certain and binding fact about the Church exists (cf. Matt 5: 37; 18: 17). But the area of obligation that antecedes the fact must not grow into a burden. It must not overtop our awareness of the sovereignty of God. It is God who must remain at the pinnacle of any hierarchy. Given our free acceptance God must himself be the guarantor of our acceptance as one of responsible, free adults. With our acceptance goes our perseverance. Only God guarantees that.

In 1983 the revised Code of Canon Law was published by Rome. How does that fit into a non-lawyer's view of the hierarchy of truths? Some remarks may help an orientation of the mind. Law, including Church law, must attempt to fit the realities of the society for which it is framed. In the case of the Church it is especially true that its law can in no way be a reduction in its substance from the given empirical Church as it is now, or even as it was, with such and such an empirical form. Equally it cannot neglect such structures as exist. Yet from its empirical inheritance such law inherits the strictures passed by Paul on the Law in Israel. Of itself it may try to put men right before God. Of itself it will fail. The point is illustrated by a reported remark of Paul VI on the subject of the legal penalties of excommunication. 'People,' he said, 'had a new motive for staying in the Church of today and that was because they loved the Church and no longer feared her.'[57] The observation that love had replaced fear meant that the Law no longer derived its sanction from society. Theologically speaking we can say that, insofar as the Law was the occasion of love or even elicited love towards the Church, it was doing so through the sanction it derived from its transtemporal reality as a mystery of faith. The Pope too was obviously thinking of the work of grace rather than the possible influence of legal revision. This very admission has also entered the modern canonist's mind. He and his colleagues 'no longer have at the centre of their studies the *philosophy* of law but rather a *theology* of law' (author's italics).[58]

There is in the very business of promulgating Church law a lack of a genuine Christian fit. Pope John Paul II implicitly admits this when he grants the impossibility of transposing 'the image of the Church described by conciliar doctrine into canonical language, nevertheless the code must always be related to that image as to its primary pattern . . .'[59] Thus basically it is not and in Church law cannot be, man who matters, but it is God. Paul VI was contrasting the fear of the Law out of legal sanction, with the love in faith of God's mystery. Augustine had seen it too:

> So what is the difference? I will tell you in two words. The law of works commands with menaces what the law of faith begs for in believing . . . By the law of works God says: 'Do what I command'; but by the Law of faith we say to God: 'Give that which you command' (*De spiritu et littera*, 22).

There is thus a thoroughly Catholic agreement that the Law to be right for salvation must correspond with the God-given inner transcendent vitality of the Church. When it fails to do that, it is a mere relativization of that life. It remains condemned to sterility.

That is just how our way of union with the Church should also be judged. If we do not correspond with the inner transcendent vitality of the Church, then we are sterile. 'Identification' is the popular term for this. I suggest that it is a dangerous one. If we push that idea of identification with the terrestrial, pilgrim Church, then we give back life to a seductively fallacious half-truth that the Church is the perfect society. It became a post-Tridentine theological placebo, but it threw right out of balance the more profound ideas of the Church as mystery, as People of God, or as Mystical Body of Christ.

Of course we are committed to a visible, pilgrim Church, in its daily empirical form, a Church of sinners. But our commitment is one of honest integration rather than identification. The difference is important. With structures we can and do integrate. It is to everyone's peril that we identify with them. And it has to be admitted that the Church, to use de Lubac's phrase, in 'its temptation to idolize itself' does sometimes propose identification.[60] But actions in the concrete Church do not escape from sinful circumstances and motives. Nothing can oblige us to think that such a state of affairs is necessarily impossible. As Augustine in the context of Donatism so clearly taught us, the wheat must remain with the tares until the harvest. But the empirical Church likes to forget just why it was right over Donatism, and just why Donatism was wrong. Nor would Augustine have us gloss over flagrant scandals, such as the recent history of the Vatican Bank. It is his point that in spite of historic scandals there is an abiding factor of holiness dispensed through and only through Christ in the Church. So we do not have to identify; we do have to integrate. That goes for the empirical Church. With the Church of the Kingdom, of God's eschatological coming, of Christ's judgment and submission of all things to his Father — that is different. There we can do no other than identify. The process begins even now in our continued purification and absorption into God.

Again it must be said that, if we were literally to be identified with the daily workings of the empirical Church, then the radical Christian freedom inherent in faith would be brought to nothing. The charism of truly spiritual creativity would be lost. So also would its power to enhance our lives. The Church itself would lose its radical responsibility before God and men. The significance of this bi-polar situation must not be missed. It serves to show that once more we are in a situation in which respective truths and their realities are hierarchical, a part of that order transcended only by God who is our ultimate in the eschatological future and in the process of our continued becoming as Christians.

Considered in whole or in part, however, the Church is a created reality, and once recognized in its empirical form the obligation of adherence cannot be gainsaid. Here we are at the root of our experienced life as Christians. We are at the root because of the pressure of the absolute future in faith and in grace. We should like to identify the sense in which, in the words of St Paul, we 'groan inwardly as we wait for adoption as sons . . .' (Rom 8: 23). We certainly long for a Church without temptation and without sin, a Church in a totally single and exclusive appurtenance of God. But since with the Church we are only a partial project of what we shall be, the time is not yet. Our present condition was described by Arthur Koestler, who was then not thinking theologically. Our present self-transcendence, he thought, is a power of man that is both the glory and the tragedy of the human condition. For both of these 'derive from our powers of self-transcendence'.[61] This power in us, whether inside or outside the Church, is without God's help ruinous. It can be harnessed to creative or destructive purposes. It is 'equally capable of turning us into artists, but more likely into killers'.[62]

Koestler is thinking literally of the situation within the social body. But we may ask what happens when artistry and creativity in faith are blocked, refused, or destroyed. Identification with Christian societies and their particular ideologies can go wrong. A gross example in our Western history is that of the Inquisition. Another is the current distortion of religious identification or adhesion, as it is known to us in Belfast. The Stalinist purges, the Stalinist imposition of 'social realism' assumed that identification with the Party was always achievable. Yet identification deifies. In 1980 *Pravda* found the comparison between the Soviet Union and Nazi Germany 'blasphemous'.[63] That is nonsense language in the West, but a plausibility in the Soviet Union, where the citizen must be deemed to have so far identified with State and Party that any rejection is a rejection of the ultimate. It is thus that in *Pravda* the word 'blasphemy' finds its plausibility. Outside its own thought system the use of the word seems insane; but in part it is the insanity of the conscientious. 'The word of madmen is a saint run mad.'[64] Eichmann for one was a conscientious bureaucrat.

In religion absolute neutralism and isolationism are impossible. For one cannot engage in the process of becoming by being neutral or being in isolation. Man must be interdependent. In his interdependence he must while believing believe as a 'part whole who, *qua* whole, enjoys autonomy within the restraints imported by the interest of the community'.[65] That may sound banal enough. It may seem to be at some remove from the hierarchy of truths. In fact this dual function, that of being the 'part whole' is to be found at all levels of the community, and 'such an ideal society could be said to possess "hierarchic awareness" '. Koestler is here offering us a simple sociological factor which is the counterpart of the theological condition of the Church believer. The ecclesiology *of communion*, as Thils calls it, which we have now inherited from Vatican II, gave the whole Western Church the possibility of re-opening for itself the understanding of a divinely orientated hierarchic awareness. Such an awareness can not only allow pluriformity, but it can see its importance. The hierarchy of truth of which God alone is the source is and can be the only hierarchy which is transcendent. Within that transcendent hierarchy or order, Church forms and doctrines are to be found. By that fact they are secondary with respect to the transcendent order or hierarchy.

STAYING IN THE TRUTH

If we look at our theme from the point of view of the Church of authority and jurisdiction, it has to be said that it is only through the Church's transmission of gospel truths that we can know the doctrine of the hierarchy of truths as it presents itself to us. It must also be said in this connexion that the Church is herself by no means a merely quiescent sign of God's truth among men, she is also a real active presence of that truth and a grace-bearing presence, creatively 'speaking the truth in love' (Eph 4: 15). That is a process which must reach to the stature of Christ. So the Church as well as being a power and an authority to transmit and to preserve is also a source of vitality and growth. Thus even when Christ commands, and the Church proposes under his command, she does so in the context of vitality and growth. To that we must add that when in the continuum of history the Church's faith includes 'a binding "yes" and an unequivocal "no", that also takes place in the context of the Church's vitality and growth'. It is not possible 'for the Church to stay in the truth' unless it operates within that vital continuum. We cannot doubt that the Church may exercise her binding power; but it cannot be doubted either that any such exercise makes sense only within the concrete, ongoing, historic process of growth.

That is worth saying because it would be a very incomplete way of looking at the Church merely to see the *magisterium* as a one-sided affair. It is not as though the power resides with the Pope and the bishops on the one side, and on the other there is the passive lump of community obedience in its belief without initiative. The *magisterium*, as it has now been referred to for a century and a half, has had before its eyes the special responsibility for preserving the apostolic character of the Christian faith. It has therefore tended to think of itself somewhat exclusively as a *magisterium* brought into operation after the event.

But that hardly corresponds to 'staying in the truth' as within the concrete, ongoing, historic process of growth. We must not forget that life and growth surround and feed a process which may or may not have to be checked. And the power of the *magisterium*, which is present before as well as after the event, is a power of service for the Church. It is the vital power of discerning the true gospel witness to Christ. As such it is every Christian's power and every Christian's responsibility. It follows from the very conferral of baptism and confirmation. For what is concerned is that life which enables the Christian to give witness. Insofar, then, as he is informed by the genuine charisms of the Spirit, every Christian is empowered to give true witness and thereby becomes part of the *magisterium*.[66]

Now by the experience of prayer and reflection in faith, that share in the *magisterium* takes on the great seriousness of being properly *theo*-logical, i.e. it has a relating effect to God himself. This very high gift is one for all the faithful who will answer the call to such seriousness. That is why the mystical tradition of the Church must always be taken seriously. It is also a contribution to the full *magisterium*. Nor obviously in this sense is the scientific theologian to be excluded from his share in the *magisterium*. He too seeks genuine gospel witness and to the whole Church. He speaks of God, the One Truth, valid and presented to all men; and he speaks of Christ the one particularity, the only possible particularity in which all men may share. The experienced and loyal Christian theologian cannot speak of Jesus Christ except in consciousness of the universal witness which he has before him. He cannot of course command agreement. But he should not have to plead so much that his aims be taken into account. His responsibility as a universal witness is built into his life. It is worse than an offence against fair play to try and manipulate his sincere contribution or to attempt to stifle it in secret. (In passing we may say that we have yet to hear a genuinely theological argument on behalf of the continuance of secret ecclesiastical censorship.)

What should be abundantly clear is that we need an abiding balance and a genuine dialogue, in fair weather and in foul, between the *magisterium* (ordinary or extraordinary) and the continuing mature witness of those baptised and confirmed believers who form its completion. Since Vatican II this cannot seriously be in doubt. All reports of our National Pastoral Congress of England and Wales (May, 1980) tend to show that this event was a brilliant example of what the baptised and confirmed can indeed offer towards balance and dialogue. Above all it must not be the end of a process for the Church owes it not merely to herself but to her Founder that there should be no diminution in her growth in faith to his own stature.

So, first, the hierarchy of truths must make itself felt. It may perhaps cause an overspill of witness beyond Church structures. Who could regret it? Witness is rarely tidy. And even within her boundaries it will be seen that when the Church aims at preserving the purity of God's Word through the hierarchy of truths there will be two effects. *First* the Church will be helped to find the right weighting for what she is trying to say. She may at times have to admit that what she feels bound to say must be provisional.

Secondly, that very hierarchy helps the empirical Church to acknowledge that she herself does not penetrate the mystery of God. Without the hierarchy of truths she cannot even delineate it. In the varied, if not *de facto* pluriform, condition of today the Church needs to know and acknowledge much more clearly the limitations on her own knowledge in faith. Touching her own structures the Church surely has but a relatively uncontrolled future. More clearly than ever before the Church may yet have to share in the kenotic ignorance of her Master when he was on earth.

The question cannot be avoided. Can the Church not admit it in perfect doctrinal safety when she simply does not know? She might well have done so in the case of Galileo. There are, for example, areas of morality which in their total implications are simply ungraspable. Is this not plausible of contraception, genetic manipulation, nuclear disarmament, Latin American political involvement? Areas of ignorance would enhance the hierarchy of God-centred truths where knowledge becomes more clearly its own witness. Would not a *sancta ignorantia* be publicly appreciated as part of the awe and *pietas* which the Church can show to God and to the children in his image, her members. Of more importance, would more room not then be left for prophecy within the Church? And could a theology of liberation not be considered at least in part a form of prophecy?

It is clear from the phenomenon of repeated and world-wide papal visits that the intention is to bring the 'centre' to the 'periphery' (Roman words and concept of structure). No doubt too the cohesive unity of the structured Church is at stake. But we should not forget that there is a periphery in two senses to the Church.

In the Roman Church the first is clear from its very geography. The ruling Pope now tours his provinces with manifest intention of consolidating structural unity and popular loyalty. The second sense of periphery concerns people rather than structures, the mind perhaps more than the heart. For now a conscious evaluation of the centre-periphery relationship takes place. This probably takes place among groupings which tend to be lay, to have some connexion with religious orders, especially to be associated with religious education and schooling.[67] It must not be forgotten that it is the result of such evaluations which tend to be the longer lasting influence. Nor must it be forgotten that such groupings have been on the side of liberal change, and that they feel less bound to existing structures and territorial Church government.

A quite different type of peripheral Church is to be found where life is under external constraints. In different ways and to different degrees Churches in the Eastern European bloc fall into this type, as well as national Churches in Latin America and in the Far East. Random examples would be those of Czecho-Slovakia, the Western Ukraine, or Lithuania.[68] Central America hardly needs a mention. In Zaire the succession of bad times and better times keeps one in mind of the 'pilgrim' character of the Church. This is a type of periphery in which loyalty to the *catholica* is sorely tested. These conditions can drive a peripheral Church either to greater outward, and perhaps inward, conservative solidity as in Poland. Alternatively, as in Latin America, the harshness of life can lead to polarization within the Church. We can admire the human quality of loyalty especially to ritual and structures; but the price can be grievous. The deeper insights into faith will be denied to Christians who, forced to concentrate upon ways and means for survival in the *status quo*, are the less free to understand what a hierarchy of Christian truths might mean for them.

With non-Roman Church bodies the Roman Church has not yet accepted a co-ordinate role. It is not yet, for example, a member of the World Council of Churches, nor in the United Kingdom of the British Council of Churches. It is content to await developments with an observer status. If there were any serious will to loosen the log-jam, the practical endorsement and application of the hierarchy of truths could play a major witnessing role. The World Council showed a consciousness of the hierarchy of truths, when from the late 1940s to the late 1960s it strove again and again to give expression to a common Trinitarian faith lying behind its ecclesiology.[69] The 'basis' of the World Council is all but quoted in the Decree on Ecumenism (n. 20). This hint towards official initiative on the part of the Roman Church has never in fact been followed up. But it must seriously be asked, would not the Roman Church be in a freer position to join with the World Council of Churches and thereby to bring to it of its own riches, if it were to find a way of following up the initiative suggested by its own Council?

It is the ever-greater penetration into the reality meant by the hierarchy of truths that should be one life-line for faith in the Churches. I do not mean to prophesy that a great Church will that way emerge from generally divided Christian bodies. But if in a process of growing interaction and dialogue, we remain faithful to a genuine experience of the perceived hierarchy of truths, even though now we can only in pain look upon ourselves as an afflicted *catholica*, then that same *catholica* may more recognizably emerge as the *catholica* of Christ.

A NEW SENSE OF PROPORTION

When we use the formula 'I' (or 'We') 'believe in' (or 'believe that'), we express our own commitment to what we shall say or recite next. We also convey our sense of awe and reverence towards the realities and mysteries we shall then name. Between Christian bodies we share that respect for our 'confession' of faith.

Within this attitude of respect we accept that the same beliefs recited by another may be held with equal sincerity, but with a relatively different hierarchical weighting or evaluation not as to truth, but as to importance. Doctrinal relativism in this sense becomes a necessity. It was quite basic to the teaching of Jesus to recall men to a sense of proportion and to a hierarchy of religious values. This he did in confrontation with the interpretations of the Law of the Scribes and Pharisees and to the extent that he promulgates a new Law, namely that of love. Much that Vatican II demanded also amounted to a new sense of proportion, so that we could again hold in respect and awe, as genuinely due to faith, our continuing living truths and practices. Not that our hierarchically differentiated awareness would become a thing settled once and for all time. As I shall be saying later about man, i.e. humanity, the Church *is — in its becoming*. Revision within renewal must continue if the believing community is to remain an organism having life. The 'riches of Christ' are 'unfathomable' or 'immeasurable' (Eph 2: 7). The way he is for us will strike us first of all. That is variable because we are variable. It was an exaggeration, but an understandable one, when Melanchthon said that to know Christ is simply to know his benefits. It was a minimalist judgment on the other hand when the young Augustine said that knowing God and the soul in prayer was the total of all that could be desired:

A. My prayer is completed.
R. Then what is it you wish to know?
A. All that I have asked in my prayer.
R. Resume it in a few words.
A. To know God and the soul; nothing more.
R: Nothing more?
A. Absolutely nothing (*Soliloquies*, I, 2, 7).

With Melanchthon and Augustine, however, it is possible to sense the awe and respect which they feel before the mystery of Christ and God. It is also possible to sense that they possess a hierarchic awareness and that they are aware of its correspondence with the hierarchy of divine truths. The Christ of God and his benefits, the glimpse of God who is the total beatitude of the soul, these are mysteries before which wonder and reverence are an inescapable quality in the believing response.

Yet even in these instances the 'Yes' in faith is not only a believing assent ready for knowledge, but a believing assent in which knowledge brings the desired good thing, namely the benefits and the beatitude. Nor does that efface the awe before God. In glimpsing the way God is, we can have only reverence and awe, but we cannot separate that reverence and awe from our desire, since in knowing the way He is, we also know the way He is for us.

Nowadays pluriformity makes a synthesis of the kind achieved by Thomas Aquinas an impossibility. If that is so, and if we pursue the idea of the hierarchy of truths, are we simply going to omit some things in faith and retain others as one might shed some cards from a card index? Are we going for an agreed minimum at the cost of the ambit of revealed truth? Or is the process to be one of a certain boiling down to a few basic insights? Would not these methods simply be a form of error in the faith? Omission would surely imply misrepresentation. Boiling down would surely amount to a betrayal.

Yet the expression of the Christian faith is not merely about words, not exclusively about things out there that the words signify. It is also about the life being lived by the believer. The well-used episcopal defence mechanism whereby nothing must be said or done to disturb the faith of 'simple people' contains this important factor: Catholic believers are all in the same boat for the good reason that faith is for living, and for living together. Not even a theologian can or should live his faith in total isolation from the good widow Rafferty with her rosary beads. The good widow needs him.[70]

In the age of casuistry this interaction was, if not better understood, at any rate commonly taken for granted. Suppose an eventuality, they always said. Suppose a rough fellow near to death. He wants to be baptized, and time is short. May he receive baptism, the sacrament of faith? He is hardly able to articulate a belief in God who is One and who is Three. Should he be baptized? In perfect agreement with Vatican II and the hierarchy of truths, they thought: Yes, he should be baptized for God's gift of this sacrament has a divine purpose, the salvation of the believer. Equally the Christian faith of the sacrament must somehow also be there. But how? There must be a faith that the good God exists, and that somehow he is to be this believer's happiness. It looked minimal enough. Should not the notions of the Church, the Bible, and the Sacraments be included? Not really necessary, they said. It is the purpose and promise of God which counts. After all Heb 11: 6 had said: 'For whoever would draw near to God must believe that he exists and that he rewards those who seek.' In that solution the hierarchy principle could not more clearly be seen. In fact a stricter opinion came to prevail, and the need of an explicit belief in the Trinity prevailed. Even so the affirmation of the Triune God sufficed.

It is not the rights and wrongs of an ultimately casuistical debate which concern us. It is the agreed principle of the hierarchy of truths behind it. The hierarchy beams on God, and applies to faith as a form of life. It was the second factor which in the course of time got overlooked. The truths of faith acquired an official grading or rating, known as their 'Notes', 'Qualifications' or 'Censures'. The items of faith, it might be said, came to take an importance in their grading independently of the connexions between them which basically were the reason for the grading.

Here again tidy Aristotelian thinking was to blame. In the sixteenth century a system was laid down for the West whose very strength was also its weakness. The trees took on so much more importance than the wood, that the reason for their being where they were, was forgotten. It was Melchior Cano (d. 1560) who laid the foundations. His importance is that he came to dominate post-Tridentine theology until well beyond Vatican I. Dependent even on Cicero for an understanding in rhetoric of the way theology works, he knew he had to give the theologian the tools so that when at work he could know where to find, how to place, and how to judge. For Cano the last all important element was concerned with that quality of certitude which would produce conviction. As a result the truths of the faith had to attain a gradation of authority to carry conviction. Is this truth *de fide*, or is it not? Should the theologian be prepared to give his head for it? How should a judge of the Inquisition evaluate a proposition?

Cano had personally taken papal infallibility on board. For him it fitted the system; and one had to be armed to survive and carry on living in the 'new' and 'special' republic, which the Church, the perfect society, turned out to be for him. The grading was doubly important. For the representatives of authority and for the theologian whose job it was to discover as well as to prove and confirm, Cano intended that there should be a certain rational flexibility. But his system became a strait-jacket. In pre-Vatican II theological manuals, truths were graded into fourteen or more slots, and it is hard to believe one's eyes now when reading the *New Catholic Encyclopedia* of 1966 which actually finds it 'extremely regrettable' that there was not greater uniformity.[71] Here was a systematic use of the hierarchy of truths which resulted in placing the 'authority' supporting a truth before the very purposes for which the truths were available to man.

Alas for the tidy mind, the degenerated system of 'Notes' and 'Censures' has happily gone or nearly gone into oblivion. As some sort of scaffolding it may yet be revived of course; but the view of the Church which supported it no longer reigns supreme. So the scaffolding can no longer dominate as before. The genuinely sound purpose of the scaffolding, however, remains. It was to ensure that the edifice of our faith always grew upwards towards the reality of our saviour God. It is this abiding dynamic (scaffolding is much too static as an image) which ensures that the hierarchy of truths can never in the course of any abridgment, give us an impoverishment, let alone a reduction in our faith. Yet, says Rahner, 'The Second Vatican Council's teaching about the "hierarchy of truths" says that not everything which is true must for this reason be equally significant.'[72] There may be a shortening, a verbal telescoping, but rightly used the hierarchy should lead us to express ourselves with greater profundity about the things believed and with a greater genuineness of adhesion and commitment in what we profess. The hierarchy is there to bring out the ordered connexion between the truths. It is this sense of the connexion in reality that ensures that the remaining significance is a heightened one. It is only at the opposite pole that we find reductionism.

The following significant factors for the believing Church and for the individual believer seem to me to emerge:

(i) Faith in our Saviour God is also faith in and of the Church, a faith present and shared in a common ground of differentiated awareness. Further, what is known about God and his salvation arises from no other point of awareness than that which from above commands all the rest. So it is paramount and in commanding the rest makes it by comparison the mere small change of our dialogue with the Creator, Saviour God. There can be no theology from below in constructing a hierarchy of truths.

(ii) Our faith is both obedient and free. It is a response to a command and to a promise. Its living and permanently unchangeable foundation is Christ, so that even the *Yes* or *No* demanded by his created Church always corresponds to a lesser reality than the reality of the concrete *promise* which is offered. That promise cannot in substance be negated by any created interposition.

(iii) The command of faith from God in the Church continues the Lord's own mission to evangelize. The guaranteed strength of that mission is no less than a strength grounded in the uncreated witness of God. It is only this which has a claim on absolute commitment.

(iv) In the faith-life of the community and of its members, there can be neither a truth nor a command that does not have its place within the hierarchy of truths, which hierarchy is both declaratory of a specific truth's relative importance and of its normative value.

(v) The thrust of truths of faith in the world is authentic insofar as God, the *Prima Veritas*, shares in these very truths by disclosing them. This authenticity cannot be measured by Church structures or the applause of men.[73]

AND OPENNESS

As an event of the 1960s Vatican II has already fallen into a distant perspective. Critical reactions themselves can now begin to be evaluated. Let us remember that the impact of Church Councils has usually made its way across not merely decades but across centuries in a contentious fashion. After Chalcedon (451) the Monophysites were beaten into heresy. Today the West has almost forgotten them. In 1054 papal Legates excommunicated the Patriarch of Constantinople. The definitive breach was scarcely noticed at first. But thereafter polarization between East and West widened and widened. It was only in 1965 that the papal excommunications were lifted. That move at least registered a mild change in the general climate of opinion. It is to be hoped that the almost surrealist visit of John Paul II to Istanbul in November 1979 will be remembered as some sort of milestone on the way to reconciliation. Two Church Councils have failed, Lateran IV and Florence. In the Latin West the Council of Trent was followed domestically by waves of a conservative backlash even. One has only to mention Jansenism, Gallicanism and Febronianism. Nearer to ourselves Vatican I drove the objectors into Old Catholicism.

After Vatican II, I see the hierarchy of truths having both a negative and a positive force. Negatively it provides for criticism of views, official or not, which rely too much upon a doctrinal short cut, or which offend against Christian freedom. Positively it is the hierarchy of truths which can act as a safety net around weightier doctrinal decisions so that they may always be viewed in a wider perspective than seems to be called for.

But the hierarchy of truths offers something even more enriching. It helps us to cope with a tension in the Church. On the one hand it enables us to renew the privileged patristic outlook upon the Church, so that truths shall always be living truths for living the Christian life. On the other hand we have inherited an image of the Church leading us into a static, museum-like version of the Church. It is unfortunate that in the tensions of Church life the *perfect society* image has detached itself from its theological root. That root was the claim to a vicarious possession of the authority of God. Such an instance of delegated authority was deemed perfect. But the hierarchy of truths tells us that only God and his Christ are above instances. The terminology and the model could be only relative.

Now a body intended for witness must witness variously, and the monolithic system that looked foolproof turned out to be stultifying and had to be dropped. Vatican II has enabled us to start again. But that does not mean that we now have a foolproof insurance against ever again getting our priorities wrong. Each situation has to be explored anew. The hierarchy of truths cannot be made to rest secure like Hope on her anchor. At their meeting in Ghana, Pope John Paul II and Archbishop Runcie of Canterbury acknowledged this point quite emphatically. They said that they believed 'that the time is too short and the need too pressing to waste Christian energy by pursuing old rivalries and that the talents and resources of all Churches must be shared, if Christ is to be seen and heard effectively'.[74] That Christ should be 'seen and heard effectively' comes near the summit of any doctrinal agenda that any Church, and particularly the Roman Church at Vatican II, has to write. There we have the nub of the 'means of salvation'.

Perhaps indeed the nearest we shall ever come now to a foolproof insurance against wrong priorities is the common respect expressed in Ghana for the shortness of available Christian time, and the pressure of human need.

In the obsolete system of 'notes' or 'censures' attached to theological propositions it used to be said that the proposition that God willed all men to be saved (cf. I Tim 2: 4) was 'proximate to faith'. Such a weak embrace of the gospel was unfortunately under the influence of the most restrictive version of Augustine's predestinarianism. But in today's experience of urgency, so well put in the Accra statement just mentioned, the old particularist certainties about the 'elect' or the 'non-elect' have gone.

We cannot say that there is or can be any human situation which effectively rules out the divine will to save. Vatican II's

Constitution on the Church treats the famous text of 1 Tim 2: 4 quite positively and then adds:

> Those also can attain to everlasting salvation who through no fault of their own do not know the gospel of Christ and of his Church, yet sincerely seek God and, moved by divine grace, strive by their deeds to do his will as it is known to them through the dictates of conscience. Nor does divine Providence deny the help necessary for salvation to those who, without blame on their part, have not yet arrived at an explicit knowledge of God, but who strive to lead a good life, thanks to his grace (*Lumen Gentium*, n. 16).

Here an openness is offered to us. It is endangered by today's polarization of opinion within the Churches. It is endangered by a fear of pluriformity. By means of the hierarchy of truths and the scope given to it through the Council's declaration, a renewed and clearer expression of the Church's essential mission should be brought home to us. By it the Church should become more herself to herself, to all Christians and to all men of good will. It is the essential involvement of humanity with God which is at stake. God is the One. Men and women are the pluriformity.

CHAPTER TWO

Suffering and the Creator God

In our first chapter we pleaded for a recognition of order and proportion among divine truths. Within the ambit of true faith, let us be reasonable, we said. The *fides* should be ever *quaerens*, and so should be the *intellectus*. God wants this humanity in its rationality to be humanly human. One thing could overturn such an account of the divine-human relationship. It would not be sheer thinking, nor sheer believing. It would be that concrete, raw and brutal reality, the human experience of suffering. The faith of a fanatic can give no account of it, nor can the reasonable resignation of the coward. It is an evil lottery that remains with us.

Not that theology, or a philosophy of religion, has remained silent on this subject. It has probably said too much, said it too confidently. A sort of shorthand theology used to say that suffering had a redemptive value, even that suffering conferred merit before the Lord. Such a theology is now a sick theology, and it offends against human dignity in the image of its maker. The truth is, as we know all too well, that suffering can corrupt and pervert, can tear asunder and bring in despair. And it kills. It is now beginning to appear that massive unemployment can induce suicide. From one point of view the two ends of suffering are suicide and genocide. In between one can point to famine, as at present in Ethiopia. Our speculative question here is whether, when we see Christian truths even in some hierarchical fashion, we can also see a way of bringing back reasonableness, let alone worth, dignity and solace, to our human condition. Does a sense of proportion in faith still allow us to hope in God and somehow to do honour to man?

The old effort at rationality was called theodicy. Its shortcomings are now well known. If we insist on trying to 'justify God's ways to man', we land ourselves in an area of implausible abstractions, and we put forward a God who conveniently for himself tends to look the other way. Whether the mystery, it should never have been called a mere 'problem', can be penetrated head-on is highly doubtful. But the language used suited the derailment of the 'problem' at the time of the Enlightenment. The new line of reason was inadequate and has given theological thinking on the point a bad name. The Enlightenment removed the 'problem' from its matrix in a living faith about God, and preserved it as a museum piece. God's most mysterious relationship with man was 'secularized'. The perspectives being altered, the God of any sort of salvation history was left behind. The result was that thinking on the subject became confined to abstract language, and 'theodicy' became 'a purely theoretical undertaking'.[1] Even on the theoretical plane the problem came to defy 'the application of all rational principles'.

Suffering is not a 'problem' out there, unless perhaps to relief workers. It is a mystery in here. It is immediate, it involves. It continues, the paradox of it, to relate God and man. As we become absorbed in it, we find a double directionality. It goes out and up (for the sake of a word) towards the most supreme reality we know. It also comes in and piercingly divides ourselves from ourselves, so that we doubt our own self-consciousness in its presence. Knowing ourselves in suffering, knowing suffering in ourselves, and then knowing God within that circle, remains an agonizing experience.

KNOWING EVIL AND KNOWING SUFFERING

'How did I get this?', asks the hospital patient. The whence and why of evil and suffering is a first reaction after the spasms of protective flinching elicited in the nervous system. The what and the how of suffering must belong to a further stage, even though in one logic they are more elementary.

Let us do a little direction-finding. Pain and suffering do belong to medical writers as well as to philosophers. When doctors give their minds to a question in general anthropology they come up against the topic soon enough. They have to deal with the apparently purposeful mechanisms of alarm and evasion which the body exhibits. At the level of biological utility we can all see what they see.

We can even see a grander design. Life in general needs protection and help in its self-perpetuation. So we can argue that 'death, pain and the risk of suffering are intimately connected with the possibilities of new life in general, and the emergence of conscious, and especially human life in particular'. And it may also be the case that in an impersonal world with the sort of order we detect in it, that pain and suffering will be inevitable for 'conscious and self-conscious creatures', if they are free.[2]

But in self-conscious existence that argument comes to a full stop, when we take into account the scale and quality it has to stand up to. Can genocide, mass famine disasters, and the nuclear holocaust be slotted into that argument without a qualm? The astronomer, or the macro-biologist like Teilhard, may consider the matter with some indifference. For the concerned theologian the impersonal laws of an evolving universe are not the locus of the redemptive God's activity. Nor can the same theologian be satisfied with the idea that such general laws, involving such destruction and death, are acceptable as a means for the purpose of 'soul-making'? They do not seem to tie in with any desirable perfectibility which the rational creature under God's revealed love may attain to.[3]

Such questions belong to a world of optimistic reason that has gone. We may still seek for an overarching order or orders in the divinely revealed truths, but we are far from thinking that they can be picked up by inspection of a mechanistic and rationalistic universe. Our cosmological horizon, in the human sense, is no longer bounded by a world of nature philosophy. If God is open-ended, emergent and continually active, then so must man in his image become and remain. The outer husk of nature cannot set bounds to that, otherwise the redeemer God is no redeemer. It is, I submit, sheer suffering which discloses that. So we are not to be bounded by a working cosmology. We have to think of theological ends and theological beginnings.

We have to turn again to God the Creator *ex nihilo*. In the ontology of the Christian faith of the west, it is held that the creative action is from nothing and that it takes place in entire freedom. As theological points each illustrates the other. When we are considering suffering I think the traditional thought model of the *ex nihilo* creation still has something to say. A scientist considering the notion of a *creatio continua* may find the older Hebrew model from chaos to cosmos more congenial. It may cosmologically speaking be preferable. But the anthropological horizon of suffering is different.

Thus the scientist may face with equanimity the thought that one day the earth will be reabsorbed into the sun. But the theologian faces a more proximate, and in his language more human, drama. Under the threat of nuclear extinction from a human agency how does God appear now? We know that for his sons in God's image the *ex nihilo* of hominization's origin has some meaning. Can we not also see a meaning within the threatened *in nihil*? For on one plane, the human one, the Creator *ex nihilo* is also the Redeemer. And there is an *ex nihilo* of redemption just as there was an *ex nihilo* of creation.

That is why I think we must in theological fashion face up to the blank of the human *in nihil*. Does not that voidness itself take the mind back to God? But then how? I come back to God as to our related interest. The good Creator God binds us totally to him in his creating. Now surely, just as he was then, he remains the good-one-for-us. That is not a fiducial guess, an extra to the Creed. We would depart from the Creed, unless we were prepared to admit that belief in the good, almighty Creator God is an interest related statement. It is ultimately God's Word that says so. It also says to us that the positivity of the two *ex nihilos* was a positivity of goodness and love. For in love the creature was made and redeemed. Thus in face of a final catastrophic suffering we are led to explore the lost positivity in the *in nihil*, by comparison with the positivity of goodness and love in creation and redemption.

So the focus is still on man, the sufferer in God's image. Can that image in all reason and goodness go into a human *in nihil*? Does the Christian faith leave us accepting that the *in nihil* of the nuclear holocaust implies an evaporation of human good in the threatened extinction of men? Of course we know too little of eschatology, but we hear the positive groaning of creation, and we have heard of the promise of submission of all things to Christ. Furthermore beyond history the New Testament sees a living ground of something that has been active though hidden in all history. History is not here cosmological but human. So the relationship with the good Creator is seen as a lifeline threaded through all, never as a blank, never as an *in nihil*. The scriptural truth is that the positivity of the *ex nihilo* becomes active. Classical theology can see it this way. The goodness of the Creator, whose act is in his Logos, who redeems in his Logos incarnate withstands destruction and maintains his image.

That still does not claim easy intelligibility to be seen in all suffering. But equally it is not a counsel of despair. It does not say, 'Forget it. The time will come when there is no sense in speaking of a relationship with the good Creator. Total godforsakenness is all.' We are speaking of *our* God, whose being is *being-for-man*, which makes our being (body and soul) a *being for him*. From the black hole of the *in nihil* we still have to say the good Creator does not lose us from the sphere of his *goodness-for-us*.

In spite of all, the nuclear holocaust cannot be thought of as outside every sphere of providential goodness. In the worst of his sufferings we may hear the Christian, or the anonymous Christian, cry out, 'Where is God?', but he is also saying, 'Where is my good God?'

The Bible looks at this more concretely still. The relational side of the origin is clear: 'The Lord God formed man from the dust of the ground, and breathed into his nostrils the breath of life; and man became a living being' (Gen 2: 7). Hominization itself has a Godward significance. It is that of a creatureliness in life. This life is on our earth. At this point already God's action is revealed to us as the beginning of his fatherliness. Man does not come from outside or above the earth. As God's son he is set free above all to receive God's Spirit, that he may perceive he is in the image of God. And there is no reason to exclude his bodily existence from this compenetration by the Spirit.

It is the whole man who is related to God. From the *ex nihilo* to the inbreathed Spirit there is, theologically speaking, only one connecting link. It may seem tenuous, but it is God's. It is the refusal of nothingness in God's creative act. The prior weighting in favour of man's existence is not man's, but God's. It follows from what we have been saying that this prior weighting in favour of existence is also a prior weighting in favour of a good. At the same time it was a prior weighting with a risk. A risk for man, and a risk indeed for God himself. If creation is from goodness and out of love, then it is also a risk to goodness and to love. It is not an *a priori* thought that God risked suffering 'in, with and through his creation as it brings into experience new and hazardous possibilities'.[4] We shall use that idea again. As can be seen, when we speak of risk, God's risk, we imply the possibility of suffering, God's suffering. That there is also a risk for man is clear. This man-for-God has the power in himself to turn himself into a man-for-man. But the point of the way I have been developing this argument is that there is greater intelligibility and significance for man in the possibility that God takes a risk in goodness and in love.

We are now moving in the direction of a famous doctrine. It is that of the so-called *theologia crucis*. It accepts a high doctrine and significance of what Jesus did on the Cross. It tries to take to itself the full intellectual consequences of both the incarnation and the cross. The eternal and impassible One suffered (ho apathēs epathen). We shall have more to say about the implications of this doctrine in Chapter Four. But far back behind it lies another idea. It touches us now. When we say that in the very idea of a creation of the rational creature, there lay a risk for God himself, our minds are working not, as it were downwards, from God to man. Rather our minds are working backwards from God to God, God in his incarnation to God in his creating. We are working back from the only experience we have of God revealed which is not merely human-like, but fully human. It is so fully human that it is an experience of suffering. Concretely, God in creation risked the Cross on which he died.

When the Colossians are told something of the theology of the Christ in whom they believe, the Christ, Son of God's love has a role in creation as well as in redemption (Col 1: 15–20). The Son is so pre-eminent that creatures owe creation as well as redemption to him in whom they have believed. The creational risk of the cross is implicit but present. The divine risk was the greater one, but one that triumphs. While as for man, the biblical death of turning to dust (Gen 3: 19) does not imply simple annihilation. The foreseeable and foreseen human death *in nihil* is not an absolute. The death, as Bonhoeffer suggested, is the death of only one sort of man, that of the pseudo-man, the *sicut deus* being.

The divine risk carried some contingency, which was mysterious, within it. Much less mysterious is the contingency that falls out wrong for man. But the Bible, even when it admits that, continues to weight man's destiny on the side of the good. The all-important factor is that of the relationship between man and God. And here the good God continues to hold out a relationship in sheer goodness, indeed in ecstatic love. Of course the curse of death lay there too. But we must look within it. What lay there? Not annihilation, not as *in nihil*. It was rather the promise: 'The death of Death — that is the promise of the curse.'[5]

One consequence for our thinking when we join beginnings and ends is this. We cannot stand outside this revelation of God's Word. If we do we make ourselves God's accusers and we abuse his standing promise. Again theodicy fails. Only if we start with the assurance that God is the good creator can we find a way. Socrates already sensed this. 'If it were necessary either to do good or to suffer it, I should prefer to suffer than to do it,' he said. He did indeed refuse the means of escape when they were offered him by Crito.[6] Thereby his realm of noble ideals was left intact. But the question was not put wide enough. Pascal and Kierkegaard have changed it for us. The suffering that comes our way, or threatens our lives, is no longer just an incidental, just an unfortunate accident that hits us. The suffering that was without, whatever its scale, is now a reality within. For any religious experience involves us in ideals, even in basic good things like human dignity, which mysteriously are a part of our religious existence. Pushed to a typical paradox Kierkegaard finds that the more of suffering, the more of religious existence there is.[7]

It is not now we, who examine and test life or God on the subject of suffering. God is the 'examiner who in faith and in the love that a man has for him, must push matters to the extreme (while himself suffering in love more than the candidate)'.[8] So now the dilemma of suffering takes on a quite new logic, the logic of sheer *religious* existence. We may not go all the way with Kierkegaard. But we can see again how theodicies are bound to fail. They reach out to the wrong God. They should be stretching out, or better looking within, for the *God-for-man*. Through suffering he speaks to the Christian. Through suffering the Christian seeks for the grace to reply. The rational theodicy was impervious to the very dynamism of God's creation in love. Equally it is impervious to the God who promises. The argument between Socrates and Crito, noble as it was, cannot embrace the *God-for-man*. Theologians have given Socrates the same advice as he gave himself. To a living Socrates perhaps one can do no other. But the Christian must be brought back to creation in love, and to the promise in hope. Does he have to make suffering constitutive of religious existence. A merely conceptual answer is no answer. What the Christian knows is that there is no other existence at all which is pointed to by suffering, and if that existence is human it will come to be religious. In this century it amounts to a de-sacralizing of man and of religion if we consign the whole of our answer on to another world or the next world — if we say that is where the balance of dignity and felicity will finally be restored. The nuclear holocaust is about an obliteration and de-sacralizing now.

But the middle sort of person who suffers is neither Socrates nor a saint. Even if he is a Christian trying to respond to the offer of a fundamental vision of God, the suffering he endures may block his vision. The struggle within the Christian to see clearly and to look in the right direction comes out of the Christian existence as such. We can now see more clearly how at least three of the historic main lines of thought have failed to rescue the thinker as sufferer.

(i) The best established and most familiar view is also the one most criticized today. Coming from Plato through Plotinus and Augustine it had acquired great authority. It says that evil and consequently suffering, considered as an evil, is either the absence of being or the absence of good, or again it may be a privation of being or good. It had an early critic in Epicurus (d. 270 BC) whose logic has been difficult to get out of our systems. Either God wishes to remove evil from the world and he is unable to do so; or God neither

wishes nor can he do so; or thirdly he does wish to do so, and
he is able to do so. That seems to exhaust the logical
possibilities. We are then left with the uncomfortable
conclusion that in the first two hypotheses God can by no
means be the all-powerful God of faith. The third possibility
is strangely inconsistent with the facts of life as we live them.

But it is possible to get round the disjunctions of Epicurus.
You may say that beyond the area of his disjunctions, there
exists a transcendental order of things to which his
disjunctions cannot reach. Thus there may be gradations of
being some of which are beyond the scope of the *either/or*'s of
Epicurus. Or again we may try saying that we are relative
agnostics in the sense that God must in himself always be the
provident God, but we cannot know exactly how. Or again
that this is a world essentially admixed with evil with an
inbuilt sin-situation which now pre-empts the *either/or*'s put
before us by Epicurus. Then Epicurus would not exclude,
and could not do so, all the possible aetiologies of evil and
suffering.

But the believer has to go on asking. Can it be true that the
God who creates and saves merely in using the so-called
permissive will is really looking the other way? Does that not
look like a sleepy intellectual device for putting God at a safe
dualistic distance? Does it not also make the epidemic of sin
and guilt which hits us vanish by some mental retrojection to
a point before our human history?

This first view is at its feeblest when it puts on a rag of an
argument from the beauty or harmony of the world. Since
the mind can hardly encompass the extent of real and possible
human suffering of the world, it appears an almost
blasphemous irrelevancy now to say that without its dose of
evil and suffering, a nice moral balance could not be achieved
in the universe. The mind cannot be asked to leap from
genocides and nuclear holocausts to the notion of a greater
harmony yet awaiting discovery or revelation. It is true that
the argument was given popularity by Augustine. But
having adverted to the runaway character of evil he was
unwilling to draw the human consequence in his thinking
and too willing to follow the logic of the argument that sin
and evil are a nothing.

(ii) But the intellectual system of Christianity might have

gone from bad to worse. For the mental alternative to this wrapping around of suffering in a greater harmony or order is to accept that somewhere behind creation there is a primal cleavage and antagonism between good and evil. Certainly it was with help from Augustine that such a view has been permanently proscribed. The struggle, as in Manichaeism, between light and darkness, or between good and evil, cannot be a radical constituent of the universe. Not only would the good God not be the all powerful God, but then totally untouched by suffering he would not be the *God-for-man* either.

It is true that at various times Christianity has given more or less hospitality to a hell, to an almost irresistible devil and various demonologies, as well as to a deceptive-looking opposition between two totally opposed moral kingdoms. It cannot be denied that these as a dualism are adumbrated in the Bible. But it must also be remembered that in the New Testament Christ operated a transformation. That leaves the human situation in process of finding the victorious end of history which is good, while already in the midst of an ongoing human history. The traditions of the 'two kingdoms' have not always shown that they are part of a process.

What Augustine never faced is implicit in what I have been saying. It is this. The world has now experienced, is experiencing and will experience such an excess of suffering that the concept of an overriding order is no longer compatible with the idea of the *God-for-man* who is otherwise to be found in Augustine's God of love. The mind now negates the simple concept of an overriding good order. Suffering can no longer be universalized as evil, made into an abstraction and be allowed to spirit itself away. We cannot, as Surin points out, escape 'the sheer particularity, the radical contingency of human evil'. Surin reminds us that one can even with Ricoeur speak of ' "the bad faith of theodicy" ' which ' "does not triumph over real evil but only over its esthetic phantom" '.[9] We can no longer stay with the idea that there is in eschatological time a final and radically good solution to the threat of the *in nihil* which in the meantime needs to be seen as a merely interim affair. There must be another perspective. Without it there can be no sense in which the *in nihil* comprehends a *felix culpa*.

(iii) A third possibility in our attempt to satisfy the mind over evil and suffering might even be suggested to us by some biblical expressions. We would then be tempted to place as it were all the hardness of human destiny on none other than on God himself. It would amount to saying on our part that God's absolutely sovereign will could be no other than that which is told us of his justice. The Old Testament metaphors would then take over. They would present him as an oriental despot and we would have to justify this view of the divine. Eventually we would have to say that God can and does will man to suffer, simply because, and for no other reason, it is his good pleasure. In Isaiah is God not simply the predestining potter, who has the right to do what he will with his clay?

Our thinking would be reinforced by what Paul apparently made of such a text and after him what Augustine even more harshly made of it. Further we would then accept Augustine's handling of the case of the twins Jacob and Esau quite simply in terms of a positive and negative predestination. The oriental despot, accountable to no one, just decides the fate of two individuals solely in accordance with his good pleasure. Then nobody can cry 'injustice' for the immutable *apartheid* between the twins is settled by the immutable will of God.

Indeed traditional western theology went a good way along this line of thinking, until Karl Barth taught us 'that in creating God chooses good and rejects evil, which henceforth has the character of being denied and opposed by God'.[10] God now reappears as a moral agent, and on this principle discussion could be started afresh.

This is a good point at which we in this chapter should look around us, for we mean to consider suffering in the light of creation. So let us see Barth going one step further. When God rejects a possible evil and selects a possible good, that implies something we have already been hinting at. It is this question of weighting. Whatever the question of the election of the twins by God may mean, it certainly must take account of the fact that destiny for the rational creature, with all its attendant risks, must be weighted in the direction of good, and of good for the creature. God in his rejection of evil is not in some merely dualist fashion opposing himself to a *nihil, das Nichtige*, lying outside himself. God does also remain supremely free with an intelligent freedom. For by it he does bestow his own intelligibility in part upon the rational creature. Equally it is his supremely loving freedom, which bestows goodness out of spontaneous love.

Where the rationality of humanity impinges upon us most lies in the fact, as Barth insists, that all is done in the light of the incarnation of God's Word. Thus none of God's choices can ever be considered in abstraction from the incarnation of the Word, his Son. Once this is accepted, it is clear that the total freedom or justice of God can never in the slightest be considered as limited, or still less despotic. That must of course be rejected as unthinkable. It offers nothing from the *God-for-man* to the *man-for-God*.

Additionally it is clear that the despotic God cannot be the God in whose image man is created; and the de-humanizing suffering of this world cannot be allowed to escape both God and his rational creation in his image. If it did so, it would become another independent principle of evil. It would also destroy the idea of God's image in man, for this image shows itself in the brotherly relationship between men, and more intimately, as Barth holds, in the relationship between man and woman. Christianity cannot at bottom accept a despotic God, because in consequence man loses his humanity as man. That he apparently tries to do in the concentration camps, the gulags, and in the possibility of nuclear holocaust which threatens to devalue God and to de-humanize man.

To switch our thought back to God, we must still see the will in God as lying within an inner divine necessity. But it is a necessity to be identified with his transcendental existence and his self-affirmation for us. His own self-direction is to good and to love. An arbitrary will in God not identified with his goodness and love would not be the will of God as *Deus totus totaliter*. We may not lessen that goodness because we cannot see our way back to him.

(iv) So we have mentioned the possibility of some sort of limitation in God and we have found that we had to reject it. But there is a further supposition which can be made. Let us suppose that the rational creature, as we know him, is not merely a neutral, unaspiring, undesiring personal being. At all events, if we take seriously the revelation of a *God-for-us* we cannot see man as merely neutral in regard of God or of his neighbour.

The electing, purposing God creates his *man-for-God* as man ready now for aspiration and for love. Here again creatureliness implies a relation towards God which persists. It is a relation arising out of the relaxed divine letting-be. It too has its image. The creature thus let-be runs the risk as his Creator ran a risk. He runs the risk of the reality which is let-be, a relaxation, a loss of happiness. But even that is still a risk weighted towards a prior good. It would be nevertheless, as we suggested, a weighted risk with a bias towards the prior good. It would have to be a risk within a framework, that of the divine offer of love.

Of course if love is given on the terms of a divine letting be, then the returned love is not on terms of equality. Then on the part of the creature the liability in the risk is clearly the greater. The concrete events of experience only confirm the point. So the total disproportion between God's love of us and our love of God may indeed expose us to pain and suffering. If we listen to Romans 8, the risk is a universal as well as a religious one. There, man is yearning in concert with a vast creation which is groaning in travail and expectation for the final divine disclosure.

May we not here have the rudiments of a theological theodicy? Creator and created reality are juxtaposed. The Creator's love and risk are answered by the creature's awareness of risk in love.[11] This very awareness is an opportunity and locus for a greater understanding of the creation–Creator relationship. There is no need now to speak of evil as an absence of being, as in the Augustinian tradition. At the same time the relationship between creature and Creator circumvents anything like a radical dualism between good and evil in suffering. God is not despotic, nor is he looking the other way. Above all creatures are looking Godward. Paul moves us into a mode of thinking in which faith and hope are now stimulated to wider theological horizons. They are quite consonant with today's expanded consciousness of an open-ended universe. As Käsemann says of the passage: 'Only Christ is exalted. Disciples are still stigmatized by his Cross and must occupy the place on earth which he has left.'[12] And the expanded horizon shows that in the now of suffering we may also live in eschatological time, which means that there is a theological simultaneity between the suffering now and the glorification (cf. 2 Cor 3: 18 and 4: 16).

It is now a secondary matter whether or not we push back an aetiology of evil into a Fall story, into a pseudo-time, an *in illo tempore*. Since in a mysterious resolution pain and suffering are moved forward in faith and in hope to a final reality, this movement shows us an existence still weighted in favour of love and of the good. By it man can still be humanly intelligible even in the midst of his suffering. He is not in any religious sense basically de-humanized now. Or better, the monstrous de-humanization, which we know, is now given a transformation. I still do not think we should imagine that we have now discovered a silver lining to the black cloud of suffering. The total cynicism of the Grand Inquisitor is in a sense never answered. But in pain and suffering there may be the discovery of a deeper set of relationships. The death of Maximilian Kolbe took on its intelligibility in the new relationship to men which he explored by it. For many people that is a plunge too deep to be contemplated. But we must acknowledge that he taught us in suffering what an embracing loving deed could be in its very depth. In being so impotent it was an ecstasy of love. The creature meeting the Creator joins in creating anew. In this concrete sense of taking creation and redemption together, of bringing the divine mystery into the human mystery, I submit that we do have an open-ended approach to theodicy — always on the condition of course that it is a theological theodicy. For that reason we are continuing to point in the direction of the theology of the Cross.

But we have not yet finished with beginnings. It is my belief that the very first article in our Creed is relevant to anxiety and perhaps suffering. Through our affirmation that the Creator God is the all-powerful One, we are keeping the risks and anxieties of life at bay. 'Observe,' says Augustine, 'how quickly the words [I believe in God the Father Almighty] are spoken, and how full of meaning they are. It is God and he is Father: God in power, Father in goodness. How blessed we are who find that one Lord God is our Father.'[13] Augustine is commenting on that Creed [R] which goes back to the closing decades of the second century. By then the Roman Christians had become aware that, not only is God our Creator and in that sense our Father too, but that he was also our Father in the sense that he was the almighty One who could assuage anxiety and lessen the dread of suffering.[14] Christians of the first three centuries had been exposed, as we are, to a world dread, and we may believe with Dodds that they did in fact take some of it on board.[15] It was not to be philosophized away. I would argue that the ancient way of understanding that first article of our Creed is most relevant for us today.

Before passing to our next section we may summarize the four views we have just discussed. The first view was a logically neat one, but it does not satisfy the demands of a revealed Christianity's *God-for-us*. The second view in the end offends against the Christian faith. The third restores to us some opening of the mind for the revelation of God. The fourth view relates us once more to our Creator God who is our Redeemer, and it prepares us for the *God-for-us* who reconciles even in suffering.

EXPERIENCE AND SUFFERING

So when we say the Creed we are not leaving our world of apprehension and suffering behind. It is part of our affirmation of God that we believe in him for us in our troubled state. Like the neophyte reciting the Creed we both profess and ask. The same is true of the theological effort. Our own personal history with its preoccupations follows us into the continued effort we make. We ask and re-construct all in one. It is either personal or general, human experience that makes us ask.

To take a famous example. 'Lisbon,' said Voltaire, 'is plunged into the abyss and Paris goes on dancing,' So he was writing within ten days of the famous earthquake at Lisbon in 1755.[16] There can be no doubt. Voltaire was moved. But he was moved in a form of anti-*credo*. He had his motives. For one thing he wanted to sneer at that English poet, Alexander Pope. In Voltaire's judgment Pope had missed his cue and in his observation had failed to mention God. For good measure Voltaire was not above a gibe at Rousseau as well whose mental solution to the problem of Lisbon was to make some sort of calculus. On one side you added up the evils of the event of Lisbon, and on the other side you added up the evils of the *status quo ante*. Which then was worse for the population of Lisbon? Voltaire will have none of this. His humanism goes deeper.

> Le présent est affreux, s'il n'est point d'avenir,
> Si la nuit du tombeau détruit l'être qui pense.[17]

The question of thinking, *l'être qui pense* and his rationality is Voltaire's clue. Pope was wrong. Rousseau was wrong. You cannot both be the thinking being and conceptually leave out God. There cannot be a lesser of two evils when one of them is a destructive earthquake. Human value (*l'être qui pense*) cannot be subjected to such a disorder, human degradation and darkness, even the escape of a demonic force. It added up to this. Were there no future, then there would be no more of man. To use our jargon. That earthquake implied a dysteleological suffering on a genocidal scale. It meant no future, no rationality. Take away rationality and man is no more.

In spite of his readiness to sneer Voltaire was surely on the right lines. Suffering is *sui generis*. It is not to be classed with any phenomenon in the range of human experience. It is as such an *unicum*. Thereby it provokes a question, as Voltaire saw, in an order of things which is also, truly or falsely, unique, namely that of religion. The evil of suffering unquestionably touches. It provokes the cry of scandal.

When we see it joined with the innocence of childhood it becomes *the* scandal. Contemplate Anne Frank's Diary, or see a group of spastic or mongoloid children in their efforts at play, or think of the new-born infants rescued from Calcutta's dustbins by Mother Teresa's helpers — a cry escapes us, of scandal and of protest. These things must not be.

But the horror without and the sorrow within make the mind, as with Voltaire, spring to and for, or against, God. Either he exists, then he must be accused. Or he does not exist, then his priests and defenders must be put in the dock. From the believing tradition Paul and Augustine had already constituted themselves Voltaire's answerers. How dare he? Who is man? He cannot become God's accuser.

Yet the Christian mind cannot be confined by that simple answer. In personal faith and hope and charity, the Christian is turned to his personal God, turned in a continued quest, if we fuse Augustine and Barth, to the beauty of a personal Thou. In its constraint or violence the mind struggles to remain above the personal threshold. It cannot for long endure the fancy that there exists no Thou who is a listener:

> What agony I suffered, my God! How I cried out in grief, while my heart was in labour! But, unknown to me, you were there, listening . . . You knew what I endured, but no man knew.
> (Augustine, *Confessions*, VII, 7)

There may be violence (mental, moral, physical), alienation — from self, from other selves, even from one's own culture. The suffering may be in an enclosed and vicious circle, or racial hatred, total personal grief, poverty, endemic disease, famine. We may with nature suffer in its pollution and spoliation. Moltmann, the current theologian of the Cross, sees even deeper into circles of 'senselessness and godforsakenness'. Then all future and all purpose can go. Then the Christian must seek, and seek how those circles shall be broken. His beginning is simple as ever it was in that Creed. The Father is almighty. The breakthrough will be personal.

It is true that in appearance the endurance of suffering may seem like an attempt to come to terms with an impersonal force. The greater the violence the more likely that seems to be. Rape and violent death destroy personal inviolability. Moral rape and the forcing of religious opinion illustrate the point better. Runciman's *History of the Crusades* concludes with the opinion that those enterprises virtually amounted to the sin against the Holy Ghost. How could he say that? The acceptance of a religious faith is a personal interiorization within the spirit of man of a relationship with his god. It is the most serious thing man can do to or for himself as a person. The old moralists looked for and found the worst sin they could categorize, and they called it 'hatred of God'. I never saw the reason until I met a certain case of advanced multiple sclerosis. An Italian woman school-teacher had suffered for long years. Though still comparatively young, she had come to the point of despair. She began to destroy the only horizon of her own existence as a believer, which she was. It had to be in the language of hating God. In struggling to free herself if only mentally from this sub-human thing or presence, which was the disease, she had to tear at the heart of her own existence. She did so in the language that came to her, the hatred of God. The personal God, interiorized in faith, as intimate to herself as herself, was now depersonalized and turned into an instrument with which to rend herself so as to avoid that other final destruction. Needless to say, I took this as a privileged insight into the condition of suffering and by no means or in any sense a sin in the language of the old moralists.

Perhaps at its most impersonal suffering should be given a different name. Simone Weil calls it *malheur*.[18] The distinction she makes is so sharp that the word she selects should be retained as she chose it. *Malheur* is above all an uprooting, an equivalent in its own way of death itself. Yet it is a presence continually felt because of the threat which cannot be avoided of sheer physical pain. There seems to be a threshold between it and suffering, and when this is passed, *malheur* can persist in life for decades. This capacity it has to perdure even among the innocent is allowed by God, and it was *malheur* in this sense which constrained Christ to pray that even he might be spared. Simone Weil observes without mentioning a theology of the Cross, that *malheur* may be an experience in the absence of God from the soul and at the same time with a feeling of revulsion towards the self.

That brings us to the dissociation which we shall have to mention. Job is an example of this, and he shows how in time the subject may come to take on the role of complicity in the presence of *malheur*. In its extreme form *malheur* implies besides physical pain, distress of soul and social degradation. In some ways this last factor may be the most hurtful, because without that sociality the subject may suffer depersonalization. It is of course fed by common or garden weakness of the flesh, by inconstancy of soul. Indeed the worst, namely suicide, may occur since we all depend upon sociality and our appreciation of it, for our general feeling of existing at all.

Once *malheur* as a distinct state, which we can place in parallel with suffering, has been pinpointed and identified, then Simone Weil can say: 'Knowledge of *malheur* is the key to Christianity.' Yet in the strong sense such a perception must be impossible, and it is just as impossible to know *malheur* without having passed through it. Paradoxically it is accessible only through supernatural favour. That being so, we have to admit that being compassionate in the full sense is the prerogative of Christ alone. Only he is the one who can transport his existence into the very being of the victim of *malheur*. At this point one passes on to the mystery of the divine love incarnate.

Would it not then be true to say that the shocking thing about suffering, as in his twisted way Voltaire was quite capable of seeing, is that it mocks God, the personal God? It does violence to a perhaps unthematic consciousness of God within. But the resulting state has importance. We have a characteristic state of revulsion. It takes a special form, which I would call a *not this* recoil, a retroaction away from what is now inflicted. On the other hand there is a concomitant and frustrated yearning for a precious *but that*, which has now been defaced, destroyed or simply removed and is now lost.[19] My example taken from a pseudo-hatred of God tends to show that in suffering we can identify a constraint or violence on the self. This is such a destructive violence that at its grossest it can point to or work for no sort of unity in the subject. There may be, as with the saints, a submission or endurance on a heroic scale. But so far as the infliction is concerned, prescinding entirely for example from grace, the consequence can only be a false interiorization, an attempt to combine the impossible tension, *not this — but that*. Even in prospect it can be seen how this is an untruth, a disvalue to the self, a negation not only of the self but of its ground. The place of God may of course be in some sort taken by patriotism, freedom, liberation, and the struggle on behalf of human dignity. The powerful symbol of sacrifice has evoked heroism in the Judaeo–Christian tradition as in others.[20] We must treat heroism even in its Socratic form as exceptional. The fact remains that the friends of Socrates were inconsolable.

No theological anthropology has yet shown how genocide should be approached in the spirit of sacrifice. No parallel reflection has ever emerged to cover the hideous inaction of the Western foreign offices when they were appealed to on behalf of German Jews in 1942. History has recorded 'acts of heroism performed by starved, tortured, hunted Jews inside and outside the ghettoes and concentration camps during the Nazi rule of Europe'. But besides these, history also records 'the mysterious passivity of the Jewish communities in face of the Holocaust'.[21] We must respect the adjective 'mysterious'. Any attempt to pinpoint the exact locus of suffering is only the roughest of direction-finding. The victim interiorizes, tries to swallow his lot as best he may. The interiorization is at least a matter of degree, and then on no simple scale. It may run from the cowardly or the passive to the heroic, from the sincere and the true to the twisted or false. But what calls for our respect is this. Even within an area of false interiorization, when suffering is the issue, something still human remains to be disclosed.

First: we must insist that through the relationship, that really subsists, between the sufferer and God, it is God also who is attacked. In that perspective the being invaded by suffering can just be made intelligible, for the victim does have his future in his very need for God, deprived as this may be. Within a false or distorted interiorization there is still some beaming upon God. This basic reflection has found little or no place in the classical theodicies. They have neglected a core issue in suffering, namely the attempted rending of the ongoing self. That rending lies in the apperception of the self at its deepest level. The destruction may not take place in a direct line we can point to, since it touches the self's dialectic with others, the world as well as with God. The false interiorization may aim now at one, now the other, or at all three simultaneously. It is in any case aimed at the individual's characteristic as a person, the destruction of the basic relation *ad alterum*. We cannot go much deeper.

The martyr in sight of his end, the mystic under conditions of crushing duress perceives what may affect us all. The intelligent appreciation of the self as personal is an appreciation of the inherent gift of the *ad alterum*. The *ad alterum* as to others and the world, finds its deepest level in the *adaltereity* within. 'The intelligence,' says Plotinus, 'when turning towards the One does not go out towards a Being different from herself, but enters within herself, for God is no other than the interior depth of things.' If this is a personal panentheism, it brings us face to face with the fact that the destruction of the good *adaltereity* in suffering, which is inflicted, is nothing less than a blasphemy. There is no room here for an armchair theodicy of the omnipotent will inflicting just punishments upon a *massa damnata*. The theologian must pursue the thought that the Creator God, and good Father God of the Creed is also the God who, having suffered on the Cross, now suffers with and in the sufferer.

Secondly: we may come down to a more perceptible state. What of the rending or splintering by the pseudo–interiorization? It is not to be located merely in a destruction of concentrated consciousness, nor in its purposive attention, nor even in the extinction of a vital possibility of judgment. It is not that the sufferer cannot make *differentiations* any more. The transparent lucidity of Socrates remains both an ideal and a possibility. The point is rather that the sufferer's judgment is, as it were, differentiated for him. What should be active in him is made passive. He cannot escape from the *not-this-which-I-suffer is my right and good*, but *that-over-there-which-I-have-lost is my right and good*. This differentiation is forced upon the subject. It is followed by a clouding and eventual rejection in a spontaneous judgment of the mind. The sufferer does not simply nod his head at that differentiation forced upon him. He drops his head. Now the helpless sufferer is torn from the possibility of integrating his situation with himself. He can give it no meaning. He can make no nexus. Choked and blinded he is submerged. At Auschwitz the terrible passivity of suffering communities was marked by the helpless leaps to the ceiling for air as the gas filled the chamber.

I submit that no one can think of the holocaust and be satisfied in his mind that these monstrous evils could be docketed and ticketed as a privation of good, or as a punishment for sin.

Thirdly: let us take the element of the *not this but that* under a common denominator. I would borrow the term *alterity* ('altérité') from Denis Vasse. He uses it to express a condition of the suffering subject; and it is amenable to experiential and psychological description. Dysfunction and a certain rending or cleavage is an accepted sign of the presence of suffering.[22] The subject's ongoing self experiences a feeling of inner interruption, even of suspension over a void or gulf. In this state of confusion emerges a process of alteration. That the sufferer interprets as 'I am different', 'I am not myself'. Through this obscure process of alteration, in fact mediated by it, there emerges a pseudo-Other. That pseudo-Other becomes a state of *alterity*. Denis Vasse allows for, but does not make much of the further element of the *but that*, which I think is important. But he includes the desire for life which, for me, can well correspond to the *but that*. The subject is 'affronté au désir de vivre et à la mort'. It is 'le cri d'un sujet naissant' and the call to live is now not according to 'leur propre image'. It is created by the *not this*.[23] So *alterity* is, I think, just what is thrown up by the forced differentiation, or by Vasse's 'altération', to be found in the *not this but that*. Indeed it is surely exhibited at that very point where the sufferer *is* the sufferer and nothing else. *Alterity* is the threat and more. *Alterity*, because unacceptable and because *ex hypothesi* irremovable, acts as an effectively malignant process and presence, an effective signifier of destruction.

When it begins to get to work, it is not precisely the threat or the act of an external strange reality. My enemy may inflict suffering. He is not *in* the suffering. The evil of *alterity* lies in this. It offers a relational possibility. Yet I cannot relate to it. *Alterity* in suffering cannot be loved without perversion. At the same time I am not of course suggesting that *alterity* is the essence of suffering.[24]

Let us take it for granted that in practice the inimical *alterity* in suffering does threaten and does invade. It does this to the person as 'subject'. Worse, we might say, it does this to the subject at the point of arrival at the level of free, loving personhood. The sorrows of Werther make that clear. Above all we cannot forget that the form of that *alterity* is one of violence and that its action is to destroy integrity. Even the gross symptoms and syndromes of some cancers suggest this. The inherently destructive power of *alterity* does away with the integral man, whose very being before God lies exactly in his possibility of becoming the integral man. If man's being lies, as I take it to do, in his becoming-for-God, then the instability of bodiliness and spirit gives a toehold to *alterity*. That makes theologians, like Luther, who conceive of man as being a battleground, plausible. *Alterity* at this level destroys by the process of release.

Schoonenberg speaks of a sharper eye, that we need, to get a 'comprehensive idea of nature below and in man'. He lists disorder, failure, deformation, deformity, illness, decay, death and violence as phenomena which demand a sharper eye in theological analysis and interpretation.[25] He must be right. I believe the sharper eye must come in our making a conscious effort to blur an old, but now increasingly, irrelevant distinction. The difference, to put it crudely, between physical and moral evil is no longer what it was. The limits of the *actus humanus*, which is moral, as against the *actus hominis*, which is mainly, since it lies outside a narrow sphere of voluntariety, without basic human significance, are not longer sustainable. The passion (*pathos*) of man for which there is an ultimate moral responsibility in the race, cannot be left out of account. Alone, the problem of Third World starvation has changed our apprehension of responsibility for suffering and with it our responsibility for the fearsomeness at all levels of the invasion of *alterity* in human life.

The same is true of the modern threat to the person as person. Considering man as spirit, as free subject, as the responsibly independent individual, as an embodied self, and as socially interdependent and as creative, it is clear that invasive *alterity* has a thousand points of entry from subliminal advertising to the tortures of the Latin American prisons. We know that all this goes deep, because the biography of the sufferer then becomes a story of disintegration. The usual metaphors to describe suffering do have an ontological sense: incoherence, being uprooted, overthrown, transfixed, rent asunder, racked — all these make the point expressively. Mysticism and heroism apart, the disintegration implies that the person in his or her wholeness can no longer be, and that love itself is no longer possible, now that the ground for self-commitment has gone. So has free subjectivity.[26]

Fourthly: we must ask, ontologically speaking and empirically, is not the most threatening of the characteristics to be noted in *alterity* that of unfreedom? On the individual scale the extreme risk at which personal oneness and the dynamism of love is put must be clear. *Alterity* forces not only into unfreedom but into a regression into the self. The exceptions we have acknowledged are the heroic ones.[27]

But in 1988 the question of human suffering before *alterity* in the sight of God cannot be left there. Where suffering means unfreedom the Christian conscience must be stirred. I take the risk of one remark suggested by the witness of Liberation Theology. Is it not the case that in Latin America the preaching of a Christ Liberator arises out of the experience of an almost total *alterity* within society, the causes being economic and cultural as well as social? In these circumstances Liberation Theology works at two levels. It must. First there is the level of social analysis which forms the anthropological base to be incorporated into properly theological reflection. The second level is to be found at the point where theology undertakes its own work of hermeneutics. In Liberation Theology we know that this amounts to a socio-economic analysis seen through the grid of the gospel and Christ. Now the interesting thing is that at both of these levels the element of *alterity* plays a role. In the first level it is pin-pointed by the situation of massive human repression. In the second it has the function of a release mechanism in the dynamics of dialectical 'transformation'.

The Liberation theologian is at once struck by the destroying power of *alterity*, an *alterity* he sees as inducing a massive process of de-humanization. It amounts to the destruction of historical man in the experience of a crushing *alterity*. The theological conscience that says this, is both an I-conscience and a We-conscience, thus accepted as the one and only possible conscience.

It seems that here we have yet another reason why we cannot accept evil or suffering to consist merely in the privation of good or in non-being. Indeed the Liberation theologian may add, that, if we are satisfied by such a theory, we add to evil and suffering in confirming a repressive *status quo*. The only thing to do is to relegate the ancient theory to the status of a residuary concept. It once fulfilled a logical function, but can no longer be utilized.

It is also quite inadequate to the demands of the theological concept of the Kingdom, where transformation must reign.

The *alterity* in suffering, human division and regression, sin and death — this *alterity* can be treated only as a reality to be transformed. The Kingdom has its orthopraxy which demands it. It could be argued that if orthodox Church language is at bottom incapable of reconciling man with man and of destroying *alterity*, then that language must be relativized, just as the poor carpenter of Nazareth relativized the religious absolutes of his day. *Alterity* is only thinkable as a reality to be overcome through the death-to-resurrection process, even if that should have to take place *within* the Church.

I add a short point to this witness given by *alterity* in the perspective of Liberation Theology. It is clear that *alterity* may be individual or communitarian as we, in the Old World, have known it. What is new was latent before. A threat to the individual is perforce a group threat. That is the contention of the analysis that high-lights class-warfare. The *alterity* is clear. The unfreedom is clear. It is not surprising that there is a prophetic call for clarity over the role of Christ the Liberator.

TWO FIGURES

Let us now turn to two figures of suffering, Adam and Job. Both are types. Each appears as the sufferer in his own psychodrama. I venture a few quite partial remarks about each of them with apologies to all exegetes. Adam and Job also belong to the whole of the history of theology.

Adam is our primordial human symbol. He is man, mankind, man with whom God takes a risk, gives him his partner and then plays what is almost a game. Adam belongs *in illo tempore*, to our paradisal youth. The good Creator makes him body in spirit, spirit in body, of earth and divine breath, in his own image and likeness. The man moves in a fairy-tale garden which he dominates. To what purpose? Is the aim not to bring him into history? We are watching almost a game with horror stakes. For in the middle of the picture it is not Adam who is there, but the oriental tree of life. It is a tree which relates, the tree of life, and Adam has life.

As Bonhoeffer says, 'it cannot occur to Adam directly to lay hands on the tree of life'. But fatality lurks all the same.

There is another tree, the tree of the knowledge of good and evil. This tree is different. It is a tree of plurality and differentiation. But relationality reigns. Adam is addressed by God as man, and addressed in freedom. Relationality holds. Yet the limit is there: 'in the day you shall eat of it, you shall die'. Bonhoeffer, whom I am still following, points out that the ultimate division of good and evil is one that can also mean 'full of pleasure, full of pain'.[28] These alternatives too are related. For the tree looks forward to a time beyond innocence, towards an adulthood where pleasure and pain are not inevitably separated. What will be is that *tob* will not 'exist without constantly being submerged in *ra*, the painful, evil, mean, impure'.[29] Nor of course is *ra*, evil a reality without 'a glimmer of pleasure'. Relationality ensures that there is no good without evil from now on, nor is there any evil without good. It is only when the split between them is complete that we leave the realms of relationality: 'When the debased itself takes on form, man has lost his manhood and we say that he is ill.' What we cannot know is, 'how the deed was done'. For us now there is no *illud tempus*. Our world is one of sundered relations. What Adam's sort of history became, ours now is.

In fact Adam among us reinforces the contingent relationality we live in, with all its limitations and unfreedom. Good things have become a curse. In Adam's affliction with *alterity* the other possesses power against us, against me to the extent that it is an *alterity* by which I must die before God. It would be dishonest for the Christian to proclaim that he can suppress such a death in the name of the Resurrection. Rahner says the Christian is marked by a 'pessimistic realism'. The theologically portentous death with Adam is as much part of our death as is the death of Christ.[30] And we have to admit that in asking for 'transformation' we are asking for a piece of 'realized eschatology' now. And why not?

But here we have to observe that the suffering of death as an experience is part of the world of splintered relationships. And the animal that suffers goes into hiding. Man is not an exception. As Adam shows in our primitiveness our suffering induces shame, a reality and form of experience which after all can only subsist where there is division and *alterity*. Adam, as Bonhoeffer teaches, brings it with him, for 'knowledge, death and sexuality' are now destined for suffering. By shame we are lost between the division felt in guilt and the loss of oneness and self-possession. Above all the division is between *tob* and *ra* first of all seen in Adam's relationship with Eve. By that condition alone it touches man's relationship with God. The creative gift becomes the destructive gift. Bonhoeffer echoes Augustine when he writes: 'Man's own life is to preserve and propagate itself in the destruction of the other person. Man is creative in destroying. In sexuality mankind preserves itself in its own destruction.'[31]

I believe it is best to admit, with Rahner, to a pessimistic realism. Suffering is our theme and its tragic perspective is to be glimpsed even in the question, 'Adam where are you?' The truth is that suffering implicated in guilt and shame does not merely run into some fateful *alterity*, or even into a self-inflicted *alterity*. It runs into *alterity* in the now-changed relationship with God. The very question of a theodicy is theologically speaking a question posed by the supposition of the impossible *alterity*, that which confronts the dependent reality. It is impossible in the sense that the dependent reality, the might-or-might-not have been of existence, finds *alterity* in him who for him necessarily is. It is an *alterity* that to all appearance cuts off the life-line of existence itself. In the Adam story the dependent existent then makes things worse. 'The woman Thou gavest me . . . she gave me.' On the face of it a mere complaint perhaps; but in reality is it not a question to the good Creator God. In the circumstances it seems to say, it is he, the Creator, who should do the justifying. In a sense that is what we, like Marcion, have tried to make our theodicies do in their turn. To quote Bonhoeffer again: we fall back 'on one art learned from the serpent, that of correcting the idea of God, of appealing from God the Creator to a better, different God'.[32]

In fact does not the suffering of the Yahwist's Adam go straight to the point and show just how to locate suffering under the good Creator God? In the amalgam of suffering, guilt and shame we are told of there is a force of evil which takes on a quasi-unity, a quasi-positivity also. The Greek empty slot theories of evil do not really fit at all here. But it took some time for this to register in the West. Leibnitz set his mind to try and defend the Christian God against the quasi-unity subsisting in evil and consequently in suffering. Kant saw the point more clearly, and standing away from the empty slot theory faced the positivity of evil quite squarely. It is Schelling who goes further and posits the dualism of good and evil in God himself. Thereby he rejected the empty slot theory outright.[33] The truth is that once an appeal is begun away from the God-for-us of revelation, and back to the God of the philosophers, there is no reason why one should appeal to a better God any more than to a worse one. The art learned from the serpent enables us to do just that, for the serpent knows of a 'nobler God' who does not need such a prohibition.[34]

The second biblical figure I shall offer may take us a step further. I am thinking of the age old hero and paradigm sufferer of the Bible, namely Job. In later tradition he became holy Job, if not Saint Job, and the point about him gets misplaced. He is surely a paradigm of enduring faith, in the sense of fidelity with belief, rather than merely a paradigm of patience. But that is by the way. Job is here a most useful paradigm for us, because he is, almost by definition, the man of innocent integrity. More than that he has a lucidity, which rules out that common phenomenon of self-anaesthesia in suffering. He too possesses the noble transparency of Socrates. Together with his lucidity that helps him to make clear to us what his contribution will be.

He is indeed any innocent sufferer of our day, who might be brought to ask what sort of God is that God who is pleased, or placated, or satisfied — or even is simply permissive — before the suffering of the innocent?[35] The case for what I am saying should be carefully constructed, but I risk putting it roughly.

In his perspicacity Job is one who sees. He sees: 'the terrors of God are arrayed against me' (6: 4). He sees that innocence does not ecape, for God 'destroys both the blameless and the wicked' (9: 22). But he gives us most help with the theophany of Chapters 38–42. So what does the man above all register in his seeing, and what does he not register? He knows that he is being offered no argument or explanation for the suffering of the innocent. Against that he has to set the fact that it is the good Creator and sustaining God who is to be identified 'out of the whirlwind'. First of all he has to be identified as the one who is present, and then as the one who himself is total wisdom and power. Thus Job confesses the divine transcendent power and its purposes. This he can do because of the realized hope expressed in the second cycle of speeches: 'without my flesh I shall see God, whom I shall see on my side' (19: 26–7). In the lesson to the whole poem Job somehow sees that the hope just formulated is realized: 'no eye sees thee . . .' (42: 5). Of course the author of the work knows that no man can see God and live. Job's vision — it is not likely that it is eschatological — is that of a comprehension sharpened by spiritual experience.

He comprehends that in the *alterity* of suffering there is a divine element or even presence to be discerned. He perceives what we must reject, and we do. There can be no radical dualism separating an essential evil on equal and hostile terms outside God himself. He also rejects that there can be any radical dualism within God. In advance Job flatly rejects Schelling. But what Job positively does see is most important. It is that *outside history* there is, as it were, no locus of God's justice dominating that history. There cannot be a tyrant justice dominating human history from above, as there eventually will be in the Augustinian divine justice, which does dominate the wallowing *massa damnata*. For Job there is rather an element of rationality to be identified. It is not directly about God. It is about the way we understand the history of the world's sufferings. Basically, that constitutes the beginnings of a theodicy through history. Augustine would add a theodicy to history. For Job it is a matter of sensing the divine even within the threatening created *alterity*, which is the destroyer. So the divine rationality of the world lies not so much in its static physical laws, as in the inner reality of a residual homogeneity with its dynamic Creator. Job sees that so strongly in suffering that it amounts to a presence.

I am tempted, when that is said, to leave Job with his silence or with his vision. But it is hard to resist gilding the lily. Once we admit the presence of an inner homogeneity in human suffering with the divine, then is there not an intelligibility within the feeling and the will afflicted by the suffering in the human predicament? There could still be a lifeline. A point is made about Job by the Gnostics of Princeton. Should we not grant also that in Job in addition to or as an enhancement of his faith there is something else? Could the man not be something of an agnostic? Job, say the Gnostics of Princeton, is 'the first hero of an inventive faith, a faith which creates a new dimension, when the irreconcilables are reconciled like the two stereoscopic images which give rise to the third dimension — Job's stereoscopy is semantic'.[36] This may be so. But, then, how does Job do it? He does it, by his refusal to go beyond the evidence, a refusal to justify God so that he, Job, may continue in his faith. Then indeed Job's relative agnosticism has two good effects. He refuses to turn himself into an atheist. He refuses to find an alibi for God. The result should have been a precious one for later theology. Job, the semi-agnostic is left with his God, a God present to him nowhere else but in his suffering.[37]

But we must not leave Job without a theological remark tying back his vision of God to our parallel theme of creation. The Creator, for Job, is the free Creator. That is not a matter of speculation, of giving the Creator a fine attribute. Rather a quality in creation takes the mind back to the Creator as free. There is a wonder about creation and it takes us back to its origin. There are, for example, 'the nature and instincts of wild animals which evade all rational comprehension'.[38] There is thus a primordial creator-freedom 'which hurls one into a feeling of one's own nothingness'. Moreover there is a bond between the Creator and humanity. It is deep and mysterious, but 'people feel themselves addressed and seized in the depths of their being by God's rule, even though they do not understand it'.[39] In a sense this is a deepening of the point about Job's, and our own, potential insight into history. There is a bond between Creator and rational creature in history. It is one of comprehension, if confused and mysterious on our side, and its very weakness may cause our attempts at theodicy to become a guess at justifying ourselves, an anthropodicy. Even so not all is lost. For neither theodicy or anthropodicy can make sense or have anything to say without some connexion with its partner.

Of course the theodicy of Job is a piece of unfinished theological business. But in remaining unfinished it still gives the opportunity to construct or reconstruct. It points to the

Cross of Christ, where the focus must again be on the combination of guilt, pain and suffering, the *impossible alterity* of God, and the victorious swamping of his creation by the love of God. We must now try and point ourselves in that direction.

THAT DARKNESS CAN BECOME LIGHT

It is possible to say that, although suffering is an evil thing, the good man must suffer. But that statement could mean one of two things. He 'must' suffer, because it is our view of man which says that he must. Thus for example, he 'must' suffer because learning comes through suffering, and there is no other way than by suffering that such a learning process gets through to our essential humanity. The *pathei mathos* in other words of Greek tragedy.[40]

Alternatively, and perhaps additionally, one could say the just man 'must' for theological reasons suffer. He must for example take up his cross and follow his Master. The 'Master' was dedicated to a 'vocational suffering', so must the disciple also be. Both those ideas have had their appeal in the past, and they doubtless still have an appeal. The Greek tragic ideal seems to mirror the history of human experience. No doubt we all do learn something by what we have suffered. But ever since Lucian's satiric dialogue, *Zeus Catechized*, awkward questions have been asked either of Zeus or the Fates.[41] What type of necessity binds us to such a learning process? As to 'vocational suffering' I am not at all convinced that in an unrefined state it has any place or any significance for the Christian idea of man.

Let us abolish one thing, the simple notion of vocational suffering. It is far too close to the idea that it is God who wants us to suffer, any simple version of which is repugnant. In the practical effort to lead the Christian life the very notion does harm. That of necessity men or women should take upon themselves to expiate by suffering needs very close inspection. No doubt heroic things have been done by the vocational volunteers. But encouraging the idea that the repayment of a debt to God incurred by all gives us an enclosed, fixed, and basically sterile view of the relationship between God and man. As François Varone argues, such a 'religion' can be destructive of authentic gospel faith and piety. I believe he is right, for such a closed system offers a mechanism based upon the repayment of a transcendental debt for which the payments are finite and can never match the scale of the debt. The business of such repayment can hardly be the stuff of a genuinely divine vocation. Debasement inevitably takes place. Thus for example the Cross of Christ comes to be utilized as a pseudo-masochistic symbol.

Thus, too, the idea of suffering as a necessary satisfaction to God comes to require the mechanism of a counterpart. Historically that has favoured the growth and perpetuation of a carefully selected priestly caste. For apart from the self-sacrificing heroes there must be others to form the regular mechanism of sacrificial appeasement. Hence history has indeed favoured the priestly caste to whom the power is given of satisfying the divine demands. Of course sophisticated Catholic theology does not talk like that. But it would be a pretence to maintain that the social and psychological mechanisms which give a handle to Varone's critique are non-existent in the traditionalist layers of the Catholic Church today. Where we must differ from the sixteenth century is by putting our own house first of all in theological order. The truth is that a distorted theodicy does lead to a distorted *praxis*.[42]

Nevertheless the whole gospel must be kept. How does it, or even can it apply? Where is the genuine human correlate of the sufferings of Jesus? Are we to try and correlate for example the film clips and documents of the Nazi extermination camps, the victims of Hiroshima, or the famine-doomed populations of Africa with the sufferings of Jesus? The mind hardly takes this on board.

Has not human suffering now moved out of the scale of human intelligibility? Meaning in it has got lost. These things can only in part be an accusation against man, still less an accusation against a divine vocation. We are only beginning to seize upon the mystery of their quasi-Satanism. The nuclear threat is race-wide. It is difficult even to find a word which will stand up against the terror scale of life under a totalitarian régime, still less against that of the Holocaust. But a word can be the thin end of a wedge of rationality and even mental protection. It may preserve some intelligibility

and meaning for the race. We have in fact seen the growth of
a new word recently taking over the defence of a basically
ancient Christian concept. We know it as *solidarity*. The word
began, I think, to make its fortune with Max Scheler.
Among the intellectuals and theologians of Poland it seems to
have been well established, before it became the name of a
movement or a 'union'.

The matrix of the idea was biological: 'any part of a living
cell has the power to become any organ and to enter into the
role demanded of any cell, so long as it has not yet acquired a
determined function through an already completed formation
of the organ in question'.[43] The idea was elevated by Scheler
to become a principle, and indeed a social principle. But
especially and most significantly *solidarity* is ethical in
reference. And that interests us. For it is in its moral aspect
that in face of guilt we do all indeed feel guilt. The principle
goes even deeper. Primordially and from the springs of our
own being (*ursprünglich und von Hause aus*), we take upon
ourselves the common responsibility for all the ascents and
the descents in the moral and religious state of the
collectivity's world. That is a process we undertake in the
state of *solidarity*.

The process operates by relying upon a real mental
sympathy present in the human organism. If *A* loves *B*, there
is normally a necessary response in *B* for *A*. The response
may of course be refused or concealed. But the process
already begun necessarily continues. For the existing love of
A for *B* by a solidarity in natural sympathy now grows
outwards for *C* and for *D*, and then for *E* and for *F*. Indeed it
proceeds to a *quasi* infinity. But what of hatred, injustice and
sexual deviance? Indeed they may spread in the same way.
Violence also. All this may happen below the threshold of
awareness. When Scheler sees us as liable to be infected by
one or other of these streams, then he also sees us under God
as responsible for each other. The spread is such that only
God can be the judge. Paul has made the point. To be judged
by human beings is a small thing. There is so much more that
is at stake. One cannot even be judge of oneself; but the
responsibility is there. 'I am not aware of anything against
myself, but I am *not* thereby acquitted. It is the Lord who
judges me' (1 Cor 4: 4).

Scheler's insight may be judged to be somewhat romantic. It nevertheless does provide a further shaft of light into some classical Christian doctrines such as the infection of the race with a sin, or the sin-situation of origin, as well as the doctrine of the mystical body of Christ. If it seems that the ideas of original sin and the mystical body are lacking in any form of experiential correlate, then it may well be that the principle of *solidarity*, which runs in two directions, may be offering us a clue. By *solidarity* there is a common felt apprehension that one's ideals and values as well as disvalues are those of the collectivity. The result: *Mitfühlen und Mitwollen tragen hin die Gesamtwerte*. Perhaps too it is even more important for us that in *solidarity* the individual is the responsible representative of the collectivity and he can and must live up to it, or be responsible for it: *das Individuum ist Organ der Gemeinschaft und zugleich ihr Repräsantant, und ihre Ehre und seine Ehre*.[44] Significantly Max Scheler also uses the concept of the stranger-Ego, der *Fremde-Ich*, to structure the ethical formalism he needs. But, and here is the largest hint of all for us, the stranger-Ego, like *alterity*, is, if seen in a larger perspective, part of the transcendental order of love. For love can in Scheler's view, descend as well as ascend. And we can see that it is love which is called for in the profoundest sense, so soon as we begin to reflect on the presence of *alterity* in the existential reality of suffering.

At bottom to say that there is *solidarity* in suffering, as we often do, is in fact to say something quite paradoxical. If the precise effect of *alterity* in me, when I suffer, is that I can have no part in the aggression implied upon myself, then how can I in any sense speak of *solidarity* in suffering? No, suffering is a disvalue which cannot be shared, for it lacks intelligibility and meaning as a basis of sharing. The other disvalues of suffering equally prevent sharing. But does an argument from the principle of *solidarity* lead anywhere? My short answer would be: I think it can be made to do so. It gives us a basic determinant in the search to find ourselves and our fellow men. It is a ready correlate in living man for the one who now represents man, the second Adam. 'Anthropology,' says Dorothee Sölle, 'and christology are related as question and answer.'[45] The Christ as our representative is not a substitute for us. He is our *pro nobis*. He is for us as the one unique instance where *alterity* does not deprive the sufferer of intelligibility and meaning. He becomes the supreme meaning and intelligibility through the *alterity* expressively transformed in his Resurrection. Thus there is one instance in which *alterity* is not merely in part transformed as it may in heroism become: an extreme of *alterity* becomes an extreme of love. We have no other such thinkable instance.[46]

The uniqueness of the transformation in Christ is not a matter essentially of the quantity or quality of his sufferings. The uniqueness lay in the person, or subject who suffered, and in his acceptance of it as a culmination of his being the representative in *solidarity*. There are signs of this reality in the gospel. Companionship was significant for Jesus. It was the Pasch 'with my disciples' that he wished for (Matt 26: 18). Poignantly that hand was 'with me' in the dish (26: 23). He was mysteriously to drink the cup again 'with you' (26: 29), and the Gethsemane scene of dereliction twice related a 'with me' (26: 38: 40). A desire for *solidarity* with his own in the most human terms is there in the passion story. Is it different from our normal desire to allay the first effect of the impersonal *alterity* in suffering, just as it begins to enter in and to destroy?

The beginnings of the destruction wrought by *alterity* are hinted at in the story of the unbearable cup of Gethsemane (Mk 10: 38). Had he really been, or was he remaining totally free from the idea of equality with his Father? At any rate Mark's insight as to how far *alterity* went seems to show Jesus, to use Barth's famous phrase, 'in a far country': 'remove this cup from me; yet not what I will but what thou wilt' — ou ti egō thelō, alla ti su — (14: 36). We notice the *not this but that* of *alterity*. In the same expression we note the overcoming love by which *alterity* is vanquished and transformed, transformed in the divine unity by which the Son loves the Father. But Jesus is the human representative. Consequently in that overcoming love he overwhelms the world with his Spirit. The reality of the event is both Trinitarian and incarnational. On the incarnational side *alterity*'s invasion of human *solidarity* as an ineluctable destiny is destroyed.

This is the point at which to say why the simple and in some way naive terms of *alterity* and *solidarity* have been preferred in this chapter to the classical symbolic language of the New Testament. We might have spoken of enmity, slavery, divine wrath, or of sonship, liberation, reconciliation, or of redemption, propitiation and sacrifice. All these throw precious shafts of cross-light upon the one mystery. And those shafts of cross-light have been built into theories. But I accept a criticism made by Schillebeeckx: 'This both weakens and "tames" the critical force of the crucifixion of Jesus. Suffering as suffering (in whatever way) takes on a positive theological significance . . .'[47] For a time we should look away from that significance and in a different direction. It is not 'suffering as suffering' on which we should build. I hope that we can agree that the spirituality of dolorism is a dead end. Theologically, if we remain trying to build only upon an analysis of suffering, we try to build a theological parallel to a philosophical theodicy. Such thinking makes no theological progress. I have to plead that progress means we accept a simple divine *a priori* for our reflection. It comes to this. God does *not want* suffering. God does not want human *alterity*. God does want human *solidarity*.

Solidarity I think teaches us two broad things about suffering. In the concrete it points to an obvious *not yet*. *Jésus sera en agonie jusqu'à la fin du monde*, said Pascal. And he added: *il ne faut pas dormir pendant ce temps-là* evoking the lost *solidarity* in Gethsemane. There is in other words an ongoing, hence also future, human correlate to the divine *a priori*, and it is the unending agony of Jesus in his body.[48] It does not leave him alone: it should not let us alone. It should be an *a priori* in our reconstruction. But his first lesson unfolds another ambiguity. The *a priori* of the unending agony gets separated from its real and concrete condition. The inward looking side of the Churches is only too good at doing this. It looks selectively at the agony of Jesus. 'A Polish Jew has declared that the name of "Christ" always makes him think immediately of *pogroms*.'[49] Is it necessary to evoke the problems of Central America? This sometimes heartbreaking human *a priori* lies under the divine *a priori* of what God wants. 'But God shows his love for us in that while we were yet sinners Christ died for us' (Rom 5: 8). Here *alterity* even in the ambiguities of the human *a priori* is vanquished. As Käsemann points out, this is a divine act of power, the same power of the good God whose creation was *ex nihilo*, and who now from the nothingness of the Cross (one might again say *das Nichtige*) 'puts an end to wrath'.[50] Now in face of the continued agony of Jesus in his brethren that creative power of God is not confined in a temporal scheme of things to the *ephapax* of the Cross. We are speaking of a re-*creation* and, in re-creating from a human *ex nihilo*, the God-for-us renews his promise. In that promise he again assures us that his deed is the death of death. His will to extinguish *alterity* has been expressed in his deed. As Simone Weil puts it: 'the Love of the Father is to be found at one of the extremities and the love of the Son at the other. Cosmic order is to be found *between* them, and the contact takes place *through* him.'

That brings me to the point where I want to say that our attempt at a logical placing of suffering is verified in the one supreme instance in which suffering regains intelligibility and meaning. The suffering of the Jesus of the gospels lucidly accepts the deadly threat to his own existence. The fearful anguish of the *not this but that* was experienced in the gospel version of Gethsemane. The threat induced by that *alterity* became a fact in the death on the Cross. He died on the Cross and there the unfreedom of *alterity* became total.

Yet that *alterity* became a good going beyond the event. Again it is Simone Weil who shows us how that distance may be crossed. For in her view we have our part in the distance separating the Father from the Son. The pain of separation can be love. 'The distress of the abandoned Christ is a good, because it is love.' The paradox goes so far for her that in a thoroughly mystical vein she says: 'In the extremity of his *malheur* he can almost be entirely absent. For us on earth that is the sole possibility (*l'unique possibilité*) of perfection.'[51]

Consequently it would appear that the Christian is entitled to say: God's *a priori* remains good in face of all the ambiguities of the human *a priori*. So belief in history is for us still a serious option, indeed the only option. Only the reality of a suffering God can help. The God who participates possesses *solidarity*, and that he does so is vital for us. He participates in humanness. And that human *solidarity* in suffering, which as *solidarity* arises primarily from the being of Christ, is itself part of a divine movement. For love re-creates human *solidarity* in a movement that goes from infinity to infinity. Being divine, nothing less, it has opened out the self-enclosed block of *contingent alterity*. Saying that by no means solves the problem of suffering. It does something towards showing that a transformation of the condition is a possibility. Even more it is a concrete possibility expressed in the martyr symbols we know: Maximilian Kolbe, Martin Luther King, Oscar Romero of El Salvador. The totally transforming power of the divine movement of love in Christ expresses itself in a moment of suffering and sacrifice. Still mysteriously, but all the same in reality darkness can become light.

ON THE CONTINUING SCANDAL

In one way the Christian view of suffering does transfer the scandal of suffering from the creature victim to the Creator God. It moves the scandal to a state where scandal continues, but with a difference.

Having said that, we must also say what does not happen. We do not say, man is not guilty but God is. We do not say the indifferent and serene God has now repented of his indifference. Nor is it said that *alterity* is swallowed up or eternalized in the perpetual self-identity of God. Nor is God so far removed, and so dualistically removed, from his rational creation that there is no 'ongoing or outgoing interaction with the created universe' — one may add, of suffering.[52] We must, in my view all follow Thomas F. Torrance in thinking that the 'Incarnation has opened up for us knowledge of God himself as Triune, and that John of Damascus has enabled us to see that there is room for newness in the unchangeableness of God'.[53] For more reasons than one we can now reject Peter Lombard's *Deus non factus est aliquid* as inadequate, and against Frances Young, for example, we can maintain that there is a sense in which God does have a biography.

The point that God cannot have a biography was made probably in the third century by an unknown cartoonist in stone. A *graffito* found on the Palatine of the early Christian era shows the figure of the crucified, dehumanized, that is to say with an ass's head. The inscription, as *graffiti* can be, is mordant: 'Alexamenos worships his God.'[54] This scandal to faith had of course been foreseen by Paul. Only believe, he says, and the preaching of the scandalous truth represented by the *graffito* is in fact the very *dunamis* and *sophia* of God.[55] This core of Christian preaching comes back to us every time we need it with greater force. Faith has to be structured upon a Christology, like Mark's, which makes the cross central.

By the doctrine of the Incarnation suffering does pass to the Cross and to the Crucified God. Alexamenos, not the cartoonist, was right. In early Church tradition it was easier to see the sheer power of the transfer to God on the Cross. We now have to make the effort to see that it is the God of the atonement who is identical with the Creator God. But Paul would not speak of the 'power' and the 'wisdom', if it were not enough of a shock to find that even God is so involved. Here is a difference with the thinking of the ancient world we should still try to bridge. In Augustine's way of thinking, for example, punishment and suffering would always go together. It was natural that they should. That the subject of suffering was a sentient, self-conscious subject should have received more qualification than it did.

Today theology has a different and new problem to cope with. Put simply, it is clear that the ancient world did not have to ask itself what suffering would entail for a million, for six million (Hitler), or for ten million people (Stalin). For us the sheer effort to stretch the sympathetic imagination that far is impossible. To make a strategic nuclear war or nuclear holocaust take on reality we have to use the euphemism of the 'game'. The idea that nuclear strategy can be wrapped up in a game, provides us with a mental buffer and shields us. But behind calculations that are made there is, whether they are serious or jocose, a certain, inner human truth. To it corresponds the factor of human *solidarity*. We cannot euphemize such subjective human suffering with the buffer mechanism of a 'game'.[56]

To remain with the question of suffering, we must ask, where we can locate reconciliation and atonement in the subject/victim of suffering. It has to be not merely a reconciliation and atonement with God, but also a transforming reconciliation with the dead *alterity* of suffering. In this scandal where indeed can the divine power and wisdom be recognized? Where can we expect to see that human subject, as subject, caught up into a process of transforming change?

In theology it is often good to question a question. Can
there be *a where*? Can we expect *a where* along the linear time
of this subject engulfed by *alterity* and weighed down to
death? Ancient and modern doctrine tells us to look towards
two parameters. One is the concrete presence of experience.
The other is the effect of *prolepsis*, an anticipatory yet present-
making appropriation of the full reality of God's end-time. If
God's love acts now in man, it does not act in a mere *nowness*.
God's act will be supremely free, supremely in process,
supremely in the form of the future, in the light and reality of
the final image of this child of his love. Prosper of Aquitaine
had the formula: 'Tales nos amat Deus, *quales futuri sumus*
ipsius dono, non quales sumus nostro merito.' That was
quoted by the Second Council of Orange (AD 529).[57]

There is nothing arbitrary about that. God's deed of love is
essentially through the Cross and Resurrection.[58] It is the
eternal *now* of the Resurrection which brings forward the
sealing-value of the end-time. That sealing takes place in man
or woman, so that the measure of him or of her is not the
measure of 'a man' or 'a woman', but the prototype is God's
love itself. Concretely God's offer of love is an offer in the
passion of suffering, of *alterity* itself, so that the human
passion or suffering may be transformed. God did not write
finis as the smoke came out of the gas oven.

Suffering, which is of now, must nevertheless receive its
end-time dimension. By his engracing love its dimension is
that of realized humanity. That is so important that nothing
must be thought out of reach, for whatever it is, it can be an
imitatio Christi. In the God-loved sufferers there is a human
convergence in the basic human *solidarity*. It is the one
established by Christ, so it is never fully sealed off. Christ
creates 'one new man in himself in place of the two' (Eph 2:
15). New with God, it is a new relationship with man.

I think we may try and conclude our task of direction
finding in the following ways:

(i) The objective deed of God's love is, in the Christian
interpretation of it, expressed in a grace, or a graced
relationship. We should look in the case of suffering man to a
first effect in that man's concrete reality, in man *talis qualis
patitur*. That concrete reality is the subject of the suffering. It
follows that if we can locate the basic condition of the

suffering, then we can locate the event of grace. Somehow, and this is the most difficult part, that grace will be found in experience. Somehow and somewhere guilt is transformed into love and suffering into loving reconciliation.

(ii) God's love must be seen as in history and offered in history. It must consequently possess an historical form such that:

(a) it is a free and boundless historical offer, as well as ultimately the sole command;

(b) that it has the form of a communicable transformation from suffering to love;

(c) that it proceeds from an *ex nihilo* of love to a new and restored love;

(d) that it heals, perfects and restores unity in place of *alterity* in such a way that the wholeness of a divine meaning is restored to the suffering creature. By it the residual capacity to answer the divine call of love may be awakened;

(e) that the *not this but that* of suffering now becomes the matrix or springboard, since man is historically engraced, through freedom from unfreedom in the transformation bestowed. Thus *solidarity* with God and man is a movement, as though from a non-movement, within a movement. It is *this* sufferer who is restored;

(f) that the subject's humanness in being the locus of his restored love be nevertheless open to verification, by which I mean that God's deed verifies itself in ravaged man, as man in project. Being henceforth known by the gospel 'fruits', being found in charity, joy, peace, patience would be such a form of verification. Here a proleptic sense of 'eschatological verification' as applied to man's anthropology seems to me possible. Knowledge of the truth and reassurance of the heart should be ours *now* (1 Jn 3: 19).

This effort at concrete direction-finding has necessarily been largely put in terms of the individual. These are only an indicator. We should think wider. The first question to be asked should concern the suffering and lost communities of the world. On emergence from suffering will *solidarity* be theirs? The effort to think on their behalf has begun in Liberation Theology, some of which has the charism of prophecy. When we concentrate, as we have been doing here, on the subject of suffering, we must clear up a misapprehension for which our tradition has in part been responsible. It in any case contributes towards indifference. There can be no theoretical justification for community suffering on the simple reasoning, promoted by Augustine, that the guilt of the race gives no ground for complaint or reproach. In face of the holocaust, the Third World or Latin America no such idea can be entertained. What can be said is that the lesson of Adam is more open-ended in spite of Augustine, than that of Job. It is to Adam the man of the mass, that the Trinitarian God offers his transforming love on the Cross.

God's history with man is not merely the history of a presence, as with Job, it is a circular movement. It comes from God and it goes back to God. That *alterity* appears at the point of the break in that circle is clear. But the divine movement continues nevertheless and in an enhanced form. Irenaeus and Athanasius saw a continuity in the divine action, creation leading in to redemption. They saw that God touched man down to his roots. We still have to see the creative irruption of the Cross, as creative of the community. The imagination barrier caused by numbers must be broken. In the divine movement *alterity* can never have a final place. The Holocaust past can dispense us from thinking about Hell. The Holocaust possible makes *apocatastasis* an irrelevancy. The theological imagination has now earned a holiday, but only because 'the "boundary" of transcendence is experienced in suffering and transcended in active hope'.[59]

CHAPTER THREE

Christ Relevant

We have discussed Christ in relation to the hierarchy of truths. As 'foundation' or 'basis' for that order of truths, he was clearly and in a logical sense relevant. But each believer makes his hierarchy for himself far less from some doctrinal architecture which he has studied than from his own living experience of the Christian faith. It is not necessary to have a mental solution to the Christological debates of this or of any other century in order to profess and live the Christian faith.

Existentially and personally the believer has his own hierarchy of truths in which Christ is paramount. The Christ as basis for me may prescind from arguments about the uniqueness, the ontology, the myths, and perhaps even from discomfort with the forms of worship encountered. Somehow the 'mind of Jesus' is put on, though a seriously misleading form of worship or liturgy might perhaps be the most damaging distraction of all. Commonly the eucharist appears as highly relevant.

RELEVANCE

The relevant Christ does come to the believer in the awareness of his own human condition involved as it is in the offer of God's revelation. That is not to erect into a form of special awareness an awareness of Christ in faith which is general. It is to say that in apprehending the Christian revelation, we are also aware of a recognizable Christ quality or form in our very awareness. The succession of articles in the Creed is held together by two things, our perception of their relatedness to Christ, and our perception of that relatedness to Christ as relevant to us. If I attempt to answer the question, 'What does Christ mean to me?', I find I do so under the guidance of those two overriding perceptions. They gave me an overriding personal interest in getting my

answer right, so far as I am concerned. The mysterious
Christ, 'foundation' and 'basis' of the objective hierarchy of
truths, is also the foundation and basis of my existential and
personal hierarchy of truths just as I have lived them from
day to day.

Living from day to day may indeed suggest relevance, but
it is not the nub of the matter so far as faith is concerned. I
beg leave to quote myself:

> So we must give our minds to the question of relevance, a much
> abused but indestructible term. I have the habit, at bottom, a
> lazy one, of fussing about that word in pupils' essays on
> Christology. 'Relevant to whom or to what?' I say, hoping to
> push on with one of the old debates in the subject, *anhypostasia,
> kenosis* or whatever. But today students are not to be put off so
> easily. 'Relevant to me', they answer. The trap in the question,
> 'relevant to what [i.e. doctrine]?', is disdained. 'So, what makes
> Jesus relevant to you?' I ask. Again, no hesitation. 'Experience',
> they answer. 'Not faith?', I ask. '*If,*' I am told didactically, 'my
> faith is an experience of, or an encounter with, someone, and
> that someone is Jesus, then, yes, you can call it faith. Otherwise
> not.' I try again, 'Isn't that a bit subjective?' And, 'What about
> me?', I add. 'My experience of Jesus *as an experience* is surely
> different from yours. I may never have experienced or
> encountered Jesus in any sense that would satisfy you. How then
> can we agree or disagree about what the relevance of Jesus is?' I
> get that pitying look reserved for the fifty-plus cleric whose
> deplorably scholastic, and therefore (please note) *profane*,
> thinking makes him a rather useless piece of furniture for the
> household of the faith — or rather for the experiencing
> community.[1]

Most fortunately on both sides of this discussion we want
Jesus Christ to be relevant. So the dialogue has a chance.
There is an admission, usually implicit, of a common
personal interest or value for us all. Thus the mysterious
Christ 'foundation' and 'basis' of the objective hierarchy of
truths is indeed acknowledged also as 'foundation' and 'basis'
of the quite personal hierarchy of truths. The foundational or
basic Christ can hardly be approached, as it were, from the
outside. It is not sufficiently underlined in Christological
discussions that our perception of Christ is both in faith and
in grace. Yet the New Testament and our worship and

liturgy offer an effective grasp and being grasped by the Christ who is *pro nobis* or *pro me*.

That is not to say that Christ is only relevant because interest-related or value-forming. The point is not an aesthetic one, though of course it might be that. The interest or value is profound. There is no harm with Tillich in seeing it as an expression of our 'ultimate concern', of our total committed seriousness. So the intellectual relevance remains. Christ is as intellectually relevant to us as he was to Nestorius, Cyril or Leo. I do not agree with Andrew Greeley for whom the irrelevance of Jesus is more obvious than his relevance. It is not because he was irrelevant that he was murdered, if anything it was because he was too relevant. The danger here is that we separate the deed or fact of Jesus (his death and resurrection) from the word of Jesus (his preached message of good news) in the first place, and then we go on to separate his word (singular) from his words (plural, not the message but its medium). In fact Greeley does not consistently sustain his paradox and rather takes it back by saying: 'The message of Jesus is relevant precisely because it provides the underpinnings of conviction about the basic nature of reality without which we shall never be able to change the world.'[2]

I have been talking about 'us'. Admittedly that is dangerous. Moreover, to insist that something is dangerous carries an inbuilt risk. In the case of Christ it is called a scandal; and it is a double scandal. For there is about Christ a 'scandal of particularity', and there is a 'scandal of imparticularity'.[3] It serves no purpose to ask which is the worse.

But both are present, and both are a risk because of relevance. The relevance of Christ means that Christ will be the man for all the human family at all times and seasons (imparticularity). The relevance of Christ also means that he will be the man for this Church however large and for this chapel, however small. He will also become 'my man' whom I opt for at a revival meeting — or equally the wonder-worker of a miraculous statue, the social worker for me and my mates, the great lay-man when priests pullulate, and the liberator if I am a freedom fighter (particularity). So we have to face the confusing phenomenon that relevance can universalize Christ to the extent that he can become a world-principle, an abstract cosmic existent. (The Teilhardian Omega Point is surely cosmic, but is it mine?) At the same time relevance can so particularize Christ that he becomes a privatized or personalized cipher. Lord Beaverbrook saw Jesus as the Divine Propagandist. And we are all invited to see Jesus as the Jesus of my experience, my piety. Relevance invites it all and more. The imparticularity may dissolve him into an abstraction. Particularity may fragment him into 'First-personalism' or into the 'Me-Empire'.[4]

The New Testament takes both risks. It knows that we need more than a plausible biography of that particular carpenter of Nazareth. But it does give us a *Jesu*-ology. At the same time it also gives us a, or rather several, *Christ*-ologies. It knows that Jesus must not only be chronicled and theologized (Synoptics), but that he must also be theologized and chronicled (Fourth Gospel). The relevance we shall seek in this chapter looks rather to the first option. An example of how I would look upon this is to be found in Bishop John Robinson's *The Human Face of God*. I would like to quote myself again:

> Now Dr Robinson and I have a near common acquaintance. He does not name her; but I think I recognize her in our English situation. A good Catholic with *mantra*-like habits of prayer, she is also absorbed in good deeds of a churchy kind. In America she goes to lectures. 'Does Christ get in the way?' Dr Robinson asked her. ' "No, but he gets in my daughter's way", and she went on (in her native Californian): "How can I speak of what gets me without turning them off?" ' (*The Human Face of God*, p. 13).
>
> I am so glad Dr Robinsin heard about the daughter. She worries me too. Stained glass and statues are of no use to her any more. That is not so serious, but Dr Robinson knows that it is the thought-forms behind the stained glass and statues which are the trouble. So he undertakes to eliminate the cobwebs and dead-ends, in order that the daughter shall not be 'turned off' and shall recognize Christ as a fellow human being relevant to herself.[5]

But there is more to it than that. Let us say, the lady, it is clear, can look after herself. Her daughter sets the problem, at least our problem. Where and how will she come to see the relevance of Christ for her? Can she come to see him not as a fragmented, particularized Christ, as it were tailor-made for her own image of herself? Can she grasp at Christ in such a way that neither she nor the Church builds a particular empire out of him? Can her belief start again and remain the continued belief of Christ's body, the *catholica*?

Certainly there is instrumentation by which that can be done. Yet nothing we have said so far can help. We have left out the theological truth that any revealed faith in Christ is at the same time *in grace*. There are various ways of looking at that. But in the normal way of life, faith in Christ and God's grace go together. They are facets of one reality within the subject who believes. And the state is one of newness, for 'the righteousness of God has been manifested . . ., the righteousness of God through faith in Jesus Christ for all who believe' (Rom 3: 21–22). Now this perception of Jesus Christ in faith to the believer is linked with and is part of the *charis* of God. Grace now enters in, and for Paul it joins with a perception of what the crucifixion means for the believer. Paul's method is here to zoom up with his theological camera to that vital moment in the believer which joins the gift of justification with the cross, and by the same device he emphasizes that this is the beginning of the new life of justification. *Charis* is here brought up to a sharp point. But that sharp point is just where the Jesus-faith or the Christ-faith begins. The insistence on the cross and its dramatic impact does remind us of what a very great deal of the theology of grace quite simply forgot, namely that grace and faith are both realities of experience. Indeed there is a whole theology of grace as experience to be found in the New Testament.[6] We must allow, as in principle Schillebeeckx does, that the Californian daughter may independently of revelation find her 'way back to natural experiences as a kind of preamble to faith, an openness for deeper experience of the senses'.[7] Yet since we are speaking of faith as experience, neither we, nor the Californian daughter, can be sure that an approach to Christ is strictly only a preamble. For, if the experience of the senses in question is somehow also an experience of the self, it is extremely unlikely that she will ever know when 'deeper experience' is, or begins to be, illuminated by Christ in grace.

The theme of the cross and of tribulation met with so early on in the new life carries with it an enormous counterweight leading to hope and optimism. The ordinary Christian now participates through a common vocation in Christ's sufferings and triumphant raising. These form an unthematic portion perhaps, but a real one, in the stirring apperception of faith deep down in its personal roots and experience. The Californian daughter's deeper openness in crises on the way to and through adulthood will not be bounded simply by a maturity factor. The participation will be one in the experience of grace. The whole reality, however much or however little a matter of experience, we can call christiform.

We do have the habit of thinking that the 'mature' adult is the one upon whom age has conferred an adequate psychological balance, and that this is the sign of the present grace. The idea remains an attractive one, of course. Tension and conflict appear to be charmed away in the 'season'd perfection' of grace. But that is not the point about christiformity in grace, The question we should ask is whether the developmental factor is, or is not, *the exemplification* of the christiform life in grace. In short, is a 'season'd' maturity the real meaning of the gospel invitation to the christiform grace to which God calls us?

The collapse of our culture of statues, holy pictures and stained glass on the one hand, and the immediate hippy appeal of Jesus the nonentity in the 1960s surely told us to think differently. The Christ–grace form in our lives is not merely a matter of measuring up to a mechanically acquired perfection which comes to us with time. In practice I can of course continue to say to myself, 'I have fallen short', or 'I should have been more balanced and mature in that situation', or again 'I should have been more generous and wiser than I was'. As an *ad hoc* way of coping with daily life that may work well enough. But, if the repeated use of such a way of thinking leads me to suppose that in spite of my passing inadequacy I have reached a certain stage of christiform maturity, or that by now I am myself satisfactorily endowed with a certain stage of perfection, then I am misleading myself theologically and, very probably, psychologically as well. The static model is wrong. When St Paul gave us the example of the athlete, he was inviting us to measure ourselves against the project of ourselves as *future* victors. Even in our apostolic work we should strive to see ourselves not merely as established centres or foci of activity, but as projects of an outward-looking service (*diakonia*) of Christ and of the brethren.

OUR SEASONS AND OUR PROJECT OF SELF

So we must be ready to correct the static view of ourselves in grace. If we fail to see it as constant growth, then we shall not so clearly see that our very existence in grace is all of Christ. We shall fail to recognize in him our immediate vivifier. We have to recognize him as the doer and energizer of our growth in conformity with him.

The corrective in question is justified by the Pauline idea that we are not yet anything, but are still *waiting for* 'adoption as sons'.[8] In other words, grace both has come and is still coming. To make sense of that, we must see ourselves not merely as isolated individuals, but as members of a community of hope in the Spirit. Without a life in the eschatological community, our christiformity in grace is incomplete. In fact, if it were not the grace of his body in which we grow, the growth itself would be no growth. Equally, that is why a spirituality which relied entirely on a one-to-one correspondence between Christ's seasons and our own would be a defective one. His one deed for us is irreversible and he unchanging. By it he elevates our plasticity into an existence in freedom. We are his project, too, which he draws into existence and to which he gives of the perfection revealed in his one season. It is that which continues to emerge in our lives. '*Being made perfect* he became the source of eternal salvation . . .'[9]

The *project of self* is thus a workable model for our thought; and the corresponding psychology of the idea is not bad either. It has distinct advantages over the *nature of self* model. It allows too for all those concrete, formative influences on our lives, known or unknown to us. It seems to me that we should not deny the role of such influences in the advent of Christ's season upon us. They go on playing their role, and in so doing witness to the fact that our perfection is indeed a matter of becoming rather than being. Thus, when we offer this life to an alloplastic moulding in Christ and his grace, we should not think of the daily grind as of a series of events of which we can take a cross-cut and call that our season. We should think rather of our seasons and their tensions as an internal growth factor within our lives, the condition *out of which* rather than the condition in which our christiform grace is finding its form *in his season*, not ours.

Thus these tensions are not merely a regrettable external situation hostile to us, and over which we have no control. The tensions are part of the growth, 'growing pains' which should be viewed with optimism. 'My power is made perfect in weakness'.[10] In spite of the suddenness of his own conversion, Paul allows for continued struggle as a dimension of the bestowal of grace. The christiform project, which we are, has to be realized *in and through*, rather than around and upon, our own existence. Though all of God, it is still our emergent reality.

Many of the theologians of grace (Paul, Augustine, Luther, Newman) had an intuition about a complete 'twice-bornness' which was the irreversible event in their lives. Grace, when it came, brought a trauma of change and difference never to be repeated. The theological value of that suddenness is not easy to estimate; but it was the suddenness which struck them, a suddenness in conversion. What they were getting at was, I think, the irreversibleness of grace, irreversible in its action upon us as it comes from God. Again that irreversible character implies something about Christ's action in his season upon us. It is teaching us that his action upon us is not only his temporal, last act, but that it is also his final act upon us in the sense of being ultimate in significance. More than that christiform grace is not and cannot be. Our own self-realization can therefore by no means be an achievement 'by seasons season'd'; it can only be the acceptance of and growth in that being, whose single season was ultimate with the ultimacy of God.

There remains of course the linear, biographical programme in our own history which we must play out. There is our experience of the struggle, the active affair. An example in the synoptic tradition is a good one. The rich young man is given a programme: *go, sell, distribute* and *follow*. If he accepts, the subject will proceed from one state in life to a new Christ-inspired one. The behaviour sequence enjoined is

to be a bit of his biography in linear time, and it is proposed
to him as a condition of his perfection. But giving one's
possessions would not of itself constitute that perfection.
Something else has to be present, and to be paramount. Had
he accepted Christ's call, the perfection would have been
constituted only by love.[11] Nevertheless we also have to say
that adversity, self-spoliation and unworldliness are basic
conditions, and in them we shall find our seasons.

To such an extent does God, as it were, protect us, that even
those conditions have their unclarities. Here again our
christiformity is protected from an invasion by techniques.
Techniques of self-spoliation and unworldliness, were they the
whole story, would bring back again *our* seasons and would
minimize his.[12] I said that the unclarities are there to help us.
There are for example, important unclarities and paradoxes
about the kingdom. Is it here, or is it not? Is it visible, or is it
invisible? Does it arrive of itself, or do we storm it? Is it
restricted, or is it universalist? What such paradoxes of the
kingdom effectively demonstrate above all is that the kingdom
can never become a possession of ours, never *our* season. For
Paul that is why we must rid ourselves of the impious boast
(*kauchēsis*). That is why he forbids the boast that is possessive, or
the boast over origin. We must have a *theologia crucis* which
alone averts the possessiveness distorting the very christiformity of grace, lest it be in danger of not being God's grace. That is
why he chose 'to bring to nothing the things that are, so that no
human being might boast in the presence of God'.[13]

Here again we see the Christian reason why the seasons of
the creature are not, and cannot be, the means of its 'season'd'
perfection. For the same reason not even a developmental
theory based on tension and crisis will do. Of course we do
grow when in tension and crisis; but the growth itself comes
from something beyond that again. Growth comes in the
'word of the cross',[14] and that refers not merely to the
destruction of life, but to the unique life in Christ which
comes in the completion of the cross, namely the
resurrection. For our part, obedience to his word must bring
us beyond the possessive boast, even the boast that we
possess Christ. Our pseudo-wisdom has to become folly, so
that in his season Christ can become our new wisdom, 'our
righteousness and sanctification and redemption'.[15]

I would like to think that in our considerations we have reached this point. Our seasons in christiform grace do not matter unless they share in *the season (kairos)* of the crucified. The engraced season-process of man is impossible without the engracing season of the Man-God.

GRACE'S FORM AND FINALITY

Our christiform grace from Christ on the cross cannot be incoherence, still less selfishness. *It can be* 'abandonment, oblivion, uselessness, insignificance'. Such kenotic forms within ourselves are not un-christiform, because of the spontaneous love and will of the Saviour to obey the Father's will. That after all is what gives the apparent formlessness of those 'emptyings' their true form.

Why is that? The answer must surely be that the form which Christ gave us in his season (*kairos*) was a form of crucifixion and resurrection, and it was final. For, once we accept his season (*kairos*), we live also in an age to come (*aiōn*). The life of that eternal age is the divine one. On this unified view of it, we can see more easily what von Balthasar meant when he wrote: 'there are not really three counsels, but one — to *one* form of life, nor are there really three vows, but only one vow — to vow oneself to the crucified form of love, as to the one and only form of life'.[16]

Yet, 'since it does not appear what we shall be',[17] we in our seasons remain to ourselves only a project. Such project-talk would be misleading, if it took away the form of love, and made us merely formless again. (We cannot give ourselves form of course; but we can in thankfulness look for that emergent form of love in our formlessness.) Our seasonal formlessness is given its coming form in his own season. Our seasons are in reality not merely phenomena of a rectilineal time, they are absorbed in his trans-temporal *kairos-aiōn*. There we can safely project, because in the truth of the incarnation true form is no projection, though the mystery of his abiding love-form for us is still opaque. In that sense he is still 'found in human form' and 'humbled' in his season.[18]

But it would not do to think that in accepting the season of the Lord, we are merely stunned by the imposition of a final death-form upon an otherwise formless life. It would not be right to translate the idea into the language of psychological dynamics, and to say that all we have to do in our Christian living is to super-impose the Christ-death-symbol or the cross upon the otherwise polymorphous perversity of our instinctual life. Death and mortification in the old Christian sense do have something to do with it, but they are by no means the whole story of our christiform grace.

What we must never forget is that the season of his death was also the season of his resurrection-life, a Spirit-life. So also with our internalizing of this mystery and our acceptance of its form. When we do internalize it in our faith, we make real in ourselves the call to a life-fellowship with him in the Spirit. Thus his interiorized season now becomes ours indeed, but not merely in the sense of an individual or personal enhancement. It is a perfecting in fellowship (*koinōnia*). Because the Son in being 'lifted up' has acted out his obedience to the Father and his love in the Spirit for God and men, so the form of that love in us now becomes trinitarian. We must now think of our real existence in the *kairos-aiōn* as of an existence in the trans-subjective sense. That existence is no longer merely *ours-mine* but *ours-ours*. In that sense we are sons in the Son and in that sense temples of the Spirit. That is how his season in us is already a divine and eternal one. It happens, as the fourth gospel points out, by the fact of believing. Hearing his word and believing in him already enable us to live in the sphere of 'eternal life', having 'passed out of death'.[19]

And this trans-subjective mysticism of time and season in eternity is the mode of our communication in the Spirit. When we accept and will our mutual interdependence, then comes the intimacy of his season, then is the proximity of Spirit existence, the divine indwelling.[20] By the love-given form of grace can we be Spirit-filled, and by the same form ever new resolutions of the life-death tension vivify the *I* and *not-I* into the *being-with* that we must become. The negative acts of our existence, though we still trail them along with us, have their positive values enhanced. A project is being realized. We thought it would be ours; but our possessiveness vanishes. We thought that in being possessed by Christ we would possess the All. In this field of divine inter-personality, 'God is "the centre of centres" in an interlocking web of free spiritual relationship in which the all and the personal are no longer exclusive'.[21] In realizing the project of ourselves, not statically because we are growing and living, we transcend our loneliness and isolation as well as our passivity and selfishness. For it is *his* season which is the sphere of this realization.

AND THE WORLD'S SEASONS

So Christ is for all men and to live in them. In this lower world do even we, his Christians, take in what that means? 'Yes', we say, 'he is to be given to all men', though we go on to add, 'but he is not yet given to all'. 'The end-time is not yet' is a reflection which shields and insulates us from the final form of the christiform grace offered to the world. But if we do not try and deepen our sense of the Christ-for-all, then we have to ponder the condemnation of the Laodicene church:

> I know your works: you are neither cold not hot. Would that you were cold or hot! So, because you are lukewarm, and neither cold nor hot, I will spew you out of my mouth. For you say, I am rich, I have prospered . . .[22]

It is a condemnation among others surely of the proclamation of our Christ through the framework of a friable triumphalism which says, 'he is mine and cannot be yours'. Christians have been so much tempted to make their historically-conditioned Christ their own, that they have been obliged to maintain a fictitious universality for him. That characteristic has been given its proper name, 'the scandal of particularity'. Kittel first called attention to this danger, an exclusivism of outlook about Jesus which leads us to contradict the basic universalist appeal of Christianity.[23]

It is a charism of this century that we have reacted in a healthy direction. The ecumenical movement has drawn strength from its effors to bring home to us the 'scandal of our divisions', especially in the mission fields. But behind the institutional problem there lies a doctrinal one. 'Is Christ divided?' asked Paul.[24] It was a protest of horror at the absurdity of a fragmented Christ parcelled out among empire-building sectarians at Corinth. That he and his christiform grace are shared should be clear. That is the meaning of the Christ mysticism just outlined above. Yet in practical living, the 'scandal of particularity' is such a scandal that it operates on nearly any level we like to think of. It is a piece of selfish religious indolence as old as the New Testament itself. There can be no petulent hugging to ourselves of our Christ in a world with arms outstretched for him.

At the same time there is a paradox involved which must never weary us. On the one hand we say that the Christ is The Man, who resumes in himself all that is in man, and on the other we say and preach that Christ is present there where our Church is present. One reason why the paradox is wearying is, of course, because in practical living we do not care to resolve it. Not even our basic preaching does so with gladness. Indeed, we do preach a lordship of Jesus over all worlds and all men. But we maintain some form of anathema to him who understands Jesus otherwise than our Christian Church proclaims him to be. So when we run into such spontaneous movements as those of the Jesus–people of the 1960s we find them intellectually and theologically null. 'Unitarians of the second Person', we might call them. But the very tragedies of theological history should make us look closely at any re-birth of the Spirit in man. The New Testament churches knew something of spontaneity, and in their earliest phases something of social radicalism. They certainly knew something about concentrating on immediacy of experience.

Whether it is by contamination with a world-season of generalized and somewhat unfocused desire of a Jesus only dimly to be recognized, I do not know, but we Christians are now asking more than ever for a personal encounter with Jesus. We exalt it as such, and pin it on to a philosophy of an 'I-Thou' relationship. As a result we are performing a balancing act. The public preaching of the traditional Christ must be maintained and adhered to in all its orthodoxy. On the other hand we recommend among ourselves the esoteric experience of the 'I-Thou' relationship. In the first stance we secure an objectively expressed faith at the cost of particularism. In the second we encourage the swallowing up of our expressed faith in experience and awareness. 'Only connect'; 'be sensitized', we think, should be enough. In the first mode of behaviour the danger is one of possessiveness, particularism, sectarianism, while in the second the danger is an abrogation of objectivity.

Undoubtedly since Vatican II world pressures have played upon the believing Church so as to elicit from it the lively tensions which underlie its life of faith. Ministry and prophecy in the Church are once more in tension. Institution and 'undifferentiated comitatus' tug against each other.

> After Vatican II we are experiencing, it would seem, the juxtaposition and alternation of the second model with the first. Any attempt to put into action the concept of the Church as the 'People of God', or as a 'servant' body, is clearly drawing on a different model from that suggested by the highly structured organization (we have known since for example Vatican I).[25]

If what I have said about tension and growth in christiform grace is true at the personal level, then we may expect that the grace of christiform belief in the Church will be vivified according to the same law of tension and growth. I believe this to be the case, and conclude that the tension in church-faith and its conditions is simply the emergence for our time of the form of love for the Church, which for her too is the vivifying cross. And by our inside tension we are recalled to the universality of our Christ in his destiny for all men. In practice, whether we live inside or outside the Christian milieu, the tension from within should make us all the more concerned with a Jesus for the world and for all its seasons.

Perhaps we should remember more often that at first Jesus proclaimed not his own lordship, but the rule of his Father. The disciples themselves began their faith-experience in the resurrection-Christ with an awareness of his lordship. Through the death-life form of the cross, they now saw their messiah as the heavenly one, whose activity here on earth was a royal anticipation of cosmic finality.[26] Even therefore in the reassurance of the resurrection the disciples looked forward. There was no resting in their faith as a faith entirely of the present. The reason why they did this was surely because the master had taught them to do so.

But the future is not the only way to focus our belief. We do not have to despair of a present christiformity in grace, thinking that it cannot touch the world or ourselves. Neither continuing church crises nor world crises, nor our own personal perplexities should overwhelm us. It may be true, as Joseph Comblin writes, that 'In fact the average catholic is a being frightened by the evolution of modern man'.[27] If that is true, and I suspect that for many a pew-bound catholic it is, then again we should look back to the New Testament. In Paul's churches of Ephesus, Colossae and Philippi, the Christians were indeed frightened beings. Their domestic version of Christianity could not prevent a feeling of cosmic anxiety. The political and social world seemed infected with demonism beyond what they could bear. They were afraid of their own future, afraid of what the 'principalities' and 'powers' could do to them. Like many an African Christian, who in a death and life emergency sends for the witch-doctor, they wanted to make doubly sure. Paul had to insist again and again that the exalted Christ has somehow already subjugated the 'spiritual powers'. Perhaps it was, as John Bligh writes, in the sense 'that he *could* (author's italics) at any moment reduce them to powerlessness'. They were 'created in him and for him'; and even more, Christ 'exerts his power over evil powers through the spiritual gifts he imparts to believers'.[28]

There are two conclusions of immense importance here. The *first* is that the present season of the world does not escape from the lordship of Christ which emerges in and through the tensions. The *second* conclusion is that it is *his Lordship* indeed, but that the believers (church-institution as well as church-community) all participate in his mission. When there is true ministry in the Church, and when there is true prophecy, and (best of all) when these two are fused in one witness, then the lordship of Christ is truly proclaimed. At the same moment, as with us in our own individual seasons of growth, the seasons of the world are swallowed into the cosmic season of Christ. I doubt if we ever have a certain assurance of when and how this takes place. If we did, the scandal of particularity would finally be set at nought.

A famous verse of Paul reminds us whence came the lordship of Christ and whither it must return. That reality is set even beyond the stage of our last enemy, death. 'For God has put all things under his (Christ's) feet.' In the end-time, 'when all things are subjugated to him who put all things under him . . . God will be everything to everyone'.[29] Of course the end-time is not going to show us a hidden limitation upon the lordship of Jesus. It is going to show us that when there can be no more process, his lordship will be complete. All the world's seasons will now become one with his season, 'as the Son now brings the entire creation into the obedience of sonship, thereby mediating it into immediacy to the Father' nothing will, nor could, be more final than that act.[30] Nor can any created reality escape it. The end will prove to be the beginning after all, for in the Son's procession from his Father, the end boundary of all reality is also the generation point of all reality. In that trans-temporal season of the 'all in all', the world of God will be disclosed as God's world.

CHRIST AND MODERN DOCETISM

Until recently, what the gospels had to say about the humanity of Jesus satisfied us well enough. The baby, the child, the adolescent (mostly hidden) and the grown adult made their regular appearances in our liturgical and prayer calendar. Each time one of those figures came round, it was a familiar *alter ego*. But it was an *alter ego* with an occasional touch of unreality. There was one question a priest might hear in counselling or in the confessional, and it ran like this: 'How can I pray to, or model myself upon, even expect understanding and sympathy from, a sexless Jesus? Unless he knows my difficulties from within, it is unreal and even useless for you to propose him to me as friend, or model, or forgiving Saviour.' Today the question often has to be met in the form of a flat denial of faith. 'If your Jesus was as sexless as the Church has presented him, then he is just not normal, not human.'[31] The situation is a serious one. Jesus was, it is true, proposed as an *alter ego*, because he was fully human; but some may now believe, that when it comes to the all-important question of sexuality Jesus apparently cannot help them.

Richard Egenter puts his finger on one factor we should not neglect.[32] The complaining believer, for once, is reacting against the artistic sentimentalizing of the figure of Jesus, a process which is very much in need of analysis. Think of

Holman Hunt's *The Light of the World*. Think of the mass-produced statues of the Sacred Heart, tasteless, poor-spirited and above all sexless objects. The observation even holds good for the vastly popular and brilliantly meretricious painting, *The Christ of St John of the Cross* by Dali. Popular piety had until recently been fed for about one hundred and fifty years upon *Kitsch* — an art style you do not define, but you do recognize it. Religious *Kitsch*, especially catholic versions of it, litter the planet. It is of course different from *folk-art* or *pop*, in which life and vigour are sustained. The social effects of *Kitsch* need to be studied, and its implicit effect upon sexuality. *Kitsch* is weak, save in two respects. It encourages submission and obedience, and it is strong in repressing or infantilizing sex, which is different from sublimating it. It has been unmistakably powerful and popular. We must not forget that in religious houses such statues were for decades the object of regular private, if not community, *cultus*. [33]

I see the question of *Kitsch* as a particular, but common, condition which introduces us to more general problems. It must do so because as a religious conditioner it is meant to affect the individual subject as a whole. These 'pious' objects were meant to encourage our 'zeal', our 'sorrow for sin', our 'love of the rule', our 'desire for the missions'. These are orientations for the whole person; and, as with religious objects generally, they are normative and prescriptive: in that the example embodied in the object is held up as a pattern for conduct. It is clear that individual as well as social sexuality were, and are, involved in such a situation. They were involved in the variety of lily-bearing statues, and indeed in the many sexual ambiguities implicit in the *Kitsch* versions of the Sacred Heart. [34] Modesty powder and special garments for the bath are still within living memory of convent life. The use of chains and disciplines has been entirely reconsidered in non-monastic orders and congregations; but that still leaves the problem of co-existence among generations of religious whose outlook and 'formation' now differ widely. Religious, who have to move freely in the sex-permeated atmosphere of the city, are aware as never before of a pseudo-ideology of sex, through advertising and the mass media, which is in conflict with an ideology of chastity that has yet to be rebuilt *as an ideology*. *Kitsch*, with its drained humanity and hidden violence, will remain suspect.

Herzog, quoted by Egenter, is of course right when he points to the strong subconscious influences of sex on the most widespread pieces of *Kitsch*. Our Lady of Lourdes, or the Immaculate Conception, 'here almost always appears as a sweet girl, more precisely a curious combination of courtesan and goddess, for these images make nothing of Mary, the Mother of God . . . but rather the feminine part of man's soul — still in a primitive state — his undifferentiated anima'.[35] The particular theory behind these remarks does not matter. What does matter by way of introduction to our theme is that *Kitsch* is an expression of a totally inadequate response to the Christian faith. In its weakness it displays fear of total doctrine, here the maternity of Our Lady. In its hidden violence it flees from independent and mature moral decision; hence also from grace. In its fear of the human body and of sexuality it is patently docetic in tendency. It preaches and teaches a Jesus who was not even recognizably human.

HE WAS THUS AND THUS

The situation is not as well-established as it was; and from time to time one can hear extravagant reactions, which do not help us in our main task. Our commitment is to confirming others in their faith in Christ. If, in some merely secular fashion, we were simply trying to restore to honour some historically lay-figure more or less accurately portrayed, we could then afford to be disinterested in how he was represented. We could afford such an attitude, so long as it did not interfere with a substantial loyalty to the institution in question. Whether even then we should be so disinterested is another matter. But we Christians take it upon ourselves to go so far as to aid in the search for a mystic counterpart to the individual believer, a counterpart who will be thought of as the object of the believer's whole unitive life, and in whom he will, so far as may be, come to be totally absorbed. We dare to hope as we busy ourselves with our apostolate, that the motivation of our fellow-believers will be determined by the Jesus they find in this spiritual and in some degree mystic union. We will insist on the necessity of learning from him, of listening to his inspiration at all times, and indeed of being so conformed to him, that he becomes a kind of control in our lives. We will be satisfied when we hear of the need which is felt for the spiritual *alter ego*, or *spouse*, especially in the celibate believer's life. We shall recommend that a certain presence of Jesus be felt in the community so that it may remain at peace with itself in face of any form of external aggression. It is true that, since we are ourselves believers, we shall by the same token absolve ourselves from any suspicion of 'manipulating' others through the type of Jesus-figure we present, since we are convinced that in our sincere obedience to gospel and tradition we are entirely guided by an objective state of affairs.

That last phrase could obviously be discussed at length, but would take us too far away from the present subject. It is enough to say that there is no way of helping the brethren except through the various religious and cultural environments in which we encounter them. We can do no other but start with our own cultural equipment and use what means of creative criticism we possess. That is why I mentioned *Kitsch* to begin with. It would be good to think that, though we may have to give way to *folk* or *pop* in religious art, and perhaps in theology, we need never again give way to *Kitsch*. We cannot in fact continue to disseminate it, and at the same time not be conscious of 'manipulation', once we have seen something for ourselves of the critiques of psychological anthropology (that is, the overlapping interests of psychology and anthropology) and cultural psychiatry (that is, the relationship between socio-cultural factors and emotional disorder, or emotional organization in general).

But if progress has been slow, that is partly because in the Catholic Church we have dragged our feet. When the practice of psycho-analysis became generalized, and while the chief works of the Freudian corpus were making their appearance, a negative reaction took place. As Michel Meslin remarks, we were first treated to a violent denunciation of Freudian materialism. Then, in so far as Freudianism made an impact as a coherent theory it was declared to be an unacceptable reductionism of the Christian faith. Polemic was shocked and vigorous. The danger seen in psycho-analysis seemed, however, to diminish when priests and nuns appeared to benefit from treatment. The polemic cooled off;

but, and this is the important point for us here, it still seemed
quite impossible 'that the love which a believer had for his
God could, in the slightest degree, depend upon his urges or
his sexuality'.[36] It is here that the question of sexuality in our
Christ-faith and Christ-devotion has to be thought through
with tranquillity. I quote Meslin again: 'it is clear that after
Freud, "believing" (or "living the life of faith", *croire*) no
longer means exactly what it had meant before'.[37]

I suggest that at first sight the problem breaks down into
four areas, though they overlap, especially *areas one* and *two*.
Area one has to do with the question whether or not we can
make any historical statements about sexuality in the life of
Jesus. *Area two* is concerned with statements of our historic
faith about Jesus, when we say, preach and teach that he was
concretely thus and thus in his life on earth, or is concretely
thus and thus as the risen and eternal Christ. *Area three*
concerns the meaning of the humanness of Jesus *for us* in our
faith; that is to say, the meaning, that on reflection and
interpretation, we think he ought to have for us, rather than
the meanings which may be foisted on him. *Area four* has to
remain a programmatic and interpretative one. We are still at
the stage of reviewing the questions which have to be
explored, rather than coming up with a set of answers.

Area one can here be dealt with shortly. It asks the
question, 'Did the Nazarene prophet-carpenter, called Jesus,
have a sex-life like ours?' The question obviously begs a
number of others, but Bishop John Robinson settles the
matter satisfactorily for our purposes:

> In all this, of course, the issue is not what historical remarks we
> can confidently make about Jesus of Nazareth. The answer is
> quite clearly, None. We do not know anything for certain about
> his sex-life. As Dennis Nineham has reminded us, the gospels
> 'do not even think to tell us definitely whether or not he was
> married', though a book has recently appeared with the title *Was
> Jesus Married?*, which is not in fact as mad as it sounds. The
> gospels do not exist to provide answers to these questions.[38]

There is really no difficulty with the arguments against
saying that Jesus was married. First, the gospels say nothing
about it. Secondly, the anti-erotic bias of the New Testament
churches came early into Christianity; and we can suppose

that if Jesus had been married that tendency would have been checked, or at least that there would be some sign of dissent. Lastly, when Paul invoked his *right* 'to be accompanied by a wife' (Greek, *sister as wife*), as the other apostles, and brothers of the Lord and Cephas', any tradition that Jesus had been married would have clinched the point he was making.[39] (I tend to think there is something in this last argument, though Catholic exegetes have in the past preferred to suppose that Paul was maintaining his right to subsidiary female help; translate then, *woman as religious sister*.)

It is hard to see that much more can be said about *area one*. Questions like these: What was the emotional stance that Jesus took towards the women in his life? Could he have had latent homosexual affects? Was his relationship with his mother satisfactory from the point of view of his emotional development? Had he, as is not rare in religious figures, no trace of an Oedipus complex? Such questions certainly do not belong to my *area one*.[40]

Area two is more complicated. Mainline Christianity, in its statements of faith in Jesus, has held to an historical Jesus; and in its high-point, Chalcedon, it held that the historical Jesus was 'co-essential' or 'consubstantial' with us. Nicaea had already said he was 'co-essential' or 'consubstantial' with the Father. It is worth noting that at the time of Chalcedon the commoner phrase was 'co-essential' or 'consubstantial' *with Mary*. The 'historicalness' and reality of this particular man Jesus is thus brought out strongly by his singular and individuating relationship with Mary. But in its stand against Eutyches, the Council went further. Eutyches had already agreed that Christ 'was from the flesh of the Virgin and that he was Perfect Man'. Now the council demanded that Eutyches commit himself to saying: 'If the mother is *co-essential with us*, [Christ] is also . . .'[41] There was an implication here which Eutyches could not face, namely that Jesus was fully co-essential with us.

The hesitations of Eutyches survived him, and as late as 1442 the credal section of the Decree for the Jacobites insisted that Christ was *passible*.[42] The common view was that he *took on* corporeal infirmities such as hunger, fatigue, pain and death. But those were, so to speak, 'clean' infirmities. Diseases were different. Theology and medicine get mixed up in St Thomas's view of the matter. For him disease has to be excluded from the list of Christ's possible infirmities, because diseases are partly caused by original sin and sometimes by the fault of the individual, such as inordinate eating habits.[43] It was also common doctrine that as a human being Christ was not ignorant, that he did not sin, indeed that he was radically incapable of sin. All that is a *second area* picture of Christ. And, as we noticed, the contemporary world-view, including the medieval idea of what constituted human perfection as well as health, were contributory factors. One cannot ask of a world-view that it shall be in advance of its time.

After the Reformation and the Enlightenment, theologians had to struggle and are still struggling to produce a picture of Christ which is humanly credible. Here, it is enough for us to satisfy ourselves that there is ground for hope that they will one day succeed. Why? The answer is in part a methodological one. Just because *area two* statements are different from *area one* statements, there is room for manoeuvre without disloyalty to the gospel truth about Jesus. *Area two* gives room for manoeuvre because, as we can now see, different thought-models in that area are not only legitimate but necessary.[44] But we need not fear that such models and their implications are merely an excogitated mental spin-off of our own. The New Testament itself carries within it a variety of Christologies, as is now generally accepted. They complete each other of course, and are not in contradiction. We thus find that *area two* overlaps within and without the limits of New Testament thinking. In seeking to correlate our views of man and the world with those of the New Testament writers, we thus have an open-ended situation on both sides. But what we have to respect, and where the danger signals will be hoisted, is in those places where the New Testament writers have a better hold on *area one* than we have, when they make *area two* statements. We cannot go behind that.

There is at present no ready-made *area two* set of conclusions about the sexuality of Christ, or indeed of the psychic background of the beliefs of the early churches in Christ. All the data of the problem cannot be satisfied. But the open-endedness we have mentioned is encouraging in a situation which contains many a paradox. Professor C. F. D. Moule opens up one of them for us. It is the paradox of the human 'continuity and discontinuity' in Jesus. According to the New Testament writers, the *humanity* of Jesus is both 'continuous and discontinuous from the rest of mankind'.[45] As being the entire human race, as 'this man', as the 'new man', the 'sinless' man, even in the language of the New Testament he is discontinuous with the human race. How then should we see this in terms of the emphatic statements implying continuity? Moule does not say, for example, that Jesus could never have 'looked lustfully on a woman'. He does say that the sinless side of Jesus is in play because 'the set of the will will negate what might have been looking lustfully on woman'. Here is an *area two* argument (in part conditioned by historic New Testament faith, in part conditioned by a theory of the human will), which attempts to supply for a blank among the *area one* statements. The result remains at the stage of an open-ended paradox.

How does that affect us? It means, I think, that statements of historic faith from any period of our doctrinal history still leave us with a task of interpretation. We have to interpret the humanness of Jesus not by means of an ancient instrument from some museum of psychology appropriate to New Testament, patristic or medieval times, and not in the long run with some mint-new instrument of our own day (though in the short term I see no reason why that should be neglected, if it helps). What we have to interpret is the humanness of Jesus as a religious symbol. It must emerge as a symbol that speaks and 'gets through'. I quote Meslin again:

> . . . it is absolutely evident that today we can no longer talk of symbols in merely historico-cultural terms. If, as Ricoeur rightly felt, the symbol gives us ground for operational thinking, then there is all the more reason to find out why and how we can make the transition *from* our analysis of the properly human symbolizing function *to the result* of the operation which man forever practises in the different cultures.[46]

To put that into the terms of our problem we can say this. We know Jesus as Saviour, Redeemer, King, Teacher, Shepherd, Mystic Bridegroom, Sacred Heart and Infant Jesus of Prague. At any rate we think we do. But none of those

symbols is native to us today. We know that with some of
them we can make the transition of which Meslin speaks. We
do not advert too closely to the difference between those that
do work, and those that do not; and, perhaps worse, we have
not specifically inquired why Saviour and Shepherd
apparently do make the transition, while Sacred Heart now
does so less, and Infant Jesus of Prague hardly at all. To keep
the right symbols alive we must know what we are doing
from the human end: that is, we must have a sexually
intelligible Jesus, if the *transition* is to be made to the 'properly
human symbolizing function'. The idea of sexual intelligibility
rather than the idea of mere sexual similarity seems to me to be
the relevant one. We shall come back to this. In the meantime let
us open up the question of *area three*.

HIS HUMANNESS FOR US

Area three could be labelled *his humanness and us*. It is the area
in which we must try and take a stand, whilst it draws on the
New Testament. The Jesus of the New Testament, we must
remind ourselves, even when its theologies are highly post-
resurrectional, was *a man* with a genetic history, a biological
and psychological history interacting with other human
beings. Even his most glorious-sounding titles relate to one
who should make sense to us, in so far as the meanings of
these titles are enfleshed in his concrete existence. That
existence attracts and polarizes us, even though its inner
psychological drives and structures are largely concealed
from us.

   In trying to make up our minds about the religious meaning
for us of the problem of Jesus and sexuality, we must after all
look for a soberly religious answer which is governed by the
New Testament. It will incidentally be necessary to see
whether we continue to put anything in brackets, and to state
why we do so. So first of all a general remark: from all our
evidence concerning the religious movements of first-century
Palestine, one thing is clear, namely that any religious teacher
or leader showing the slightest sign of 'permissiveness' could
never have become plausible, and attracted a following. On
any sane interpretation of the historical tradition surrounding
Jesus of Nazareth, he was both popular and plausible. Fasting
and the desert played a part in his life; and as a result he could

afford to shrug off the efforts at a smear campaign against him. In the company he kept he ensured that his respect for the law should not interfere in any bigoted fashion with his social relationships. His respect for human beings contradicted the tendency of his time to relegate women to an inferior status. [47] As Dodd says of the passage on the woman taken in adultery: 'Compassion for the woman is no less marked than scorn for her accusers, but the final words have an astringency which rules out any suggestion of "permissiveness".'[48] All that we shall ever know in a direct factual way is that he was not 'permissive'.

Now that fits in with the rest, for sex obviously was then, as it still is, a central religious issue. It is true that there have been times in the history of the Church, when a horror of the flesh has obscured Christ's role as healer, de-alienator and Lord of a man's body. That does not fit the New Testament view and will not do as a genuine *area three* view of Christ. But still there are factual blanks about the New Testament Jesus, as we know him. We should not forget that in some ways we know him best as a teacher. As a teacher he could be stricter than his religious opponents. When he held that divorce and oaths were sinful, he was stricter than strict Jewish practice. 'We should not get a true picture of him if we failed to hear people who were shocked by his severity exclaim, Who then can be saved?[49] But when all that is said, we should remember also that it is a Jesus who takes his own line that we hear as a teacher. Only minimally does he engage in casuistry. In general he appears as a religious liberator. But, for our purpose, in what sense a liberator? 'Permissiveness' has been excluded; and it has never been shown that 'permissiveness' is a genuine and human form of liberation anyway. But he must be a religious liberator even in respect of sex. In what sense? I think he does *two* things both as teacher and healer: *(a)* he *liberates from* sin, where sin, a religious matter, is involved; and *(b)* he *liberates for* love of God, our Father, *for* love of the brethren, and *for* the realization of the project of self which is disclosed in him. To the modern that may seem restrictive and in part mythological. But, if *area three* reflections are to keep their New Testament aspect, that is the only honest answer. From a broader theological standpoint also we must say the same;

for, while with the Bible and much of Christian tradition we can see an overlap between sex and sin, we cannot possibly see an overlap between love (in the religious and profound sense) and sin.

To go back to speculation about Jesus himself, what we say excludes any possibility that Jesus could be alienated from himself. Lostness from God in Jesus would contradict the New Testament and all our understanding of it. Are we then definitely excluding anything which must find its place within the sphere of what constitutes man? Did he then possess that dark, irrational area of existence in which, and even more through which, we grow in grace? I think he did, and I think that such an opinion can legitimately be made within *area three* and its regard for the New Testament. If he was hungry, thirsty, sad, ignorant, and liable to that crisis in mind and resolve which is implied by Gethsemane, then he was not a stranger to the dark, irrational region.

Here it would be easy to embark upon a guessing game, but it must be excluded. We can reflect rather upon the consistency of his non-aggressive attitudes where his personal interests are concerned. (His zeal for his Father is another matter, for it is that of the authentic adult collaborating with God, rather than appropriating him, and there is no doubt as to where Jesus's ideal lies.) His inner concentration seems positive and relates to something which has to be said or done later on. And, if we add to that the consistent balance of Jesus in his relationship with women, we can say that we have a convergence of signs which suggest that in him we can see a very high degree of successful adjustment to reality.[50] Now, if I am asked, does that not mean that *area three* has simply brought us back to the plaster and paint of *Kitsch* with which we started, I am bound to reply, No.

Let us now move away from the three areas discussed and try in *area four* to reach tentative interpretations which will keep what we have said in mind. Any interpretation must be religious. It is not enough to say that, as Jesus showed no signs of guilt, anxiety, tension or aggressivity over sex, therefore he must be a suitable antidote to what we think are disorders in ourselves. Many schools of Christian spirituality have proposed a doctrine of the imitation of Christ. We are not in a doctor fish situation, on any theory of grace or conformity with the divine exemplar. The effect he produces can therefore be neither magical nor automatic. Such an idea is not even a religious one.

In an obscure way it somehow underlies two opposed tendencies from which mainline Christianity has had to recoil. We have on the one hand the prurient believers who have recoiled from the flesh, and on the other the reductionist humanist, who must at all costs see some measure of sex in the life of Jesus, so that we can all feel better on recognizing ourselves in him. It would seem that a similar psychological mechanism, the projection of guilt, is at work in each case. The mechanism is a device by which the afflicted can come to terms with the reality they need in their lives. It is, however, not compatible with the Christian belief in Jesus. But the dilemma which such Christian variants have tried to meet is relatively simple: *either* we feel so guilt-ridden in the experience of our own sex-lives or in being deprived of sex, that we can only bring ourselves to worship an unreal *Kitsch*-type of Christ, *or* we are so sex-guilty that we must have a sex-laden or sex-joyous Christ as our own familiar surrogate. Neither position allows for the particular Nazarene carpenter, who is the historic figure of our worship. Making Jesus inhuman in the first alternative is as mistaken as making him, in the current vernacular, 'sexually normal'. The latter phrase is, in the sense intended, quite inapplicable to a religious leader such as Jesus was.

Such conjectures are also bad thinking about Christianity. When we insist that the question of Jesus and sexuality is a religious one, we are not suggesting that it is religious in a merely individualistic way. Faith in a reality called Jesus of Nazareth is a faith in the context of historic believing communities. Nor, to find an easy solution to the problem, can we de-sacralize Jesus, and then weave a sexual fantasy around him. The larger context of belief in Jesus includes the phenomenon that sex and sin overlap, and that sex can symbolize sin.[51] We have to be cautious here. The symbol does not have to be the thing, and historically the connexion between sex as a symbol and sin as a reality, has sometimes been stronger and sometimes weaker. There is no need to canonize the whole of the tradition. What we still need is an

understanding of why the symbol works. There is a paradox
here, for the Church has in fact stood firm against
Manicheeism, Catharism and Jansenism, and has not denied
that sex and the flesh are a human good. But on the other
hand, where theology has so far feared to tread, has been
over a principle of the Greek Fathers about the reality of the
humanity of Christ. *What was not assumed* (by Christ) *was not
healed*, they held. Later theology never inquired if that was
true of human sexuality.

This is where there is speculative work still to be done; and
it must be done on a jointly human and religious stand. It is
possible that the Western sex ideologies of protest (for
example, 'sexual politics'), and of a sexual–mystical character
(the neo-Freudian sex mystics of the 1960s) can still be made
to stimulate some genuine thinking on more realistic lines.[52]

Today it is important, I think, to relate the general
perplexities in this field to the basic gospel situation. The
person of Christ and his message can more clearly convey to
man what his potentiality is than can the do's and dont's of a
morality which is in any case looked upon as shifting. There
are several reasons for this. First a Christ-mysticism is a
communicable reality. Such a mysticism is securely based,
and, as the life of St Paul, its greatest propagandist, shows
clearly, there is no need to lose touch with the reality
principle in living out such a mysticism. In its acceptance,
and even in the concomitant wish for death, there is an
implicit acceptance of the fact that gross sex–deviationism is a
pseudo-existence. In Freudianism, the role of the death-wish
is controverted. As one of the symbols of Christ-mysticism,
it has an assured balancing role once it is projected through
the cross onto a death shared with Christ. Here the ideal Son
with whom we identify is accepted by his Father, and the
perfect sublimation becomes an ontological as well as a
psychological structure.

At the same time we are enabled to come to terms with the
fact that there is no paradise now. Today's culture suffers
much and struggles much to disguise that reality from itself.
Sex and drugs are one formula. But against this, mainline
Christianity must stand firm. It has no mystical form of a
paradise-for-now to proclaim. The task is always to renew
the gospel of growth in grace, love and union with God, and

man and the world; but growth implies a term not reached. Hence there can be no human perfectibility which leads merely 'into that simple health that animals enjoy but not man'.[53] Christianity could obviously not say that; and even Freud held a much more sober view of perfection. On reflection, it was even more sober than the somewhat static or mechanical view of 'Christian perfection', which, after debasing the dynamism of Aristotle, settled down to a snug existence in manuals of spiritual perfection. Freud rejected the view that it is even possible fully to free a person from internal conflicts to perfect him. But the mirage has long been with us and we have projected a schematic normality upon Jesus, which we know that we ourselves shall never attain. The really religious aspect of the matter should have told us that we were looking in the wrong direction. The Epistle to the Hebrews repeatedly associates the perfection of Jesus with his suffering and the resolution of his life crisis.[54] Here, if ever, we are talking about the concrete Ego of experience, which is also the concrete 'I' of everyday life. Here, in the realm of theological conclusions, we find ourselves much nearer to Jesus as healer. It is the concrete 'I' in sexual distress with which religion is concerned.

LIKE SEEKS AFTER LIKE

The reason why we can involve the Jesus of our religion with the problem of sexuality in man must therefore be viewed along the line of person and personhood. Those who try and make Jesus a talisman or magic touchstone fail, because they take Jesus out of the context of religion. There are of course resemblances between sexual attitudes and religious attitudes. Sexual attitudes help to structure the person; and the believer and lover of God is none other than the concrete structured person. That does not mean that all sexual attitudes can be related to religious attitudes. Some are destructive. Oral sadism is in the end destructive of human love. Religious oral sadism of the Savonarola type is destructive by its bigotry and violence. Human sexual love, considered as a personal endowment, is quite different. In this perspective there is a vertical line transcending the finite human relationship: now sexual love relates through the *other* to the One, God our Father. This vertical line is surely disclosed in Jesus in such a way that sexual affectivity is neither distorted nor denied. That seems to me most important, and one must look for an illustration.

Jesus, we say again, is liberator as well as healer. He promises that his yoke will be a light one.[55] That must hold good for sexuality as for the rest. In the first instance, Jesus liberates from the casuistical thraldom of the sabbath law. In that he shares his lordship with God.[56] The point is that it is precisely with God, our Father, that this lordship is shared. Authority is now taken away from the rabbis. Jesus is thus himself the liberator, and the one who is commanding Lord. But he gives an enabling command. The result therefore in the realm of human sexuality cannot be a licence for perversity as a form of liberation. It can only be the establishment of a relationship in sexuality which is open to the basic possibility of personal encounter, and through that to the possibility of the essentially religious relationship with the Father. That is how the enabling command must work out. 'The living Christ,' said T. W. Manson, 'still has two hands, one to point the way and the other held out to help us along.'[57] Such a process is no form of sex homoeopathy. It is still, however, what this man Jesus does; and he does it as *a man*; that is, with all the characteristics of the race in compassion and love.

So we must reject the argument that only *like cures like*.[58] I see nothing in well-considered Christology which ought to make us think that the incarnation ought to be a sort of philosopher's stone for sex. If we turn again to St Paul, we can see that it is not *likeness*, but *sameness* on which he relies. For him the graced condition of any man, and, as we are talking about a personal relationship with God, *through our sexuality in a large or narrow sense*, that graced condition is a total negation of any human boast (*kauchēsis*). The likeness of sex in Christ to heal sex in us is a human projection; in other words, it is our doing, not God's doing. Now the principle, already mentioned, that *what was not assumed was not healed* relies on *sameness*, not likeness, with us. Christ's consubstantiality or co-essentiality with us points, not to a situation within him of incoherence or perversity, but rather to the possibility of realized structuration. He is not merely a specimen of schematic normality. He is in his human structuration perfected personal love itself. The man, our Saviour, was the same as we are in the sameness of structured personality, in that which relates us as sons in the Son.

To anyone who says: 'Ah, but you have now put the question of sexuality in brackets and have forgotten it', I must honestly reply, *Yes* and *No*. *No* in the sense that the matter remains subsumed in the vertical line of personality, and in the sense that it is left *ad agonem*. At the same time, I must say, *Yes*, in the sense that crisis and struggle are the normal ways in which we think about sexuality from day to day. I have not suggested that liability to guilt, anxiety and aggressiveness are removed, nor that it is through those factors that our distress impinges upon us.

It is probably true that the element of aggressiveness is the one which appears to us to be the least compatible with our idea of Jesus as healer. It goes with domination and, when imposed, in any circumstances in which sadism may be suspected, can have no place in the perfected structuration of love, especially of love which involves the divine. Non-violence is surely of the essence of what we call the supernatural. We are here in an area of considerable ambivalence. The neurotic subject projects his inner conflict on his religious outlook and becomes socially aggressive. God or Christ will then always be ready to punish. There is no denying that sickness may lead in that direction. But for our present purpose this must remain another topic. In our line of thinking we have opted for the non-violence of moral strength and love to be found in the structures graced by Christ. What happens then to the aggressive element latent in sexuality? 'Aggressiveness,' says Jean Lhermitte, 'can become the most effective motive in spiritual progress.'[59]

Would that be true even in the area of Christ and sexuality? I take an illustration from the personal study of that massive and constructive theologian, Paul Tillich, written after his death by his psychiatrist friend, Rollo May. Paulus, as his friends called him, loved women sensually but not sexually. Nevertheless . . .

He could talk about sexuality in public so long as it was not personal confession. And talk about it he did, with a frankness and honesty which stood out radically indeed in faculties where most professors spoke as if they had never heard the word sex. It was in Paulus' lectures that I first heard of the 'love bite', that moment of hostility and aggression which occurs at the climax of sexual intercourse. He believed that, even though partly aggressive, the sexual act in the orgasm is still a giving of the persons to each other. It is the tension between the aggressiveness and the giving which produces the ecstasy of sex. From Paulus I also heard of the 'union of opposites', of which sexual intercourse is a symbol — the straining of the totality of one person to become wholly absorbed in the other person.[60]

What is said there can be taken as symbolic expression of what I am trying to suggest from a theological point of view. As we know from the Song of Songs and from many high points in history of mysticism, human love is a symbol of the divine-human encounter.[61] Our residual, but sublimated aggressiveness, may yet contribute to the 'union of opposites'. It would take us into our next chapter to show how this can be verified. For the moment let us return to the thought that in and through sexual tensions on the part of the believer, the offer of Christ is still for a mystic union of persons. St Paul had no hesitation about mixing Christ mysticism and sex to insist on the need for sublimation.[62] It is clear that the union in question excludes paradise now, the lapsing into perversity, and regression into infantilism. It would also be true, as I wrote in a sacramental context, 'that the use of such symbolism' [as that of sexual love] 'for the ordinary believer as for the mystic has to be accompanied by a sense and practice of sensual purification. There would be nothing odd in that. The Christian as well as the Freudian traditions recognize that there is always a role for Thanatos.'[63]

It may be felt that I have argued a severe view over the humanness of Christ and sexuality. If I do so, it is because I see no substitute for the objectivity of the Church's faith in Christ. Questions can be asked only about the real, objective Jesus Christ of Church faith who was the Nazarene carpenter. Nor can any offer to relieve sufferers from anxiety, guilt, or an aggressiveness connected with sexuality be anything but a religious *placebo* unless it is grounded in the being of the Christ who was and is.

All that could be done here was to sketch a line of thought.

Much remains to be worked out. The technical casuistry of the past concerning sex is no longer helpful and is falling into desuetude. Christians still ask for help in avoiding humanist reductionism, and from folk-lore concepts of guilt ranging from ritual impurity to socially secular transgressions. The holy touch view of Jesus was simply wrongly focused on a not-given sex-factor in his life. It was equally unhelpful to concentrate exclusively on the all-pure sinlessness of Jesus at the expense of the far more communicable fact that his life was wholly one of humanly personal love. There is no need to think that our relationship with him is merely a psychological identification. It is far more. The force he communicates, the offer of surrender to God that he makes — all this adds up to the situation of a Christiform grace-relationship. We can then say that the sex-liberation offered by Christ is to be freely embraced in the sublimating death-life of the cross. It is there that love speaks and discloses; it is there that we find communion in deed, and it is there that love, to use the language of von Balthasar, gives of itself as form.

Christ, I have been saying, is a therapist for our wounded existence as sexual beings. He is a healer, not merely because he is 'like us'. He is a healer because he is 'of us', or to use an old piece of theological theory, because he has 'the same nature'. I would prefer to say 'because he was becoming', or 'because he is the very "what we shall be" '. His healing comes not from any form of indulgence — and in any case why should we say what we know nothing about? — but because he grew into his suffering, because he agreed with, and he affirmed the cross. That was a self-possession, a process affecting our process, the fuller possession of that project in becoming which we are.

HEALER AGAINST ANXIETY

Beside sexuality this age has brought home anxiety to us, and it has done so in a new way. We are children, as we saw in Chapter Two, not only of incoherence and perversity, but of fear, affliction, *malheur*. Anyone who would be relevant must recognize that. Nor has progress in the human sciences or in religion made us rid of the condition. It is true that before the unthinkable horrors of our own history, philosophers in the

West had seen anxiety writ large in the human condition. We can come back to that. For the moment let us observe that if we are to speak of Jesus as our healer, whether particularized or imparticularized, there is a simple demand made of him. In conflict, dread and resentment, even in a formlessness of religion within and without, what can possibly be the relief that faith in Jesus can bring?

This state is different from that which used to be known as spiritual 'desolation'. Then it was the subject in his private strivings towards 'perfection' who felt himself lost. He was lost within a known and accepted framework. The framework was that of an ordered world, itself the reflection of certain absolutes. But now the uncertainty and the threat seem to concern God and Jesus as much or more than the state of the subject. The neat divisions of private and public, religious and secular, worldly and other worldly have become quite blurred. Not only does the non-religious world appear to have overflowed into the religious world, but religious thinking itself appears to revolt against its own tradition. The 'de-privatization' of religious thinking has meant a violent change in the secure framework of the life of faith. As a result, religious certainties seem to have lost their stabilizing power. Security within is apparently no longer on offer. In the Catholic tradition the shock has been hard to assimilate. We inherit from St Thomas among others a tradition of thinking that holiness and wholeness are bound to overlap, that man will surely come to terms with himself and with his world, if he will but co-operate with grace.

The idea was reinforced in more romantic times by what seemed to be a self-evidently correct reading of the gospels. In the idyllic setting of Nazareth and by the Lakeside, did not Jesus exemplify and preach a gospel of pure joy, light and fellowship? 'The vision of heaven, far from driving them (his followers) to the hermit's cell or the pillar of the Stylites, sent them out onto the highways and lanes with songs on their lips and a passionate yearning to share the good news with their fellows.' Such language we might have expected to find in any book of pious meditations for religious which appeared between 1870 and 1939. But the worm in the fruit may be detected from the fact that the romantic tradition from Renan was strong in the highly original Cambridge

theologian, C. F. Raven.[64] Yet many of us have at one time
cherished such a New Testament view. It was an attractive
mental short-cut, and it was handed us on a plate. We should
have recognized in it the 'heavenly man' of apocalyptic or
even something of the gnostic Jesus. Lazily we did no such
thing. We should not now really complain overmuch if the
romantic short cut, laid over the medieval view of perfection
and over the medieval world-view, appears to have let us
down. It seems quite reasonable therefore to talk about an
age of religious anxiety as an accompaniment to the age of
secular anxiety in which we live.

First let us risk a few more generalizations about anxiety.
In varying degrees and modes we are indeed familiar with it.
Novelists and poets have shown us its dramatic possibilities.
Psychology and sociology have analysed it. What then are
they concerned with? With the experiences of uncertainty,
with a mental disturbance or agitation which makes
judgment difficult, perhaps even with a feeling of dread for
which we can hardly account in an entirely 'objective'
manner.

But we must map out the terrain a little more carefully
than that. However widespread or familiar anxiety may be, it
is still very difficult to define or even to describe.[65] There is
obviously a sense in which it is not even an intangible thing,
not even a live abstraction like panic in a cinema when
someone has shouted 'fire'. Even when for practical purposes
we try to forget our anxiety or to put it into mental brackets,
we know that there is no *it* which we can treat like that. The
police may turn the hoses on a panic-stricken crowd, but we
cannot do that on our private or shared anxiety; nor can any
authority, much as it often may wish to, allay anxiety so
suddenly. Yet, we would think, except in states of delusion,
there should always be something it may be clearly felt or it
may be vaguely felt, to which our anxiety relates and which,
for all we can tell, is responsible for its presence.

Freud's early view of anxiety was mechanistic. But he and
his followers afterwards modified the rather simple notion
that anxiety was the outcome of a mere suppression of
somatic tension. That was clearly not the whole story.
Anxiety must have some relational focus, commensurate
with its force or not. And anxiety, it was thought, must be a

state with a natural purpose. Could it not be in the nature of a
signal informing the subject about some danger to himself? If
a neutral observer could point to a recognizably 'objective'
threat, then the signal could be called an 'objective' one. Was
there nothing 'objective' to be discovered, then the whole
situation would appear to be internal to the subject, and he
would be called neurotic. The distinction, as I have outlined
it, is of course far too crude. How for example are we to
consider the subject whose anxiety centres on the personal
values he holds, and which he feels to be threatened? The
values themselves may, or may not, be 'objective'. So the
threat may or may not be 'objective'. We must say again that
anxiety is not a thing, but a highly relational state. The easiest
and perhaps the commonest way in which it can be triggered
off is to be found when interpersonal relations are, or are
merely felt to be, at stake.

Even so it remains vague; and there are always many
unknowns. But for our purpose we can say that the more
anxiety is amenable to diagnosis, observation or control, the
less it concerns us here. Oddly, where religions and anxiety
meet is mainly on grounds that are vague; yet disconcertingly
they are, though vague, none the less present. When anxiety
can be 'objectified' or personalized, especially in terms like
'the jealous husband', 'Russian spies', or, as among the
Belfast *graffiti*, 'the Pope', then the less is the concern
expressed a specifically religious one. It is after all only by
accident, for example, that the kind of anxiety known as
'scruple' can properly be called religious.

The specifically religious question of anxiety arises when
God himself, in the least as well as the most personal concept
we can form of him, becomes invested with it. Need this
ever be so? God is after all 'our Father', and we are 'sons in
the Son'. The name of Father does not avoid the issue.
Indeed, in the Judeo-Christian tradition, God himself is even
given the name of 'Fear'. In an extraordinarily modern way,
the book of Genesis makes the patriarch Jacob call God 'the
Fear of Isaac'. Thus he can say, 'if the God of my fathers, the
God of Abraham and *the Fear of Isaac* had not been on my
side' (cf. Gen 31: 42). The idea of fear, awe or dread as a part
of man's response to God is in the Old Testament accepted as
valid. It is part of the demand that God makes upon man.

God indeed makes moral demands on man, and the God who makes these demands appears to man from across a gulf of mysterious separation. We have inherited and accepted an Old Testament tradition which expects throughout that man's relationship with God will be characterized by fear. Thus correct religious conduct is 'God-fearing'. 'There can be no doubt,' writes Eichrodt, 'that *in the Old Testament statements about the fear of God, the inward agitation produced by the mysterium tremendum*, emerges with extraordinary emphasis.'[66]

We can call that 'modern' because, among other reasons, it is a modern discovery that such basic states as anxiety can pull in different directions at once. We find, for example, that 'trustful love' is associated with 'awe' of God, and so is confidence in him. In 'encounter' with God, a moment we expect to be one of intimacy and solace, we also find 'an absolute imperilling of human existence'. Disloyalty to God imperils the self, but concomitantly there is nevertheless 'a mysterious power of attraction which is converted into wonder, obedience, self-surrender, and enthusiasm'.[67] But we can know God's will according to Old Testament teaching, and so 'quiet *confidence* in the manifest God gets the upper hand over terror'. Finally the deliberate decision to adhere to God is rewarded by our finding trustworthiness and reliability in our relationship with him.[68]

It would thus appear that even in the Old Testament the all-embracing religious character of dread, awe and anxiety is consecrated in religious experience. Thinkers like St Augustine and Pascal have never shirked from seeing that belief in God as loving and rewarding cannot be separated from a quality of awe in faith. But placing anxiety or 'dread' firmly in the forefront of religious experience has been done for us by Kierkegaard. In the Protestant tradition he more easily saw *Angst* ('dread' perhaps rather than 'anxiety') as one of the most fundamental affective human states, for it is the one which discloses how precarious the human situation is. By it we have some idea of our radical possibilities. We have a certain consciousness of our freedom. But what we really are, and what we are constrained to become, our 'facticity', that sets us in front of the most vital question — now we discover that we can hardly respond. For Kierkegaard and for

Christians since then, the agonizing question remains, 'am I a Christian?' Conscience no longer merely says 'am I doing the will of God?' The interiorizing movement has become deeper and darker, and the emphasis on will and decision is more severe. Personal genuineness seems harder to come by. Once a graduated scale of genuineness was encouraged by the efforts of casuistry, today it hardly suffices any more. That is a point worth remembering when we are tempted to bemoan the diminished frequency of private confessions. It should be accepted that in parts of the Catholic West we have a new generation, struggling with all-or-nothing demands on the part of conscience. The new forms for private confession are an instinctive attempt to cope with the situation. They touch only the surface of the problem, which is deep and quite theological. The fact is that today's anxieties are bringing some Christians, many of them Catholic, nearer to Kierkegaard's dilemma, namely that we ought on the one hand to preach anxiety as a gospel call, and the fact on the other hand that apparently no one can bear to hear it:

> The immensely powerful tranquillizing means which Luther discovered in the extremity of his *Angst*, in a fight to death in fear and trembling and temptation — this is what is to be proclaimed as the sole means for all. And yet there is not one individual in each generation with this experience.[69]

In the tirades of the *Last Journals*, Kierkegaard comes to the ironical conclusion that the lowest paganism is possible in Protestantism, while it is avoided in Catholicism, which 'has a general supposition that we men are scoundrels'.[70] Now Kierkegaard could be a master of religious caricature, not least about himself. In a sense he was wrong about Protestants, and he was wrong about Catholics. But when he was pointing to the all-or-nothing demands of conscience before God, he was indeed pointing to an ambiguity in Christian existence. God demands and loves; we are attracted to belief in him, but in the attraction we dread our total inadequacy.

I said I thought that a new generation in Catholicism was trying to face up to such demands. In the nature of things, it does so with hesitation and with an inconsistency which it is easy to deride. To me, however, it sounds more courageous than its opposite: 'that's not how we were brought up'; 'why doesn't the Church exert its authority?'; 'why are children not taught the catechism by heart the way we were?' Such exclamations betray a feeling of insecurity, of abandonment, of being lost to fatherly authority. But the question remains: when you feel insecure, which way should you face? Should it be the way of nostalgia and regression? I presume the answer should be No. And that is one reason why I connect the question of anxiety with Christ. Only a hostile interpretation of Christ, such as the Marxist one, can leave us with the persuasion that his preaching of a kingdom not of this world is merely recommending nostalgia and regression.

It has to be said very often that no one can believe in Christ as though he did so in a mental and cultural vacuum. Nor can we freeze some socio-cultural framework of the Christian past and choose to live in that alone. As a result, the absoluteness of God's demands in faith is a mediated one. But it is also tempered by the fact that he made those demands first in his Son, his expressed and proclaimed Word incarnate. And he still makes those demands in that Son whom we can only know in our own theological skins, so to speak; that is to say, in the believing Church of today. If God demands, in any way we care to suppose, awe, dread, or anxiety on our part, then it will be the awe of the man of the twentieth century, not the awe of the man of biblical, medieval or Victorian times.

But it would not be right to suppose that change takes place at a uniform rate. Our present day fear of evil does not have exactly the same shape as fear in ancient Christianity, even though the ancient Church can still be our teacher. The patristic Church, for example, was quite clear about its fear of demons, principalities and powers, divine judgment and wrath, corruption of our nature, of the race and of death. With a more objectified sense of dualism than we now have, there was an evil sphere into which man might lapse or which could reach out and grab a man for itself. '*Thrusting down* Satan and his wicked angels' was a divine operation to keep the universe in balance, an idea recently as familiar as any, in the Leonine Prayers which were said at the end of every Low Mass. In ancient times pagans especially were seen as the victims of roving devils. The fact is that 'all Christian language may turn demonic'.[71] It is the one refuge of Christian anxiety. It was an easy in and some ways satisfactory one, when the cosmos itself was an intelligible and above all an ordered spiritual as well as material reality. Fear could thus be objectified. So in a previous age of anxiety, Christianity beat its rivals by out-bidding them. It is a sound historical point that in the fourth century and onwards, Christianity 'wielded both a bigger stick and a juicier carrot'.[72] Both the stick and the carrot have lasted well. It cannot be denied. But the world-outlook which helped to form them has lost even its vestiges. What has not gone is man's anxiety, his dread. Nor on the other hand has his God and his Christ.

But when we come to the doctrine that this world is one of tribulation we come to something more abiding than the socio-cultural medium of the gospel truth. It belongs to the very message of the gospel, because it relates to the person of Christ. The impetus and authority of Jesus himself are there. 'In the world you have tribulation (*thlipsis*); but be of good cheer, I have overcome the world' (Jn 16: 33). Here the Jesus of the 'little flock' gives a message to future generations, tempted as they will be, by anxiety and uncertainty arising within and without the community of faith. Such pain and anxiety can be overcome because Jesus has overcome. Here, one can say, is the better established Catholic tradition and theology of anxiety, surely a successful rival to that other tradition of faith-experience which propounds the necessity of anxiety or dread as a parameter to the very possibility of Christian godliness.

Certainly, the theology that Christ's victory gives grace and salvation, because evil and the grounds of fear have been overcome, is well established. I am certainly not proposing that we should go back upon it. Fear of the principalities and powers, as we know from the Captivity Epistles, must now be considered a vain fear. In Christ, God has disarmed them, triumphed over them and raised us up (cf. e.g. Col 2: 15; Eph 2: 6). The world-view in which the *theologia gloriae* was expressed is that of the New Testament. In it world-anxiety could be pinpointed, personalized and vanquished.

But, as we may still be somewhat slow to see, we should be prepared to rethink the self-sufficiency and the scope of the doctrine of the *theologia gloriae*. That is not to deny the truth of the *theologia gloriae*, nor to question its perfectly valid context. Yet, our relationship with God is mysterious enough not to be wholly comprehended in one theology. God's Word and work in his Son is indeed a way of victory. But, just as Paul was left with a problem on his hands over the apparent continuance of evil and the infliction of anxiety on the part of the principalities and powers, so the simple statement of Christ's victory still leaves us with the problem of the completion of the victory. It is something like the interim period we recollect at the end of World War II, between what was called VE-Day and VJ-Day, a victory that was not yet a victory. In that case one victory completed another. In this case we may say that another way of seeing how Christ relates to our anxieties is compatible with the first. The classical name of the alternative way is the *theologia crucis*. That too has a truth value. If we take seriously the proposition that 'by the cross the "sufferings of God" reveal to the world his involvement in the fate of his creation', then we can take seriously the specifically Christian value of man's anxiety in faith.[73] In the way of the *theologia gloriae*, God's impassible serenity is a firm reassurance during tribulation. In the victory of Christ, the God who calls us is far from sin and death; in the godforsakenness of Christ, God suffered and died. He who is God knows our basic dread and anxiety.

GOD IN THE ANXIOUS LIFE

In discussing Christ and sexuality we accepted the idea that it would nowadays be wrong to continue to think, as in the past, that the believer's love of God cannot in the slightest degree depend upon his urges or his sexuality. It would be equally wrong to think that the love of God cannot depend upon anxiety. As we have been saying, anxiety has a special role to play in the structure of our belief and in our love of God as well.

Can we now go on to say that the phenomenon is observable in our Catholic believing communities? If it is true that we are in an age of religious anxiety, which mirrors the anxiety of the secular world, then it would be wrong to consider religious anxiety as a massive deviation. In any case, the signs are that we are going to have to live with it for some time to come. A few simple reflections should bring that out.

The Catholic Church has now made itself much more conscious than it has been since the Reformation that it is a pilgrim Church. The Constitution on the Church has thrown strong emphasis upon the doctrine of the 'people of God'. Whenever possible we now try in church life to insist upon the lack of difference between us as members of the Church. Priests and religious tend to feel the effects of this change more than do the pew-bound Sunday laity. The individual thus comes to ask himself, and it is done with varying degrees of awareness, about the exact nature of his or her role. The so-called search for identity among priests and religious is now a byword. When the doctrine of the undifferentiated group is so much to the fore that Vatican II can teach us that the Christian community, so far from being bound to uniformity, is to be seen as mysteriously conterminous with the whole community of mankind, then the individual must question himself and his role (cf. *Lumen Gentium*, 1; *Gaudium et Spes*, 23ff.). He must do so because the larger the group to which he belongs appears to be, the less certain to him is his identity or role within the group. The individual who was not ready for such a doctrine has been in a sense left high and dry. The point at issue is, of course, not whether or not such a doctrine is faithful to the teaching of Jesus, but whether or not a relatively sudden shift of emphasis has, on 'the purely natural' plane, contributed to the factor of religious anxiety.[74]

Again, on 'the purely natural' plane we can accept that church structures, and the structures within religious orders, have in the past made a valuable contribution to the 'belongingness want', and even to the 'power want' of many of their members.[75] A great number of clerical jokes have in the past turned especially on the latter fact. Canon Law on clerics and the Constitutions of religious orders have by no means ignored the dangers of the situation. As a problem, the matter was well in the open before the redaction of the first gospel: '. . . that these two sons of mine may sit, one at your right hand and one at your left, in your kingdom' (Mt 20: 21). The 'belongingness want' is clearly expressed and with pathos in John 13–17. Critics, who have disliked the intrusion of human nature into the New Testament world, have often complained of the notorious *Frühkatholizismus*, the organizational corruption as they saw it, which had apparently crept into the Pauline churches especially. Any revisionary reading of the gospel (such as 'renewal' following Vatican II began to be) must also protest against excesssive concessions to the 'belongingness want' or to the 'power want' of the individual. Nor can the process avoid hidden, and doubtless unwanted, threats to the individual. Personal faith and religious existence cannot be isolated either. We are driven back to the fact that, given our social needs and dependency, our anxiety about ourselves is also an anxiety about our relationship with Christ. If one asks, is that good or is it bad, then the answer must lie in the quality of one's acceptance of Christ himself.

Where groups are concerned, the same phenomenon is surely to be observed. We cannot ostracize from our thinking about the Christian life, the fact of the extraordinary growth of the Pentecostal movement or movements. We know that there are in existence groups of varying sizes and in great numbers. They cut across denominational boundaries, across clerical-lay boundaries; and it is worth noting that they tend very especially to escape from the largely male domination of ecclesiastical structures. They tend also to have an ecstatic character, and they cherish their undifferentiated and egalitarian qualities. Perhaps more obviously significant here is the fact that they try and answer demands for ministries such as healing, for mental health generally and sometimes also for deviant behaviour. Their activities, as we know, include the occasional practice of exorcism of those in 'possessed' states.[76] Here again we are not raising the problem of how good or less good such phenomena may be, nor what ought, if anything, to be done about them. Nor do we have to say anything to try and account for their presence. If we are content to note the existence of the phenomenon on the large scale on which it is to be found, and if we note the vagueness inherent in their doctrinal expressions, then we observe how easily all chimes in with a generalized anxiety state among believers. Distressing? Perhaps. But anxiety does not contradict the presence of faith, hope and love in Christ.

To exemplify the matter in the most individual, yet abstract way, let us construct a religious *identikit* picture of the 'troubled priest'. He may be in young middle age, socially and culturally well-established in Catholic ways of life. He has had a protected childhood, schooling and seminary life. No longer of the generation for whom church learning and an ability to stand on one's own feet intellectually was a respected and expected asset, he has enough university experience to feel ill at ease with the church learning he does have and which he now tends to distrust. His situation 'in the world' is, as he thinks, a second-class one; and his situation within the Church is no longer protected. The identity quest is thus inevitable. It would be easy to continue the fantasy. I merely want to suggest how in practice a responsible, believing Christian, finding himself confronted with the demands of a *theologia crucis* within his own life of the spirit, finds himself at a cross-roads in faith, and specifically in his faith in Christ whose declared follower he is. What was comforting about the old has apparently let him down, and seems hollow. The new asks for a commitment for which he is theologically and spiritually unprepared. If one considers the problem in that light, then factors such as 'a row with the bishop', 'falling in love', can be seen to be quite adventitious. The quite tragic suffering over faith-fidelity to Christ must be looked at from within.

The doctrine that 'the faith cannot be doubted without some moral fault' has led to over-protection.[77] For the present I have tried to high-light one type of situation, in which, it seems to me, anxiety in faith in Christ has to be accepted, not for its confused origins, but for what it basically *can* become, an awareness of God in life itself. It implies an acceptance of the *theologia crucis* and can always be urged on the sufferer in gospel terms: 'was it not necessary that the Christ should suffer . . .?' (Lk 24: 26).

CHAPTER FOUR

The Cross in Question

More than ever the Christian cross is now in question. In a
new way it impinges on daily life within and without its
religious context. The human hells of world famine may
seem just secular, the hells of terrorism, especially urban
terrorism, come with their ambiguous religious wrappings.
Yet where there is death, there is surely God even with the
disguise of 'godforsakenness'. I am going to suggest that
'godforsakenness' in its most profound sense is what the
cross is about.

Seeing and feeling the plight of his fellow-believers and of
his fellow-men the theologian would be a lazy fellow indeed,
if he did not ask himself some basic questions all over again.
Have we got it right about the cross of Jesus? Have we
reduced the garden agony and the cry of dereliction to a
psychodrama of our own shape and size, so as to live with it
and not suffer too much discomfort? Does sharing in the
cross of Christ refer to what I can manage and what hits the
others? Or do the human hells from Auschwitz to
Bangladesh via Northern Ireland constitute the real presence
of the cross of Christ in the world? Must it be a cross of stark
dereliction? And what of the cross of divine risk? Can you
have a crusade for social and even political justice, watch it
turn sour and end in intolerance and even violence and
terror?[1]

Reflecting that he cannot answer all those questions, as
well as a few more awkward ones he keeps to himself, the
theologian may be tempted to turn his *métier* into a spectator
sport. Real life is what he sees on the telly screen, and he
must trim his answers for that interview when it comes. 'The
Holy One,' he might say mixing his religions in his reverie,
'Blesed be He, is the Immutable, the Serene, the Impassible,
the Apathetic.' That is a corner of the religious language

game he does not encourage in the pulpit. It implies that mere mortals, we must just sweat it out. Hate, bombs and hells are all in the day's work. For the record, let them have a social gospel and even a political theology, and — well, all right — a theology of revolution to cap it. But remember that sooner or later it all goes sour. There is no social theology, as Malcolm Muggeridge once said of sex, without tears. So theories, if you like; but no practice. We must preach eternal happiness. As for what happens here below, the truth is that we are in for a long theological doomwatch.

This chapter is not meant to suggest that a revised theology of the cross will solve our problems for us. It is intended to clear some of the background problems out of the way in view of a deeper ecumenical understanding. At the same time I want to look forward and outward. I think it is vital to do so. By forward, I mean that I hope as many Christians as possible may benefit from reconsidering a Protestant answer to a basically Catholic question. By outwards I mean, and hope that what is said will have an overspill beyond the denominations. I also hope that that overspill will bring some human value to already human problems and predicaments. Down the centuries the Protestant *theologia crucis* has been kept at a distance from the Roman Catholic theological scene. A dialogue has begun but certainly not before time.

The cross does have its place high up in the practical hierarchy of truths of any Christian. Its fundamental relevance is not in doubt. But it is all the same a challenging relevance as 1 Corinthians insists. The cross, which is a part of the very mystery of salvation shares in the resurrection. Hence it is a power as well as a challenge. Indeed for Paul the cross is a criterion of relevance and of what the gospel essentially consists in. It is also that which makes the gospel intelligible. The wisdom of the cross is placed in direct opposition to the Greek gnostic intellectualism of Corinth. Under pressure Christians can have only one form of their own intellectualism, namely the Cross's wisdom, 'the word of the Cross'.[2] Put in that dramatic language from which I do not think we should shrink, we can accept Moltmann's dictum: 'Theology can receive its divine justification in Christian terms only when it continually and fully actualizes and makes present the death-cry of the forsaken Christ.'³

I am sure that theological uprightness as well as ecumenism demand that we envisage a renewal of our theology of the cross. Future Christian identity, as well as inter-church and denominational loyalties require it. So do the human hells we often pass by on our continued Christian way.

The kernel of the matter to be discussed is this. God was himself 'godforsaken' in Jesus. Our 'godforsakenness' now can be enlightened only by the 'godforsakenness' of Jesus then. Only experience of that tragedy seems to give us God. Only the God so disclosed is giveable. His inner self is thus unveiled as a self of *pathos* and of *sumpatheia*, a self of Fatherhood, a self of Sonship and a self of sealing Spirithood.

Catholicism has kept its distance from such a theology. If it takes the twin dialogues of ecumenism and secularity seriously, should it still do so? Under the entry '*Theologia Crucis*' the *Lexikon für Theologie und Kirche* carries a section by Karl Rahner which amounts to a plea that Catholics should try to penetrate the significance of the distinctively Protestant theology of the cross. It is a theology that belongs to the *rationale* of Christ's saving work in relation to ourselves. It is also a theology at the edge of the Catholic–Protestant divide. As a dialectic it is also a psychodrama to strike chords in the disenchanted Marxist.

Since 1973 we have had the English translation of Moltmann's *Der greuzigte Gott*. Like his *Theology of Hope* it was and remains an exciting theological read.⁴ It has become probably his most influential book in English. In parts it has greatness. This I put down to the timeliness of its insights. I do not think that the theological needs of the 1980s have in any way outgrown the appeal of *The Crucified God*. The late Karl Rahner has pleaded for greater Catholic sympathy with a *theologia crucis*. So this chapter proposes a renewed dialogue with Moltmann on the subject. The time has come on the Catholic side to ask more plainly, What can we do about it?⁵

It is characteristic of Moltmann that he looks beyond denominational boundaries and beyond church boundaries in a global sense. He certainly does not, because of his Lutheran inheritance, try merely to further that theological tradition for its own sake. His *Theology of Hope* was more than an

ecumenical challenge, it was a contribution made from
within a tradition and offered to all. A theologian who takes a
prophetic stance and joins it with a sense of responsibility is
nowadays challenging the secularist as well as the Christian.
Moltmann does this most effectively, I think, through a
mostly implicit 'de-privatization' of Christian belief.[6] To see
how this is done at the theological level, the reader must take
account of the 'horizontal' eschatology expounded in *The
Theology of Hope*. Before the ultimacy of a consummation in
God, the *de-privatization* of faith and hope is seen as an
essential condition of successful survival in the face of a
Marxist critique. So for Moltmann eschatology refers to a
communal 'hope, forward-looking and forward-moving,
and therefore revolutionizing and transforming the present'
(*Hope*, p. 16).

Truth comes for the believer in his reliance on divine
promises; and human reality is to be transformed by the
future on the basis of divine promises. Such an approach is a
biblical one. It also in effect implies more than an inter-
church re-consideration of man. It moves on inexorably to
the Church's responsibility *for mission* 'to the nations'. Hence
it will eventually imply not only an apologia in face of, but
also a dialogue with Marxism. For the Marxist understands
something of eschatological language. Moltmann's *Hope* was
deliberately written as a complement to Ernst Bloch's *Das
Prinzip Hoffnung, I, II* Berlin, 1959).[7] Here the dissatisfied
and unquiet Marxist can find a certain salvation for faith. In
what, though? The reply must be, in the unfinished quality
of life, in its being unfinished within as well as without the
Ego. This twist to an Augustinian perception is made
meaningful by the necessary category of hope, *spes quaerens
intellectum*. For the Marxist as for the Christian hope carries
its provisionality, but it carries also its own form of
transcendency.

It would be an over-simplification to say that *The Crucified
God* continues where *Hope* left off. What it does is to take one
step backward and two forward. So it is not a case of a
theologian who, after basing a study on the resurrection, then
goes back to another study based upon the crucifixion. *Hope*
had introduced a pivotal form of eschatology which may be
called 'horizontal', rather than 'realized', since it is the state

produced by two overlapping movements on the same resurrectional level. The 'horizontal' eschatology enables Moltmann to construct a theology, which goes that one step back as a *theologia crucis*, and then two steps forward in the sense that it issues in an *eschatologia crucis*. The cross which initiates the momentum, because it is dialectical, comes to a final consummation in God. In this sense God himself has a future.[8] Thus the meaning of the cross for the future is that the cross itself, which is the 'form of remembrance of his death', is also and paradoxically a form of remembrance *which looks forward*. In looking forward it does so with hope. We here have a cluster of truths which form the locus for 'creative discipleship'. A 'creative discipleship' in the cross is surely the form of afflicted Christianity where 'godforsaken-ness' is experienced. The eschatology involved makes Romans 8 come true with its doctrine of the 'creative expectation'. In a common Christian 'godforsakenness', God offers the cross and his promise, a new and perhaps necessary dimension for the ecumenical mind and will. Let us try to think through the basic doctrinal issues before the rest. An appropriate Catholic response must surely begin with doctrine.

THE CROSS IS PRIMORDIAL NOW

So I want to urge that we should try to enter into the mind of a *theologia crucis*, incomplete as I think it is in Moltmann's pages.[9] One thing Moltmann makes clear on first reading. A theology of the cross has urgency. The lived mind of such a tradition has an immediate impact. The Lutheran's faith in the cross, as he experiences it, comes through as the faith as well as the hope of a brother in baptism. If that stirs us less than it should, then a theology of the cross is even more timely. It should give us a norm for self-criticism besides an obvious area for discussion. Do we need to be shy of saying that the role of the cross *could be* more creative than it is in present-day Catholic theology? *It could* in the critical sense be more normative also. *It could* give more urgency to that adjustment we make with philosophical contexts, however existential and personalist.

In the concrete we cannot speak about the ultimates which concern us except in terms of the Cross. We cannot begin to evaluate what Christian destiny may be without it. Nor can we speak of our reconciliation with God and Christ's atonement without it. The Christ of the *kenosis* in Philippians 2 calls for such a theology. The Lutheran can say, 'What happened on the cross was a happening between God and God; there God disputes with God; there God cries out to God; there God dies in God.'[10] True or false, perceptive or over-drawn — the non-Lutheran theologian cannot at that point simply pass by.

The reason why a theology of the cross can never be left out, lies in the state of theological circumincession by which the Christian mysteries interpenetrate one another. Sooner or later any mental scheme or model brings us back to the most existential starting-point of all. So in some sense all Christian theology is a *theologia crucis*. Not only must theology, as a thinkable and as a thought world of reflection, be a theology of the cross, but so also must our activity, as theologizing beings promoting an ongoing process, be a theologizing of the cross. From the fact that what we are doing is characteristically Christian, then it is the cross which gives even this activity its primordial definition.

We can go further than that. When we theologize, we do so in parallel with the active habit of faith-belief. That faith-belief, just like our faith-fidelity, draws upon the grace of none other than the Crucified One. More than that, again I would say that, as our theologizing can and should be a Christiform activity in grace, it is also an activity for that reason defined by the cross. That is why theology is not only a necessary but a highly responsible activity. Pseudo-crosses have to be distinguished from real ones. The theologian must on occasion say to himself 'today's work was the work of a sinful man'. He may have to ask himself if his handling of dogmatic truth is liable to the 'sinfulness' of being unworthily legalistic, or without charity, or complacently and lazily absolutized into an ancient and no longer communicable formulation. In parentheses one is tempted to ask whether the theologian does not also have a responsibility towards his non-theological brethren. Do they not need help in distinguishing the cross from pseudo-crosses in the life of faith? But fairness, if we are drawing up a programme of theological work, demands something else as well. We should be prepared to re-think and to re-value the *theologia gloriae* of the Catholic tradition so that that too may be more ecumenically intelligible.[11]

To start by considering the matter in God (i.e. *in divinis*), it is easy to see that we are in a region where unclarity reigns. In fact it belongs to the very historic expression of the mystery we are talking about. There is a good lesson to be learned here. In the combative aftermath of Chalcedon, the leading theological personalities were not all exactly Chalcedonians. One effect of that paradigm among councils was that theological power and religious vigour passed from the Catholic parties, who after victory were content to shelter unadventurously under imperial protection and manipulation. Catholics had to wait for a century and a half before they found a new theological figure in Maximus the Confessor. It was the Monophysites who meanwhile remained in a challenging position. Chalcedon had put the ball in their court and they kept it there. At Antioch a turbulent patriarch, Peter the Fuller, successfully made a bit of history. To the famous *Trisagion* ('O, holy God . . .'), which we know from the Good Friday Reproaches, he added the famous phrase 'crucified for us'. Was that heresy or was it not? Peter made the addition in a partisan spirit, and there was trouble. Later the Scythian monks thought of a peace formula. It became equally famous: 'One of the Trinity suffered for us.' Was that heresy or was it not? Unfortunately for peace the formula, when it came out, seemed to have a Monophysite slant. It got a bad reception. There was more faction in the Eastern Church. In AD 520, 'One of the Trinity suffered for us' was condemned by Pope Hormisdas. The whole thing had been thoroughly partisan, and it took time for the Catholics to see that the monks' formula could easily be taken in a Catholic and not at all in a Monophysite sense. The light dawned after thirteen years. The Roman See changed its mind and John II restored the formula to honour.[12]

I said I thought there was a lesson here. I really think there are four. The *first* is that it matters enormously to Christian belief to know *who* suffered and died on the cross, in the sense that it matters enormously to know whether the Christian doctrine of the Incarnate God will stand up to the question, was it *God* who died on the cross? *Secondly*, it also

matters very much that we should see how on this one
question, where we are so near the heart of the all-important
Christian mystery, there is room for theological reflection.
Thirdly, it pays to try to see the other point of view. Peter the
Fuller would have been pleased with Moltmann's title, *The
Crucified God*. Pope Hormisdas would not at all have
approved. John II would have given it his *placet*, but in those
days would have had to add *iuxta modum*. *Fourthly*, what
about ourselves? Do we not sometimes try to keep the
question about God suffering at the periphery, as though it
were something too mysterious, even too scandalous. At
least over the scandal we cannot say we have not been
warned (1 Cor 1: 23).

In spite of efforts to keep the question at a comfortable
theological distance, it nevertheless comes back to us in our
terrors and 'godforsakenness'. I give two examples:

(i) The SS hanged two Jewish men and a youth in front of
the whole camp. The men died quickly, but the death throes
of the youth lasted for half an hour. 'Where is God? Where is
he?' someone asked behind me. As the youth still hung in
torment in the noose after a long time, I heard the man call
again. 'Where is God now?' And I heard a voice in myself
answer: 'Where is he? He is here. He is hanging there on the
gallows . . .'[13]

(ii)   *It's God they ought to crucify*
              Instead of you and me,
              I said to the carpenter
              A-hanging on the tree.[14]

Here in the terror and the 'godforsakenness' the mind
returns spontaneously to historic Christian faith. Just as we
say Mary was the Mother of God (*Theotokos*), so we say God
died on the cross. And we make the most of that. The
'godforsakenness' of the Jewish victim cries out its Christian
overtone. The 'godforsakenness' of the 'godforsaken' himself
can only be brought out by the understatement 'They *ought*
to crucify' him. The faith that they *did* crucify him is too
much. Human pathos can be met with reverence, or laziness,
or evasion. I sometimes think that Catholic theology has not
been immune in the last decade or so from the evasion
symptom. In 1960, when the translation of Durrwell's work,
The Resurrection, appeared there was some justifiable joy at

the discovery of a movement among theologians and exegetes, which restored to us some of the values of the Resurrection.[15] No doubt that a theology of the resurrection came almost as a welcome substitute for the well-used categories in theology and piety on the subject of the cross and sacrifice.[16] The insistence in the liturgical movement and by Vatican II on the 'paschal mystery' and on paschal joy confirmed this state of affairs. Devotions such as devotion to the Sacred Heart have diminished, and orders of men and women, devoted by name and religious practice to the passion of Christ, have been driven to doubt their own role and usefulness in the Church. In itself, of course, the 'paschal mystery' refers to the cross and death of Christ as much as to his resurrection. The first section of the decree on religious life in Vatican II speaks quite unambiguously about the redemption and sanctification of man by Christ's obedience to the death of the cross (cf. *Perfectae caritatis*, n. 1). The fault lay not in the insistence upon joy and the resurrection, but in a general inability to think through again the theology of the cross.

THE GOD–SHAPED PICTURE

So we must attend to the death of Jesus in our theology. As Rahner says, it leads us straight to the kernel of our faith in the redeeming God. Not that God was himself bound by a destiny outside himself; but he did bring about the atonement *by* and *on* that redeeming cross. It was God who redeemed us so. How strong, then, is our theology of the cross as a *theology-of-God-suffering*?

To take up again the monks' formula, does the phrase 'God died on the cross' mean 'one of the Trinity died on the cross'? It is tempting to say 'yes, of course that is the faith' and then to add 'and that is all there is to be said'. Analysis is still important here and we have to be patient with it. When you say 'One of the Trinity died on the cross' you could mean a number of different things according to your theology of the Incarnation. Thus: (*a*) you could mean, 'the name we give to him who died on the cross is "one of the Trinity" '; (*b*) you could mean, 'One of the Trinity, who had the personal appearance of being God and man, died on the cross'; (*c*) you could mean, 'One of the Trinity whom I abstractly consider as one and the same person having the nature of God and the nature of man, died on the cross'; (d) you could mean, 'One of the Trinity, who is the psychological subject of the experience of dying, died on the cross'; (e) you could mean, 'One of the Trinity, who is the ontological and psychological subject of the experience, died on the cross'.

Full Catholic tradition in the West can be satisfied only by the last of the above meanings (e). Thus, if you use the Chalcedonian model of two natures in one person and if, within that framework, you ask 'Who died on the cross?' the only satisfactory answer is the one which says that the person, who was the ontological and psychological subject of that death is Jesus Christ, His only Son, Our Lord, that is One of the Trinity. To mean less than that, as in examples (a), (b), (c), and (d) does not (in the metaphysical tradition working upon Chalcedon) avoid Nestorianism.[17] I labour the point in no apologetic spirit, but because it is here that Moltmann challenges us to draw a further conclusion. If we really mean what we say in accepting (e), then what is our answer to the question, 'Did the death of God affect God or did it not?' Rahner for one, holds that 'if it is said that the incarnate Logos died only in his human reality, and if this is tacitly understood to mean that this death did not therefore affect God, then only half the truth has been stated. The really Christian truth has been omitted.'[18]

At first glance, the 'really Christian truth' must be bound up with a dilemma. If when talking about the cross we are making a 'statement about God himself', then two things seem to follow. On the one hand we appear to be speaking of a God who must be less than God if he is the full subject of suffering. On the other hand our central religious truth about the redemption, and its symbol the cross, become depotentiated if this God does not suffer. We should at once notice the thought-matrices of the two statements. They are different. In the *first* instance of the God who cannot suffer, we are talking about God in abstraction from the matrix of revelation, prayer, liturgy in which we know him. In fact we abstract from God as he is known to us in salvation history. In the *second* instance we are talking about God precisely as he is revealed to us in salvation history.

The dilemma presented by these two lines of thought has

been usefully clarified by Jean Galot.[19] Thus the first line reminds us that in Aristotelian terms God is *actus purus*, the impassible, the unmoved mover. In such a line of thinking the concept of suffering must be unthinkable. For it implies either that God changes, or that as a reality God is composite, suffering and not suffering. Yet in this philosophical view God must be total unblended simplicity. A suffering God on the side of the sufferer is then unthinkable. First, he cannot at the same time be both a God of happiness and unhappiness such as suffering implies. Secondly, neither change nor composite existence can be attributed to him, and both are implied in the notion of suffering.

It is clear that this classical outline of the Aristotelian God cannot, in spite of an obstinate tradition, by itself do justice to the Christian tradition of faith in the personal, redeemer God. Galot has to come down in favour of the prior notion of a biblical God, the God of revelation who is saviour. It is after all in the first place the Bible which invites us to see God as the God who suffers. The Aristotelian categories cannot now simply be forced onto the biblical data. Let one quotation from Isaiah stand for the rest:[20]

> For a brief moment I forsook you,
>   but with great compassion I will gather you.
> In overflowing wrath for a moment
>   I hid my face from you,
> but with everlasting love I will have compassion on you,
>   says the Lord, your Redeemer   (Is 54: 7–8).

Now the Bible does not contradict itself when it shows God as successively the eternally faithful One, and nevertheless the One adapting freely to the changeableness of man, his own creation. Galot emphasizes the good biblical doctrine of God's free commitment towards man.[21] That makes it all the more important that the doctrine of a compassionate God be not diminished or just whittled away. I must not of course suggest that Galot goes so far as to see God the Father suffer as does Moltmann. What he does is to emphasize the power of the Word in the Incarnation 'to enter freely into a certain mutability'. Similarly he brings out how the divine compassion is a distinct reality insofar as it belongs to God's free engagement in the Incarnation.[22]

The nature of God's suffering can be known only by use of the doctrine of analogy. That implies differences between our suffering and that of God of course. But there remains a basic similarity (*une similitude foncière*) 'without which the biblical assertions would lose their scope and meaning (*leur portée*). At the same time the divine attribute of immutability persists, and it would not be unfair comment to say that the consequence is some sort of di-polarity in God by which he is the Necessary Being and possesses that free activity 'which can neither add nor subtract from the divine perfection'.[23] It may be said that this last point does not display any profound development. Yet Galot should be given credit as one on the Catholic side, who has performed a most useful operation of extrication or disengagement. He does not contradict the classical tradition on the divine immutability, but he does at any rate free the revelationary perception of divine love, suffering, and compassion from it.

Nevertheless at the point at which he leaves the argument, Galot still leaves us with the dilemma between the two lines of thinking we have mentioned. There remains an *a priori* reflection in Aristotelian terms. There remains also the second line of thinking, the biblical and personal understanding of God. *Either* simplicity, immutability and impassibility, *or* faithfulness, mercy and love — the incompatibility persists.

It is to be expected that when we face the problem which our dilemma leaves us with, as we try to wrestle with it, so more and more we tend to concentrate on the clearer, if more abstract, attributes such as simplicity, immutability and impassibility. These abstractions take on the appearance of definability, and seem better to reward our efforts to think about God as a graspable thought-object. As is well known, there are many senses in which God is not a graspable object of thought. If he were, we could not have the co-existence of 'an affirmative or kataphatic, as well as a negative or apophatic theology'.[24] But we do have the habit of trying to turn a mystery into a problem with the result that impassibility seems a better intellectual fit in our God-shaped mental picture than, for example, compassion. When, however, we put ourselves in prayer or worship before the God who comes to us in mystery, and whom we now objectify in the images of salvation history, we find no difficulty with the God 'of mercy and compassion'. This in a sense catches us on the intellectual hop distrusting ourselves. Because in our own personal, historical experience of the *ordo cognoscendi*, attributes such as faithfulness, mercy and love are the more accessible ones, so we tend to think, in our attempts to misobjectify the divine, that these are less objective than more easily definable abstracts such as simplicity or impassibility. This is where a *theologia crucis* invites us to adjust our theological perspective. The death of the Incarnate is there to remind us that the more accessible attributes of faithfulness, mercy and love belong to the divine personhood, and that in God they have as much claim to be considered absolutely and ontologically as the famous attributes with the negative prefix, or those that belong to the 'omni-business'.[25]

The idea of God, moreover, disclosed by any theology of the cross is governed by the distinctively Christian matrix of experiences we share. Across the ages, applied theology in preaching and liturgy have biased us away from the idea of an *apathetic* God, one who for example need never have been born, or suffered and died. Balancing the redemptive *pro nobis* as making the incarnation somehow dependent upon a sin-state in the world, the Scotist thesis of an incarnation, which is connected with creation as its final cause, is always making its re-appearance, partly because of biblical support and partly because of our totally Christ-orientated attitudes in prayer. Eucharistic prayer, for example, in being the summit of Christian prayer, resumes and prolongs the all-pervasive attitude of prayer *per Christum*. It was within an already established orientation of this sort that Christians entered the philosophical world of, let us say, Middle Platonism and Stoicism. It was here that they found the philosophical afterthought they needed to communicate their doctrine of God. Celsus jibed at them for favouring the idea that the passing phenomena of human history could affect the realm of eternal truths. If God came down to men, that would imply a change in God. How could divine claims for Christ be taken seriously? The Stoics knew very well that to keep a religion serious, you had to clean up the luxuriant anthropomorphisms by the process of allegorizing them. God must be isolated from any process or history.

That isolation is poignantly illustrated for us in early Christian iconography. How could the dead body of the crucified one convey that this was indeed the divine Logos who had suffered and died? The full consequence of meaning (e) (pp. 139f above) as the 'one of the Trinity suffered . . .' is accepted. Some solution to this problem was needed for Christianity interpreted itself as a religion of the cross. The Christians Tertullian had in mind were always crossing themselves. But how to cope graphically with the problem of the 'impassible who yet suffered'? From the second part of the sixth century onwards come the earliest dateable depictions of the Crucified One, and they probably reflect earlier types from Asia Minor. 'The *Christus* crucifixus, who according to the body is sleeping the sleep of death, is also shown in his Godhead as wakeful in presence of the Father . . . The *Crucified Christ* was depicted as the immortal Logos and that is the only way that the wakeful faith of that time received him.[26] Graphically the problem was solved by showing the dead Christ, his side pierced with the flow of water and blood, *with eyes open* showing him as the God untouched by suffering. Thus the Cyrillian theology of the impassible one who suffered was sustained.

The category of *apatheia* protected the personal unity of him who suffered. It was a good logical defence within the Church against the Nestorians, it ensured no confusion between Christ the Incarnate Logos and the gods of paganism, and it kept piety on the right lines. It was a doctrine to be reinforced by the medieval use of Aristotle's 'pure act' to describe the divine being. It would be worth inquiring, however, to what extent *apatheia* has been taken in an over-simplified and popular sense. The doctrine that God is Father, and God is Son and God is Spirit may well be compatible with a less simple view of impassibility than popularized Stoicism. It is not *as such* the dogma of the Trinitarian Godhead which forces us to immunize the divine *actus purus* against all possibility of *pathos*. The Stoics themselves can give us the hint. 'For none of the various Stoicisms,' writes Edelstein quoting Alexander Pope, 'does *apatheia* mean freedom from compassion, a "virtue fixed as in a frost".'[27]

★

THE LIVE TRINITY

Moltmann's book looks at that in another way. He makes much of the cry of dereliction on the cross. As I understand him, we should take the cry as a high point expressing Christ's existential situation. To take it like that seems to me perfectly fair. It is an expression of abandonment which stands as a *pars pro toto* for the whole passion and death. It does so independently of any special exegesis and, by reason of its setting, independently also of other scriptural support. The cry of dereliction puts the abandonment of the Son by the Father well in the centre of our Christian mystery.

It prevents us also from acquiescing too easily in the idea that the self-oblation of Christ was an undemanded spontaneous and generalized act of love. Of course it was a spontaneous act of love; but the New Testament evidence is strongly in favour of a *mandatum moriendi*. Christ died out of obedience to a command. This is an old topic of discussion and I think that Moltmann's arguments give more plausibility to the idea that a *mandatum* was indeed part of New Testament belief. The consequence of that situation is for Moltmann a quite precise one and the main conclusion of his book. Putting it my own way I would say this. At the very moment when God is about to be disclosed as God-to-man, and that moment is on the cross, then *in his abandonment* he is disclosed as the triune God. We should not think he is then present only as Son, and suppose he is absent as Father and Spirit. The open-eyed Cyrillian Crucified One is a good depiction. It rightly suggests that the Son in his abandonment is present before the Father; so also, of course, with the Spirit. But that is a consequence which is not drawn in the Cyrillian tradition because of its insistence on the fixed impassibility of the divine.

What we must not do is to detach the heart of this mystery from God its absolute revealer. The mystery is not about an absentee Trinity. In his chiefest mystery as Incarnate, God is not concealing, but revealing. Then, one may ask, what of the abandonment? Is that a mere psychodrama on our part? It is not. It becomes factitious if we insist on considering the divine triunity in a tritheist fashion. If we wish on to the three persons, *as persons*, autonomous centres of activity; and, if we insist on thinking of them as independent subjects who each know, and will, and have consciousness, then the abandonment of the crucified by God does become reduced to a merely projected psychodrama on our part.[28] In that situation we are caught. There are two impossible choices open to us, and we know we have to reject both. We can have the mythology of a divine tritheist struggle. *Or*, we can have the gnostic psychodrama of the powers and spheres in which every symbol can in a dream-like way be transformed into any other symbol. Finally we are left with no Christ-event on the cross.[29] I prefer to go back to the ancient iconographical statement. There the part symbolic, part realistic *crucifixus* is open-eyed though in death. The effect is to show that the suffering and death of the Incarnate in part mirrors, and in part is mirrored by, the living Trinity itself. In his dereliction the *crucifixus* discloses not merely the fact of the divine triunity. He discloses also the compassionate and suffering presence of the God who is Father, God who is Son and God who is Spirit.

An old argument can be brought up here to the effect that such a view is 'modalistic'. It is a complaint that has been levelled at Barth and at Rahner. We must content ourselves here with a lame remark, namely that in this sort of theologizing it is quite impossible to please all parties. What we are attempting to do is to penetrate a little more into a divine mystery, not to rationalize it more. It is, of course, desirable to avoid on the one hand a definite revelational positivism (Barth), and on the other excessive dictation from a philosophical realism of the person (tritheist personificationism).[30] Moreover what we have to do is even more subtle than merely trying to balance an interpretation of God's word with our own mental categories. We are invited to the harder task of first hearing that Word, and then of trying to interpret it.

Of course what I have just said may seem a way-off, far-fetched piece of arguing, just tailor-made to indulge and even entertain theological hair-splitters. Moltmann will not have that. The Trinity and the cross affect us where it hurts in living and dying. 'Our "possessing" God must repeatedly pass through the deathly abandonment of God (Matt 27: 46; Mark 15: 34) in which alone God ultimately comes to us because God has given himself in love as love, and this is realized and manifested in his death.'[31] That need by no means be a question of over-dramatizing our own existences (we may not all have known Auschwitz), it can for Catholics be exemplified even in the old 'spiritual' requirements of 'abandonment to the will of God' as in Pierre de Caussade. The mystery of the cross has been offered to us in some form in our lives, and Moltmann is virtually saying: 'Take a grip on your reluctant theological heroism, and through the cross you will see yourself marked by the abandonment of the Son by the Father. By that fact comes a disclosure for your faith and hope. The triune life is disclosed, and with it the eschatological future of your God as he will be.'

As this age demands, Moltmann goes further still. It is part of the complaint against over-conceptualized Trinitarianism that its static concepts of the Godhead gave us, perhaps, a God *who is*, but who somehow *fails to exist*.[32] Unless you were a mystic, something was missing. A Christian movement, under Teilhardian inspiration, has tried to supply the vital element by exploiting the category of evolution. One might say that such an effort has been paralleled by the process theologians with their view of a 'dipolar' theism. In their 'dipolar' theology of God, there are two aspects of God stemming from himself to us. In the first aspect God is the primordial, eternal and supreme cause; but in his *other* aspect God is 'the supreme affect'. In this latter aspect God can relate to and include the universe in process. It is just here that Moltmann offers us yet another possibility. In place of a creative or emergent evolutionary category and in place of two descending lines of divine intelligibility he offers us a vision of overlapping divine movements. As I see it, there are two root advantages of this offer: *first* it is a prolongation of a theology backed by a mystical insight; and *secondly* because of his strongly revelational Trinitarianism his view is more biblically based and makes the most of the biblical categories of history and eschatology. For God too has a history, a history we can call 'of God', or 'in God'. 'The cross does not bring an end to the Trinitarian history in God between the Father and the Son in the Spirit as eschatological history, but rather opens it up.'[33]

In that history the 'sending' and 'delivering up' of the Son are its beginning. The 'resurrection and the transference of the rule of God' to Christ are its middle, and the end comes 'when the Son hands over this rule to the Father'.[34] That last phase of divine history is, of course, the doctrine of 1 Corinthians 15. As it stands, that last phase refers, for Moltmann, not merely to one, but to *one of two* consummations. An outer consummation takes place in the giving up by Christ of his dominion over the 'powers' and 'death' to the Father. But there is another consummation mirrored by the outer one. It is the inner Trinitarian consummation which corresponds to the consummation of the world. It is the consummation of the Father as Father, and the Son as Son, and the Spirit as Spirit. Thus the process and dynamic aspects of the Godhead are wholly triune.

In contrast with the 'bipolarity' of the process theologians, we have a 'bipolarity' located rather in the relationship of God to creation, but so located that it must disclose the existent movement of the divine triunity. If then there is movement, can we not speak of a *pathos* in God as between Father and Son, as in the Lutheran tradition? Or perhaps in more mitigated language as between God who is Father and God who is Son.[35] It is, of course, if we stick to it, inherent in the classical doctrine of the immutability of God as pure act that there can only be a negative answer to that question. But, if we listen to Moltmann, the biblical prophets are telling us that the answer is, Yes. For the prophets really speak of God with human history as the baseline. 'The prophets had no "idea" of God but understood themselves and the people in the *situation of God*.' In this view of it, there is a divine *pathos*, and man, when he is angry or suffers or loves or hopes, enters into a *sympathetic* union with God. 'The prophets never identified God's *pathos* with his being, since for them it was not something absolute, but the form of his relationship with others.' But God, in remaining free, remains affected by his covenant relationship; and human history affects him.[36] What Moltmann's analysis suggests to me is that we have a theological task ahead of us to explore in what way we conceive of God's perfection in his decision to create, to choose human history and to opt for human freedom. The paradox, which the cross brings home to us, is that the disclosure of God's *pathos* is made in the moment of abandonment.

I have tried to draw attention to three main points which I think a *theologia crucis* forces on our attention. The *first* is that there is an extraordinary timeliness in a theology which is fully alive to the *godforsakenness* of Jesus on the cross and to the *godforsakenness* of man in anguish today. *Secondly*, the history as well as the very conditions of Christian theologizing show that we cannot refuse to accept a theology of the cross which is a *theo*-logy in the strong sense. *Thirdly*, we have to accept that it is in the full sense also a theology of God who suffers. The *crucifixus* is fully and wholly the personal God. His abandonment is an abandonment by God. The proposition that God suffers must then be given its deepest Trinitarian implications. We have a mysterious movement in the divine triunity itself. *Pathos*, 'suffering' is in man, and it is in God. In my next section I want to draw attention to one form of the doctrine of abandonment to be found in the Catholic tradition.

PATHOS AND CONSUMMATION

In the Catholic tradition the idea that there is *pathos* in God must be sought in mystical theology.[37] At one point we come near to the doctrine itself, although explicitly *pathetic* language is avoided so that a *theologia gloriae* shall never be excluded. Of course one can find passages in Catholic writers which simply dwell with excess upon the state of dereliction of Jesus (e.g. Bossuet, Chardon). That is not what I have in mind. I am thinking rather of an adumbrated theology of the divine *pathos*, such as we can find among the seventeenth-century mystical writers dependent upon the Cardinal de Bérulle. Here we find ascetical theology relying upon something very like the idea of *pathos* in God.

Thus, when the aspirant arrives at a certain level of spiritual self-spoliation, an accepted part of pre-mystical asceticism, he is counselled to achieve 'disappropriation', a stage similar to 'annihilation' or 'interior abnegation'. It is here that we come across an interesting parallel with Moltmann. The purpose of the ascetic stage in question is 'consummation'. Moltmann uses the term especially in an eschatological context; but the Catholic reader should be prepared to find that some aspects of the term 'eschatological' in Protestant authors correspond to an older Catholic use of the term 'supernatural'. Thus for Moltmann, eschatologically speaking, man is consummated in God, and God is consummated in God. In Bérullian theocentrism (Condren's version) we find the same double form of consummation, human and divine:

> We therefore should belong . . . to God in this intention of Jesus Christ, *that He may consummate us wholly in Himself* . . . in honour of God . . . as *He abandoned in* God His Person and His Human qualities (*exinanivit*). It would *not* be in reason that the Virgin's Son, being offered up to God, should be *consummated by fire other than Himself* . . . and thus it should be *God who reduces and consummates* all that we are . . . Jesus Christ indeed offered Himself to the Father also to be *consummated in us* . . .[38]

In some ways we have an even stronger doctrine than in Moltmann. Certainly there is the double consummation of man in God, and of God in God. But not only is the believer who abandons himself in Christ consummated in God, but Christ is 'consummated in us'. Without the finality of the eschatological emphasis of Moltmann and of Paul, do we not have here an implied doctrine of the divine *pathos*? There is a hint of the destruction theory of the divine sacrifice, which I do not think is entirely absent in the *theologia crucis*. In the Bérullian outlook, though, 'consummation' takes on something of a divine conquest as well; and the weakness of the doctrine is that it draws no specifically Trinitarian conclusions. The Trinitarian emphasis is better preserved in the mystical tradition which is attached to the name of Bernard of Clairvaux. Here the erotic language of the Song of Songs is exploited to express the visionary's intuition of the tacitly intra-Trinitarian *pathos* of love.[39]

I have chosen the illustration from Catholic Baroque mysticism partly because it is quite proximate to the traditional piety, whether one approves of it or not, that is well known to very many English Catholics. Traditional Protestant piety for its part has always lived with some form of a *theologia crucis*.[40] From its origins Protestant piety has been nearer to personal theologizing also than has much

Catholic piety. 'Vivendo, immo moriendo et damnando fit theologus, non intelligendo, legendo aut speculando' was the young Luther's slogan. 'Vivendo, immo obediendo et patiendo fit Catholicus . . .' might be the weaker counterpart we have all known. But, because both attitudes are anti–intellectualist, they leave unfinished business to be done. So Moltmann criticizes his own tradition and tries to think the thing through further.[41] He keeps up the pressure against metaphysical theology, not nowadays a very difficult bulldozing exercise. You can without difficulty oppose the positivistic meaning to the transcendental one; and you can resist metaphysical conversation even when the argument leads in that direction. But you have to take a stand somewhere, if you are going to theologize at all. Moltmann seems to me to combine *two basic strands* in his theologizing while he allows for others also.

AN EXISTENTIAL WAY

First there is a quite marked existential strand of thinking, and it is consistent with the personal motivation Moltman has for writing such a book as this one after the classic work he produced on hope.

> The hells of world wars, the hells of Auschwitz, Hiroshima and Vietnam, and also the every-day experiences which make one man say to another 'You make my life hell', often suggest that the world as a whole should be thought of as a 'house of the dead', a house of discipline, a madhouse or a *univers concentrationnaire*, and not the good earth under the gracious heaven of a righteous God.[42]

Such a formulation of the problem of evil takes it out of the simple category of being an objection in theodicy against the existence of a good God. It is no longer a case of stating one fact out there, in order to put in doubt the possibility of another fact out there, of saying 'if there is no good providential government of the universe, then there can be no First Cause'. It is much more like saying 'atheism is my good, because theism has been my evil'. As Moltmann puts it, 'Here is an atheism which demonstrates itself to be the

brother of theism.'[43] It is in effect the existential stand of a
Camus, 'I rebel — therefore I exist'. Now, there is something
to be teased out of that attitude, even though its obvious
implication destroys theism. If you say, 'I rebel, therefore I
exist', you begin to shift the absoluteness that belongs to the
divinity on the 'I' or the 'we', and on to 'my' or 'our'
existence.

But if, in spite of the logic of such an existentialist stand,
you are, like Moltmann, in search of the religious idea, you
will get more than does the secularist existentialist out of the
religious symbol or situation. A rebellion of 'mine' or of
'ours' on the cross of today's hells, can disclose rather than
appropriate divinity; and it can make 'me' or 'us' a surrogate
for the crucified God. Thus in the worst of *our* dereliction it is
his divinity which is the issue, not merely some potential of
ours for deification. We do not, like Camus, see 'God vanish
on the Cross'. We must see 'Christ's death on the Cross taken
up into God', for 'only this change of perspective indicates
why (my italics) the night of Golgotha gained so much
significance for mankind'.[44]

I have underlined Moltmann's 'why'. So long as we even
try to supply the reason sought for in that 'why', then we go
beyond existentialist description and aim at religious truth.
Like many strains of piety, Catholic and Protestant, and like
Luther himself, Moltmann in his existentialist leap towards
the truth of the cross leans towards Monophysitism. I say
'leans' only to indicate a direction on Moltmann's part. The
same can, of course, be said of the great Pauline 'delivering
up' passages (see Rom 8: 31 ff.; 2 Cor 5: 21; Gal 2: 20 and 3:
13). In the moment of 'their deepest separation' there is a
deep 'community of will between Jesus and his God and
Father'. The 'godforsakenness' is historical. The 'surrender'
is eschatological.[45] The result of this most existential of all
existential moments 'is the Spirit which justifies . . . and
even brings the dead alive, since even the fact that they are
dead cannot exclude them from this event of the cross; the
death in God also includes them'.[46] Such a Trinitarian
theology implies neither Patripassianism nor theopaschitism
in 'death of God' terms.[47] What such a theology does on the
conceptual, rather than on the existential side, is to give some
symbolic (in the profound sense) meaning to the Rahnerian

principle of 'the identity of the Trinity of the *economy of salvation* and the *immanent* Trinity'.[48] If you disapprove of Rahner on this point — and, as an unshakeable *theologus gloriae*, you have that right — then you must also disapprove of Moltmann's position. But I can still recommend that you read Moltmann, for it will help you to disapprove of Rahner *en connaissance de cause*. The *theologia crucis* remains one of the subjects on which Rahner, so far as I can tell, remained always cagey and allusive.

But we must not be unfair to Rahner. He has a method and a systematic anthropology which are quite different from Moltmann's, a point insufficiently stressed by Moltmann. The point is that here we are gazing upon opposite edges of the great Protestant–Catholic divide. The respective views of God differ, because the respective views of man differ. It is foundational to Moltmann's position that as a *theologus crucis* he *begins* with an experience of God and faith *in the cross*. For Rahner a *theologia crucis* is not a matter of systematic theological foundation. Its place *per se* is not in the transcendental method as such. Nor does it lay the foundations of his teaching on grace and the atonement. The *theologia crucis*, in so far as it operates in Rahner, proves to be in the nature of a 'supplementary correction' (*eine zusätzliche Korrektur*). Because of his 'existential exigencies' (*die existentielle Not*) historical and concrete man, in his life of the spirit, needs that correction. It is the total reality of the redemption which demands a *theologia crucis* in the sense in which a straightforward theological account of a defect in the divine creation does not.[49]

COMPREHENSIBILITY

The *second basic strand* we are concerned with touches the need for a rational principle in theologizing. It is obvious that the contribution made by any reconsideration of a central topic must to a large extent be in function of its capacity to exploit rational principles. All that is acknowledged by Moltmann, and it is really the justification for the first section of his book, 'In Explanation of the Theme'. The technique is to combine an analysis of the dialectic to which the believer is subjected in faith with a critical, or better neo-critical, hermeneutical theory. We have already seen that faith in the cross is subject to a dialectic in experience. That is, faith comes through the experienced contradiction, and thereby God comes to the 'godforsaken'. Such a healing faith is subject to the old law of therapy, *contraria contrariis curantur* (Galen). That does not exclude the older principle which operates in faith-knowledge, namely the principle that *like is known by like*. The first, so far as I can tell, is meant to be the first stage of the second; but the exact relationship between the two does not seem to be worked out. Clash and contradiction indisputably do in experience come first. So much is that the case that, in the 'godforsakenness' of the cross, God is not merely disclosed to the righteous but to the godless.[50]

It is therefore quite wrong to think that we have a smooth transition from the cross to the resurrection, or that there is a single, one-way flow of significance between those two events. 'As a process and as an event, the resurrection was so to speak a light into which it was impossible to look directly.'[51] The New Testament churches did after all understand the resurrection through the cross.

Again those two events are a good example of the two overlapping movements which characterize Moltmann's view of the theology of the cross. But it should be noticed that they overlap in a contrary direction each to the other. Thus, 'we read his [Jesus'] history both forwards and backwards, and relate both readings, the ontic-historical and the noetic-eschatological'.[52] A simple example from English history may help, so long as it is not pressed. Let us ask, then, 'what happened in 1225?' To that question two 'readings' are possible according as we reply: 'the final ratification of Magna Carta', or 'the constitutional foundation of British, American and other Parliamentary democracies'. In the first reply we are trying to say *what happened* on a certain historical date (*ontic-historical*). But in the second reply we are referring to a whole series of events and a concomitant state of affairs which is world-wide, but their intelligibility in our referring to them comes only by casting our minds back *from* the world-wide democratic horizon *to* the England of 1225 (*noetic-eschatological*). In other words, from an open-future, multi-national situation we are able to interpret *what went on* in the event of 1225. Of course, the example fails in many respects; but it was not chosen entirely at random, for in its open-ended futurity it embraces apparently, and so far as the name goes, apparently irreconcilable, forms of political existence. Marxist states call themselves democratic, and so do liberal-capitalist states. Now in the counter-movement of the *eschatologia-crucis* we have a locus of the interpretation of futurity common to the sacred and profane. It is in this sense that we can defend ourselves against Celsus, and claim that history is full and real. Why is this? The reason is that the double movement, *cross-resurrection* and *resurrection-cross* gives us real open-endedness for the future. The future in function of the resurrection is not mere 'future history and thus a part of transitoriness, but eschatologically it is the *future of history*'.[53] That is why in the hells of totalitarianism there is still hope. It is not a mere human goal or idea, nor is it the human community which can produce *a future with a future*. The Marxist, who says that in the communist eschatological future the party will disappear and the lion will lie down with the lamb, has nothing more to call upon than an idea encapsulated in a future which remains profane and therefore closed. It is only an engulfing eschatological movement like that of the *resurrection-cross* which can make the future entirely open-ended for man. The disenchanted Marxists have opened a way here. Moltmann quotes Ernst Bloch: 'Indeed, the end of Christ was none the less his beginning.'[54]

Unless I am wrong, that is a paradigm of how man must understand himself, even in his secularity. The *noetic-eschatological* aspect is profane as well as sacred. It is not a hard-nosed statistical business, for interpretation can never be that. History is always an 'unfinished world' (Rosen-zweig), but its consummation is above all to be seen in the 'dialectical identity of eschatology and history' (W. Benjamin).[55] If all that seems too arcane, then let us say that what we are pointing to is a parallel. The movement and counter-movement of the cross and resurrection are familiar to us in sacred or 'salvation history'. On the other hand the only bearable way for secularized man to view profane history is to see the same movement and counter-movement there too. Without them there is no future that is thinkably human. The argument is not a causal one. It does not say the sacred must cause the profane to make it human. Nor does it say, because that is the way we find profane history, so we must also find sacred history to be that way. It says rather that if we look, we can see striking similarities in the respective sets of movements, which we find are parts of the respective sacred and profane histories. There is in consequence between these two histories a quality of mutual comprehensibility. Each can enlighten the other.

THE CROSS AND HEALING REASON

The Catholic with an inbuilt theological bias towards seeking a theory of the perfectibility of man, can now find dialogue on the *theologia crucis* an easier enterprise. Thus the correlation, which Moltmann is willing to envisage, between the idea of man under the cross and the idea of man as distilled from, for example, Adorno and Horkheimer (contributors to the neo-critical, social school at Frankfurt) provides a desired basis for discussion. That does not mean that on either side the parties to the discussion need adopt the thesis of the absolute autonomy of man. But if they can come to a basic understanding of man in society, by which they can pin-point instances of radical human non-freedom, they are then jointly talking theology. It is worth while to uncover hidden despotic structures, which act on society as an organism the same way as repressions or inhibitions act in the psychologically disturbed individual. Compulsive urban terrorism, especially if it has a religious colour, surely is worth such an analysis. The old thesis of man *vulneratus in naturalibus* is an insight to be studied now if ever in the concrete, without shrinking from its religious and human implications. At last, if we do that under the cross and with our critical faculties alive, redemption and justification may mean something. Even liberation and de-alienation could cease to act like trigger-mechanisms towards violence, and be given a human meaning. These things belong to the counter-course of history which we preach in 'the kingdom' and in our 'eschatology'.

But 'true life is in the midst of false life' (Adorno). Neo-critical analysis can in the concrete help us to see what is meant by saying that the messianic or eschatological good time is not simply an era to be tacked on to the end of a secular history. The first quarrel with Marxism is not whether or not it is atheistic, but whether it is human. As the neo-critical analysts and the Christians can now see, no eschatology means no human existence. A piece of technicolour spin-off from the exhausted tale of human history will not do either. Our Christian eschatologism must be genuinely religious. It must be about the recognizably holy and unholy, about loving and hating, and about good and bad. It must also point to these realities in the here and now. Marcuse, quoted by Moltmann, brings us back to the job in hand. There is a 'scandal of qualitative difference' between the true and false worlds. I suggest that for both sides in the common discovery of eschatological humanity, the scandal has its cruciality, or cross-form, less in the mere fact of difference between the true and false worlds, than in the *continued co-existence* between the true and false worlds. Redemption must work there. A good abstraction, one might say. No, rather a vital programme. But the programme needs its rationale, a *theologia crucis*. That is the sense in which I find that Moltmann has tried to grapple with the need for a rational principle. In so doing, I submit, he has at least shown the way.

Having achieved so much, it was normal that Moltmann should conclude with a chapter on 'Ways Towards the Psychological Liberation of Man' and another on 'Ways Towards the Political Liberation of Mankind'. Some of us have already begun to give their minds to the 'political theology' of such writers as J. B. Metz, to the stand taken in Latin America by the Brazilian and Chilean Hierarchies; and to the phenomenon of Liberation Theology. After the partial censure imposed by Cardinal Ratzinger upon some of the writings of this school in 1984 we have been encouraged to reflect further. But I leave evangelization and politics on one side as opening too vast a subject for a few paragraphs here and now.

Yet Moltmann's chapter on psychological liberation and theology does prompt a few simple remarks. We are surely aware that in the matter of a dialogue with psycho-analytic thinking the official Catholic attitude has been one of dragging its feet since the seminal works of the Freudian corpus made their appearance. There have been exceptions, of course, but they have not yet been significant enough to cause reflection on a large scale. In this country I doubt whether the late Fr Victor White, O.P., has yet come into his own. The time is right for him to be presented to us once more, and for us to reconsider his significance for today. He was before his time. The general picture is that denunciation in the early years was followed by a certain sullen acquiescence in a new *status quo*. When priests and nuns appeared to benefit from treatment, then less was said. But an important factor was never generally accepted, namely — as we have already had occasion to quote — 'that the love which a believer had for his God, could in the slightest degree depend upon his urges of sexuality'. [56]

When it was feared that all such analyses would *reduce* the faith to the size and shape of human drives, then there was some justification for the suspicion. But it should now be clear that this is not the issue. Interpreting concomitant factors does not, of course, necessarily imply the elimination of the object under examination. It enables us rather to see the object in a clearer light. Moltmann is right when he says: 'Psychological hermeneutics is an interpretation and not a reduction.' [57] The reason why Catholics did not see this point quickly enough was partly conditioned by a doctrinal factor. We had concentrated too much upon, and had unthinkingly lived by the unfortunate formulation of the nature 'fallen but restored' (*natura lapsa sed reparata*). It was indeed a useful safeguard to a straightforward notion of the supernatural, but it affected our day-to-day thinking about grace in the concrete. It meant that we were in the habit of thinking that grace operated only at the level of the decent abstraction, the *natura reparata*. Thus continuing disorder in human life could have nothing to do with the grace. To suppose otherwise would be to de-divinize grace and even to under-humanize it. What place, for example, would grace have in a life liable to schizophrenia? [58] Yet the schizophrenic is offered faith, and receives the offer in his condition. It will be fully *his* faith, often expressible in a clouded way. In the perspective of a *theologia crucis* there is no need at all to think of such a grace as somehow de-natured. The cross, which the schizophrenic is living, carries him forward to be engulfed in the resurrection wave which brings a resurrection-restoration with it. The double movement is there, sometimes imperceptibly, sometimes it gives an inkling of its presence. As the movement and counter-movement is that of the crucified God, grace is the offer of a living therapy, and may even come to be the offer of a genuinely human freedom.

So while we insist with Moltmann that the cross is still present, we can be more optimistic about man, and more God-minded about human anxieties. Why is that? Moltmann comes out with a challenging paradox here. 'Suffering in a superficial, activist, apathetic and therefore *dehumanized society* can be a sign of spiritual health.'[59] Spiritual health in the midst of disease is recognizably part of the counter-movement of the resurrection cross. Thus, as in Belfast, where emotional disorder reaches epidemic proportions, faith in the cross is still healing faith. I give an impressive contemporary example:

> A spokesman from Roman Catholic Teachers in West Belfast said yesterday that it was tragic enough to have to pray for those children who had died in sectarian killings. But to have to pray for children using guns was worse.[60]

There we can see spiritual health in the midst of a dehumanized society. Freud said, 'as long as man suffers he can still achieve something'. He was speaking, of course, at the level of symptomatology. The meaning and the future of such suffering is only brought out by a *theologia crucis*. The truth emerges that without a faith in, and without some experience of the cross, we can neither love nor be loved, we can neither know nor be known, and we cannot recognize the social idolatries of our day for what they are.

OPEN-ENDEDNESS AND TRINITY

In conclusion we must now try to ask ourselves how open-ended is Moltmann's approach, and how open-ended our response can be. In which directions must Catholics push their thinking in order to achieve an ecumenical penetration in faith? Let us pick out a few salient points.

The basic divide in Catholic–Protestant discussions always comes back to their respective understanding of man. One's radical optimism (to choose a word almost at random) about man's capacity to accept God's redemption and salvation makes a difference to one's account of one's faith in God himself. Moltmann's approach to the experience of the cross does something important to diminish that divide, just as in 1957 on the subject of justification the Küng–Barth dialogue did achieve something.[61] Suffering the cross before understanding the cross is not a piece of *a priori* reasoning, it is a necessary piece of common Christian experience.

On the other hand the Christian not only suffers the cross as a piece of prior understanding to its theological penetration and disclosure, he also brings to that complex experience of faith his culture and even his *Weltgeist*. The question is, to what extent and with what mind may he do so, and still remain in obedient faith before the cross? He may do so in order to safeguard and preserve as intelligible the mystery entrusted to him. I think Moltmann agrees with that. May he do so in order to penetrate the mystery? More discussion is needed here. The Trinitarian disclosure in faith is God's. I would propose that we can follow a good tradition and call it deiform and Christiform. To the objection that I have now introduced an unwarranted element of Alexandrian theology, and with it the Catholic doctrine of justification and grace, I must reply that like a theology of the cross any doctrine of grace and inhabitation is, of course, subject to the movement and counter-movement of the *eschatologia crucis*. The cross is the undertow of the engulfing resurrection–cross wave. So it is with grace. There are two sides to its being the *quaedam inchoatio gloriae* (Summa Theologica II, II, 24, 3). There is the undertow and there is the wave. *Our experience is of the undertow:* 'it does not yet appear what we shall be' (1 John 3: 2). The converging lines of our theologies are by no means blocked.

Certainly much of our discussion concerning the Protestant and Catholic mind can also turn on a matter of degree. How far, one must ask, is the cross in our theologizing (*a*) one of the categories among others affecting all that is believed (an *id quod normans*); (*b*) an experience category in believing (a *modus quo* also *normans*); (*c*) an inbuilt systematic regulator adjusting our interpretation in faith to (*i*) the possibility of authenticity, and to (*ii*) our lostness from love or 'godforsakenness'. The extent to which it is one or all of these things can be discussed as a matter of degree.[62]

In our understanding of the Triune God as he is disclosed

to us, we must reflect again and again on our religious living. The roots of our knowledge in faith are in our living as well as in the articulation of our faith. A developing doctrine of God must draw upon our history, our personal history as well as our community history, for, if salvation history means anything for the believer, he must be able to correlate it with his own and with his community's experience.

But there are two well-known dangers here which are not exorcized by theological rhetoric. The *first* is inherent in Moltmann's stand. It is, of course, the danger of subjectivism. The most appropriate response to the hells of our day may indeed be to say: 'only the experience of the cross yields a disclosure in faith which says anything about the Triune God'. But, if we go one step further and say that the experience of the cross *confers the meaning on* a Triune disclosure, then we are talking not mainline, but Gnostic Christianity. The truth would then no longer be a vision of reality as it is, however much a reality of love and even of *sumpatheia*. It would be the projection of our own inherited psychodrama on to God. I cannot see that the cross discloses a law of eternal dying and becoming in God. 'What Hegel called a "speculative Good Friday", which empowers reason to take over and administer the word of God' is another facet of the subjectivist danger.[63] It would be a takeover by us, were we to claim the discovery of a secret law *in divinis* which disclosed an inner tragic form to God's love within. In von Balthasar's view it would 'displace' God's absolute Love and set it aside by knowledge.[64] I am convinced, however, that that is not what Moltmann is trying to say. In fact by being willing to correlate the implications of the Trinitarian cross disclosure with a psychological as well as a political hermeneutic Moltmann already begins to mitigate the subjectivist danger.

The *second* danger is always with us in the Western Catholic tradition of thinking about God. The Fourth Lateran Council enunciated a salutary warning doctrine, namely that 'between the creator and the creature no similitude can be indicated such that the [corresponding] dissimilitude is not the greater'.[65] The warning was in the first instance meant to apply to such attributes as unity in God. But the principle should surely be seen as polyvalent. I do not see why it should not equally well be applied to the divergent models and methods in speaking about God. If any truth can be called multi-dimensional, then the truth of God revealing himself as triune can surely be called that. Each model and each method will evoke more differences than similarities. In invoking the theories of the Frankfurt school, Moltmann may have given us a lesson. We may be hammering away too hard at the perpetuation of a formulation of God-doctrine too bound up with our own inbuilt experience and view of society and of ourselves within it. The differences may be greater than the similarities, a point neglected in the social theories of the Trinity. If that is the case, you may say, all we have to do is to be tolerant and ingest the outside differences as gracefully as we can. All is grist, why not? Unfortunately tolerance, like patriotism, is not enough. Even thinking establishments have too great a capacity for absorption. The radical freedom to which we are called in the Trinitarian cross-disclosure would be negatived. Repression from within would be at work again. The love-disclosure would be swallowed in repression. There is something in this point. We shall only find one locus of communion (I would now call it), where the similarity is guaranteed to be greater than the dissimilarity. That locus is the God-given gift of the crucified God, just because it was God who was crucified. In that sense the cross is unique as a disclosure category. It will modify; it will not repress. 'For it is precisely in the Kenosis of Christ (and nowhere else) that the *inner* majesty of God's love appears, of God "who is love" (1 John 4: 8) and therefore a trinity.'[66]

I end by turning from dangers to the providential invitation offered us by Moltmann. A conscious Trinitarian theology of the cross must be the most fruitful ecumenical preparation we can make for the future. Why is that? The answer lies in our need to be engulfed in its dialectical movement. If, with our brethren in Christ's baptism, we desire that our faith in God shall be both the same and sincere, then only in the 'godforsakenness' of the cross can we find where is that faith, and where is God.

In that light we Catholics should rethink the patristic doctrine of participation in the three divine persons. It is a doctrine with dialectical roots.[67] It is a doctrine consummated in a Trinitarian disclosure and proposing a final hope:

> Our return to God could not otherwise conceivably have been
> performed by Christ the Saviour, than through the communion
> and sanctification which takes place *in the Spirit*. For that which
> binds us back with, and in some sort unites us with God is the
> Spirit. It is in receiving the Spirit that we participate in and
> communicate with the divine nature, and that *by the Son* and *in
> the Son* we receive *the Father himself*.[68]

CHAPTER FIVE

Sacramental Intimacy, the Hinge of Salvation

It is a well-worn idea that sacraments embody God's gift to man, and that they enable man to open himself to God. To make even those two simple remarks we have already had to use our imaginations, and have in the process called upon familiar picture language. The sacramental imagination in practice can be more or less poetic, but it will always be at work nevertheless.[1] Now the imagination easily sees God as somehow above us, and so we think of a sacramental relationship with God as taking place up or down a vertical line. That is not all by any means. Our sacraments are anchored in history, so we also use a horizontal line to take us backwards and forwards, as though (and here again we use the imagination) history were a lengthy *continuum* of human events *out there* only waiting to be explored or recalled to some practical effect.[2] The upward look seems to make the sacrament effective, and the backward look provides a form of guarantee, while, when we look forward, we think can somehow see that our insufficient performance here and now will by and by be made good. When we want to pull these disparate ways of imagining together, we find a way of synthesis, and say, 'sacraments are an extension of the Incarnation'.[3] The spatio-temporal life of the divine Jesus seems to give us the form of a supremely effective, though *interim*, divine–human encounter. We can readily imagine that the encounter is continued for us in words, rites, gestures which have been divinely empowered, and being so potentiated are the infinitely extended gestures of their divine–human source. But the vertical line and the horizontal line are still there.

In this chapter our concern is with the way sacraments try to overcome distancing effects. The divine transcendence and our use of imaginary distance on a vertical line is one. Time and the horizontal line is another. These imaginary axes are only the outer limits, as we see them, of sacramental experience. The image of the 'extension of the Incarnation' gives us another dimension of the imagination, and is perhaps a pointer to a vital characteristic in man's sacramental experience, proximity. There are many images we may use to project the locus of a divine action; but the nearest may have a lot to tell us. Distancing images help us to see ourselves in relation to the divine transcendence; and we cannot do without them if we want to avoid idolatry. But sacramentality as an incarnational reality brings us another way, a characteristic one, the way of intimacy.

I hope that this chapter for the reader, who has not considered sacraments in this light, will be seen as something of a modern prolongation of Tertullian's idea: *caro salutis est cardo*. It is the human body which is the hinge of salvation.[4]

TIME AND TIMES

Let us start by looking at some of the effects of juxtaposing past, present and future. Do we not try to join together in an imaginary horizontal line the past charter–event of our present sacrament together with the future end–time? These realities, or rather the symbols we use for them, we try to bring together into a brighter field of consciousness while the sacramental event is taking place. We do not try and repeat the past literally. We know we cannot do that. *Bis idem non idem*. What we do is to try and see how the past acts effectively on the present. So we make a ritual, imaginative, reconstruction, using a narrative recital of, for example, the Last Supper. Here narrative is most successful; but the future we have to treat a little differently. Narrative is possible of course, as in the *Dies Irae* of the Requiem Mass, but I suspect that today verbal anticipation can come to sound a little empty and its effect on the here and now a little weaker than it used to be. So in prophetic style we improve on narrative and make our own once more the acclamation or call to the coming Lord. The directness of the early Christian *Maranatha* ('Come, Lord') helps to overcome this difficulty, and has now successfully found a place in our new Eucharistic

Prayers. It seems to me that it is the quality of directness, which above all enhances the sacramentality of the eucharistic event. We seem to be in possession of a moment of quite special sacramental creativity, when we try and fuse the boundary moments of our imagination like that of the Last Supper and the future coming of the Lord.[5]

Do we have a special reason for trying to make past, present and future coalesce in this way? I think there is a reason and would put it this way. Are we not using a mimicry of spatial contiguity by this temporal coalescence of the imagination, and so attempting to cut down a vast and overpowering religious universe to our own size? Have we not constructed an imaginative theology of distance in time, and then do we not find it necessary to bring it back to a single point in individual or in community experience? There is certainly a therapeutic value in the process. We are able to allay anxieties (not all of them conscious ones), some of them bequeathed to us by threatening prophetic or reforming figures in our religious past. Their uncompromisingness can be too much. When by word, by gesture, or by iconic representation we can de-absolutize their threat or command, or when we can somehow by the same means identify with them, then we reach the comforting point of the familiar and even the intimate. And there is comfort also in numbers; so in the shared experience of the community we find the re-assurance to be all the more effective.

I suggest that in the fusion of boundary moments, past and future, our present experience affords a species of transtemporal contact, in which the use of the spatial imagination is also called into play. If we pay attention to what Casel had to say about the 'rite-form' (cult *eidos*) in liturgical mystery, we can see that he has described something of the mechanism by which immediacy takes place.[6] Casel's reasoning is of course different from mine, and his support is that only of an hypothesis. For the moment I do not want to be side-tracked away from the observation that in the temporal coalescence of sacramental experience, the imagination is enabled to achieve a most precious immediacy of felt contact.[7] The theological reason for such 'sense and tangibility', if we are to believe Casel, must be attributed to the Logos and Pneuma of God in the world; but his impression of 'tangibility' across time-barriers is a clear one: 'We see it in faith and *gnosis*, that is to say we *touch it*, make it our own . . .'[8] Outside a sacramental situation such language might be dismissed as a comforting piece of fantasy life. But that is not a piece of rationalization which fits the human experience of sacramental phenomena. For one thing there is a simple and basic form of immediacy, which comes about so spontaneously that we do not think about its effectiveness. Indeed we sometimes despise it, but I am convinced wrongly. The fact of ritual repetition is what counts here. Repetition is of course quite basic in any behaviour situation, but for the religious purpose in ritual and sacrament it becomes formalized as it does in music, dance and literature.[9] The result is that we are by no means just confronting ourselves with ourselves, in our talking or acting, as though for our own comfort we had to gaze at ourselves in mirror-fashion. We are not talking merely about a form of canonized narcissism. For, even if narcissism has a place in the psychological origins of the performance, that is a stage which we, as individuals or as a community, learn to pass through as we learn to cope with reality. For one thing we do not repeat without remembering, so that the qualities of the first experience come to belong to the second, and in a precipitated form, perhaps, they find their place in the third experience and so on. And in the charter-event our remembering has its object well-defined or definable.

Repetition has a further quality: it is able to achieve *two forms of contact*, leading especially in a communion (which I shall call *consummative* sacramentalism) to a form of intimacy: the *first* is between the dramatic past, the charter-event, and the present experience (as with the Last Supper and the eucharist), and the *second* is between the subject's own past experience and his now present repeated experience of a previous re-enactment. It is fashionable to emphasize that the latter form of repetition must be a fully conscious and committed experience. So much the better of course. But the common condemnations of 'mechanical repetition', 'passivity' and vague dissociation in community experience run the risk of psychological naivety.[10] Religious persuaders should not forget that the believer, like everybody else, has psychological needs. The psychologists can give us a reason that is as good from the theological point of view as it is from the psychological. 'The neurotic compulsion to repeat is a sign that a situation in the past is still unfinished in the present. Every time enough tension accumulates in the organism to make the task dominant, there is another try at a solution.'[11] *Caro salutis est cardo*; and we should not be put off by the word 'neurotic' in this connexion. As the authors of my quotation point out, the reasoning is as good for a healthy organism as it is for an unhealthy one, since in any event the 'warm play of the imagination is in general not dissociative but integrative'. We may agree. It is not the rules we have about the repetition of sacraments which explain the phenomenon. They merely express what I have already called the *prescriptive element* in the sacramental situation. Behind the fact of these varied imperatives lie the needs of sacramental man.

As sacramental man changes and develops amid the vicissitudes of his own and of his community life, his needs build up, and it is repetition which helps him to cope with the 'unfinished business' of earlier personal experience. It is surely quite basic to any idea we have of human contact with the divine that it involves a situation for the individual of 'unfinished business'. Some might say that it is an 'unfinished business' *sui generis*, and that being religious or supernatural it is a sort of psychological luxury. Once again we must not be side-tracked. For the contention cannot be avoided that that unfinished religious business is like any other unfinished business. It may be more or less objective: it is certainly as personal, if not more personal, and more fundamental than any other unfinished business. Thus for the Christian repetition in the religious sphere is far more than the mere continuance of the ordinary 'unfinished business' of personal living.

We said that the *first* form of intimacy lay in the connexion produced between the dramatic past and our present experience. The connexion is a real one and arises in sacramental experience out of a need, a need which is met sacramentally by what I would call the *consummative*, as distinct from the *instrumental, mode* of sacraments. The drift of the distinction should be clear enough for the moment. I shall have something more to say about it later (cf. pp. 179–86 below). Let us say now that, if there is a *consummative* sacramental mode, which is fairly evident in communion for example, then in some of its aspects it will resemble the basic human need to be fondled. One could object that this is a concession to infantilism and no recommendation for adult sacramental practice. But there is more to it than that, and it is the reason behind the phenomenon which interests us. The desire to be fondled or, if we transpose the matter, the need for *consummative* sacramentalism is *not* simply in response to the *pastness* of the present situation, is *not* simply a piece of infantile nostalgia. Concern is still, and realistically so, with the present. As Perls, Hefferline and Goodman say: '*neither* the desire *nor* the image [of the past] is past *because the situation is unfinished*' (author's italics). So it is also, of course, with our dramatic past in sacramentalism. We are always harking back to Calvary and its enveloping arms, or to the Last Supper with its feeling tone of intimacy, because our situation here and now, evoked by those past events, contains today's 'unfinished business'. Our theology and our practice tell us that in respect of the charter-events, our sacramental lives are full of 'unfinished business', a sacramental analogue of Colossians 1: 24 ('I complete what is lacking in Christ's afflictions'). Objectively and out-there, we accept the perfect *ephapax*. But we are still pre-occupied. Hence we re-enact, we re-present, not once but again and again until we are ourselves *consummatively* absorbed in the process. *Quoad nos*, though not in a theological sense, *we repeat*. As the desire and the image of the past remain present, they still have the power to envelop and to fondle. But the process has an aim: in the immediacy and contact produced by repetition we cope with the 'unfinished business', which as a community and as individuals we live with. We need the charter-events to become our own in the sense just described.

The *second* form of intimacy lies in our handling by repetition of our desire for and image of our own past sacramental experience. Possession, contact and intimacy are all at work. Thus it becomes '*my* Sunday Mass', '*my* last confession', '*my* last communion', '*my*' or '*our* wedding anniversary'. Time has given distance to the images of earlier experience, they now have to be de-alienized, so that by re-call and re-enactment the feeling of contact or of being

fondled may recur. It would not be true to say that in the
intimacy of contact, either with the charter-event or with
one's past experience, 'unfinished business' now becomes
'finished business'; rather I am trying to suggest that there is
here by intimacy or contact a feeling of absorption in a
transpersonal reality to which the 'unfinished business' itself
calls us. The experience of present intimacy is the present
image of it. One cannot say that the result is either true or
false. That is not the point: the result is human and in being
human also sacramental.

In passing we ought to say something more about
sacramental repetition. Where the symbolic content is so
highly charged, as it is in the eucharist, then from the
conceptual point of view the believer is being challenged in
the *here and now* experience beyond the point he can cope
with. There will therefore be another form of 'unfinished
business', namely the continued exploration of the mystery
of faith, of which the unfinished psychological business will
be a normal analogue. 'Unfinished business' should in this
context be put differently; but in order to keep the idea of
intimacy in focus I neglect other theological materials, which
would not make the point so directly. One might take for
example the theology of the eucharist as offering. The
believer makes an offering of himself along with Christ the
victim. Precisely what he is doing is vague to him, and must
remain so. It is true that, if he abstracts from the conceptual
difficulty inherent in the term 'offer', he can still detail his
gifts, his powers and activities, and apply the term 'offer' to
these. But he is still operating in a conceptual and theological
cul de sac. He knows that the more he details his qualities and
powers, the less he is in fact talking about himself. If he really
means to 'offer himself', he must include, however he may
put the notion to himself, his *unknown* and *irrational* identity.
Now his anxiety can be relieved, for the more his unknown
self can in a mysterious fashion be fixed or placed in the
symbolic situation, then the more adequate will seem his
participation. 'Offering' now includes in its scope his opaque
and unknown self, which can fuse or make contact with the
opaque and mysterious symbol of the eucharistic victim. The
point is that identification with or in another, familiar,
unknown gives comfort, immediacy, and even intimacy so

long as the matter is considered from a psychological point of view. Jung makes the point in a pioneering lecture on the Mass: 'our *psyche* in reality spreads far beyond the bounds of consciousness . . .'[12] We may add that it is because the psyche does so that we have the possibility of sacramental intimacy once more. So the piecemeal attention, which is all that we can pay to the awesome claim that, for example, 'the eucharist is the focus of all the great realities of the faith', is complemented upon the theological as well as the psychological level. 'Active participation' can have a Jungian basis and a symbolic superstructure.

That situation too is enhanced by repetition. The believer is able so to feel and hold within him the old image of his sacramental experience, that the present one becomes somewhat defused of its charge of awesomeness, which can now be ingested by the imagination and become an intimate reality. In all this there is of course a feeling of religious inadequacy, sometimes going as far as 'scruple', on the part of the believer. That also has its purpose: if it were not present, the sacramental experience in question would not be highlighted in the centre of consciousness as indeed it is.

It might be objected that I am here substituting experience for faith. I have no desire to do that. Indeed, so far as we are considering the satisfactory effect of repetition in the sacramental situation, I would hold that the life of faith strongly persists and descends far lower in the scale of consciousness than the protagonists of an exclusively 'committed faith', or 'engagement', or 'authenticity' would be willing to admit. In other words, in the believing community and for the believing individual, I have no objection to the old doctrine of *ex opere operato*, which in the circumstances seems to me to make psychological as well as sociological and theological sense. On anthropological grounds Professor Mary Douglas has made an effective counterblast against the assault on ritualism as such.[13] We can still go along with all that, and yet remember that when an individual or group clings through thick and thin to the form of sacramental behaviour *as form*, then the way of intimacy is open to abuse. We may cling to our religious, sacramental form as to a teddy bear, that is to say as to a 'transitional object', like the child which clings to a soft piece of blanket or to a cuddly toy. These objects are substitutes for body contact with the mother, after the time when such contact was possible and necessary for the child. Religious behaviour is by no means the only department in life where that can happen. Where sacramental behaviour is concerned, the attitude would be a sign that the intimacy offered by sacramental life has not been satisfactorily internalized. Excessive use of cult objects could well be viewed in such a light. But I would not agree to criticize in a blanket manner persistent adhesion to ritual in face of change on the simple ground of 'infantilism' or 'immaturity'. We have inherited a situation far too complex for that. In many matters we doubtless all cling to transitional objects, and do not notice. That does no harm. The trouble arises in religious sacramentalism when the transitional object has been over-socialized. The historical quarrels over the reception by the laity of communion under one or two kinds have been much conditioned by over-socialization of one or other practice. When that happens sacramental *prescriptiveness* can become implacable.[14] At the same time we should charitably remember that devices, such as transitional objects, are developed to cope with the harshness of separation from the familiar and yearned for past. The distancing effect of time is responsible for our distress; and the mode of intimacy is the most normal therapy.

THE 'GREAT TIME' AND NOW

I believe that another way by which Christian sacramental liturgy induces the feeling of proximity or intimacy is by means of the imagery, which recurs in various forms, that an earthly liturgy is either paralleled by, or participates in, a heavenly liturgy.[15] The notion is a cherished one in theology and devotion. At first sight it looks unhelpful. Why should a celestial *Doppelgänger* effect make our earthly liturgies more bearably cosy? Surely 1 Corinthians 2: 9 has warned us; but we affect to ignore the warning. We 'project' our symbolic furniture and its activities into the heavenly courts following the Apocalypse of John, but in an anodyne fashion. It is easier to say how than why we do this. We 'project' but in a dream-like way; and the result is the construction of a vast projection-screen, which in turn proves to be an admirable

mechanism for our needs. The mechanism of projection is
that 'it is attributed to objects or persons in the environment
and then experienced as directed *toward* you by them instead
of the other way round' (authors' italics). From the religious
point of view it is no objection to say that heaven is not part
of our environment; we might as well say the same of
conscience or the moral law, which are also used by us as a
'projection screen'.[16] However, it is not my business here to
say that I, or anyone else, can prove that these realities exist.
All I have to say is that for religious purposes such abstract
and intentional 'realities' need a mechanism, if they are to be
practically related to ourselves, and that a satisfactory
mechanism exists in the phenomenon of projection. Thus we
know that we should treat the doctrine of heaven with awe,
as we do the doctrines of conscience and the moral law. But
awe is not enough. It creates distance and anxiety; and heaven
has enough of a normative aspect about it for practical
purposes to demand that we come to terms with it. Our
imperfect consciences apart, we are aware of our imperfect,
indifferent or bored, religious performances. We think we
have reason to feel anxious about our liturgical and
sacramental defects. So the imagination experiences the
perfect heavenly liturgies as directed towards us by way of
paradigmatic completion or perfection. Once we are familiar
with this self-directed projection, the threat can be
assimilated and its expression becomes part of us and in
familiar intimacy we cling to the mental furniture. Erik
Peterson gives examples from the history of monasticism
which illustrate the point.[17]

I said there was a dream–like quality about the projection
mechanism of the heavenly liturgy. The experience of
mounting to a height, peculiar perhaps to this experience of
familiarization, is a common dream experience. It has been
studied among others by Mircea Eliade. He notes that 'upon
the planes of ritual, ecstasy and metaphysics — ascension is
capable among other things, of abolishing Time and Space
and of "projecting" man into the mythical instant of the
creation of the World, whereby he is in some sense "born
again" being rendered contemporary with the birth of the
World'.[18] There is of course a common prejudice against the
allusion to dream materials but their increased use by

anthropologists seems to me to suggest that caution should be two-sided in this matter.[19] No theologian could pretend that the symbolism alluded to by Eliade is unfamiliar. One would expect the themes of the paradisal 'Great Time' or 'first time' to find their place in baptismal liturgies and theology also.[20] Re-birth we are also familiar with (cf. Jn 3: 5; Tit 3: 5; 1 Jn 3: 1), and it is closely accompanied by the theology of co-baptism in Christ's death with the believer's subsequent growing together with him (cf. Rom 6). All these themes and mechanisms produce a coalescence of the time element and a feeling of spatial contact with the primordial past. One can, if one so chooses, reject the notion that we tend to anchor the present in the past, though I would think the proposition needs a good deal of discussion.[21] What does seem to me important is that we should evaluate for ourselves the effect of the juxtapositions alluded to. Have we not once again come into a category of feeling that can in the long run only be described spatially as one of contact and, allowing for dream associations, as one of intimacy?

There is a somewhat rhetorical point about recall of the past, which I am not at all sure that I want to urge, namely that the past can in its very deadness produce 'a spiritual vertigo, if I cannot lay hold of an eternal somewhat to save the world from absurdity, from utter unreality'.[22] Specula-tively I find an 'eternal somewhat' a subject on which we are not likely to have semantic agreement. We can do better nearer home, and this is where the ritual or sacramental situation can help us. For in ritual the anxiety, which the linear concept of time may occasion, can be dealt with. That substitute for the 'eternal somewhat' is a very ancient one, and embraces in the use of 'cyclic' time, an achievement to be found in cult 'which consists of diverting for the human consciousness the straight line of time into a circle, in which the same thing recurs, the present moment is preserved, and the terror of the transitory is assuaged'. Lohfink points out how, if we live in the rhythm of such a cult (and I would argue that Christian renewals of the paschal mystery attempt just this), then recurrent festivals provide us with a reassuring structure of consciousness. I would argue that sacramental repetition, through the immediacy and contact we are describing, surely does the same thing. It is in the genius of

Christianity as well as of Israel to synthesize the cyclic with the linear concepts of time, so that the *Urzeit* of linear time (Exodus–Canaan, the paschal mystery of Christ) is brought into the lives of the faithful by the immediacy of cyclic repetition. 'Each generation could begin to live anew through this, as though it were now happening for the first time'.[23] Nowadays the popularizing of the thought-model of 'salvation history' will have the effect in repeated liturgical and sacramental practice of reassurance. The sacramental imagination can take a short cut, can be contented in the present feel of a continuity of God's action touching us now.

As to the anxiety caused by the past we can take Hepburn's point: if we do not deal with it creatively ourselves, then no one else will do it for us.[24] The reassurance we have gained may in itself be one to which we have no logical entitlement. On this I think two things should be said: (*a*) whether or not one can solve the problems attached to such a mystery, one still has to live with it. Sacramental man through his feeling and verbalizing can come to terms with himself and with his world. He may well be in such a state that a logical guarantee attaching to his every experience of the kind could only be a luxury. (*b*) At the same time the stronger and more reassured he becomes, the more he can take up again the problem of his religious existence. Indeed he is offered the opportunity to do this every time he receives a sacrament. As Karl Barth says, 'we are faced with the problem of the doctrine of the Trinity, every time baptism is validly administered in our Churches' (C.D., I, 1, p. 435). The problem that should really be taken up here is the problem of man's freedom in the situation of sacramental intimacy and reassurance. I would content myself with saying now that through man's free option for God in his faith, his freedom in sacramental life can be enhanced rather than diminished; but that is another argument. For the moment let us agree that it is an advantage brought by the reassurance of sacramental intimacy that sacramental man can live, and live more securely, with his problem. It may be that in sacramental experience freedom is only dimly experienced. But theological anthropology will say that to be profoundly free, man must have an object which transcends time, and that object must be God. If Christian sacraments are what they claim to be, unique

among human gestures, then one would expect the way of
transcendence to be present somehow in the way of
intimacy.

BODY AND SPACE

The daily effort to achieve and accept some inkling in faith of
the divine transcendence through the see, touch, hear world
of sacramentalism will quite obviously make use of the
dimension of space besides that of time. Space has after all
long been peopled with religious symbols. Again we must
continue to acknowledge that we are using the imagination.
Although the philosophers and theologians, who have
explored the use of time and space in a sacramental context,
have not always observed it, there is a difference between
using the imagination and reasoning about it. When it is said
that sacraments give grace the way a jug pours out liquid, or
as a purse gives ransom-money to free a captive, or indeed
when it is said that these notions are ridiculous, then we
should not forget that the receptacle notion of space is in part
a work of the imagination, and so obviously is the parallel in
the second example between human bargaining and the so-
called 'occasional causality theory'.[25] On inspection we shall
probably be as dissatisfied with the imaginative as with the
metaphysical view. What we must not do is to forget which
category we have used, and try to apply one in criticism of
the other.

Sacramental man, however, as such is both less and more
sophisticated than our reflections on him suggest. In
sacramental living he can go to the heart of the situation
without bothering himself with abstractions. It is, I think,
the way he understands and experiences his own body which
makes him able to do that. In practice and in experience he
does not need, though he may take satisfaction in, reflections
which are necessarily at one remove from the fact of his
experience. In that he is less sophisticated. He is more
sophisticated when by the superimposition of symbols he
structures his use of the imagination by the very use of the
imagination. I do not think the process is a luxury. It comes
into play because of the need we have to cope with the
problem of space. To do that body consciousness comes into
play, and of all processes body consciousness is perhaps the

hardest to objectify. It is not hard to objectify because of distance or remoteness, but rather because it is so near. In fact the process becomes one of almost second nature. We make use of the bodily imagination for most purposes in life, whether we are thinking about ourselves or about other people. We also do it in talking about God on whom we bestow a body like our own. 'Then I will take away my hand, and you shall see my back; but my face shall not be seen' (Exod 33: 23). So the priestly writer finds he cannot describe communion with God, unless he gives God a body like his own and uses the language of bodily contact. The speculative theologian need trouble himself no further: we have here an anthropomorphism, a regrettable if not inappropriate way of talking about the divine. But that is not the whole point. The writer is talking about God *and* man, a relationship and one that can grow or diminish. The language of the degree of contact between two experiencing bodies, or embodied selves, is highly appropriate.

In fact if we want to believe that acceptance or rejection comes into our relationship with God, then we shall use bodily language. We do it between ourselves. If we try and avoid it, we drop into an exaggeratedly rational attitude; and that turns out to be a piece of protective armour so as to avoid the risks inherent in the prospect of acceptance or rejection by the other person. Such rationality depersonalizes. In a philosophical search for objectivity it is clinical and appropriate. But as a sacramental being man is trying to stay personal, and indeed capitalize on his personhood. Such is the behaviour between man and man; and sacraments are there to ensure that as between man and God we need not fear language and thoughts that belong to bodily gestures and contact. Language is once again mildly indicative. One may 'embrace' an idea, a project, an attitude; one may 'open one's heart to another'; we 'offer the hand of friendship'. Such expressions are so common that they are almost neutralized and we scarcely advert to their bodily basis. Erik H. Erikson gives a few examples involving rejection: ' "he makes me sick", "she pierced me with her eyes", "I could not swallow that insult", or, as the song has it, "I'm gonna wash that man right out of my hair".'[26]

If we were on the defensive, we could say, I suppose, that

all such examples do is to show us that it is difficult to talk about concrete realities, and that as a result we naturally drop into the most ordinary and nearest way of talking. It is the best way to avoid the effect of remoteness induced by abstraction. That we must do, since we are trying to talk about a concrete here-and-now situation. I think that, if we are still talking sacramentally, there is more to it than that. The sacramental situation is not merely an effort to avoid remoteness. It is the most *particular* situation that exists, a case of experiencing the 'scandal of particularity' itself. The point could be elaborated. It is the talking and doing situation that interests me. Here we are expressing and experiencing the most particular and unique object-experience we can find. At least we think so. It is Strawson's thesis that ordinary language has two basic categories for particulars — material bodies and persons, and among particulars the central position is held by material bodies. 'They appeared as the basic particulars from the point of view of identification.'[27]

So, when we wish to express the experience of communion with our God, he offers identification by contact with his sacramental body and sacramental blood, and our own bodily contact with him must be by eating and drinking. So also with the bodily contact involved in other sacramental actions. It could not be of a more particular *hic and nunc* and tactile variety. Thus in addition to eating and drinking, we have washing with water and cutaneous rubbing with oil. The anthropologist can assimilate to these functions the extraordinary particularity of the bodily killing of a victim. Catholic theology has much wriggled in the past to avoid what, in the abstract, seemed to be the unacceptable crudeness of the idea of the sacrificial death of Christ in the Mass. 'Immolation theories' are now out of fashion. I would not wish to see them restored. The point is that human beings *can* think of the killing of another human being as sacramental. At first sight this looks far from what I call the way of intimacy. The connexion lies in the shedding of blood.[28] Not only is the process effective of immediacy and union, but also of communication. However grotesque and horrible the idea may seem, ritual murder, as a gesture, achieves some species of intelligibility. And the marking of the human body is commonly recognized as showing passage to a new life. It is very odd in any context but the present to think that ritual circumcision, branding, flaying and the cutting of finger joints are forms of communication for the right individual in the appropriate society. The clerical tonsure, which has not long since disappeared in some Catholic countries, had the same role.

My point in this section is a very simple one: when the symbolic religious imagination has to manipulate the category of space, it is forced to do so in terms of actions or activities done by, or done to, this particular human body.

THE CONSUMMATIVE MODE

In sacramental language and behaviour it is, I suspect, sexual union which is the hidden but operative symbol more often than is commonly thought. Before making the point that it is the act of intimacy *par excellence*, and thus a remarkably apt one for expressing the way of intimacy, I must take up again the distinction between the *instrumental* or *consummative* modes of symbolic expression. The body, as the classical theologians well knew, can be used as an instrument for doing or for communicating. The *consummative* mode was less amenable to their sort of analysis, and I think they missed the quite basic point that it is because the body is capable of *consummative* experience for the embodied self, that it is also capable of the natural sacramentality which they perceived in the *instrumental* mode. If it is asked why Satanism and ritual murder cannot be sacramental, my reply would be that because the *instrumental* mode is here used in total dissociation from the *consummative* mode.[29] But sometimes when the classical theologians were less afraid of their own mythical imagination, the effective, sacramental and sacramentally *consummative* aspect of the human body became an occasion of extraordinary insight.

I give one example: the seventeenth-century exegete (Cornelius) a Lapide saw the production of Eve from the side of Adam as the completion in man of the divine Trinitarian life, the highest mode of intimacy he could think of. This very beautiful mysticizing of the sexual union as a theological projection need cause no surprise. It fits very well with the common theological generalization that, because man is made in the image of God, the very dignity he has even as a sexual being makes him a sacred being, capable of self-transcendence in sex, an act of imitation of the intimacy of the life of the eternal Godhead.[30] The lesson for us here is that there is no reason to think that there must be a final elimination of bodily and sexual language or attitudes in man's sacramental state.

Still it is true that Western man more readily recognizes sacramental activity when it is more obviously in the *instrumental* mode, as in washing, purifying, preparing and blessing food and drink. The one exception in which he at once recognizes the *consummative* mode as sacramental is in communion. I think it probable that he makes the distinction too sharp between the *instrumental* and *consummative* modes, since the human body may play its part in either mode. Victor W. Turner records a practice among the Bengali Sahajīyās, a sixteenth-century revivalist sect, which seems to me to show the *instrumental* and *consummative* modes appearing in the same rite. The Sahajīyās had elaborated liturgical actions and repetitive mantras 'which culminated in sexual intercourse between fully initiated devotees . . . who simulated . . . the love-making of Krishna and Rādhā. This was no mere act of sexual indulgence, for it had to be preceded by all kinds of ascetical practices, meditations and teachings of accredited *gurus*. It was essentially religious in nature, treating the act of sex *as a kind of sacrament*, "an outward and visible sign of an inward spiritual grace".'[31] Professor Turner evidently feels no hesitation in using the word sacrament of such a rite in such circumstances. The use of ascetical practices suggests to me that the sect managed to combine the *instrumental* and *consummative* modes of bodily expression. The Western reader may find that example strange, if not profane. One must simply say that it is not profane. In passing one may also add that if it seems quite foreign to the Christian tradition, then without going too far afield in the history of Christian deviant behaviour there are already recorded specimens of 'over-ripe' decay in American Catholicism.[32] But in making something of a debating-point, I am not of course suggesting that for our purposes religious decay is unimportant. The state of decay, or for the matter of that the state of inchoateness, in sacramental behaviour is useful to us insofar as it brings out elements, which may always be present in a sacramental situation, but which in the accepted sacramental life of the ongoing community may be overlaid. The very *instrumental* mode itself may obscure what is being done, or what it is intended to do. The *consummative* experience *as experience* may obscure the real religious objectivity of the sacramental situation; and the existence or enhancement of the live, and creatively-live, relationship between this man and this community, between this man and this God here and now may find no effective expression. Any example of an aberrant sacramental gesture would show this happening.

I conclude, all the same, that sacramentalism is essentially bound up with bodily language and experience. Further I think we should also admit that the more the sacramental situation is a communion with God, or a *consummative* situation, then the more probable it is that, besides the symbolism of bodily ingestion, there will also be present the overtones of sexual union. Since we are discussing the place of bodily intimacy in sacramentalism, then we must acknowledge the existence of the various forms under which we think we detect its presence. What we have also to recognize is that bodily communication must also be of an appropriate degree on an appropriate scale. Only the life of a religious community will *in the long run* be decisive for determining its effective significance. If the way of intimacy were to be totally abjured, then we would have to ask whether sacramentalism could at all survive as a religious event in human existence. We do not appear to have any other way than that of intimate behaviour, language, or structured gestures to express what has to be said and done. When we look at sexual rituals in any religion we must keep that in mind. In any religious tradition in which love, human and divine, plays a high doctrinal part then clearly it would follow that (*a*) any attempt at sacramentalism which ran counter to the expression of love itself would be insignificant, and (*b*) any expression or use of sacramental symbolism which was not open to a relationship of love with God and our neighbour would, to the extent that it failed in openness, be defective. The punitive methods of the Inquisition which attempted to teach a religious truth through a distortion of bodily contact were of course no sacramentalism but an impiety. Similarly, if we wish to judge the association of sexual activity with sacramental behaviour, we shall ask if the situation is expressive of genuine love. The Christian answer will be that in marriage the condition is verified, but that otherwise it is not.

Even so love in the religious sense has been found to be inexpressible without the use of some symbolism of body contact. I do not mean merely cutaneous contact, though that cannot be excluded. But it is not an impossible extension of the term contact to say that there is in religious behaviour a visual contact, as in the glances exchanged between the guru and his disciples, or between the hierarch and the worshippers, or between the fervent preacher who, like an actor, is 'collecting the eyes' of his congregation. The 'word', the 'book', the 'gospel proclamation', the 'rite' — all these things imply an auditory as well as a visual contact, which at privileged moments may call for an engaged response in the form of an acclamation, or an antiphonal response from the congregation. Ritual progressions, placings, signs of blessing, impositions of hands, tactile anointings, the putting on and taking off of special dress are also forms of contact and scarcely need discussion.[33] I merely want to suggest by these reminders that gesture language with its unending play on various forms of intimacy is all of a piece with the *consummative* act of 'eating his body' and 'drinking his blood'. At bottom we should bring ourselves to admit that the claims we make for our Christian eucharist are such that we are proposing the highest form of religious intimacy possible, and that in recognizing how it overlaps with cognate forms of human intimacy we have only more to learn.

Tillich looks for a metaphysical substratum. In sexual rites it is not so much, he argues, the element of sex, but 'the mystery of being' which 'manifests itself to us in a special way'. One can dismiss the idea of course. Or one can take Tillich at full strength, so to speak, and follow him throughout the ramifications of his doctrine of the 'ground of being'. He will go so far as to say that it is the 'ground of being' which 'explains the rich use of sexual symbols in classical Christianity'.[34] For my purpose it is enough to say that Tillich has managed, in what for me is simply another rich symbolic overlay, to suggest that the all-pervasive and necessary need for sacramental love-talk and gesture is bodily. The way of intimacy thus appears as basic, but I would say that there is another lesson in Tillich's overlay. From his appeal to his doctrine of 'the ground of being' we can conclude that the religious use of sexual intimacy is not an end in itself. That is important and may help us to clear out of the way one of those indigestible bits of rationalization in religion which makes consistent thinking difficult.

We all know that in the case of the mystics and mystical writing the use of sexual symbolism has achieved canonical status on grounds that can vaguely be called privileged. For the mystics, so the argument runs, in their entirely different and privileged state of divine-human intercourse the use of sexual symbolism is intelligible and permitted as a perhaps regrettable necessity. But, if there is anything in my point and in Tillich's, there seems to be no reason why we should go on thinking that the mystic by way of holy exception is entitled to turn the sex thing on its head and make an irreligious proceeding into a religious one, but for himself alone. There is no need to suppose that for him symbols have suddenly lost their meanings or connotations, so that the mystic cannot possibly mean exactly what he says. The point will now rather be that in the perfected human and mystical state the full range and meaning of religious sex symbolism can be drawn upon in a completed or more perfect way. What is true of the mystical state will also in its own way be true of sacramental symbolism. We have to allow that there is a scale or progression in the range of available sexual symbolism. At some place in the scale, there begins a band of symbols given us by nature in the great range of experience and play of intimacy which makes such symbolism valid for religious purposes, whether they be those of mystical or of sacramental man. Here there is an invitation to a feeling of intimacy which sacramental symbolism cannot afford to ignore. The validity of the process arises not by means of a holy disinfection, nor because the symbols have now lost their power, but because in sacraments, as in the mystical state, the divine-human love-relationship is that which *informs* — the hylomorphic image is helpful — all the rest.[35] We can thus think consistently about the religious and the non-religious situation, and may after all conclude that D. H. Lawrence or Norman Mailer grasp or express the essential less perfectly than do the Song of Songs or St John of the Cross.

There is still, I think, something to be gleaned from St Thomas Aquinas here, though we have to be a little indulgent about his biology and his historico-theological aetiology. In the paradisal state, he holds, human intercourse would have been one 'of greater sensible delectation' (Summa Theologica, I, 98, 2, ad 3); and further, the reason why woman was taken from the side of man was so that she should be more intensely and inseparably loved by him (Summa Theologica, I, 92, 2). The paradisal state for Aquinas, it must be remembered, was not a less real or less natural state of affairs than that we know now. For one thing it was the state that God wanted, and more richly endowed than the one we know. In the paradisal state two things appear together: one is the greater and more intense communion with God, and the other is the 'greater sensible delectation' in the communion of human love-making. Indeed Aquinas goes even further and declares that in the state of innocence continence would not have been praiseworthy.

But we must try and be clear about what in St Thomas's viewpoint is congenial to us. He has no intention of being permissive. But he is broad-minded in the sense that he does not shrink from a conclusion, if it is demanded by his premises. Does that imply in this case an exaltation of the human sex-drive? It does, I think, imply greater esteem for it in the human family, but on one condition, namely that it is subject to the unhindered use of reason. For St Thomas that is what distinguishes human from animal sex behaviour.[36] The paradisal state implies an enhanced use of reason unknown to us. Now it is useless trying to make St Thomas say more than he does say; but I think he says enough to give us a lead. In the post-Freudian era there is nothing bizarre about suggesting that concomitantly with the life of reason the sophisticated Westerner is stimulated to make use of and explore the familiar realms of the symbolic imagination by which he also lives. In fact in doing this he is only acknowledging what he has been doing for centuries. How does his religion help him in fact to come to terms with the trauma of birth, and with the anguish of death? By use of the symbolic imagination which elaborates and familiarizes itself with the language of Christian revelation. The mystery of the Virgin's maternity; the mystery of Christ's calvary and death: we ingest and embellish these symbols and thereby live with our own mysterious anxieties surrounding our own birth and death. At different times the Christian imagination has explored the mysteries of 'the Holy Family', 'the Hidden Life', the 'Divine Infancy'. The historical data are few. The explorations have been in the realm of the symbolic imagination, and the reward has been a sense of intimacy.

About the mystery of sex what I am finally getting at is this. This awesome mystery, at once remote and yet near, both repellent and attractive, itself symbolizing death as well as life, is made familiar in the full life and experience of sacramental intimacy. It may of course be true that the use of such symbolism for the ordinary believer as for the mystic has to be accompanied by a sense and practice of sensual purification. There would be nothing odd in that. The Christian as well as the Freudian traditions recognize that there is always a role for Thanatos.[37]

One remark about Christian marriage may suitably end this section. Together with the eucharist it is after all marriage, which, by reason of its symbolism, has most claim to being called a *consummative* sacrament. The fact that the Roman church decided to canonize the consensual theory of marriage might seem to militate against the point I want to make. It did so in the twelfth century when Pope Alexander III decided in favour of the Paris lawyers against those of Bologna. Paris held that marriage is effected by consent while Bologna held that it is effected only through consummation. But if a simple opposition is set up between the theological symbolism of the sacrament and what has been called the 'essence' of the sacrament, then from my point of view matters are over-simplified. The symbolic theology of marriage has existed since the New Testament. Christians did not adopt a rite for marriage, distinct from contemporary pagan ceremonies, for a long time.[38] It would be a false emphasis to insist that the canonization of the consensual theory removed the element of intimacy from the sacramentality of marriage. For the purpose of this discussion it did not do so; nor in the long run did the decision to make the sacramentality of marriage stand or fall by consensual 'validity' by any means exclusively restrict sacramentality to the consensual element as such. Were this the case, then the distinguishing Christian symbolism of the union between Christ and the Church would be devalued. The question of the relationship of the consent and the 'bond' to sacramental intimacy is another one; and it might profitably be pursued. Here we must content ourselves with observing that marriage, in and through its legal forms as well as through its sociology and folklore, is a sacrament of ritualized intimacy. Legal history leaves it to theology to continue to explore the basic symbolism of the sacrament from Scripture, and especially from Ephesians 5: 21 ff. The situation leaves plenty of room for an exploitation of the overlapping symbols. The *New Marriage Rite* brings out in action how the symbolisms of marriage and the eucharist overlap, a creative piece of liturgical thinking.[39]

POTENT MEDIATION

In my last point I want to borrow a well-known antinomy from the sphere of theological anthropology, and to suggest that there are ways in which the factor of sacramental intimacy may itself help towards a resolution of the antinomy.

The sexual imagery mentioned in the last section, which attracts and repels, seems both holy and profane, is in itself a pointer. The fact is that theological man, and quite naturally also that part of him which is sacramental man, is caught between two sharply contrasting models of himself. Man before God may see himself in two fundamentally different ways. *First* he may see himself as the free, responsible, active agent of God. In this guise he sees himself as Adam's successor in divine sonship, the high priest of all creation, bishop-overseer mediating the domination of God, *par excellence* the creative male, his partner of the other sex remaining a theological loose-end. As a view this is an optimistic one: the final evil is an interruption of the chain of mediation, the evil of disunity. This first view fits in well with the outlook of a Teilhard de Chardin for whom a combined love of the world and of the divinity is the basis of a renewal of the doctrine of the sacramental universe. The sacramental principle can then be extended to the active responsible agency of man in the cosmic process, through whom love mediates increasing divinization with a mediation of unity. The way of intimacy is then both microcosmic and macrocosmic, and is in operation and effect strongly marked with Teilhard's optimistic perfectibilism. The gradual, sacramental unification of the cosmic process through love mediates increasing divinization. With such a vista the sacramental symbolic imagination can operate as widely as possible. I do not see why the pure Teilhardian should very much hesitate to choose one ready-made symbol rather than another, so long as the process continues.

But there is a *second* view of theological man, which affects sacramental man also. It contrasts sharply with the previous one. Here the image of man is rather that of an 'impotent reactor', a creature of alienation, a child of wrath, the Augustinian man of historical theology in stark opposition to Pelagian man as depicted in his self-sufficiency.[40]

Hence even sacramental man is partly potent mediator and partly impotent creature. In the role aspects of baptism, confirmation, and the priesthood he receives an enabling mediation. In the healing aspects of baptism, penance, anointing and even marriage there is the remedial nature of the imparted grace and divine relationship. Symbols such as water-washing, insufflation, and consecration with oil have a sense of life-giving contact, which, when personal, amounts to a form of intimacy. Equally the strengthening and healing value of food and drink, water, anointing, and of the human partnership between man and woman is itself effective through the sense of intimacy induced whether by ingestion, contact or union. My suspicion is that in the Christian sacraments we have inherited a ready made 'audio-tactile' culture of great comforting power. Church practice would be foolish to abandon it at this juncture. If that power came merely from the mechanism of intimacy, the Christian would have little claim in comparison with any other sacramental religion, and more sophisticated intimacy techniques might in any case obscure what Christians claim they can offer. It will always be necessary to come back to the Christian community's original audio-tactile contact and intimacy with its Founder (cf. 1 Jn 1: 1). In its revelational form the audio-tactile intimacy of Christian living draws, or claims to draw, strength from the divine Jesus as from a charter situation which is still effective now. Unless the Christian apologist constantly recurs to that claim, he cannot sustain the position of Christian sacramental particularity and privilege.

What then should be said of the way in which even sacramental man swings between the poles of potent sacramental mediatorship and helpless theological infancy? I think two things can usefully be said: (a) that, while the swing between those two poles is another and a good way of expressing the human condition, in practice sacramentalism (and sacramental man knows this) makes allowance for a wide variety of kinds of human perfectibilism; and (b) that so far as sacramental man is concerned, the way of sacramental intimacy is also one of very great variety, which the believer and his community are constantly re-shaping to their needs.

I can pick out only a few aspects of sacramental life which seem to me to illustrate the point. Today there is in various ways a current craving for a return to bodily contact: insofar as it is the expression of a theological model of man, it is nearer to the image of the impotent creature than to that of the courageous mediating man of Teilhardian perfectibilism. The craving in question is now an acknowledged phenomenon. We may or may not like it; but it is a craving and a human one.[41] Does our sacramental system take any account of such a situation? Much of what I have been saying was meant to show that it does.[42]

There is, however, one example upon which a little insistence is worth while. The Western urban conglomerations with their increasing encapsulation of family units into high-rise buildings are said to increase the need for proximity and contact and to encourage aggressive, anti-social behaviour especially in adolescents. In this context there is, it seems to me, a significant piece of sacramental practice with all the necessary reassurance attached to it. It is the practice of infant baptism, a practice that illustrates an important dictum of Dr Morris's very well: 'Love first, freedom later — is basic not only to man but also to all other primates.' If there is anything in my contention that sacraments have a way of intimacy, then we may have here a disclosure of the very human attitude of the Church, and of sacramental man himself, when he is willing to go along with the situation in which he finds himself.

'Love first, freedom later' transposed into terms of sacramental life should mean that we have in infant baptism a powerful factor for the later life of the adult in grace. I would argue that, just as the forgotten intimacies of mother and child are themselves extremely powerful in later life, so the intimacy aspect of the gesture of child baptism remains, perhaps a less forgotten, strength in the grace life of the adult. Once again Tillich has something to say which is to the point: 'the presence of the New Being in a community precedes everything he [the infant] is and knows'. 'According to the multidimensional unity of life in man, the earliest beginnings of a human being in the mother's womb are, in terms of potentiality, directly connected with the latest stages of maturity.'[43] There we have a theological reason for saying 'love first, freedom later'. In his chosen context Tillich is indeed speaking of love as well as of faith, and in his system he can speak of love in a serious ontological sense as being 'multidimensional'. I am persuaded that we have here one of the roots of sacramentalism itself, and that this is the area in which we should look if, as an exercise in theological anthropology, we wish to get a little nearer resolving the antinomy of the two images man has of himself. But now we are in the narrower sphere of sacramental man. In this sphere would it not be apposite to say that the practice of infant baptism is as good an example as one could wish for, of the Church's multidimensional comprehension of love, and that here more clearly than elsewhere the mother image of the Church is one of profound personal intimacy to all of us? The zoologist can observe that 'love first, freedom later' is an indispensable condition for successful motherhood among primates. If the axiom is a true one biologically as well as psychologically, it should also be verified theologically of sacramental man. I am not of course saying that you have to be an infant to be baptized, or that unless you are baptized in infancy there will be something lacking. I am saying that baptism is concerned with an intimacy of love, and that in the evolved condition of an ongoing community life the intimacy of love belonging to the mother and child is a most precious inheritance, all the more precious in that by infant baptism it has been sacramentalized. In the new *Rite of Baptism for Children* the symbol of the Church as protecting mother has now been extended so as to find a place throughout the rite. The texts seem to give greater importance to a need, almost instinctively felt, for spiritual and sacramental intimacy in infant life.[44]

I take marriage, then, as another example of the way in which a sacrament of intimacy contributes towards the resolution of the two contrasting theological images of man. The relationship of man and woman in terms of Trinitarian life has already been mentioned.[45] That human symbol of the intimate life of God is made more explicit when referred to the divine self-giving by Christ. Husbands are to love their wives, according to the classical sacramental text, 'as Christ loved the church and gave himself up for her' (Eph 5: 25). There are many ways of taking these words, but the clear reference to the passion and death of Christ would simply never be overlooked. Sacramentally speaking the passion of Christ has always been seen to possess an operative role; and so it is here. Père Bro, a sensitive writer where sacramental symbolism is concerned, is quite correct in saying: 'désormais dans le mariage chrétien, entre l'époux et l'épouse, il y a le sang du Christ'.[46] The blood of Christ is of course a mediating life-blood as well as a sacrificial price. It is in the mediation of the theandric act of his death that Christ is the symbolism of marriage and passes on his mediating life. As Père Bro also observes, the death of Christ on the cross is the marriage pact of God with mankind. We may add that the Christian marriage, which re-lives in its own sufferings the sufferings of Christ, re-lives also in its happiness the exaltation of the risen Christ. In doing all these things it re-lives the *exitus* and *reditus* of the divine life and its re-creative effect. In marriage this only takes place through the multiform vicissitudes of the sacramental way of intimacy. Another mediatorial aspect of marriage is to be found in the symbol, now a favourite, of marriage as the 'new society'. Professor Macquarrie speaks of the sacrament of marriage as 'providing a bridgehead into the world'. Here the 'new society' is shown on the social level as having a mediating value of sanctification for the world itself. 'If these most intimate communal relations can be "sanctified", that it to say made whole and healthy, then a decisive step has been taken toward eventually sanctifying the larger social relations that lie beyond.'[47] This outward, growing, creative view of marriage shows how sacramentality, even in the way of intimacy, has a self-transcending value.

The reverse theological figure of the indigent and impotent creature of God is also reflected in the way of marriage intimacy. In the very demand for exclusive and perpetual consent there is also a call made upon and a gift given to the infirm will. In the surrender in intimacy of individual independence a strengthening of the partner, and ultimately of the giver, takes place in imitation of the gift of Christ of himself to the Church. In the all-important task, which the individual has, through a personal relationship to grow into and reach his own mature psychological ego, there is to be found the marriage symbol of the total self-giving of Christ. That symbol through the way of daily sacramental intimacy proves to be the paradigm of the therapy which the weakness of the partner needs. The love between the partners, which in this sacrament becomes Christiform in the way just specified, then lives through the experience of total self-giving, of which the term is the arrival at the stage of the mature ego symbolized by the exalted Christ who emerges from the self-giving of the cross. If we could rid ourselves of the romantic (and Freudian) idea that falling in love is a form of neurotic infatuation, for which therapy will give more or less adequate relief to the symptoms, then we might see the process rather as one of growth and completion through the crisis stages of life, a growth just ready to be 'informed' by the sacramental symbolism operating in the experience of marriage. The life of marriage is not merely the new life of an evolving 'new society', it is also the healed life of an ever-perfectible partnership in which a stage of relative maturity can sooner or later be descried.

CARO SALUTIS EST CARDO

It should not be necessary to state that what I call the way of intimacy in sacramental behaviour is (*a*) by no means the sole way or the exclusive way; (*b*) that, as conveying a partial insight, a description of that way by no means replaces any theory of sacramental efficacy — it is not meant to do so; (c) that because the way of intimacy can only be described in the language and behaviour of man with man, it by no means suggests that sacraments are not divine-human events.

Nor is anything said above meant to derogate from the fact that Christian sacraments receive meaning only in faith. At the same time the fact that sacramental man, in Christianity, is also a believer does not mean that his religious life is a two-tiered affair, the one above, a life of intelligence and faith, and the one below, that of sacramental touchings and the like. The intimacy we have discussed is at its peak points known and recognized as part of an intellectual assent. Yet, even here we may remind ourselves, knowledge in faith is knowledge by connaturality, and the wheel comes full circle when we reflect that that knowledge too is aided by contact.[48] And such is sacramental man in his way of faith.

The lessons to be learned from an observation of the way of intimacy are perhaps the following: (a) that even the way of intimacy is not one clearly delimited homogeneous phenomenon. Cultures are heterogeneous to each other in many ways. Observation must always be renewed. But because intimacy, even in its sacramental dimension, arises from and is polarized to inescapably biological, as well as psychological, energies and drives, there remains a human constant, and in that constant rather than in variation and overlap can sacramental man find himself and his God. (b) Vague phobias about the nature of intimacy in religion had best be exorcized in face of a vast historic religious approval of sacramental intimacy and in face of an increased knowledge we have of ourselves.[49] There is no reason why church thinking should not be much more sensitive. (c) The situation outlined here is so fundamental, its mode being the mode of the Eternal Being itself, namely that of love, that we must conclude: a Christianity without sacramental intimacy would be like a Christ without humanity — a phantom of the Docetists.

CHAPTER SIX

Sacramental Interiorization, the 'Yes' to Communion

First I should perhaps enter a belated word of warning. I shall make no attempt to clear up the general confusion that exists between the use of such terms as 'image', 'sign', 'symbol', or the misunderstanding that continues to enshroud the word 'myth'. To do so would involve us in epistemological as well as heuristic and psychological problems, which would demand treatment in their own right. We hope to start and continue with the observable phenomena surrounding well known religious signs and symbols; and theory, when it is brought in, is meant to appear merely as congruent with the phenomena.

THE PROCESS

When we speak about interiorization, we have to admit that we can recognize in our own sacramental talk and behaviour an *outer* and an *inner* element. We seem to take quite readily to speaking of an 'outward sign' and of an 'inward grace'. To reject such talk we have to make an effort. Luther's idea in *The Babylonian Captivity* that a sacrament was the Word of God *made perceptible*, and thus a pledge of promise to help faith and quieten the conscience also possesses an outer and an inner element. Calvin indeed laid greater emphasis upon the *inner* working of the Spirit in the heart of the believer, but the *external* and *visible* sign is still there. Among believers there is a general recognition that they are talking about an objective state of affairs when they use such language. At the same time there would be agreement that this is the language of theological reflection meant to bring some sort of coherence or logic into the varied uses made of symbolic gestures and words. Thus theologically we can speak of washing with water as an inward cleansing or as expressing an inward life. Here theology is using only two out of the many uses to which water is put by symbolic imagination.[1]

As to what exactly is meant here by interiorization, I must confess that I would be hard put to it to find a satisfactory definition. The term is meant to range fairly wide, and by no means to be restricted to some such process as conceptualization. I am thinking rather of any reaction of the organism on presentation of a symbol. This can be taken to cover any psycho-physical response, or interest arousal, and should allow for reactions ranging from the merely sensory and motor-rhythmic to intellectual comprehension itself. More loosely I can say that by interiorization I respond to an attraction in the situation. I can also interpret and translate a situation, and I can give an interior adhesion, or renew an old belief or commitment to the meaning which it conveys or celebrates. It may be that watching a Salvation Army procession and hearing the band, I will feel the itch to march in time with the rest, to chant the slogans or the hymns, and finally to sink my identity in the common one so far as to wear the common uniform. Sight, sound, word, or gesture may do the trick.

Interiorization may, or may not, be accompanied by abstract reasoning. I may speculate or argue with myself whether the proposed or accepted adhesion is on general grounds reasonable; but I need not do so. If the march I am watching is in celebration of an event or of an occasion, I may or may not advert to the exact nature of the celebration. The fuller, the more human, the interiorization the more will I now accept responsibility for the meaning, or the proffered commitment, indeed for the gift as I may think of it, which is now entrusted to me. The world-view of the believer makes this a more intelligible situation than might at first sight appear. He believes for one thing in the transcendent work of God in the world. These sacramental occasions, these moments that initiate interiorization, are really only a sort of re-infection of God as the transcendent power in the created world. We are indeed talking about a threshold of breakthrough that constantly recurs. That is all the more credible if one thinks of God as *causing to live, to grow, to incarnate*. It is thus in the rhythm and form of effective symbolic presentation that the divine creative presence finds its response. Sebastian Moore asks the question, 'Does God break in?', and answers it by saying, 'No, God breaks out'. The reply is not meant to be exactly in spatial terms, except insofar as one needs them to talk about an epidemic. He points out that the right symbols cannot be thought up, they emanate from human life. In this he is powerfully supporting the view which here I am trying to propound, namely that in sacramental realities man is drawing upon himself and his most intimate human experiences, and that in the long run it is in the experience of himself, *as an experience of himself and of his world*, that man allows the sacramental hinge of salvation to operate.[2]

When we say that the operation is human, we must also admit its claim to spirituality in the believer's or in the metaphysical sense. That shows itself in the by now familiar way. With *the other* I will now remember (*anamnesis*, the *descriptive-narrative* element); and with others I will acclaim and call upon the transcendent power (*epiclesis*), and I will join in the common acceptance of obligations that properly belong to this celebration (the *prescriptive* element). Paradoxically there is no acceptance by the individual of the divine epidemic unless it takes place in such a spiritually human condition that *the other* is present beside the self.

At the same time in speaking of interiorization, I do not mean to suggest that once we have made the distinction between the interior and the exterior of the sacramental event, the distinction must be taken as hard and fast or total. The more a sacrament is *consummative*, in the sense already explained, the more will its exteriority and interiority be perceptibly compresent to us. The more the sacrament is *instrumental* the more the way of interiorization will prove to be a process rather than a mode of compresence. Overlap there can always be, and the reason for this state of affairs is that the religious imagination, like the mythical or the symbolic imagination generally, has an integrative power. It has the power of bringing together or of effecting union by fusion or conflation, as well as the power of dividing and separating.

All that is at no remove from the bodily aspects of our existence as the way of intimacy told us. When we speak of a way of interiorization we are still not much further from the body. But of course there are levels or stages of interiorization. Our attention may be focused on some quite exterior process such as washing. Even if I don't see the dirt removed from the skin in baptism, I can allow an imaginary cutaneous reflex of reacting to liquid to give me some information. With my belief in a real presence, the swallowing of what looks like bread or wine may suggest a most mystic union with the divine. Familiarity with the process of eating has led me to a mystical penetration through the process of interiorization in which bodily imagination has, more or less vaguely, played its part. But if the imagination is disciplined by some reflection the process can be even richer. There may be a double reference available to the imagination by the presentation of the symbol. The referent, let us say Calvary, is absent but the eucharistic symbol moves us to it; yet the absent Calvary is thought to affect us now, so there is a movement back through the symbol to ourselves. That is an example of sophisticated interiorization, a work of the imagination disciplined by faith, theology, aesthetic impressions and the socialized behaviour of the community. The overlap defies a single effort of logical analysis.[3]

But the process of interiorization, as a process, also embodies a conative and volitional–affective side. Nor in that form is such interiorization restricted to the religious sphere. If human commitment is involved, then interiorization is to some extent conative. The bi-centenary celebrations for Beethoven involved no mere *anamnesis* of his legacy in music but also a re-dedication by performers and audiences, and the effort to spread appreciation and affection for his work.

Interiorization is also at work in the dedicated lives of professional men. The vocational roles of a doctor, an advocate, a leader in public life are instructive. In different degrees, as in the case of the priest, it is expected that the role will be interiorized by a form of commitment. Thus a strike by doctors, nurses or teachers can be viewed as to some extent a denial of the interiorization through commitment of the vocational role. The case of the defecting priest is sometimes viewed with greater consternation. And theories constructed to show that the priestly role is a temporary one, in the sense that it lasts no longer than his deputation to a particular ministry, are often viewed with horror. It is felt that such a theory diminishes and devalues the extent to which society demands, through its ideology, the conative and volitional interiorization of his role by the priest. From a dogmatic point of view this observation is confirmed by a remark of Hans Küng's: 'This non-repeatability [of the priestly character] relies on the *unique* and *definitive* character of the beginning that God has enacted with man in Christ, and which makes repetition senseless . . . all the more so for a sacrament of initiation.'[4] If ever there was a claim to an interiorized situation, it was made by the Word incarnate in himself and in his acts. Their analogue in our sacramental life is good insofar as it is also an interiorization. But it is not *any* interiorization, it is that of our radically human history and committed personal biography.

We can also add that anyone who is looking for a practical argument on behalf of maintenance of a *status quo* situation for the priestly character, can also say that, if you agree that the priestly role and character depend solely on the actual deputation to ministry, you give the man less to interiorize. That is no theological argument, but it is a reasonable conclusion from empirical observation.[5]

On the other hand if we look at the theoretical side I think we have to admit that *a priori* Christian tradition is an exacting one: it does seem to demand a thorough-going acceptance of interiorization of the priestly role. The early historical theology of the subject must be left to the specialists; but writers on this topic are perhaps too shy, or too intent on the discussion of hard-won historical nuggets, to notice that in the fully sacramental world of holy sights, sounds, touchings the priest is associated with the most biologically critical phases of life. In the sacramental society it is the priest who is wanted to be near at the time of birth, near to the crises of adolescence, even sex and marriage, near to traumatic events in community life, or near to celebration. It is the priest who is concerned with guilt, sickness and death. I am of course speaking of the sacramental community in its Christian setting. (It is for the sociologists of religion to discuss the extent of decline and what they take to be its explanation.)

I am thinking of the phenomenon of thorough-going

interiorization as a surviving or waning phenomenon. It is my view that *a priori* reasonings on this matter are more empirical than is thought. Karl Rahner says: 'For we may justly call sacramental all divine supernatural reality which takes place in history and is therefore present to us in sign.' The Western and Eastern Christian priesthoods have made a powerful contribution to that statement. Rahner himself very rightly sees that the priesthood, though of course partly institutional and institutionalized, is also thoroughly human in being the visible cultic expression (in sacrifice and prayer) of the *inner* religious attitude of man. By using the word 'human' I do not mean to suggest that the interiorization of the priestly role is significant only in terms of human behaviour, though according to Rahner it belongs 'to the normal enduring institutions of human life'.[6] Indeed, a social anthropologist might well quarrel with that particular generalization. My point is that the historic Christian priesthood of East and West discloses very human and earthly roots, which have *de facto* contributed enormously to the interiorization of the priesthood as a personal and as a social institution. Rightly or wrongly the interiorization has been a massive one, which has in one form or another swallowed up periodic revulsions. The historic issue of celibacy is indicative, for the point surely is not so much whether by an act of common consent, neglect, or simple authoritative *fiat*, there shall, or there shall not, be a celibate Western priesthood, but whether interiorization of the role shall be accepted as so intimate as to make the appeal to the individual successful.

I have mentioned the priesthood because it is such a striking example of sacramental role-interiorization. Baptism with confirmation, and marriage are also role-conferring rites, which make demands on the recipients' willingness to interiorize. The test lies in the realm of *prescriptiveness* flowing from the sacrament. Baptism, we are told, marks the beginning of a new life with corresponding ethical obligations. So also does marriage. It is enough to remember that the palmary doctrinal passage in Ephesians 5 is in fact part of an exhortation to better conjugal relations.

NEGATIVITY AND BEYOND

So far I have been trying to say that there is an observable process of interiorization in sacramental gesture and language. That I think to be the case whether sacraments are to be considered as events or happenings in one's life, and whether or not the role or status acceptance connected with those events is considered from the point of view of an individual's biography. But it is not only the theologian who is free to approach the matter in an *a priori* way, it is also the philosopher. 'Cult in the Christian community thus appears as a concrete process of interiorization', says Henri Chapelle, one of Hegel's recent commentators on the master's philosophy of religion.[7] It would be pretentious to follow the dialectical reasoning in which that observation is enshrined. Nor, obviously, do I intend the present use of the word interiorization to bear the heavy dialectical weight laid upon it by Hegel. It seems fair, however, to claim that the precisely Hegelian movement of thought is favourable to the more simple approach to cult and sacraments I have in mind. When I read that 'the Christian cult then appears as a twofold negation of the extrinsicism of dogma and of the believer's immanentism', I must agree for that is surely what the double polarity in interiorization is all about. The believer accepts his sacramental symbol, but is not wholly absorbed taking in the *descriptive-narrative* element to the detriment of his own active participation. The comparison with viewing a film or being in a theatre will not do, not at least unless there is a genuine locus of creativity for the sacrament, *qua* sacrament, where interiorization of a doubly effective kind takes place.[8]

But not all is positive, transitive and creative. Negativity is required for the dialectical process to be recognized, and this may be verified in the logic of psychological experience. Interiorization to the point of disclosing or effecting a divine presence will also follow the law: 'unless the seed die . . .' Hegel and Freud seem to combine here. The age-old arguments over the need for the death of the Saviour in Christian soteriology have tried with differing success in logic to follow the same psychological law.

What really happens at or in this point of negativity is the next somewhat mysterious question. For Bernard Bro the next step is '*to embrace negativity and move beyond it*'. Here I think is one of the decisive anthropological foundations of sacramental life.[9] Bro connects his point with 'this all-embracing image, which man has of himself', and 'which cannot be regarded as ultimate. It must be relativized or shot through with negativity, or tragedy will ensue.' Such negativity Bro sees in the life circumstances to which man adapts through Christian ethical experience. If I understand him, he is saying that only through the acceptance of the need to negate our basically infantile perversity can we sufficiently relativize our self-destructive dynamism, an inner self-orientated aggressivity, which otherwise will reign supreme. For that is what happens, when a project becomes our be-all and end-all and we work for it in an entirely unfettered way. The old egotism of self-assertion holds an incoherent sway, but eventually we experience a fatal discrepancy between the desired image of ourselves and the reality. Frustration follows, and then an intolerance of our own self-frustration. As an 'explanation' I believe that is on the right lines. That is why I think Thanatos has its rightful place in both sacramental symbolism and in its *prescriptiveness*. At this point I would join Bro and go a step further with him. In living our lives we need negativity, usually in the form of a contradiction of the pleasure principle, as a motive or drive. We find it most commonly in the form of repetition. In sacramental interiorization we have a sound parallel. Not only we, but the creative moment needs its negativity. It comes partly from the *prescriptiveness* that belongs to the sacraments; or, as in life, it comes from repetition which can also fill the bill.

Embracing negativity and moving beyond it is after all one of the basic operations in infancy. Here we have an ontogenetic basis, it would seem, of what I am calling interiorization. The infant's own body and the world of its environment have to be differentiated. How does the child do this, except by the gradual discovery of a within and without (the basis of our interiorization) of his own body? Children's drawings show how preoccupied they are with this very discovery, and they show how emotionally charged it is for them. From that fact Le Men deduces the importance that has to be given to the within and without (interiorization again). We are familiar with the fact that a special piece of ground or place acquires holiness by being enclosed, an enclosure as such, a house, a city.[10] All these are accepted as delimited and protected sanctuaries. But we are also familiar with the ambivalence of such symbolism. Places of privileged access may indeed be holy, but in the event also prison-like. Positivity and negativity do not fail each other.

As to interiorization, in which we are interested, Le Men is helpful. For the infant definitely relates space to his basic emotions, those of desire and fear. Interior space, within the child himself, is that on which the highest value is set: 'c'est une nécessité biologique et biophysique'. Thus even today, when physiology teaches us otherwise, it is still the heart which is the seat or centre of the affections, and as such a piece of infantile spatial interiorization.[11] All the same the conquest of space is important, for one thing it belongs to the learning process in the infant's life and leaves its trace as a personal achievement. Le Men draws attention to the importance of the achievement of a vertical posture at the age of three or thereabouts. At that stage nothing seems more implacable than height or verticality. Its conquest in addition to being a postural symbol of later conquest in life, also proves to be the symbol of liberation (ibid.). Once experienced this achievement remains an ever ready mnemonic pattern which will serve as an interiorization even in religious life. We shall have to return to the question of ascent as a form of sacramental interiorization.

BINARY OPPOSITION

Interiorization can, I think, be glimpsed in another way and by another mechanism. The phenomenon I have in mind is the one known as *binary opposition*. It is a very basic ritual element common to other traditions besides Western ones, though by no means confined to ritual or sacramentalism. Even in the history of Western philosophy it is to be found at the dawn of Greek thought, and there can be little doubt that it has influenced our ways of thinking quite profoundly.[12] In our common socio-cultural encounters we take the matter entirely for granted as does the Judeo–Christian tradition throughout. The simplest example concerns the difference between the left and the right hand. In the Bible for example 'in no single instance is the left hand given a position of honor, superiority or righteousness'.[13] Further, 'Christian ritual is predominantly dextral in all its aspects; that is in addition to clockwise and sunwise circumambulatory movements of the priests with the altar facing the east'.[14]

It is true that the liturgical axiality of churches used to be more important than it is now, but the tradition was significant enough, for the right hand was associated with the east and the left with the west. Thus the eastern end of the church was orientated towards the dawn, the light, and the risen Christ, while the western end was the exit towards the setting sun, darkness and the profane world. Westward facing altars have to some extent, though they need not have done so, confused the issue. In few sacraments is there no sign of the cross, although the movement from right to left, the more ancient one, is puzzling. Twin shrines are not uncommon either, although here it is the polarity rather than the handedness which is significant.

So far as one can tell these binary oppositions, even the crudest, exist because somehow the opposition is there crying to be resolved; and, as I think, by a process of interiorization. Of course it is possible that sociality is a very important factor in the perpetuation of such binary oppositions; but it would be surprising if that were the whole story. As an 'explanation' it would hardly do justice to the exceptionally large variety of subjects and gestures which binary opposition affects. In any case opposition demands acceptance in some form, or rejection. To do either of these things some logical process must intervene even at the symbolic level. Some apparently opposed symbols are accepted as coming together, while some are not. Variety itself suggests this. Peter Rigby in a very clear article shows how dyadic opposition, starting with the left/right dichotomy, extends to sex, cleanness, ritual, fire-making, sowing and husbandry, geographical orientation, sickness, death and health, witches and poisons, kinship, economics and politics as well as affinal relationships, duties in life as well as marriage.[15] It looks more and more as though we are right to suspect that the basic dyad of binary opposition has a role to play in the interiorization of outward symbols, especially when we find that dyadic classification is not enough. Anthropologists have been forced to resort to more complicated *schemata*. According to Turner there is no single hierarchy of classifications that may be regarded as pervading all types of classification.[16] But he also admits that binary pairs seem to persist, however much the classifications prove to be in different sets.[17] What I suggest is that the more complicated the sets of classification, the more interiorization is needed, while the need to cope with binary opposition is itself already a sign that some interiorization takes place, if only by a process of re-arranging the pattern or cluster of symbols.

If we are asking ourselves whether or not all this is very 'primitive' and far removed from our sophisticated ways of Western sacramental behaviour, then we should beware of dismissing the life of the imagination, especially the religious one, as 'simple' or 'primitive'. 'In matters of religion,' writes Turner, 'as of art, there are no "simpler" peoples, only some peoples with simpler technologies than our own. Man's "imaginative" and "emotional" life is always and everywhere rich and complex.'[18]

To that extent Turner will concur with Lévi-Strauss in thinking that *la pensée sauvage* 'contains properties such as homologies, oppositions, correlations, and transformations which are also characteristic of sophisticated thinking'. If it is true that *la pensée sauvage* can do all this, though we have only our own conceptualizations to tell us so after we have made our observations, then interiorization at the level of the structured imagination, whether 'primitive' or 'sophisticated', seems to me the only conclusion. After all the properties mentioned are in themselves all amenable to some kind of logical control. In a religious context they will be amenable to the same sort of logical control, no better and no worse, than we are accustomed to use with our own inherited symbolism. To an outsider in anthropological matters like myself, it does not seem that the experts have arrived at the stage of a generalizable 'explanation', but it does seem as though their analogies point in one way. In an ostensive, rather than deductive, fashion they are introducing us to a *methodic psychologism*. For Durand the method is one of convergence and is pragmatic, that is to say it is definitely non-metaphysical. Thus the argument is not in the form, A:B::C:D; but it is rather in the form, A:B::C^1:D^1. This seems to be particularly apt as a way of describing the interiorization of the basic symbols whether in binary opposition or in more complicated form. Thus the resolution, when it occurs ritually or sacramentally, is to be found now not merely in the psychologism order of A or B, but in the cultural order of A^1 and B^1, where the oppositions may persist until resolved in the new order.[19]

The result is seen by Turner as a 'Gestalt', indeed a 'tensed Gestalt'. In his view the tension is constituted 'by ineradicable forces or realities'. I had a mild reservation about the term 'Gestalt' before, partly because it is more difficult culturally speaking to pinpoint the nature of Christian sacraments in 'Gestalt' form, and partly because of the difference between the psychologism of the elements on the one hand and the cultural order on the other in which the resolution or creative moment is to be found. Although we have glanced at Hegelian dialectic as in some way helpful, I am glad to see that Professor Turner thinks that these tensed unities are 'not quite like the dialectical pairs of opposites of Hegel or Marx, of which one party, after mastering the other, gives rise to contradictions within itself.[20] The caution is a good one. And there is another caution to be added. We must not apply to myth what we observe about ritual, nor must we reverse the process. The connection between the two is in any case notoriously controverted; but in spite of that it emerges that *to a certain degree* both ritual and myth are bound up with binary opposition. It is a matter of degree. Some experts favour a higher rate, others less. Lévi-Strauss rates binary opposition extremely high as an element in myth. Professor Kirk criticizes him for it. The function of binary opposition is for him overrated.[21]

I think we can now agree, however, that the function of binary opposition is, a common one, and that, whether or not we like to see it in terms of Hegelian dialectic, we can admit that there is a process associated with it which we can call 'going beyond', or 'rising above' or indeed interiorization. To that extent it is a fair index to the sacramental situation. Is it a necessity? Somehow I do not think that it is. Its place may be a large one, but it does not appear that it is central to the operative message of a sacramental symbol. There is still something to be said for the 'natural' symbol. A kiss effects what it signifies, in any language so to speak, and without the need of dialectic or binary opposition. Opposition may come from the superimposition of symbolic meanings. The water that washes away dirt is added to the water that gives life. The former has to do with binary opposition; the latter does not obviously do so. But at the same time, the latter symbolism by itself may have less of a hold on the religious life of our experience. The superimposition of the dialectical symbol has done nothing to destroy the one-way message of water as a life-giving element. Rather it has helped, though interiorization could have been achieved without the dialectic. When a ' "natural symbolism" . . . is immediately apprehensible irrespective of culture, then the symbol may speak without calling for its opposite'.[22] With the dialectical symbol superimposed we may go deeper and we may go wider.

THE RELATIONAL SETTING

Interiorization may thus take place by some form of resolution of binary opposition. But whether that is the process, or whether mere presentation of the unitary symbol suffices, we do in the end go beyond a mere repatterning of the symbols involved. The new significance, however, serves to bring out something else. What has happened is recognized as *for me*, and that means an engagement on my part. My engagement can be in and with the community.

There is all the difference in the world between the student of religious phenomena in his study as he thinks over the different aspects of the eucharist, and the believer or worshipper reflecting on the eucharist in which he is here and now participating. To take three typically different sets of polarities about the eucharist, we may remember that we are dealing with: past/present; one/many; death/life. The student will ask himself how it is that the memorial (*anamnesis*) resolves the first polarity, how the common meal and the sacrifice resolve the second and third. He may reflect upon the mechanisms we have been talking about, how the logic of the symbols can match with any formal logic he chooses, or where the 'essence' of the sacramental gesture resides. That is not sacramental activity. But interiorization, as an experience of the memorial, the meal, or the sacrifice is different. There is an aesthetic, emotional, and mental resolution of the polarities. The sensible and disparate patterns are in a nodal moment (more a movement than an instant) of acceptance resolved; and that acceptance comes at all levels, personal and communitarian, physical and spiritual. I see no reason to believe that interiorization must terminate in an etherealized spin-off from human experience.[23] One reason why I think this must always be true of sacramental experience and of worship is because of the continued presence of the descriptive-narrative elements which are never lost sight of. So long as our worship remains largely *anagnostic*, and gives its sacramental value to the scriptural element, then binary oppositions which can be thus indefinitely prolonged are there to be resolved and to occupy us.[24]

Although, as we said above, the relationship between ritual and myth is a notoriously difficult one from the point of view of the Christian sacraments I think there is plenty of room for manoeuvre. Our rites are rich in *descriptive-narrative*, or mythical, elements. Some are more closely central to the sacrament in question than others; but I would venture the opinion that wherever the life/death opposition occurs there we are in presence of a central element.[25] We have seen the possibility of simultaneity of functions for a sacrament expressed through the different polarities in the eucharist (memorial, meal, sacrifice). Now simultaneous functions for myth are an admitted fact. There should be no difficulty in admitting simultaneous functions for the gestures or rites that make up the sacrament. I think two conclusions flow from this for the purposes of theological reflection: (*a*) that it is only pushing one's way towards a dead-end to want to construct a theology of the eucharist as a common meal at the expense of the eucharist as a sacrifice, or *vice-versa*; (*b*) that we do not have *a priori* to claim for example in the case of the eucharistic sacrifice, that it is so unique *as sacrifice* that it can only be understood in its own terms and no parallels can help us. That is an indulgence in an unnecessary theology from above, and a generalization at the expense of the depth and breadth of the faculty of imagination in man.

Thus in the realm of the imagination and with its own structures different mechanisms can co-exist. Pluriformity, transformation, dyadic structure, and single natural symbols can all do their work. The life–death logic of religious symbols and sacraments ensures that we are dealing with ultimates. But if with ultimates, then also with our comprehension of them. The process is *for myself* or *for others*. Interiorization comes in again here. If the world is hostile, if I fear demonic forces, or even unconscious threatening figures, if I fear even my own past, then de-absolutizing, which is an obvious piece of therapy, will come with interiorization by which I can, so to speak, swallow the remaining 'unfinished business'. 'What is made sensorily perceptible,' writes Turner of the Ndembu, 'in the form of a symbol (*chijikulu*), is thereby made accessible to the purposive action of society, operating through its religious specialists.'[26] That is true of 'dangerous' or 'noxious' conditions. Professor Turner makes the natural comparison with psychoanalysis, and certainly our reflections on sacramental man do not show that he needs to take his distance so very far from the primitiveness of the Ndembu. I wonder, however, whether interiorization in the sacramental sense may not be nearer the mark. 'When something grasped by the mind,' says Turner, 'is capable of being thought about, it can be dealt with, mastered.' Interiorization, which takes place in its new relative or relational setting (e.g. the confessional), and in which death/life, or hate/love, as binary oppositions are resolved, would seem to be part of the process. By becoming a reconciled penitent sinner, in a penitent church, I can now ingest and assimilate the dreaded opposition without harm. In pathological states the patient cannot cope with the world of symbols from within, because his instinctive impulses are not able to symbolize his latent wishes. It is then that the equilibrium between the imagination and purely logical and lucid thinking is no longer maintained. In the latter case there is notoriously a diminution of personality, and over-socialized forms of thinking take over.[27] It seems to me that in both these situations we have an unsatisfactory interiorization and that provides an argument for the retention of private auricular confession.

VITAL FEELING

The rest of this chapter is presented as speculative only. It is not meant to be more plausible than the materials themselves suggest. Its value as an 'explanation' can only be partial.

I have spoken fairly often of 'the religious imagination', 'the disciplined imagination', and 'the creative imagination'. It is now time to look at these ideas a bit more closely. First I do not mean to suggest that there is a superior sort of noosphere to be called the imagination, which has an independent existence, if only we can get at it, and to which access is only possible by climbing an esoteric and religious ladder. I am sure it is more or less accessible to anyone as is, for example, the world of painting from Lascaux onwards. Indeed the symbolism of sacramental man should belong to an even more freely naïve side of his make-up, and, though I think it has a necessary discipline, I think also that that discipline comes from within rather than from without. So significance should be attained with relative ease. But atrophy may set in for a variety of reasons which do not concern us here.[28] I want now to suggest that the structured symbolic imagination in virtue of its structures forms part of sacramental operationalism.

In what follows I am relying heavily on the information and conclusions to be found in a magisterial treatise by Professor Gilbert Durand.[29] This reliance emboldens me to prescind as a matter of method from many other arguments. Can the *structures de l'imaginaire* do anything to confirm the impression that sacramental symbols have force through interiorization?

The first thing we have to note is that Durand's position, as an empirical researcher and philosopher, does not allow him to accept the relegation of the imagination to a secondary status *vis-à-vis* conceptual thinking. For him Cassirer, Freud and Jung, who have a great deal to say on the subject, still betray signs of an unacceptable dualism.[30] The symbolic imagination ('l'imaginaire') acts in fact as a balancing force ('dynamisme équilibrant'), which makes its appearance as the tension of two forces of cohesion, of two régimes, each of which classifies ('recensent') the images in two opposed spheres. When things are healthy and normal, these spheres are systematically reconciled in a sub-sphere ('sous-univers'), where the divergent polarities are bound together in a temporal fashion. This is what takes place in the course of a narrative like a myth, and the result for Durand is a 'system' rather than a synthesis (ibid.).

The coincidence of this analysis with several elements we have already touched upon is very striking. In the context of binary opposition we have noted what Professor Turner had to say about the 'tensed Gestalt' and assimilated it to interiorization. Here we see Durand uncovering a very similar phenomenon in his analysis of the structured imagination. As in the case of binary opposition a balance and tension is maintained at least in imaginative association. In place of the study of behaviour patterns, as with the anthropologists, we find that we are in touch with the realm of the imagination. In Chapter Five we noticed a similar effect in the reconciliation of past, present and future. For me the symbolic imagination, especially in its use of *descriptive-narrative* materials and by the use of repetition, achieves a vital fusion of boundary moments. At first sight Durand seems to place all the effective weight upon the narrative itself ('une histoire') as performing the work of organizing psychic moments.[31] On the merely socio-psychological plane, as Durand rightly says, it is the narrative which fulfils the need.[32] But in the sacramental situation we are in the realm of performance as well as of narrative.

From my point of view narrative does not tell us enough. The 'Sacramental Intimacy' of the last chapter has convinced me that we have to look in a less conceptual direction. In *Les Structures Anthropologiques de l'Imaginaire* Durand shows how we can in fact still do this and maintain a reasonably empirical stance. In my language we can see how we can liberate ourselves from the horizontal, successive and linear time-factor which is imposed upon us by mere recital *as recital*. The work done in linear fashion by myth may indeed be conducive in its own fashion to a form of interiorization; but it would not, I think, be conducive to a characteristically sacramental form of interiorization.

There is a symbolic device to be found within and without the sacramental context, which has two characteristics that makes it jump out of the linear time narrative into immediately benign or threatening proximity. In its fashion it also can be assimilated to the way of intimacy. For *time* in itself is a threat, and the threat is met in the imagination by coming to terms with the jaws of the dentated beast. The importance of such *theriomorphism* resides far less in the narrative than in the power it has to remove our horror of the dentated jaw of time! That is what Goldilocks does for us in the story of the Three Bears. Familiarity in such a case is a form of vital adaptation, and fear is exorcized by imaginative proximity. In any case the bestiary is the basis of one of the standard classifications of the imagination.[33] Tiger Tim can do his work mainly in narrative form, it is true; but Teddy Bear, the transitional object, is a much more effective *euphémisation* of the dentated jaw threat, and is to that extent more sacramental.

We have of course forgotten how to live with animals and now live in a situation of symbolic impoverishment.[34] But at the beginning of things interiorization was present in our own response to the sheer aliveness of animal existence, even when only brought home to us in symbolic form. Durand has an animal *quasi-Cogito* for us: 'it moves, therefore it lives'. That means that the 'animation' (aliveness) of a fish, or of a colony of ants, communicates itself to us not merely as a piece of information about another form of life, but as a vital feeling. The imagination is stirred, and a feeling of liveliness induced. For me that is already in the large sense sacramental. The hallowed image of the fish for the eucharist comes to mind, though unfortunately diminished in importance; and very few people in our parishes could say why the pelican is a symbol of the eucharist. But the bestiary has been needed to cope with the major religious themes of good and evil, heaven and hell, life and death. It is true that we are at present vilely impoverished; but enough remains to point yet once more to the imagination's work of interiorization.

The eucharistic symbols just mentioned are obviously benign figures that do not need *euphémisation*. It is the threatening figures with some shock value that jump out of the time series and interiorize themselves which do need it.[35] I think two factors point to the continuing interiorization of such figures whether benign or hostile. The first is the fact that we continue to use animal symbols in a sense that defies what we know to be the case about them.[36] The other factor is this. Beasts, benign or hostile, belong to a special régime of the imagination. In the case of symbols of the dark (*nyktomorphic* symbols), such as horses, monsters of the dark waters, interiorization is perceptible in the shock process. We continue, in order to 'euphemize' the situation, to use them for funeral rites and mourning. Black hearses, black horses, dramatic silver emblems are *theriomorphic*, and give us a shock we can cope with. Interiorization is not difficult to interpret.[37] Generally speaking sacramentalism avoids the dark, shock-tactics of *nyktomorphic* symbols. It also avoids the threatening feminine image.

But sometimes the contrast is brought out. Thus the benign medieval form of the Church, Christ's bride, when seen as a female figure in contrast with the female form of the Synagogue, is shown as smiling and open-eyed. It is regrettable to our ecumenical taste that the blind-fold face of the woman, not seeing and threatening darkness is the Synagogue's.[38] In the case of the Church the female figure has been sublimated. More normally *féminisation*, even if it is concealed, means the advent of something threatening and fatal. I do not deny that there is much to be debated here of course; and no doubt social factors have played an important part in attributing a sinister role to woman. 'The idea of woman as the Old Eve,' writes Mary Douglas, 'together with fears of sex pollution, belongs with a certain type of social organization. If the social order has to be changed, the Second Eve, a virgin source of redemption crushing evil underfoot, is a potent symbol to present.[39]

Whether the avoidance of the female figure in sacramental symbolism has been a matter of slow acceptance, or rapid rejection, or gradual disentanglement must be left to the specialists to determine. The fish, the lamb and the pelican were always, I should have thought, sexless. The dove, at least in the West, has been a victim of gradual disentanglement, although it should retain high sacramental value.[40] *Féminisation* certainly has had a wavering history, although the role of the Blessed Virgin in Eastern Orthodoxy and Western Catholicism has acted as a definite surrogate. Seeing and touching have come in with holy icons, statues, weeping Madonnas, and with the phenomena of Lourdes, Fatima and Medjugorje. The transfer of woman from the *nyktomorphic* to the *diurnal* régime has also been carried through successfully. White and shining clothes are familiar accompaniments of the *diurnal* image and are common to most Marian apparitions. Bright astral phenomena (Fatima) belong, as symbols, to the realm of internalized elevation or ascension. The definition of the Assumption in 1950 should have completed the interiorization of woman in the *diurnal* régime. It is too soon to say whether enough has been done for practical results to follow, such as the ordination of women.[41] Says von Allmen, 'The only consolation to be derived from the tiresome dogma of the Assumption is its implication that the Virgin Mary, resurrected before the time, was exalted to heaven *as woman*.'[42] For scriptural reasons von Allmen is quite happy with a liturgy of the angels, but not with one of women.

The *diurnal* treatment of Mary, so to call it, is, I think, an unmistakable form of interiorization. Her association since the Baroque period, following scriptural suggestion, with height and light is a proof, for 'the process of imaginary gigantization' is always accompanied by an implacable, blinding light; and celestial light is of course a common religious phenomenon.[43] The question we are really left with is whether the continued use of feminine symbols in Western Catholicism will persist as genuinely effective. The devout must have faith. If I have a suspicion that the time of the best effectiveness of *féminisation* as such is running out, it is because the genuine ambiguity of woman, her most effective strength as a symbol (a 'tensed Gestalt' perhaps) has been for cultural reasons etiolated beyond recall. That is said of course with the structures of the imagination, not with the rightness or wrongness of a theology in mind.

THE RIGHT RÉGIME

With Tillich I am convinced that the dichotomy between word and sacrament has been overplayed. Durand's analysis of the structured imagination tends to confirm this. For one thing, if we continue with the *diurnal* régime, we shall not be surprised to find that *word* is to be found among its images as well as light. Of course no reader of Dodd's *The Interpretation of the Fourth Gospel* is ever astonished to find that *Word, Light, Glory, Judgment* are all considered in close association with one another.[44] What indeed appears to happen is that in addition to, or behind, the Christian situation we find comparative religion, etymology and psychology all combining to tell us how ineluctable and ancient as well as widespread, the relationship between those *diurnal* images must be.

In non-Christian terms Mantra is probably the best overt link between word and sacrament, for it is in the fullest sense 'la réalité symbolisée et le signe symbolisant. Il est en quelque sorte un condensé sémantique et ontologique.'[45] In Mantra the presence of the divine goes in and with the word, rather as it does in the cult of icons in Eastern Christianity, for it serves as an hypostatization of the divine power.[46]

But Word through its clustering with other images of the *diurnal* régime can appear even more operative.[47] As the Epistle to the Hebrews puts it, 'the word of God is living and active, sharper than any two-edged sword, piercing to the division of soul and spirit, of joints and marrow, and discerning the thoughts and intentions of the heart' (Heb 4: 12). No doubt there about interiorization, and the author of Hebrews is talking better anthropology than he knows. Professor Durand can tell us that *diurnal* images, and the word is one of them with images of ascent (a sword used symbolically points upwards), have a cleaving, separating effect. Hebrews could not have put it better. The effect in question is called *diaeretic*. (If the term looks too outlandish, we have only to recall that the diaeresis is printed on the second of two successive vowels to show that it is sounded *separately* from the first.) Now ascent obviously signifies an enhancement of power; but in structured imagination you not only ascend but you separate yourself from that which you have left behind. This often entails a struggle, internal or external. The progress from word, to light, to sword is thus natural. So are the legions of angels, the heroic and apotropaic Georges and Michaels, who ascend their mountains or ride their chargers high. I mention them only to argue that their popularity must somehow show the ease with which such an image is interiorized.

Can we go further? I suspect that we can, but only to put the point tentatively. The interiorization of the *diurnal* symbols must surely owe much to the conquest of an upright posture in our own lives. Elevation calls for postural imitation. Why should not the feeling of a posture of ascent initiate the symbolic movement that corresponds with it, and once initiated why should it not register in consciousness for what it is? These may be very loose remarks to a philosopher; but to a theologian I cannot see that they need present any problem, unless he disdains ever to reflect upon the imaginative processes from which his job takes its start.

One could of course say that purification, ascent, power and light are in any case vague symbols of a vague state to which sacramental man through his automatic responses aspires. As Eliade reminds us, Christian tradition has its Paradise guarded by fire, or by an angel with a flaming sword (the *diaeretic* symbol) ensuring the purifying effect of the ascent. Shamanic techniques with similar intent are 'concerned with the well-known mastery of fire'.[48] There is some logic in this order also. By purification come power, or grace, or union with the divine, and at the top of the ascent there will be light. Purification may demand sacrifice, a sacrament in the *instrumental* mode at any rate exteriorly. Indeed the gospel makes one case of this quite clear. Light is at the summit of the ascent and if it is to come from a single eye and penetrate the whole body, then the sacrifice of the other eye may have to be borne (Matt 5: 22, 29). If one thinks of the importance of light, then a saying, which at first seems far from being sacramental, turns out to be concerned with the *diurnal* régime and its effect.

Purification in any case implies a sacramental attitude. If light is desired, if darkness is to be rejected, then a change must take place. At least impurity must go. In baptism, as in circumcision, we have an immediate message to tell us so. (For the moment let us suppose that role conferral is secondary.) The message is concerned with water, and fire, as well as with the knife which makes even more explicit the import of the other two purifying images. 'La circoncision est donc un arrachement violent du mauvais sang, des éléments de corruption et de confusion.'[49] So is baptism (cf., e.g. 1 Jn 5: 6), although the practice of paedo-baptism has disadvantaged the symbolism of enlightenment which even became the name of the sacrament in the second century (*phōtismos*, cf. Justin, 1 Ap. 61, 12).

But changing styles are challenging the ancient and universal symbolism of ascent coupled with light. Holy mountains for pilgrimage, steeples crowned with the cock of Christian dawn, Christ the *sol salutis* or *sol invictus* can hardly be expected to mean much to the city-dweller. Nor does an effulgent monstrance raised sixteen feet high and surrounded by a cloud of twinkling candlewicks still convey a message of a divine and holy presence. Others must analyse the reasons for change. We can only say that if a symbol is not there it cannot be interiorized, and add a foreboding that if the symbolic and sacramental value of ascent disappears, so too will the other value of purification. We may add as a *first* rider that if we abandon the combination of *diurnal* and *diaeretic* symbols (that is, those that belong to *day* and *light*, and serve to *divide*), then we probably abandon also and for good our tradition of relative dualism in philosophy and theology (Plato, the medievals, the Cartesians). The academics may try to keep the tradition alive; but they cannot create symbols, nor can they interpret as present reality what is past history. As a *second* rider I add that when such a dualism is abandoned, then the covert *sacralization* of the male symbol of sex is also abandoned. When that as a symbol is devalued, now perhaps not for the first time in Western history, then the chances of two very needful forms of sublimation are enormously diminished. I am thinking of sex and of aggressivity. Only the sacred can wipe away the tears that go with sex and war.

NIGHT AND DAY, ALIVE

We must now draw together around some typical sacramental attitudes a few clusters of images that appear to belong to the *nocturnal* régime. It is here that *consummative* sacramentalism is more naturally to be found.[50] As I have said in respect of *consummative* and *instrumental* sacramentalism these modes may overlap. What of the régimes? I think it fair to say that there will in any cluster be a preponderance of one régime over another. Two types of cluster strike me as most important for interiorization. From the side of the *nocturnal* régime they might be grouped as follows: (*a*) symbols that cluster around 'life-food' or 'life-fluid'; (*b*) symbols that most commonly cluster around the kinesthetic sensation of ingestion–digestion.

(*a*) One of the most symbolically charged elements in the 'life-food' and 'life-fluid' cluster is milk. Like the animals of the bestiary it has suffered a decline, but it is in the Christian sense sacramental. As Musurillo says, 'Christ's comparison of his word to food and drink set in train a long tradition of very natural metaphors.'[51] I would prefer to say that the Christian origins of a whole range of sacramental symbols re-invigorated them, and gave them an enhanced interiorization. The Torah was in any case compared with water, wine, oil, honey, milk. All of these symbols were to have their significance in the Christian system. In the case of milk we find it first of all referring to teaching, doctrine and knowledge.[52] But tradition by no means confined milk to an appropriate comparison with the food of infants. Hippolytus tells us that at mass the bishop would bless a mixture of milk and honey which, as we know, formed a sacramental pair with an eschatological dimension because connected with the Promised Land. Texts show that such food was considered to be for adults and belonged to the perfect.[53]

Durand sees milk as 'primordial, l'archétype alimentaire', and, quoting Bachelard, calls it the 'premier substantif buccal'.[54] What I want to point out most briefly is that milk, insofar as it is a sacramental element, is the most obviously interiorized alimentary symbol. It possesses obvious oral and mother associations, and goes with the pleasurable oral feeling associated with sucking. Indeed the pleasurable oral feeling of sucking is unashamedly exploited by spiritual masters in Western Christianity.[55]

(b) In addition to being the primary stuff of the oral reflexes, milk also calls upon the experience and imagination which surround digestion and assimilation of food. The bread and the wine of the eucharist obviously do the same thing. Durand even reaches the surprising conclusion: 'toute alimentation est transsubstantiation'.[56] He is not of course talking metaphysics, nor the language of classical theology. But he is rightly reminding us that sacramental theology is not far from the language of the imagination, and he is giving us a reason why we so easily slip into the 'category mistake' when we try and rationalize our symbolism with metaphysics. Personal experience of interiorization in the physiological sense implied by our digestion and assimilation is the best way we have of assuring ourselves that one lot of stuff can become another lot of stuff, namely myself. Here is a pre-rational perception as common as one could wish for (cf. Popeye the Sailor and his can of spinach).

But the structured imagination does not leave the matter

there. It takes a more sacramental turn. It shows acquaintance at this level with the importance of the outward and the inward elements. In earliest days of infancy and until adolescence one of the most absorbing tasks that nature sets us is the exploration of space, space as related to myself and to the other, and space as an outer and an inner phenomenon. Eventually, by whatever favourite experience he chooses, the infant estimates the space within him as that which is most precious and valuable to him.[57] That after all is where food, when it is his, must go and in his experience that is the first basic real stuff of life. 'Le réel de prime abord est un aliment', says Durand again quoting Bachelard.[58]

It is that which contacts and unifies which is most precious. Within is where the contact takes place. How it takes place does not matter. In myth, according to Kirk, no explanation is needed of the phenomenon of transformation.[59] If we take account of the psychology of childhood and its imaginative working, and if we accept how the imagination works in myth, then it seems to me that no more is needed than our common experience of spatial analogies. These are the analogies which enable me to objectify the interiorization of food, so that transformation or transubstantiation into my own inner reality sufficiently account for it. The logic of such a 'transubstantiation', especially when the food or drink is a 'life-food' or 'life-fluid' is the logic of our own structured imagination tutored by the experience of our own physiopsychology. The moral we must not fail to draw at once is that, in the symbolic order of speech and *from the point of view of interiorization*, sacramental food must be a symbol of *something real and something here and now present. First* that is verified because the food is ingested and because it becomes the inner and precious '*Me*'. *Secondly*, in the same ordered structure of the imagination, the 'life-food' or the 'life-fluid' that is *out there*, can also be a precious life-reality here and now present. Why? Because it is destined to become the precious life-reality within.

In the meantime we should not forget that we are talking about a symbol of the *nocturnal* régime. The destiny of this precious reality being within, is in the secret and dark regions within me. Now the secret regions are the régime for intimacy and *union*. Hence descent within, penetration, possession are all commonplace themes of eucharistic piety, in a word we have *communion*. The mysterious cavity of cup or chalice often sums it up, and verbally or in iconography does not fail in its reference to eucharistic communion.[60]

The realm of darkness has of course another consequence in the structured imagination. Durand writes: 'the archetype consisting in sacred drink and wine achieves formal symbolic equivalence ("rejoint . . . l'isomorphisme") with the sexual and maternal values of milk'.[61] That the wine of the eucharist takes part in the same régime of interiorization through the dark, but vital, copulative union of life-absorption seems to me only too clearly reinforced by its correlative element, namely blood. Blood, the 'life-fluid', clearly belongs to the interiorized way instigated by the physio-psychological imagination. It also belongs to the way of intimacy. 'The Precious Blood' is the most interiorized expression of our *consummative* eucharistic sacrament, a high point in our theology and in our experience, as our *communion* with the divine.

CHAPTER SEVEN

Without 'Justification'

It is part of the free basic realism of the Christian life that change is accepted and even welcomed. If we can make the idea that doctrine develops our own, then we accept that there must be change. If we accept too that the Christian system is somehow a whole, then we accept that it has parts which make up the whole. And it would be arbitrary to think of the parts as somehow uniform in themselves and as developing all of them at a uniform rate. Perhaps it is in any case wrong to use the word 'system'. We can see for ourselves that faith implies an attitude and acceptance of something that is alive. If that is so, then faith can be no mere process 'of taking a position on, or of accepting or realizing existentially, a series of individual propositions'.[1] That is perhaps easier for a certain type of Catholic mind to grasp. But it is also true of the Protestant tradition. Its typical expressions of faith are about a live tradition, even if expressed in a restrictive form. The famous *three onlys* are a case in point (*sola gratia, sola fide, sola scriptura*). Christians have lived and live by these negations. They are at 'the core of the original Reformation Christianity, and they give the reason why an Evangelical Christian declared then and declares now that according to his conscience he cannot belong to the Catholic Church . . .'[2]

But in fact the *onlys* are high in the hierarchy of Protestant truths, and they say something positive. Thus the *only* that goes with faith makes the 'God alone' of Reformation faith possible. Taken together, the religious insight of the *onlys* claims to reach the essential wholeness of faith in God's work in his Son, Jesus Christ. We thus have to respect a theology intrinsic to living Reformation faith. Luther's insistence upon justification by faith as the article by which the Church stands or falls, is part of an ongoing, living reality. But history with the Protestant *onlys* on one side, and the Catholic Tridentine *No* on the other, has placed justification where it appears irremovably high on each side of the divide. But I would not agree that this existential and practical hierarchy of truths must remain an enemy to ecumenical dialogue. Complementarity must still be sought for.

IN THE ECUMENICAL CONTEXT

We may find help in this way. Before Vatican II had canonized the doctrine of a hierarchy of truths, Vatican I had already seen something of the way it should work. Vatican I already saw beyond the simple, linear or circular idea of Vatican II. It saw another dimension besides the line drawn from the top, or the centre related to a periphery. The controlling force of the hierarchy should come from outside. The effort to understand, it said, should be made 'from the connexion which mysteries bear to one another and *to the last end of man*' (author italics).[3] A mystery should of course not be considered in isolation from the others. But over and above the comparison and weighting we give to mysteries among themselves, there should always be an overriding correlation with the one single mystery, taken, as it were, from outside the simple scale. That outside control is the 'last end of man'. All should be seen therefore with eschatology as its final anthropological slant.

It affects my argument that our apprehension of the truths of faith is, to use Pannenberg's term, *proleptic*.[4] It pulls to itself and from the absolute future it takes on board a more complete category of comprehension and knowledge. Belief now includes the coming and totally renewing Christ. To that end the believing Church must constantly adapt. This adaptation in face of the coming of the Son of Man involves constant purification, the simple ditching of dispensable theological baggage. Christian anthropology cannot be other than an interim affair. Now justification both makes and falls under anthropology. To that extent it is not an absolute. To that extent it may be drastically reduced especially along the scale of existential and personal preferences, even of Church preferences. *Prolepsis* will demand that Christian man submit himself more especially to ecumenical parameters.

That does not touch foundational truths about Christ or about God. But even they have to be seen *proleptically* in the light of the end of man. So they too have a critical force. For the man who grows or declines in faith, or even the one who merely simplifies or elaborates, answers to the God calling him to his end. Now that man is always in a state of relative change, because he is *in via*. But, if his thought is properly theological, then it is liable to change. For he who attempts the thought of the Absolute is a changing subject. When the Decree on Ecumenism was accepted in St Peter's during Vatican II, there was thunderous applause. It was applause not merely for a much needed and enriching change in the Church. It was applause of self-congratulation. The fear had at last been banished that ecumenism might threaten the objective totality of Christian truth. A new horizon was welcomed. The Church was perceptibly changing and it could now re-focus its theological thinking through the very experience of change.

This touches the historic doctrine of justification more than any other doctrine. We, who live in the West, now have the right to talk to our religious neighbours of the West about an experience integral to all of us. We need to share it. For we share the New Testament God who forgives, saves, justifies, brings into holiness, renews and vivifies. We have conditioned our account of this experience which is also a relationship with God. Of course that relationship has been partly conditioned by us. When we talk about it we can do no other than historicize God's act upon us. We historicize his mighty deed in Christ, and we historicize our living of it in Church, society, and individually. Paul did the same thing, and with a form-giving genius for the rest of us. He looked back and out, and he saw that increased Jewish insistence upon the Torah had 'radicalized life in the Law'. He reacts, re-reads the history he knows. The result is the unbridgeable gulf between himself as a Christian and the Israel he leaves.

But there is a transmission of a spark he hardly suspects. It is not fanciful to agree with Käsemann about justification.[5] He speaks of a 'field of radiation and a place of manifestation' in Judaism. Paul's letters (Galatians, Romans) support the point. The radiation and the manifestation are sparked off again in Augustine and in the Reformers. What should have remained a field of radiation became a field of opposing forces. That happened to the question of justification. It is to try and run away from the field, if we insist that there is a justification in theory and a justification in practice. The theory can be nothing but a theory attempting analysis by description, in the end a description of experience.[6]

Of course there was historical logic in what happened. The critical language of Paul was still there. So was the critical experience in exploring the self of Augustine and Luther. It was part of the self-wounding of Christendom in the sixteenth century that the sick body was again exposed to those rays. It is also part of the paradox of living church faith that it can become very bookish, abstract and verbal. So it is not extraordinary that Hans Küng can think that the best thing to do with the doctrine of justification is simply to do without it.

> It has rightly been observed that the question most disputed at the time of the Reformation now leaves people in the Protestant churches just as cold as those in the Catholic church — not to mention that an agreement is being sought on this point. Does anyone still ask with Luther: 'How does man reach a state of grace?' Or with the Council of Trent: 'How does sinful man reach a state of grace?' Apart from theologians who regard these questions as eternal questions, who is there to argue about these things? Is grace God's good will or an intrinsic quality in man? Is justification God's external verdict or a man's inward sanctification? Justification by faith alone, or by faith and works? Are not these questions obsolete without any basis in real life? Are even Lutherans any longer secure in their *articulus stantis et cadentis ecclesiae*, in the article of faith by which the Church stands or fails?[7]

I am not at all sure that in the English-speaking theological world justification leaves both Catholics and Protestants entirely cold. And, if the wound persists on one side only, it still has to be tended. Catholics may by and large have now become indifferent. Christians in the evangelical and Protestant traditions still suffer and loyally proclaim their form of the doctrine of justification. The subject has now, of course, been discussed by ARCIC II.[8]

Certainly we may not try and manipulate our fellow Christians and tell them what they may or may not discuss.

But the question can always in a rational or even clinical manner be posed, as to whether too much old doctrinal baggage is good for the health. Equally no one should suggest that it is the New Testament in any form that should be left behind. But in the post-holocaust age have we time for the old battle? Paul's use of the doctrine of justification re-directed belief in God's action to his Son, Jesus Christ. The same question of re-direction of a doctrine inevitably comes in with the phenomenon of change and crisis. That means that we cannot avoid asking, can justification in its classical form still do the job it was meant to do?

We should not, as Küng does, pass on without another look at a problem which goes beyond the terms he describes. There are good reasons for not by-passing justification. *First*, the core of what justification is getting at cannot be ignored, and the New Testament itself uses other approaches. The original *matrix* of the doctrine in the terms we know is indeed now a distant one; but we cannot exclude the possibility that its specific message needs a new translation. *Secondly*, we cannot be sure that justification as a doctrine successfully isolates what has to be said, nor can we be sure that it does not conceal something which concerns us now. *Thirdly*, we should ask: from being divisive can the core of justification not become unitive? As we shall see there have been bouts of recent ecumenical discussion on the subject. We shall ask if the drift of these discussions has really been constructive. Have they not been too intent upon an ecumenism 'of the common ground'? Should we not be ready to find that justification cannot constructively yield anything under such treatment? If ecumenism should basically be preoccupied with the question, 'how to respond to the divine call?', then the 'common ground' is inadequate. The days of a step-by-step discussion may be over.[9]

Certainly if justification is nothing more than so much theological lumber it can do nothing to help us answer the divine call to unity. Nor can I get it out of my head that the Fourth Gospel, for example, favours an ecumenical leap when necessary. It sees the absolute future at that point where the significant present and future are fused: 'the hour is coming *and now is . . .*' (4: 23). Neither Mount Gerizim nor Jerusalem really matter. Ecumenism has to keep that absolute future open for man. Do ecumenical conversations upon justification do that? Let us consider the salient sets of recent conversations.

With Harding Meyer we may briefly note three of these sets of conversations. (*i*) In North America (1963–1966) and in Europe (1960–1967) there have been parallel conversations between the Lutheran and Reformed (Calvinist) churches. The two traditions of the Reformation affirmed that the doctrine of justification forms an agreed witness to their understanding of God's 'free and unconditional and free grace'. But, as the doctrine is 'of no significance at the level of controversy', it occupied no predominant place on the agenda.

But we cannot say that these instances show a uniform state of mind among the Reformation churches. For in another set of discussions justification once more became the central element in an agreed text (Leuenberg, 1939–1973). Ecumenically the reason was a most important one. It was not doctrine in the abstract but ecclesial communion which was the central issue. Doctrine might be discussed without a commitment to union; but union could not be discussed without doctrine. It was felt to be doctrine which would ensure that the participants understood the gospel and sacraments in the same way.[10]

(*ii*) On the other hand in the Anglican–Lutheran conversations (1969–1972), and in the dialogue between the Anglican Communion and the Lutheran World Federation (1970–1972) it was agreed not to high-light the question of justification. The Lutheran Confession, the Book of Common Prayer, and the Thirty-Nine Articles should suffice. Meyer's formulation for this solution is intriguingly tactful. Justification was thus 'not absent but not on the agenda'. The reason was again the issue of ecclesial union, so it was not necessary to go so far as the Leuenberg Agreement. An increased measure of inter-communion was indeed envisaged, but the question of unity in the ecclesial sense was still felt to belong to the future.[11]

Again the participants preferred to insist upon their shared agreement in understanding the gospel rather than anticipate future theological debate. This particular move is suggestive. It implies a willingness to shift the centre of gravity in discussion away from theological history to the immediate impact of the gospel. Is there not in this move a sense of the overriding criterion of 'absolute futurity' in the sense I have described?

(*iii*) There have been Lutheran–Roman Catholic conversations concluding in Malta (1971).[12] The ensuing document, the *Malta Report*, does not much discuss justification. Its importance had already been sufficiently emphasized, why then attempt to continue the theological debate? Meyer reports that many people 'feel that there is a palpable gap in the dialogue at this point'. Two factors seem to have been at work. The Malta conversations adopted the displacement of gravity similar to the one arrived at between Anglicans and Lutherans. Thus the claims of the Gospel began to take over. In addition the conviction gained ground that 'a far reaching consensus' had already been arrived at. Meyer insists that the problem of justification was indeed taken seriously in these debates and that the assertion of an existing consensus was a genuine one. What did remain for the Catholic party to find out, was whether it was an absolute necessity in the Lutheran mind that justification should remain central.[13] The *Malta Report* does one important thing for us. It makes clear that the apparently basic conflict between Lutherans and Catholics can now tactically be considered as no longer relevant between these bodies.

In addition recent studies on both sides of the Catholic–Protestant divide now make it an ignorant charge on the part of Catholics to continue to maintain that Lutheran or Reformed justification is something merely forensic in any non-theological sense, or that it is something merely external to the sinner. On the other side the Reformation reproach that the Catholic system surrendered the absolute gratuity of God's gift of salvation is now clearly seen as based upon a fundamental misreading of the essentials of Catholic doctrine. 'Catholic theologians are clear that the gift of salvation is "unconditional".' Protestant theologians hold that justification must be seen as an 'encompassing reality basic to the new life of the believer' (*Malta Report*, 26).[14] These two theological spectres have been laid to rest. Theologians are not likely to overlook the consensus on these issues now. But for them all the question that remains on the table is this. Is justification still basically central? Is it the case that if and when justification goes, it will also have to come back?

One more document cannot be omitted. The *Anglican–Lutheran Report* (Helsinki, 1982) by no means pushed away justification from the centre of attention.[15] The reason is one we are already familiar with. For, as with the Leuenberg formula, the participants have ecclesial communion in their sights (n. 62). The report holds that 'it is in view of our common situation that the doctrine of Justification takes on a fresh relevance'. 'Personal guilt', 'estrangement', 'fear', 'frustration and alienation', the loss of 'meaning in life' as well as 'no confidence in the future' are some of the reasons. It must now be accepted that we live at a time of nuclear threat, impotence before human destiny, and a 'loss of personal certainty and identity'. In all these circumstances justification with the doctrine of 'God's free and gracious initiative' takes on a fresh relevance (n. 17).

Next this report acknowledges the common Anglican–Lutheran heritage over justification, and it notes 'an increasing agreement with Roman Catholic theologians in the understanding of this doctrine' (n. 18). On the subject of 'justifying grace' the report's wording is taken from that of the *Lutheran–Episcopal Dialogue Report* (1972). Its language is indeed a judicious mixture of traditions. It declares 'that we are accounted righteous and are made righteous before God', that 'Justification leads and must lead to "good works" ', and 'authentic faith issues in love . . . [and] . . . sanctification [is] . . . an expression of the continuity of justification . . . growth in faith and love' (n. 20). Nor can justification 'be isolated from the corporate life of the community of faith', and 'the fruits of justification are manifested in acts of love and service' (n. 21). The report makes its own the declaration that, 'The Church is the community of those reconciled . . . because it is the community of those who believe in Jesus Christ and are justified through God's grace' (49).

What is striking in the *Anglican–Lutheran Report* is the greater harmonization that has gone into the formulations than was ever achieved before. Without any sign of hesitation justification is given greater centrality, and with an equal lack of hesitation the Protestant doctrine of reassurance is juxtaposed with the Catholic expression of sanctification, while faith is intimately associated with love and with works. In what sense that is a genuine synthesis need not be asked, for an open-ended line towards the future is asserted when the relationship between justification and the community is proclaimed. If one looks for prudence and 'the time is not yet ripe principle', one can still find it in the acceptance that agreement among theologians does not mean that one can dispense with the process of implementation by stages (n. 63).

From a rapid glance at these documents I would draw the following conclusion. Küng and the *Malta Report* are pointing in one direction. They are saying that justification should no longer be treated as relevant. Leuenberg and the *Anglican–Lutheran Report* (1982) are pointing in a quite different direction. They are saying that there can be no practical preparation of ecclesial communion unless justification remains in an agreed central position.

THE ORIGINAL CERTITUDE

From the doctrinal point of view we are still faced with the question Luther raised. Is it true or is it false that justification is and remains the article by which the Church stands or falls?[16] We have just noted how two opposing directions arise from serious sets of church conversations. Both directions cannot be theologically necessary, nor practically appropriate.

We cannot neglect history entirely. How much looking back should we force ourselves to do? *First* we must again take a brief look at the biblical *matrix* of the doctrine. *Secondly*, we must ask, What was it that mattered so much in the evolution of St Augustine that it could not thereafter leave the Western church in unworried repose? *Thirdly*, how was it that Luther could so powerfully renew Augustine's challenge with the result that the same challenge is apparently still very much alive? From the way of putting those questions it can be inferred that I am not so much interested in the defining, formulating or synthesizing of the elements in our doctrine. Rather I am persuaded that we should go on asking questions, in the hope of seeing further and beyond the point commonly accepted at present. We must of course continue to ask questions in gospel faith. If more space is given to Augustine than to any other authority, that is because he alone incontrovertibly bestrides the Catholic–Protestant division. Augustine's influence spread thick or thin is always with us.

(i) *The biblical reminder*. It is God who saves. In Israel the being 'just' or 'righteous' was a condition of that salvation. From the eighth century onwards, especially in the prophets, that is the language in use. Being right or just, in righteousness or justice, is especially signified by the words *tsedeq* and *tsedequah*. There is always a problem about the English translation. Sometimes it is one word that serves better and sometimes the other. When righteousness involves equal rights, then paradoxically 'justice' is a good translation. And of course God 'gives judgment' (Ps 7: 8–11). But the word spills over beyond the confines of equality, and it goes so far as to include the vindication of the helpless (Ps 112: 9; Dan 6: 27). In Isaiah 40–45 we cannot even do without the theological terms 'salvation' and 'redemption'. There are even four cases in the Old Testament where the Septuagint prefers 'pity' instead of 'justice'. In Matt 6: 1 we almost have echoes of the way the Rabbis stretched 'justice' so far that it becomes an equivalent of 'almsgiving' and 'benevolence'.

But those ideas do not present the elements which give 'justification' its specific doctrinal tensions. The problem is that of the inescapable forensic colouring to the term. God in the Old Testament judges men and nations both in history and at the end of history. His judgment passes onto men. Thus in Isaiah 1: 21 it is said that once the righteousness of justice lodged in the faithful city. It was 'full of judgment'. This means that the city once acted rightly in accordance with God's will. In 1: 27 Sion will be redeemed with judgment, and in 30: 18 the Lord is simply a God of judgment. The biblical theology of this idea collects rich connotations as the biblical texts evolve. Suffice it to say here that by the time of the complex and profound exposition in Romans of justification by faith the forensic horizon of the doctrine must not be eliminated. The point behind that remark may be seen in a simple form already in Ps 10: 14 where it is clear that if God wants to see the righteous or just flourish, then he must add to the element of judgment his active help. He must be the helper of the fatherless.

Of course it is the forensic or judicial element which was picked upon and caused Christian division. 'To be "justified" is to have the verdict of "just" or "righteous" passed upon one . . . that it to be acquitted, vindicated, *declared* right or innocent.'[17] A further element has to be added. When God is said to judge, he can also be said to look, and in that look of God's there is the forensic verdict. In Paul's mind that look of God is eschatological. So his verdict, insofar as it is of now, is also part of the *proleptic* explicitation of the end-time. The eschatological dimension, as the Dead Sea Scrolls have made clear, was not original to Paul. The all important thing for us is Paul's paradoxical insistence that the eschatologically present divine verdict does not come to us, as Israel's expectation had it, through the Law. That was true even though that Law had been God's own Law. Indeed now for Paul the justifying verdict comes to us through our faith in the person of Jesus Christ (Rom 3: 29–30).

That is a good passage in which to see how Paul's highly original and composite view of salvation has worked its way around from the idea of strict conformity with the Law on the one hand to the simple regard of the divine pity on the other. Paul was sensitive to this range of meanings. In fact he needed and possessed a variety of ways by which he could describe the mystery of salvation. But the one theory which became canonized as his, was the theory of justification elaborated for us in Galatians and Romans.

Yet even in Paul's construct, much of the dynamism behind the theory of justification came from a rejection, a negative element. That means he absolutely had to reject any pretence that there could be any such thing as auto-salvation. No legal works, no merit arising from their performance could result in grace. Outside the redemptive work which is Christ's own, there is simply no other work (Rom 3: 24). All is freely given in God's grace (Rom 3: 24; cp. 10: 3; Phil 3: 9). This negative point could easily be expounded at length from the Epistle to the Romans alone. It is in essence typically Christian and Pauline. One must ask, how it could later become a subject of such a profound division. The answer to that question has to be sought in the later historical evolution of the doctrine of justification.

(ii) *Augustine and his influence*. We must not imagine a theological void between Paul and Augustine on this subject. As with so many Church doctrines concrete Christian experience played an antecedent part. The way the Church had attempted to live the doctrine of justification was through its teaching and practice of repentance. We can only offer one example of the way things had been going before Augustine.

Tertullian (d. after 220) is significant, because he gave the theory of repentance a typically Latin approach both as to theory and practice. Moreover he set out his doctrine with characteristic vigour. Penance in his framework of thought could not but be the offsetting of sin, as one would offset a crime, namely by the execution of a penalty which attached to it. This was a way that appeared to set things to rights by one's own active performance of the penalty. Not that Tertullian in fact thought that the performance was in itself the effective element in reconciliation with God. Of itself it would not suffice to correct the sinner's enmity with God. But it could play its own role. In the concrete it would be the *satis*-faction for the crime, the adequate discharge of indebtedness, even a form of penal substitution, an idea from which Tertullian did not have our modern sense of aversion. The penalty substituted for the sin would be carried out for a higher purpose, namely for the sake of the forgiveness of Christ which would simply follow. Considered as forgiveness and the exercise of God's gracious power, the reconciliation would be uniquely a divine act. Nevertheless the human performance would be associated with that divine act. How the association should take place could already be seen in the one symbolically right action associated with the forgiveness of sin, namely baptism. After all Paul had himself already understood it as a locus of purification and divine forgiveness in one. There, clearly enough, was justification, and for Tertullian that implied a subsequent Christian life in which great stress should be laid upon moral activity. In that way something of the Roman apparatus of justice found its way, albeit theoretically, into the Western Church's understanding of God's forgiveness of sinful man.

When in the 390s Augustine turned to the Epistle to the

Romans he found himself elaborating a more tightly constructed account of justification. He gave it more internal cohesion than Tertullian had done. In a marked way his theory came back nearer to that of Paul himself. For now Augustine found himself attempting to explore the dimension of no less a theological reality than grace itself. And his version was so stamped by his own genius that it has never in some form been absent from the Western tradition since then.

With Augustine the doctrine came to be pulled two ways. On the one hand there was the direction which tempted the legal and Roman side of his mind. Justice or righteousness should surely come from a legal correctness. After all his own Africa was flooded with Roman-minded lawyers. Moreover the orthopraxy which the Law offered to Israel had been an integral part of the dialectic in Paul. The Apostle had after all resisted and rightly rejected the theological short cut of God's forgiving man without man. And from the Roman point of view Augustine still had it in mind to impress upon his world an effective Roman God of Roman justice. Hence there could be nothing against right thinking to hold that as a result of the sin of origin, it was for very justice that the infected human race should continue its existence in a state of nothing less than condemnation while bearing its collective punishment for the same.

Augustine pushed that line so strongly that Peter Brown sees his final opponent Julian depicting him as a 'tyrannical governor of a long Roman tradition, a divine Verres, standing trial again for the massive proscription of the innocent'.[18] One has some sympathy with Julian. The suggested caricature did somehow hit the nail on the head. Augustine was willing to pay the theological price for the idea that God's punishment was entirely just, even to the extent of reprobating a greater part of the human race. That way his God was the totally free and totally omnipotent God. Such was the first pull in Augustine's mind.

The second line of thinking Augustine also owed to Paul, but this time to Paul alone and not to Paul in his dialectic with Judaism. For Paul had replaced the Law as the justifier, and the replacement was the person of Christ. Here again Augustine followed. This Christ was Christ the Liberator, the title that Augustine preferred at first in this context. Later his favourite title would be the Mediator. It was in harmony with this view of Christ that he was led along into his doctrine of divine grace. Now justification takes on another aspect. As the Bible had suggested, man was indeed what he was by the judgmental vision of God. But in line with his thinking on Christ, Augustine saw the process as involving now an effect of divine cleansing and of divine healing. And when he sees the process from below, Augustine has to concern himself with man's most sensitive and fragile way of responding to God. That was in his *free* (and how was it really free?) *will*.

The question in Augustine has now gone so far that we can see a new aspect. In fact the two-directional pull we have described leads Augustine to try and contribute something to the abiding question, What is humanity, What is man? It is a matter rather more of the direction of Augustine's thought than of a definition. He has a doctrine of the nature of man and of man's states. He does not from the modern point of view succeed in producing a definition of man any more than his successors have done. What he attempts to do is to tell us finally how man in justification is healed and helped by God's grace.

Yet Augustine's man is anchored in reality. The 'rational nature' is viewed as a concrete existent, and above all as an historical reality. For Augustine, as in much modern writing, history becomes constitutive of man. It is a history in which man comes fresh from the hand of his Creator. To us paradisal man is not quite real. To Augustine he was, and that is evidenced for him by the fact that paradisal man was in dialogue with his Creator and was thus never without help, never without a live relationship with the Creator for which now grace is only a shorthand word. Paradisal man was real enough to have been offered an alternative life or existence which in Augustine's eyes would have made him still more real. His essential will would have been enhanced. But the free human sin of origin did take place. Dialogue with God and the real beginnings of freedom were broken, and selfish desires replaced the dynamism of love. The Maker's image in man was defiled. History turned to corruption. Man destroyed both himself and his free will.[19]

It is easy to underline that pessimism. But we are concerned with the next step: the re-making of dialogue with God, justification. The rational nature remains the subject of history. The question has to be faced, how continuously through its different states, is that rational nature identical with itself? Obviously it is not what it had been. But how profound was the change? Again there is something oblique even in Augustine's well-known answers. True it is that man has been 'wallowing in corruption'. It is also true that the change appears just there where man appears to be man, namely in his freedom, especially in that creative freedom, the freedom in loving. Here again Augustine does lead us to the centre. For this is exactly where Christianity continues to search for its own obscured humanity. And freedom for Augustine is about history also. Yet he saw that history is more often about unfreedom than freedom, more about the immorality of violence than about an ongoing human experience whose goal should be peace.

In that perspective Augustine brings justification round to freedom even more than Paul had done. He had in any case turned into a man preoccupied with the dialectic of decision (Confessions, esp. Bk VIII). That was a point which his own intellectual legacy, the Scholasticism of the thirteenth century hardly grasped. Augustine leaps over the centuries for two reasons. First within his own construct of man an element of indefiniteness remained. Secondly because in his diagnosis of desire and love, he saw clearly how these were subject to a relativity of the more or the less, of greater or lesser intensity. That made him a post-medieval before the time. And above all fallen man remained problematic. Even the justified man of the Church was a pilgrim away from home. That is the one certain thing about this uncertain man who persisted in being problematic. The unproblematic element lay outside him in the permanent over-arching order of created beings. For the middle ages that order was a certainty and the rational nature within it was not so problematic. But once, as in the Reformers, both the order and the man became problematic, then the believing man could do only one thing, namely seek assurance in his faith. The Reformation tension, especially in Luther, had already been prepared by Augustine.

ANTHROPOLOGY COMES IN

The drift of these last remarks is meant to help us to see that if we discuss justification we cannot avoid the greatest anthropological questions: What is man? What is Christian man? Thanks largely to Aristotle the blueprint of man in the thirteenth century, especially in Aquinas, takes on a clarity and firmness of outline hard to surpass. In the sixteenth century that very model of man would be split asunder. What then could the Catholic backlash do, as in Trent, but to oppose the new Lutheran man with a tightened version of thirteenth-century man? And he was almost a new construct. He had been firmed up with more detailed logical and metaphysical refinements.

Already in the thirteenth century Augustine's man with his *natura* had been subtly changed. As the subject of catastrophic distortions, it is true, he was not vastly changed. Yet some of the irrationalities were ironed out. Operation Aristotle proved to be something in the nature of an intellectual rescue. It was an effort to see man in independence of his irrationally different variations. The sheerly unintelligible side had had to be made intelligible. Metaphysics came to the rescue. There had to be a *man-as-such* upon whom the Augustinian tradition had hardly concentrated. Independently of the Fall, even of the restoration by grace, there must be a discussible essence of man. Such a man would answer to the unanswerable question, What? Now the concept of order itself, if you looked at order from within, could come to the rescue. That way you could indeed not get a better idea of the precise specification in the sense of the *whatness* of things. For order was itself subject to variation. Yet was there not a *natural order* in which man was a *this*? Was there not even a *supernatural* order in which he was *some sort* of *that*?

These orders of reality came from the Creator, so they were purposive. Augustine's idea of one human nature within an all-embracing order, could on the level of essential meaning now be split. *On the one hand* could not man *as such* be said merely to take part in an order which was the simple order of things, an order that, historical man apart, could yet be, or even could have been? Merely *as such* did not man's *natura* belong to an order which was — what else but *naturalis*? But, *on the other hand* did it not follow from the very nature of grace's gratuity, that once in grace the *natura* so engraced was no longer a *natura as such*? For grace was an ungraspable reality or state. It could be and was bestowed, even imparted, but in respect of the *natura* it was a bonus, a mysterious plus. From that it followed that the subject, his *natura* now enhanced, existed in a state or order of things higher than could possibly be of right or natural. That *natura* was now exceeded. This exceeding signalled the existence of a state 'beyond' or 'above'. For now its purpose or term exceeded any natural capacity, and exceeded also anything like the homogeneous historicity of the *natura*, or of its stages or *régimes* as Augustine had pinpointed them.[20]

Through his metaphysics it has to be admitted that Aquinas thus came to see man differently. Above all he saw man's final transcendence in beatitude differently. The final term also changed the whole of the order of things leading to it. In his Aristotelianism Aquinas was enabled to see that, if you can speak of man *as such*, then the historic, transient states of the race or of the individual, never are or can be *as such*. Nature raised at the end is also nature raised on the way to the end. In place of the Augustinian aided, healed and incorporated man responding to final, free ecstasy, we have elevated man participating in the highest plus, the participation in the divine good (*ad participationem divini boni*).[21] Even the final state now has a whatness. But it is a *supra* whatness, achieved by a now *supra* real existent.

There is nothing new in what we have just been saying. But what has to be stressed may be less familiar. By means of Aristotle Aquinas undoubtedly produced a coherent view or system. It is often forgotten that he did so in the open-ended spirit of Augustine. From our point of view the picture has two panels. Where Aquinas was being progressive, even secularizing, in his use of Aristotle, he was unfortunately preparing for the fateful later judgment of him, that he had been an over-systematic and static theologian of God and man. But more significantly where he was being traditional and Augustinian, there he managed to retain the dynamism of the Augustinian world view. So when he reads off what is man's end-meaning and his tendencies, then he can see man as man on the move. It is one thing to say that he saw *being* as that which is determinative of the individual. But we must at once add: because that being is a good it must fundamentally also be dynamic, for the good attracts and is attracted. And when in view of man's destiny one can see an implant in the *natura* to self-transcendence, that inclination is again a dynamic reality. Even more, in Aquinas there is a quality in love, by which the inclination of love itself is an inclination towards self-transcendence, *ek-stasis*. That tells us we have not left the thrust of Augustine's dynamism of love behind. For in Aquinas love does two things: it binds and it overcomes, and in another aspect of the same movement it goes out of itself. By this alone we are entitled to say that the authentic Thomist view of man is open-ended. It was a tragic after-effect of Nominalism that in the Reformation debate this open-endedness was overlooked and neglected. A fatal nemesis was then worked out in Trent which saw no need to expound this factor either.

At this point anthropology affects justification. For, within the open-ended view of man which he had, Aquinas did seek out how there could be a transition to a supernatural. What was the mechanism? Aristotle again came to the rescue. There was an armoury of qualities, dispositions, habits out of which the acting subject would act. These might be inborn or acquired. But they gave a leverage within the *natura*, an opening mechanism. It served for a time, but the advantage was costly.

Augustine had been sure that justification involved an infusion of the Spirit.[22] So, in the concrete why should one not understand that infusion of the Spirit as nothing else than a super-quality, or a super-habit, or a super-disposition. Man needed these things by which to act in any case. It was by these that he acted in or under the Spirit. This construct had a definite conceptual elegance. It provided a buffer between the act of God and the act of man. If it did not solve it for Luther, it provided a direction in thought for Melancthon's teaching of synergism. For the buffer would be an active mechanism; and across this mechanism God's free act in me becomes my free acting in grace. So in respect of my creative freedom, I am not a mannequin or robot. The quality is given me, but the action springing from it is mine. It comes from a God-given principle. I am still the subject of the action.

In due course plenty of snags were seen here. But we are concerned with nature and open-endedness. The construct which Augustine had left unambiguously open-ended both retains and loses openness. On the scale of the cosmic order man still retains his openness to ecstasy in beatitude. But the account of things from within becomes different. A new dynamic form appears. It is not the dyadic form, or even dualism, of the Augustinian dynamism of the loves. That is all dynamism and movement. But the new dispositions and qualities had to be inspected for their layering. In due course the layering of the qualities was misunderstood. The *je ne sais quoi* of preparedness to take off, was seen as a potency, an elevatable power, the filament in the light bulb in need of the current. Worse, the layering was seen as ontological, and the Thomist two-decker system was then and there vulnerable to attack. Misinterpretation came from two sides, from the uncritical traditionalists and from the genuine critics. Man was thought to be possessed of parallel powers or natures. Unfortunately such a mental short-cut became popular in homiletics. The preacher preoccupied with the 'mortification of "natural" desires' had all he wanted.

So decline was setting in. We should remember that where in Augustine justification could account for man's two loves being eventually healed and straightened out, in post-Tridentine tradition Aquinas was better remembered than understood. And now man was seen to be in even more of an *either/or* condition than ever in Augustine. He was either wholly engulfed in sin, or he was wholly restored. And that was ontological. In fact anthropology had migrated from the construct of a man in concrete history to a man meant to be ontological and dynamic, but who emerged from his over-exploitation only in rival discussions and dissension.

It is useful to see if only in broadest outline what happened to this doctrine of man, at least in so far as it was part of the history of justification. Augustine had above all insisted upon the role of the Spirit and of love in justified man. In the concrete that was how grace showed itself. For his part Aquinas had also to show in the concrete how justified man operated. He had a more articulated framework. So the work of the Spirit would be more articulated. He introduced the subject by saying that man in the image of God was to be seen as 'the principle of his action, as having a *quasi* free will and the controlling power over his works'.[23] It is almost as though he foresaw the Reformation and nailed his colours as clearly as he could to the mast. My point is going to be that the *quasi* is revealing. He can see that the trouble must come over free will. He does not claim that his analysis can possibly be complete. He is basically in agreement with Augustine that man is still a project to be explored.

For there is relative fixity and relative mobility. There can be no doubt about the metaphysical parameters of order and orders of created existences. They are large and cosmic and transcendental. Their stability comes from their source, the absolute constant, which is God. Within these orders there must be a correction. For the distance between man and his Creator can now no longer be bridged. To overcome strength is needed. A strength above and beyond's man's own strength must be given him, a *virtus altior*.[24] A new proportion, a new exaltation for man is found.[25] Thus we can go on to observe man in hearing a divine 'vocation' through 'illumination', 'restoration', and 'regeneration'. The mystery is such that only metaphors will do to show life within and across the fixity of orders. Within their grand design man had started as significant but impotent, at any rate the man we know. We know him through change and corruption, and through the changing structures of this man open-endedness can be described.

We cannot here even begin to sketch the theology of St Thomas on justification and grace. Nor is there room to take account of his development. A few remarks based on the Summa Theologica will have to suffice, and it should be noted that by the time of the Summa Theologica grace is for St Thomas both 'operative' and 'co-operative'.[26] Our aim must be simply to suggest that in fact the position arrived at by Aquinas on man is basically open-ended. Lonergan indeed makes a cosmological point about him which shows how open-endedness was a natural thought with Aquinas. It touches the problem of time. Thus in the Newtonian world an absolute simultaneity of an absolute *now* was not only thinkable but accepted. Not so in Aquinas. 'On this point St Thomas never had the slightest doubt: he was always above pre-Einsteinian illusions.'[27]

Yet he had to adjust and bring in what was missing. For openness he returns to the Bible. He knew his Paul, even at the cost of a little misinterpretation, he could rely on the Pauline view of transcendental love. When he uses it, then the doctrine of created grace begins to look circumscribed by its incomplete anthropology largely adapted from Aristotle. For the transcendence of divine love was a creative reality, itself creating a transcendental goodness and a value.[28] That has its effect in man. God draws the rational creature above its condition to make it participate in the divine good. That implies that God's simple love for it will produce the same good for it as for God himself. For God produces a value (*aliquod bonum*), and by his special love 'he attracts the rational creature above its condition to participation in the divine goodness'.[29] A nature, especially in the perspective of Aquinas, which is empowered to participate in the divine, cannot be considered as anything but open-ended. To say that, one must of course be prepared to agree that there is some significance in the traditional term 'nature'. But, however critically the term may be viewed, it still has to be admitted that Aquinas was far from looking upon man as a finished possessor of the divine. Thus he will say that in justification grace requires 'the illumination of the divine light'. And for that to happen, God's will must actually exercise its power of attraction and thus draw on towards himself the will of the sinner.[30] On the anthropological side, that is of the human dispositions and virtues, what God infuses must draw man to an end that is higher.[31] And lest we should think that such an end and its corresponding order of reality should form a closed system, Aquinas makes it clear that the divine call or the divine motion in justification implies a *transmutatio*. That change is to be judged more from its final and transcendental term, namely God himself, than from its merely human starting point. The only metaphor which seems appropriate to this argument is that of growth in a living organism.[32]

Once it is understood that in justification Aquinas, like Augustine, means us to think of the divine love, or of new life and eternal beatitude as an end or term which is normative for all else, then some old complaints have at once to be dismissed. Such an anthropology cannot simply be

written off as static. Nor must the long-aired complaint
about a two-decker anthropology be nailed at the door of
Aquinas either. It should in any case always have been
obvious that the doctrine of the inhabitation of the Spirit,
closely linked as it was with the doctrine of grace, implied
nothing like a two-decker system. The very place in the
Summa Theologica of the doctrine of grace should have been
enough of a hint. For it is otherwise difficult to see how St
Thomas deals with grace within a treatise itself concerned
with the open-endedness of moral action? One can only miss
that point by forgetting that the grace and Spirit which
justify, constitute the *lex evangelii* for St. Thomas. Finally
there is only one grace, and it is that of Christ the head who,
the theme comes back, makes us able to participate in the
divine nature.[33] There is no reason to think that Aquinas has
lost the Plotinian idea that the divine One gives unity-by-
participation to the participating singular.

But inevitably the Council of Trent was led to encapsulate
the idea of man in an otherwise brilliant anthropological *tour-
de-force*. Unfortunately it betrays itself into speaking of
justification as a *translatio*.[34] In this process, which should
have been further explored, the openness of Aquinas became
lost. One reason for this is a simple one. The genuine
horizons of St Thomas were too great for his commentators.
Few of them could live up to the perspective of the *agere
sequitur esse*. It had even misled Thomas himself in the matter
of the human knowledge of Christ. But here we are not
talking psychology. We are speaking of an essential,
antecedent dynamism that leads to the ultimate dynamism,
namely God.[35] Man's leading dynamic edge is the intellect at
work in faith. In failing to register the intellectualist edge to
man's dynamism, as it did, Trent also missed his essential
openness to God.

The same point is reinforced by the famous Thomist
doctrine of the 'desire to know'. Not only does this desire in
its openness aim at God himself, but it takes in, as an
engraced desire, the fact of human experience in knowledge.
Later Thomists ignored this. But from our post-Lutheran
perspective, it is of the highest importance that we value and
state the fact that our 'account of truth', is one that is
enhanced by the experience of grace simply as experience.

It is possible, as Lonergan for example did, to concentrate upon this openness in man. For it is wounded man who is closed off, and who is in need of the very openness he cannot bestow upon himself. In that area at least, if there is correspondence with grace, it will be correspondence with a felt reality or experience. For when the healing and interior liberation are there, they will be felt. Aquinas will show that openness comes in the form and also in the experience of 'the unfolding of the human spirit'.[36]

On this point we find that here history has distorted itself. Its account does not tell of an even development. First, Trent all but suppressed that earlier openness in fact, even if not in intention. Secondly the Counter-Reformation theology gave us a slanted view of Luther's overwhelming proprietorship of the role of experience in faith and in grace. Not that I should want to say that Aquinas or Bonaventure anticipated the role of experience in Luther or Descartes. But we need to accept this. The Tridentine attempt to shore up an already fragmented view of Thomist anthropology was no adequate counter-witness to that of Luther. With its now more limited horizons it offered a closed view of man which was dry and drained by comparison with a genuinely rich Catholic tradition. The historical sequel has been that Protestant man and Catholic man are and remain basically irreconcilable concepts. It is not St Thomas who is *en cause*. He is a theologian of perfectibility who sees movement and tendency. The tendency when it verges to perfection perfects the likeness to God.[37]

Before we leave the question imposed by the alleged strait-jacket of the Middle Ages, there is one more remark to be made. It is true that the abundance of analytical terminology dependent upon Aristotle could make man look like one more object in some natural science. That sort of analysis yields too much intelligibility unless it is handled by the master. It gave a handle to Trent. Like nature did not man have his causes?[38] Had not the ancient wisdom from Virgil on taught us: *felix qui potuit rerum cognoscere causas*? For Augustine that had meant that the vital causation in human history, a moral causation, could be discovered as a presupposition of history. That was not the kind of history of a Herodotus or Thucydides. But medieval historiography was not concerned with that either. History was rather a universal unfolding mystery of which one had to know the key at the beginning and at the end.

Aquinas took that for granted and his historical subject lives in a world consistent with his cosmology in which causes tend to act from above or from below. Along the horizontal line man lives in society itself mirroring the society of the 'highest by the middlemost'. But as R. A. Markus has shown, Aquinas found greater profundity in man considered as a political animal than as a social animal.[39]

Perhaps this reflection comes as a surprise. But if we think of the hierarchical dimensions of the universe in medieval cosmology, putting the regimen of society before society itself is a quite consistent thing to do. Here too there is a factor making for openness in St Thomas. It can be illustrated by the apparently obscure subject of liberty, such as it would have been in the state of original innocence had it continued. It is the logic not the supposition which is interesting. If man had continued in that state, Aquinas holds, then the question of subjection to a ruler would indeed have arisen, since there would have to have been an authority to subordinate free rational activity to the common good.

But the question then arises, would not life under a rule have meant a lessening of individual freedom. Aquinas was no totalitarian. Augustine's answer to the problem had not on the face of it been very profound, though it was perhaps also the answer of the man in the street today. It ran to the effect that indeed the ruler would have had to govern his subjects, but that he would have done so with a regard for their freedom. Aquinas attempts to go deeper and further. He takes one of the two classical possibilities, as R. A. Markus explains them. It is either possible to say that 'any coercion implies a diminution of liberty', or alternatively that it is the purpose for which a man is coerced that determines whether his freedom is being restricted or not. The first possibility is the 'negative concept of freedom', and the second 'relies on the "positive sense" '.[40] Even this positive approach may seem to the modern mind to be too paternalistic or pedagogical to satisfy.

But in the case of Aquinas it is not, I think, too specious a point to urge this. Aquinas was determined to save the idea of the man, who is rational and free. He does so with the proviso that the ruler's purpose must be the subject's good, or that it must relate to the common good. On earth it is the business of the monarch, in his direction of earthly affairs, to 'facilitate the attainment of that [supernatural] end'.[41] Copleston sees a 'somewhat precarious synthesis' of Aristotelianism and the Christian faith here, and doubtless he is correct. However the fact that Aquinas runs a risk with this synthesis is all the more of a sign that he is determined to hold on to his transcendental and open-ended anthropology. If totalitarianism is foreign to him, it is surely because of his respect for an ultimate finality that lies beyond showing that all things are *propter Deum*.[42]

FORTRESS TRENT

It would seem more logical now to turn to Luther and make the contrast with Aquinas that has to be made. But I propose to postpone my remarks about Luther and to deal with the Council of Trent (Session VI, 1547, The Decree on Justification). I do that so as to bring out the historical consistency as well as the weakness in what was eventually decreed. The process will also allow us to see the weakness in the traditional strength of the Catholic system. An interruption at this point would make it more difficult to show how it was at Trent that Catholic man was, if not rounded off, at any rate given the hard outline which came to dominate the period of the Counter-Reformation. To speak very roughly Trent was Thomist with some Franciscan refinements, a process in which the historical and mystical man of the Augustinian tradition came to be overlaid in a one-track orthodoxy. For alternative thinking such as that of the Scotists and Augustinians was eliminated from the decrees during the process of drafting.

In one sense, but only one, the Council was even-handed. It is true that communications with the Lutherans had broken down, but it would be a mistake to think that there never had been any, or that the Roman front since the Bull *Exsurge* (1521) had been entirely solid. Two sets of Roman–Evangelical conversations had taken place (1539–1541; 1546). In 1530 the Confession of Augsburg had crystallized the most benign form of Lutheran doctrine. Not only was it an olive

branch to the Calvinists, but as late as 1561 the Cardinal of
Lorraine still thought that the Confession might serve as a
basis for discussion. It must also be remembered that when
Luther was personally condemned he had not yet rounded off
his system. Many more powerful writings were to come.
Influential minds such as Cardinal Contarini in 1541 still
thought before the Council that a rapprochement was
possible.

Although it intended to act both positively and negatively
giving a primacy to a formulation of Catholic doctrine,
Trent's reinforced medieval anthropology was a powerful *No*
to Lutheranism. It was, as Jedin points out, fortress thinking.
Even in 1547 the Decree on Justification was backward-
looking. It ignored the *Rinascimento* except for its
Aristotelianism. It ignored the *Devotio Moderna*. It had no
anthropology to offer Latin America whose bishops were not
represented. It occurred to nobody to consult the great
Dominican bishop of the New World, de las Casas. And yet
the philosophical divide persisted into the sixteenth century's
Wars of Religion and is perpetuated in Belfast till this day.
The excuse, if it was one, can be put down to the relative
confusion obtaining even in Italy. A sort of Catholic–
Spiritual movement had emerged. A Manual on how to
study theology beginning with the Pauline Epistles, Romans
and Galatians, had appeared and was strong in Lutheran
flavour. No later than 1530 it had also been possible to speak
of the 'religion of justification' as a European movement 'in
which the essentials of the Protestant doctrine of salvation
had been taken over into Catholic piety'.[43]

When we speak of Trent as a doctrinal triumph, we should
remember at what cost to the Church's theology it was
bought. The Council was not theologically speaking
properly medieval, nor did it belong to the modern era. It
was a hinge between these two worlds. The fortified
positions which it maintained remained basically medieval.
Its modernity lay in the power it retained through papal
enforcement to extrapolate its medieval concept of man, only
lightly touched upon by the Renaissance.

The drafting of the Decrees on Original Sin and
Justification was eventually the work of the Augustinian
Girolamo Seripando. He shows reliance upon the Latin

Fathers, obviously upon Augustine, and then upon St Thomas. There are occasional contrived ambiguities so as to paper over the differences between Thomists and Scotists. The Decree on Original Sin leans somewhat in the direction of Erasmus, Luther's one-time bugbear. Of the sixteen chapters on Justification it is Chapter Seven which stands out. For here an attempt is made to define the doctrine, and here in the Renaissance manner Aristotle's causes are driven hard.

Better than nearly all of his contemporaries, Seripando knew the writings of the Lutherans. He saw clearly that some opening must be made towards them. It must also be remembered that Seripando was preparing this draft in an area of Catholic theological uncertainty. Opinions had diverged too much for any easy assumptions to be made. At the very beginning of the Council Cervini admitted that justification was a difficult subject just because it was unresolved.[44] It was not therefore at all extraordinary that Seripando incorporated a theory of a 'double justification'. Cardinal Contarini and the Cologne theologians had succeeded in making this presentation acceptable to the Lutherans at the Colloquy of Regensburg (1546). What then did 'double justification' imply? History has made the theory seem like a pointless compromise. But that is the interpretation of a fixed and somewhat rigid hindsight.

As the name suggests 'double justification' proposed that the process and state referred to could both be imputed and inherently imparted. This clearly went some way to meet the Lutheran position. Justification was then imputed in the sense that it was Christ's own justice which was imputed to us. An important piece of the Lutheran system would then have been adopted by the Catholic Church, for the imputed justice which is Christ's takes place by the 'happy exchange', since we have Christ's justice imputed and Christ for his part takes on our guilt. The other side of the doctrine of 'double justification' is of course the doctrine of the inherent and permanent change in the believer. Seripando had a simple illustration to explain what he meant by his theory. In order that the eye may have vision it is normally dependent upon the light of the sun. But in practice I cannot for my vision rely upon the sun without its light or upon the light without the sun. I need both. Thus for Seripando the sun may be compared to the 'imputed justice' coming from Christ. On the other hand the light in which we are bathed may be compared to the inherent justice taught by the Catholic tradition. This concession made by Seripando in the seventh chapter of the Decree was after debate wrested from the draft. The *unica causa formalis* became the official Catholic doctrine.[45]

The Tridentine man who emerges from the exclusion of Seripando's 'double justification' has to be evaluated. Has the exclusion of the imputed justice of Christ made a notable difference?[46] The answer must be that, although at first sight Tridentine man appears to be completely accounted for, yet in fact he is maimed. He shares neither in God's creative mystery, nor in an appreciation of himself as mystery. He is considered as a nature in different states, but within a medieval universe of natures. There apparent disorder is always subject to a higher reason even as far as the *Prima Veritas* or the *Summum Bonum*. The basic immutability of the ultimate reality forms the frame for the universe of natures.

It is true enough that man lives also within the theological ages: the fall, the time of the Law, the time of Christ and the Church and the end-time that will not pass. This man inherits a universal history such as we find it in The City of God or in Bossuet. From the medieval point of view the justified man of Trent lacks something important. It is the aspect of belonging to a community, the *respublica Christiana* whose place in the Tridentine Decrees the Church does not succeed in taking. Tridentine man lives in a rectilinear time-way. Room is made for the *gesta Dei* which include grace. Grace raises freedom. Is Tridentine man free? As is well known Tridentine man emerges as theologically free (to the Lutherans impiously so), but with his freedom impaired. The testing point is of course his relative freedom when entering into the process of justification. Even there, Trent will say, he is free but impaired.[47]

But we can no longer look upon Trent's assertion of basic theological freedom in man, merely in terms of the Luther–Erasmus quarrel which had preceded it, still less in terms of one of the Tridentine legacies, namely the quarrel between Jesuits and Dominicans on the relationship of freedom to grace. That history alone shows how the anthropology of nature propounded by Trent was a dead-end. Equally the Catholic–Lutheran debate in terms of Trent is a dead-end. It is clear that in spite of its classicist clarity Trent lent itself to misunderstanding and, worse, to misuse.

In passing we may remark that Vatican II, while appearing not to do so, did in fact make its own attempt to set the record straight.[48] It too tried to answer the question, What is man? The Decree on the Modern World treated of a *constitutio hominis*. Of course there is the widest difference. Openness is now plainly present. The recognition of man in the historical process, in *Angst*, in psychological and social disturbance, beset by a world-wide perplexity — all this is not merely an answer to the challenge of the 'modern' or 'today's' world, as the Council suggests. It is also an implicit self-criticism of the Church, whom Tridentine man had sheltered from a world which centuries before had begun to be 'modern'. The papal imposition of Tridentine man on the Church especially in its moral teaching had already in the seventeenth century blocked Christian understanding in the East and in the New World. Even the Galileo débâcle owes something to Trent through the misuse of that partly Tridentine enforcement instrument, the Inquisition.

Two factors might yet have saved Tridentine man for the modern world, or even for his own widening environment. But they were denied him. One would have been, let us say, the stream of Stoic reason to be found in the humanist culture with which several of the Council Fathers were familiar. But humanism could not be indulged in at the Council. The Protestants across Europe were already inclined to think that the Catholic Church and Renaissance humanism were duplicates one of the other. On the Catholic side it was felt to be part of the Catholic Reform that this image of the Church should be suppressed. It was not known how to cope with it.[49] Indeed a humanist element at the Council would soon have been engulfed by the heavy metaphysical theologizing, which seemed to be the only answer to Protestantism, so far as the idea of man was concerned. The second way out has already been mentioned. It would have involved the Council in a genuine effort to get at the Protestant mind. We have seen that Seripando was over-ruled in the Council chamber itself. The suspicious reaction which met him and was blown up by the slick argumentations of Laynez was but part of a growing anti-Protestant affect. So much so that the influential Cardinal Pole, who came close to election as Pope on two occasions finally missing the tiara by one vote, indeed died while waiting to appear before the Inquisition as suspect of too great sympathy with the Protestants (1558). In a sense the way back to the medieval fortress, as reconstructed by Trent was inevitable.

We must conclude that the Tridentine man who emerges from the Decree on Justification after the removal of 'double justification' is a dangerous anachronism. He is a nature, rather than a person, within a universe of natures. Subjection is the key to order settled by the basic immutability of ultimate reality. Such history as he had was more universal than human. At the same time Tridentine man is like a well-constructed machine. We may think that he has something of the technical perfection of a da Vinci machine drawing, but of course without Leonardo's prophetic quality.

That does not exclude some powerful theological rhetoric either. In fact that is the method when it comes to the attempt to say what justification is. The seventh chapter with its causal analysis of justification, is in fact making a bow to the rhetorical tradition in theology reaching back to Cicero and Virgil: *cognitio est per causas*. Thus we should come to know what justification is by five causes. The *final* cause is God's glory, everlasting life. The *efficient* cause is the divine activity. The *meritorious* cause, the Passion of Christ as satisfaction, is accompanied by the *instrumental* cause, namely baptism. Lastly, the nub of the matter, the all-important single *formal* cause is God's justice used in a sense which the Reformers could not accept.

This analysis is in some ways a caricature of good Thomist theology, and it belongs as much, if not more, to theological rhetoric as to logic.[50] It does not tell us whether or not justification is true, or even how it operates since for example an instrumental or meritorious cause is by no means a cause in the same sense in which an efficient cause is a cause. Still less should the catalogue of other causes have been lumped together with a final or formal cause. On the positive side we can agree that the chapter is didactic insofar as it teaches that justification is indeed entirely God's work, save for the created and significant instrumentation of baptism. Few would now be satisfied to describe a sacrament as an instrument.

Let us list a few short conclusions:

(*i*) In Trent justified man takes on a specious appearance of being successfully explained, and therefore knowable. To that extent no advance is made. The description on causational lines is by the standards of the day a patent over-complication. Insofar as the analysis is anti-Pelagian it shows agreement with Lutheran aims. It is unfortunate that the relationship with Christ is left as either 'final' or 'meritorious'. Here Luther, Seripando, and Hooker had a deeper theological insight.

(*ii*) The language of the Council speaking of *homo* (women are philosophically, if not socially, included) is in keeping with its *natura* theology. In the general sense the text sometimes speak of *nos*, but more often of *homo, homines, omnes homines*. The subject of justification is the *interior homo* of whom *iustificari* is used. His communitarian existence is described in the phrase *Christianus homo* who belongs to the *populus Christianus* composed of *fideles*.

Among them we find types of men, *persons who: qui iustificati*, or *qui per peccata*, or *qui filii Dei*. In addition to the *fideles/infideles* there are the classes of persons whom the Church or the Council now threatens: *si quis/ne quisquam*. In respect of justification itself man falls into theological classes often mentioned in pairs: *parvuli/adulti; impii/nemo pius; iniusti/iustificati*. In addition to the *errantes/nutantes* we have also the *lapsi/renati, baptizati*.

The subject of justification is nevertheless capable of reflex conscious activity, and the following phrases are about as far as the Council will go along the dangerous innovative way of 'reflecting-upon-myself': *peccatores se esse intelligentes; movere se ad iustitiam* (in preparing for justification).[51] For its own purposes the Council could come near to Lutheran language too: *dum, peccatores se esse intelligentes, a divino iustitiae timore, quo concutiuntur* . . . This simple analysis could be pushed further, but is merely evoked here to show how the Council in the language it chose to use turned its back on man's self-conscious existence for the most part, and worse it left no possibility for man to be considered in his open-endedness.

(*iii*) The passing of the Decree on Justification in January 1547 inaugurated a long new phase in Church thinking. It received partial correction from Vatican II, and it is still too early to appreciate much less analyse the extent of the correction. Certainly at Trent doctrinal concord was henceforth excluded. The refurbished weaponry of its thought came into service almost at once.

Tridentine man was again very soon to be found in the Council's treatment of the Sacraments where the Lutheran *sola fide* had again to be excluded. This was emphasized in connexion with Baptism (March 1547). The anthropology in the Decree on the Eucharist does adopt one doctrine with open implications, namely that of the eucharist as a symbol of Christian unity (October 1551). The Decree on Penance exhibits much of the anthropology which the Council wished to oppose against Lutheranism. It is there that we find the doctrine on the relationship between contrition and attrition which had preoccupied the medievals after St Thomas, officially proclaimed. It follows from the closed concept of a *natura*-anthropology that there must be an integral confession of sin as well as sacramental satisfaction (November 1551). The moral theology of Extreme Unction (now the Anointing of the Sick) follows suit (November 1551). The theological roots of the doctrine of the Mass as sacrifice of course stretch back to Patristic times, but the consolidating of the medieval doctrine of the fruits of the Mass is more typical as an application of the Council's anthropology (September 1562), while the continued reinforcement of the doctrine of communion under one kind is both a medievalism and a piece of face-saving (July 1562). Naturally enough the notion of order pervades Tridentine thinking, especially when Church life is involved, and we find it invoked on the doctrine of Catholic priesthood (July 1563).

It has also to be admitted that the role of anthropology does diminish when the decrees take on more and more, as they do, the character of moral teaching or discipline. But equally the reasoning proffered, together with morality and discipline, is entirely consonant with the *natura*-anthropology we have sketched in outline. Morals and discipline also favour what we can only look upon as a depersonalized anthropology. No alternative to it was sought.

The Council Fathers of Trent dispersed on 4 December 1563. Implementation began soon after. The thrust, doctrinal as well as disciplinary, was papal. Within two years the Council's Catechism for the parishes appeared. The thenceforth normative Roman Breviary and Missal appeared in 1568 and 1570. The Vulgate version of the Bible, declared 'authentic', i.e. official, by the Council appeared in 1593 (Clementine edition). Here were effective proofs of the papal will to enforce the reforming thrust of the Council. What is significant for us is that the measures were in effect a practical reinforcement of a uniform religious anthropology. Moreover in Catholic lands sovereign rulers for their own reasons of state themselves reinforced papal policy. This was conspicuously marked at first in Italy, Portugal and Poland.[52] Naturally the speed of enforcement varied from country to country. But Rome at its own pace and with well-embedded malpractices to suppress did eventually become the capital source of Tridentine renewal.

Renewal inevitably implied centralization. That was consistent with the *natura*-anthropology of Trent. Thus Sixtus V (1585–1590) reformed most of the Roman Congregations. Their power was enhanced, and so was that of the Inquisition, established 1542, over doctrine. The Index of Prohibited Books had already been established by Pius IV in 1564. Later the Congregation for the conversion of 'infidels' became the famous Propaganda Fide (1622). Together with these reforms there emerged a new type of Cardinal, both erudite and pious, and that, in spite of some previous exceptions, was in itself something of a novelty.[53]

But where Tridentine man was outstandingly successful was in the reform of religious orders and in the establishment of new ones. It is difficult to judge precisely what should be meant by success. But we may mention the new theological era that opened at Salamanca, the protagonist of which was the Jesuit, Suarez (d. 1617). Here a Tridentine anthropology began to see a development of its own and to acquire a notorious emphasis upon the technical freedom of the will. Perhaps the highest human value of that performance lay partly in the development of casuistry, an effort to disburden the human conscience already used by the Stoics. In another way the anthropology of Suarez appears at its best in his writings on the theory of Law.

Yet Tridentine man also had a morbid and vexatious side. In due course it surfaced with yet another reading of St Augustine above all by Jansenius, bishop of Ypres. His very famous book, the *Augustinus* (1640) rapidly went into several editions. The ensuing movement was notoriously rigorous owing little *per se* to Trent. For Jansenius no concessions to self were at all permissible. Nor should the confessor ever use his casuistical skill to give his penitent the benefit of any sort of doubt. Pascal's protests against the weaknesses of casuistry can still force admiration out of us. They combine a noble irony with a skill in putting Trent and Augustine at the service of the genuinely interior man. That was quite positive thinking by one who was a Jansenist sympathizer. In addition there was the remarkable phenomenon of the way in which Tridentine man was opened up to the world. It was more than institutional loyalty which acted so powerfully in the new mission lands of Indochina, Mexico or South of Panama.

Yet the same anthropology was ill prepared for the task it set itself. The missionaries 'felt that exotic people could become genuine Christians only if their views, customs, and worship were first destroyed ("method of the *tabula rasa*")'.[54] Glazik is also right when he says that Trent hardly mentioned 'overseas lands, let alone discussed them'. The notion of 'conquering the world for Christ' still belonged to the Crusades. The famous crusader vow had originated in about 1046 and the spirit of the thing outlived the collapse in strictly crusading interest towards the end of the twelfth century. Repeated visits by navigators to the Canaries in the thirteenth and fourteenth centuries provided a link for the same motivation and eventually also a stepping stone to the New World. The real Christian conscience of Spain and of a humanity owing little to Trent appeared, as we have mentioned, with Bartolomé de las Casas (d. 1566).[55] The same would be true of the idea of man in New Spain where the Jesuits were not pioneers. Many anthropological strands were at work together. An overall picture is practically impossible, and the Tridentine elements did come in. In Mexico baptism was regarded as essential for the Indians. That was not specifically Tridentine. Stress on confession and matrimony, however, were, and so was the doubt as to whether the Indians should be admitted to communion. When in 1555 it was forbidden to confer major orders on Indians, mestizos, and mulattoes that was in conformity with the *natura*-anthropology of the Council. The Jesuit theorist of the missions, José da Costa (d. 1600) upheld the same view. Nor is it known that any Indian ever emerged as a priest in the Paraguay reductions.[56]

No one doubts that in addition to a certain native piety, theology and church discipline in Italy there were even more tangible expressions of the *natura*-anthropology. The art and culture of the baroque and rococo periods expressed it. Thus the spread of the faith, the repression of heresy are familiar themes in painting. Such was to be expected at a time when under Urban VIII (1623–1644) the papal states reached their greatest extent. It was then that the counter-Reformation coercion in Church discipline throve against a background of increasing political and even economic power. But in Italy, as in the New World, it must be thought that the prevailing ideology was wholly post-Tridentine. In public monuments and in the pictorial arts a certain pre-Tridentine humanism survived. The feeling may have been baroque, the thinking was pre-Tridentine. The same would be true of the return to Church discipline. It was a genuine return to an order the kind of which should have been present even in the state of pre-Tridentine chaos. It was in this perspective that the *natura*-anthropology took on the shape of seemingly rational instrument, albeit blinkered by its own urge to act authoritatively. So one could sum up the case of Galileo.

Indeed the post-Tridentine Church has been accused of conserving more than it actually created. I think it is better to use the metaphor of canalization. A stream had formerly meandered, now it was made to flow in great and deep force.[57] One small local indication of this tendency may help to illustrate what I mean. In the seventeenth century, Neapolitan painting came to acquire something of that force. Much of it was theological. So it becomes clear that when authority has to be invoked it will be in the depicting of one familiar Titan, St Augustine. He was often called in aid, for his was a congenial, artistically baroque and rhetorical authority with what must after Trent have been a very modern edge. Above all his theological sociology of the states of man was clearly defined. And seen through the grid of the Augustinian states, the Tridentine *natura*-man can be shown in all the drama of his anxiety and sin. Here on canvas are the *peccatores sese intelligentes* and those who, one must approve, *timore . . . utiliter concutiuntur* (DS, 1526). As di Maio rightly says, the paintings show an agony of fear on the one hand and the assertion of meritorious works on the other.[58] Not merely Tridentine Everyman, but his painter must also feel the agony. Giordano himself and his free independence of conscience was put in question by the Jesuits, who gave spiritual direction to the Neapolitan corporation of painters. Giordano is ironical about them and can even regret the restrictions put upon the liberty of the artist's conscience. What he was really regretting was the anti-Protestant anthropology that even Catholic Naples was made to experience.

In the pictorial appeal to Catholic doctrine anti-Protestantism was of course marked in Naples as elsewhere. Protestantism was made to appear as a form of disorder in human existence by contrast with the settled order that prevailed in Catholicism. The life of the religious orders seemed to be an exemplary case of the settled *natura* account of man. Their superiority in the matter of order was made to appear in the illustrations of what di Maio calls their *corporativismo conventuale*. These mini-corporate enclaves, with the Fascist overtone given by di Maio's word *corporativismo*, were felt to be a justified object of pride to a Catholic population. Theory and practice would be shown as an achievement of the post-Tridentine Church. The Institute and its Rule were singled out to prove the point. The power behind the Rule would be depicted as due to divine inspiration in the founder, or at least to the awesome power inherent in papal ratification. So the founder of an order holding a copy of its constitutions was a common theme. Even more, when the Jesuit monogram is affixed to the shield of the warrior archangel Michael, that constitutes an assertion that the Institute has a guaranteed eternity before it. In the example given by di Maio it is clear that the surrounding assemblage of *Padri* are already surrounded by that light which goes with assured celestial promotion. And the spirit of achievement can be more specific, for in Naples this is also the period of the painting of the Madonna of Purity. Tridentine concupiscence is thus kept overpowered.

At least Naples was innocent of the fanatical seventeenth-century disease of the witch-hunt. But it knew of the 'obsessive presence of the devil' which went with Counter-Reformation popular doctrine and inspired disciplinary regulations. For the clean boundaries of the Tridentine *natura*-anthropology required that any threats to its well articulated and ordered states be savagely repudiated. 'Private, social, and institutional cruelty was reflected or even stirred up in that [Neapolitan] iconography. The theory of the Counter-Reformation demanded that the brutality of the impious should be represented.' It was thus that popes, Catholic sovereigns and men of patronage saw to it that the fortress mentality of Trent should be preserved.

THE LUTHERAN BLOW

We should now turn to Luther. That does not simply mean turning from one system to another in thinking, at least not without a definite break. It means that we pass from an abstract metaphysical idea to a quite singular, concrete description of human experience. Though the first may be seen as a system, the second cannot. It would not be adequate to say that we can substitute one idea of man for another idea of man.

We have to start in a sense where ideas and experience meet. Hence we have to say a word about faith. At once it will be clear that the difference between Thomist scholasticism and the Lutheran insight is not to be measured. In Catholicism we may speak of the assent in faith, or of an act of faith. Such specification is not possible with Luther. It would almost be better to speak of a process of or in faith.

Aquinas has seen the believer as a subject, but as one who partly in propositional form accepts truths offered or commanded by the divine witness of the *Prima Veritas*. This anchorage means that those truths will be coherent as truths among themselves. The oneness of truth prevails. The act of the believer may not indeed strictly terminate in a proposition but in a reality. Nevertheless subject and object remain clearly distinguished and distinguishable. The objects of faith to be believed have to be proposed to the mind of the

believer. Different articles may call for a different assent, as
for example in the different propositions put forward in the
Creed. That does not disturb the unity, a unity in hierarchy it
may be, but nevertheless such a unity that it can be seen to
have an apex, the truths to be known *de necessitate salutis*. But
the truths whether of ends or means are homogeneous, and
the believing subject retains a rational coherence in his
thinking.

On all these counts Luther is radically different. There is a
good reason for this. It springs from his own experience. In
that lay his revolution. His own interpretation of his own
experience produced a theological and preaching *doctrina*
well removed from the question, distinctions and thematics
which had become the stuff of Catholic theology. Now in a
new way the believing person as believer enters into *the
what* of belief. As James Brown pointed out: 'This reverses
the categories of human thought and life in all other
immanent activities, and is appropriated in face of the
objective appearances of things in all other departments of
experience, in a supreme passion of subjectivity which is
called faith.'[59] This implies an objectification of experiencing itself, of the process of understanding experience, or any
judging or interpreting that may be involved. We are not
asking here whether that is a logical, appropriate or even
useful thing to do. We have to accept that Luther's
revolutionary theology implies an equally revolutionary
Christian man.

Most significantly then this unique theologizing entered
into the question of justified man and of justification.
Subjectivity is now at the core of theological activity. What
can have no place in the Catholic system, 'temptation'
(*Anfechtung*), challenge or doubt is now constitutive and
appears at the centre. The Lutheran *tentatio* becomes
indispensable. In the nineteenth century Catholic theology
reacted against any infiltration of Kantism, and the official
rebuttal of the *théologie nouvelle* school in the twentieth
showed clearly enough that things had not changed. There
was, for example, in the encyclical *Humani Generis* (1950)
enough Roman confidence that it [Rome] was 'able to
formulate the opposing position unequivocally, and to
demarcate its own official doctrine by positive statements'.[60]

Since then the struggle for pluralism in theology has served to show that the Tridentine *natura*-anthropology and its conception of clear lines of faith and its interpretation is an ever-recurring Catholic phenomenon.

A second and more operative difference must now also be noted. It follows from the structure of the so-called act of faith. The disclosure of the object of faith will now be wholly different. There will be a passage from non-faith to faith of course. That passage must now carry over within its movement a negative. That negative contains a positivity. For the quite extraordinary novelty is this, namely that there must be an intimate and necessary connexion between two unexpected opposites, namely the 'believing in' and the 'believing against'.[61] To start with Paul, of course it is clear that he teaches that justification positively comes through Christ *and not* negatively through the Law. Faith and Law are thus opposed. So far as Paul is concerned it is easy to understand that this *and not* referring to the Law is merely a linguistic or even logically excluding scheme. He accepts the one and rejects the other. In Luther that simple exclusion changes. Christ is the one object of faith. The attitude *and not through the Law* is far from being a merely logical exclusion. It is an exclusion of course, but it is such an exclusion that it influences our faith in the positive sense that it becomes part of it. That goes far beyond saying that the Torah is impotent. It implies that faith in Christ is reached through the believer's experience, *and not through the Law*. It is this new subjectivization of the object of faith that the process of thinking negatively, the *believing against*, also becomes part of the believing. There is no *believing in*, unless the *believing against* precede within the same process. The one provokes the other. Consequently *believing* cannot be separated from *not believing*. In this sense believing is always in process rather than an act. Luther's thinking cannot be freed from its inbuilt antitheses.

So in approaching Luther we have to be prepared for a different language, a language primarily of act or action, rather than of ideas or concepts. It is almost a language of perpetuated shock reaction. Luther had indeed shocked himself into being able to explore a new profundity in man. Medieval theories of knowledge could offer no counterpart.

Believing in God and in his grace now arises out of personal experience. We cannot ask for medieval, still less Tridentine, coherence. Seeking coherence or consistency is now a search in the wrong direction.

Otto Pesch finds a benign formula. He concludes not that the opposition lies between two forms of thought (*Denkformen*), but between two intellectual styles of performance (*Denkvollzugsformen*). We should not be misled by the word 'styles'. It goes deeper than appears. At the same time we can also say that the distinction is not radical enough. When in this older language Pesch explains that, while Aquinas is occupied with *sapiential* theology, Luther is occupied with existential theology, he tends to shroud over the anthropological differences.[62] For Luther, Thomas Aquinas was just one more of 'the sophists', whom he lumped indifferently with the Terminists and Ockhamists heartily despising them all.

What mattered was the reality of religious experience at its high point, in which for Luther overwhelming temptation was juxtaposed with an equally overwhelming certainty of being freed. Out of this clash together with his study of Galatians and Romans came Luther's doctrine of justification. Reason would have caused him to despair. God's judgment should of a certainty exclude him from imparted or infused grace. Facing that negative in itself, gave Luther an irresistible force in formulating his new doctrine.

Its rationale had to be one of sheer act and corresponding verbal expression rather than one logically conceived. Otto Pesch sees in it some form of existentialism. The term is direction finding rather than precise. Luther was such a pioneer that he ought to be given his own term. Following Theobald Süss, I would prefer some label such as 'actism' or 'actualism'.[63] For one thing, as we have seen the *No* and the *Yes* of his thought must be kept together. They were together in his experience and have since then been experienced together in some later forms of Lutheranism. The Lutheran *No* to Catholicism was profoundly experienced, and it had permanence. The Lutheran *Yes* to God and Christ was provoked and to some extent sustained by that *No*. The non–Lutheran must above all seek to understand the *Yes* to Christ, and to feel in sympathy, a religious sympathy, something of the force of the no less historic *No*.

But here we can leave out Luther's Church and social challenges. There are three points to note about the theological challenge:

(*i*) The Nominalist view of human nature had left the Roman Church theologically optimistic about man. That anthropology Luther had to attack, and Aquinas was included in the package. That inclusion gave Trent a handle, namely the choice of Thomism in rebuttal. Nominalism made Luther attack with total vehemence the theory that man could actually do some good works of his own without grace. That had to be branded as Pelagian. So Luther professed a full-blooded Augustinian account of the Fall. Having taken so much pessimism on board, Luther had to mitigate it. Here justification again came in, for it was supported by the *sola fide* and the *sola gratia*. He knew from experience that there was and could be no other passage from God's justice to his mercy.

(*ii*) Not only *natura* but a whole theory of knowledge had also stood in Luther's way. The varied Catholic tradition behind Nominalism was ignored by him, but it lived on relying on its different realist assumptions. It had not been heir to Greek realism for nothing. To use Pesch's term, we might say that the sapiential tradition knew that it knew. The Augustinian and Thomist strains at Trent were epistemologically quite self-reliant. In its high Thomist version the knowledge that mattered was guaranteed by its participation in objective being.

In the case of theological science knowledge belonged to wisdom in a special way. It was not indeed the knowledge that belonged to wisdom in the sense of relying upon the infusion of the Spirit. That would be a special gift. Rather it was a knowledge which also depended upon an anthropology of *natura*, since it was knowledge by connaturality. *Natura* was the link that made the sharing possible. So the assenting human judgment shared in a connatural way with its divine object. That did not mean that study could be given up. It was nothing else than intellectual inquiry (*Inquisitio rationis*) from which this knowledge by connaturality could emerge. It was not a mystic knowledge, or an experience of the Spirit. It was the *natura*-anthropology about its proper work.

Most of the above comes from St Thomas. Its chief

distinction was its continuance in tradition as in various ways
normative. Trent did not depart from it. The chief non-
Lutheran threat later on would be the Catholic Descartes.
But Luther found a weakness. The system was not forced to
stand by a strong distinction between philosophy and
theology. With Ockham and Biel it could. In Luther it had to
do so. For him it was fundamental that philosophy and
theology are wholly distinct. But by the same token
'philosophy knows almost nothing about man in comparison'. It is 'theology from the plenitude of its wisdom' that
'defines the whole and perfect man'.[64]

So the conflict between faith and reason is sharpened. In
Luther's eyes reason is concerned with the physical world
which perishes. In later life Luther could be relatively
concessive and hostile to Aristotle at the same time.
Otherwise for him as we know, reason is a whore (*die Hure
Vernunft*), and there is 'no identity of truth between
philosophy and theology'.[65]

That makes Luther his own master. Reason is too material.
It cannot be of service to divine truths. Moreover faith as
infused by the Spirit is a rejected doctrine. For one thing
there can be no possible room for the Thomist idea of a
disposition in man (*natura*-anthropology) whereby he comes
to assent and thus to believe. Luther's God acts, he 'excites'
faith through his Word. He gives himself. In us faith takes
the Word, which for Luther specifically means that it takes
Christ. So now in place of the infused and raised disposition
to believe, we have the immediacy of an encounter — with
Christ. In this actualist perspective commitment comes
before assent. Commitment is primary.

In this way Luther lays hold of man's approach to God so
as to change the very concept of man. In *natura*-anthropology
the leading edge was given to the rationality or intellect of the
nature. The leading edge now becomes affectivity (*affectus*).
Simply put, this may sound merely Augustinian, and thus all
we have to do is to mention its corrective. The corrective was
classical and had served well. It was the *fides quarens
intellectum* which provided that corrective, or indeed set up a
creative dialectic. Luther escaped from it, and what he did
proved to be an historic *tour de force* in thought. *Fides* now
seeks *affectus*. We have a *credo ut faciam*.

It meant among other things the rejection of the classic sheet anchor gripping certitude, certitude about God and certitude over man's knowledge of him. That anchor had been the doctrine of the analogy of being. But for Luther our knowledge of God was too deficient. It could not rise to him. The only escape route must be that of experience. Above all through the Bible, and perhaps through some of the traditional elements that suggested God, a possibility, really existed. But anthropologically speaking, 'Because we have the Bible', we can understand or define what *homo theologicus* may be. With Gregory of Rimini Luther would insist upon the powerlessness of argument to produce certitude. Certitude he desperately wanted, and in the process the false certitudes of the sophists about God had to be opposed.[66]

(*iii*) But the most powerful blow against tradition was in itself the Lutheran article on justification. Luther fixed it for ever in his formula, *simul iustus — simul peccator*. It was fundamental and wholly typical. It soon showed itself as the spearhead of the theological attack on the 'ancient way'. By concentrating upon man as an experiencing subject, and no longer as a *natura*, this challenge of Luther's disregarded all 'works'. These could perhaps enhance a *natura* in a stable metaphysical world. But now in Luther's actualism man is always in becoming and always in act, so the stable basis for enhancement by 'works' disappears. Even more is this true, if man, as in Luther's discovery, was not at all homogeneous with himself. The now dyadic being-in-becoming could not be acted upon as though it were a simple *natura*. Before the question, What is man?, Luther had to see him as 'pure matter' existing in view of the 'future form', now submitted to sin and death as well as 'oppressed by the devil'. That must be the case, since for Luther the world itself is not a realm of reason, but as Paul says rather a *schema futuri*.[67] Within and without anthropology has changed. Set against the old clear outline afforded by a *natura* philosophy, we now have a dyadic creature of and in process, which though oppressed may yet emerge into a rationality that can only be of the future.

A NEW HORIZON

Yet Luther by no means stuck to being only on the attack. Movement in man would not wholly prevail, and it would be after all within something recognizable as man. There was *a being* in privation, in becoming, a power, a *materia*. That thought alone could leave room for some relics of Aristotelianism. In his mind Luther came to think that all he had done was to attack the abuses of the system, not its foundation. But there was no power left in him when he came to such an acquiescence. The power continued to come from Augustine, and much of it from the Augustinian transmission of the private theory of evil, namely that evil is simply the absence of good. To some extent it was that ancient theory which erupted in the basic paradox of Luther's theological anthropology, the famous *simul iustus — simul peccator*.

In fact that old Augustinian stream now became a full flood river. It gained greater force, perhaps, from the fact that its old inner logical tension was now going undisguised. Trent indeed tried to stem the flood with its historic blueprint of man. The result is our all too Christian and historic antagonism of anthropologies. I am saying that the roots on both sides are so deep as to have defied all resolution till now. Certainly the ecumenist of the common ground cannot cope with the profound implications of the problem.

For the clash is about our life and death struggle with religion's obsessive preoccupation, namely sin. The *simul iustus et peccator* is an inescapable pointer to man's greatest sickness. Catholics and Protestants try and face the fact that they have to live with and cope with the strange unholy world of sin. In a post–Freudian situation we know how ambiguous it can be. Catholics were initially hostile to the Freudian exploration. They had to be. Man in his fortress static state came forth to do his wicked act. But now he was threatened from within. The primary understanding of sin was undermined.

Simpler than the Fall story is that of Cain slaying Abel, a guilty and originatingly guilty act. It is entirely in harmony with Trent to see Cain passing from a state of relative innocence to that of permanent guilt and disfigurement.[68] The sense of sin is primitive and has hardly changed. The way Aquinas takes the act of murder as a paradigm is entirely consistent with this. The Catholic paradox then lies in this, that the more man is viewed as a fixed *natura* in a state the more is his disfigurement identified not with a state but an act, a movement with its consequences.

With Luther things go in the contrary direction. As we have suggested, his ontology of act and becoming give him a more dynamic picture of man as a reality but in tension. As a result he is required to see the paradigmatic form of sin as rather a state than an act. The mode of sinfulness in tension then issues in action, which is secondary to the state from which it sprang. That is consistent with two things: Luther's own experience and Luther's total rejection of 'good works'. One cannot pass from act to state, only from state to act.

Sinful*ness* is thus Luther's starting point. And here we again hark back to Augustine. His element of evil desire or tendency is demonized. Luther is clear: 'Therefore actual sin (as the theologians call it) is strictly speaking the work and fruit of sin, and sin itself is that passion (tinder) and concupiscence, or that inclination and resistance against the good . . .'[69] This theory of sin rests, as it does in Augustine, on the idea that man is moved by one of two loves. Either he is moved by a selfish love leading to wholly self-interested action against the divine law, or he is moved by a pure, benevolent, even ecstatic, love acting regardless, if need be, of self. These two principles in various forms are profoundly engrained in Western theological man. The principles and their applications are on the whole easily recognizable, and the traditions have lived by them.

Anthropologically the Christian can thus hardly separate the *what-man-is* from the *how-man-lives*. Nor can Christian man's way of loving in tradition be easily separated from his becoming more or less perfect as man. That too is a common Augustinian inheritance. At the same time, within the limits of this discussion, it is also commonly agreed that perfectibility at least *de facto* is never attained. The reasons, again traditional, are both metaphysical and moral and do not concern us here. What does concern us is the common acceptance by Catholic and Protestant of the impossibility of perfection.[70]

By this route I come back to ecumenism of the common ground. With the best will they can muster both the partners in dialogue are blocked. The reasons are not technical or ecumenical. They concern the religious identity of the partners. Catholics and Protestants have a different view of their own proper religious capacities and incapacities. The

Catholic, with the Tridentine blueprint of himself in mind is led by a mirage of rectilinear religious progress. His Protestant brother is in a contrary state. For he finds himself in a field of opposing forces. He also sees himself as more deeply incapacitated from within. His stance forbids him to see the possibility of any rectilinear progress at all. For long he has lived without the idea of any sort of mechanism along which God in the Thomist–Aristotelian fashion will act. More than that, since faith is so important for him, he cannot dispense with some version of the *believing against* so as to *believe in*. That very attitude in itself removes the possibility of the, so to call them, Catholic mechanisms.

It should be clear that an inner freedom is the issue here. For Luther freedom in the Christian man in the theological sense can belong only to God. For this intrinsically respectable reason and because of the anthropology which goes with it, it should surely appear that ecumenism must take a quite new turn. Loyalty to traditions, searching for clues in the waste land of the common ground can yield only irrelevant *bric-à-brac* with which to reconstruct. For overriding anthropological reasons the approach must be directed immediately to God and immediately to the believer.

For the paradoxes of Lutheran man, are those of a real, if mysterious man. They must now touch the Catholic, who for his part must re-admit Seripando to this extent.[71] Unless he is prepared to take on board the implications of the historic and actual Lutheran witness in faith to Christ, there will be no Catholic doctrine of justification that still lives. The price then will be that the Catholic doctrine of justification will simply fail in catholicity. Vatican II made way for this when it declared: '. . . division among Christians prevents the Church from attaining the fullness of catholicity proper to her . . .'[72] We do not have to add that a non-ecumenical Roman Church would no longer be a Church of her own insights. Catholic man and Protestant man as subjects of justification cannot be excluded from that awesome condition.

In consequence three things ought to be clear: (*i*) Catholic theology on justification is called upon to de-absolutize itself. The Catholic post-Tridentine anthropology does not now possess any pre-emptive rights over any other anthropology held by a Christian who is a mainline student of the gospel. (*ii*) the Catholic theology of justification will have to seek how it may displace from the centre some of its own axioms. Key concepts like 'state' and 'act' will have to come up for revision, as also 'desire', 'consent', 'work', 'merit', 'nature', and 'maturity' and 'adult'. (*iii*) the Catholic theology of justification will have to be carried well beyond the frontier established by an illusory ecumenism of the common ground, and brought into an area with a new horizon. Put shortly this theology may have to seek its own death, so as to rise again.

De-absolutizing, or seeking a new horizon may have to be sought from outside as well as inside the ambit of ecumenical dialogue. The reason that must be said is that qualitative as well as relational thinking needs to be brought into play. When the Protestant has said that by his doctrine of infused grace, the Catholic has contradicted the common doctrine of the *sola gratia*, he has done the Catholic a service. He has urged that grace above all relates. It has not yet reached Catholic preaching how the mysterious quality of grace above all *relates us* in our concrete living to a new centre of gravity, the loving God. But it should have done so. More room should already have been made for the God-to-man and the man-to-God relationships. At the same time we are almost wholly unaware of the man-world set of graced relationships, because we still basically fail to see that the total field of grace-love is a bi-polar field of crossing currents, God-to-man and man-to-man. In such a field of forces Luther's actualism can become a theological process in grace and love. The horizons, above all, must change. Can ecumenism begin to pray that we may be 'lifted up into the bosom of the Father . . . clad in the finest raiment, our feet reaching out below the garment, and Satan bites them when he can . . .'?[73] If the ecumenist's thoughts can genuinely become Godward, then mere human relativities may fall into place. Of course in the concrete all is not rationality, and our love still needs purification. But in the ongoing process of human becoming and open-ended rationality justification can be taken into the perdurance of man's dyadic tension.

INVOLVEMENT BEYOND

Hard things can become easier. Until recently it was hard for

the Tridentine man to enter at all into the theological world
of Luther. Recent writings have in part tried to say how
much that is Catholic is to be found in Luther. Professor
Gordon Rupp agrees that this is so and that it is a good
thing.[74] In consequence Catholics should not be told that the
harmony they postulate between 'nature' and grace is not
what it seems to be.

A popular example could be taken from the banal side of
auricular confession. The equation is set between the
confessing of sin and the cancellation of sin, with the danger
of forgetting repentance and forgetting the forgiving God.
So the pin-pointed catalogue, the 'how far can I go, Father?',
the mechanical performance of the work of penance — these
things (how they could be is another matter?) are not the
elements of an adult dialogue between an adult penitent
believer and God, his Father. There is certainly a new
Catholic consciousness of God as the Other. It is perhaps
thin-spread, but it is present. It can appreciate that the
Lutheran theology of justification is neither simply wrong,
nor milk for babes. James McCue in an illuminating version
of the *Sitz im Leben* of Luther's version of justification says a
necessary thing:

> The doctrine of justification is addressed to those who have
> recognized God's law in all its fullness and radicality as
> addressed to them and meant for their lives, who have tried to
> live up to those demands and have experienced the depths of
> their failure.[75]

The Catholic theologian now ought no longer to be caught
up by the dilemma *either my/our system* of thought is able, *or
no other system* of thought is able to support me or us in our
efforts to see further into God's truths. For Christian
theology is also part of man's dialectic with God. It cannot
avoid that dialectic, as it continues to take the truths it seeks
seriously. Corresponding with that privilege it is under a
constraint, a higher constraint both more human and more
divine, than a *magisterium* can impose. Theology cannot itself
escape a measure of the contradiction which it discovers in
justification itself. The contradiction flows from the open-
endedness of the subject, who is in dialogue while he yet

reasons and explores. Anyone who has followed the treatment of Catholic theologians by the Roman *magisterium* since *Humani Generis* (1950) does not need to have this spelled out. For the engaged quality of theological thinking places it under the same law as the gift of salvation. The issue is clear in the Epistle to the Romans. There salvation does not come to man in linear fashion. We cannot say that in Romans God's righteousness is simply to be equated with God's love. There is a fusion of two moments in God's salvationary act. One of them is God's act of creation in itself.

In reading Romans the Catholic has to be especially aware that the acting God is not the God 'Up there where man does not exist'. The Creator God who is the Saviour God of our Bible is not a philosophical God at any stage. Thus in Genesis God is not simply even God the father of all men. In the Yahwist's account of creation the author's interest is 'completely directed towards those relationships in which *man is completed* to recognize his humanity from the very beginning'.[76] These relationships spring from God's interest in and address to man. Further God in creating improves his first version of man by giving him a partner. In a further way God determines man by relating him to the earth. Thus God from the beginning conducts dialogues with man. The divine decision in which dialogue becomes dialectic for man is clearly seen in the Priestly version, but the Yahwist and Priestly writers are agreed upon the many-sided dialogical element of human existence. With God, with his partner the man must be in dialogue, and only so can he recognize others as brother and as person. But crisis comes and so does condemnation together with the mystery of death. One thing is clear about that mystery. Yahweh is involved in the challenge or temptation (*Anfechtung*) it poses. That is the dialoguing God and challenging God whom Paul proposes as Saviour, so the constriction to man's faith does not entirely come from within himself. And yet in Romans it is also clear that man's salvation in its very dialectical form is somehow not outside him. God's sovereign decision also itself works in Paul, Augustine and Luther from within. So it is in his hiddenness that God enters into the sinner's rejection. His turning on the Cross to the sinner-believer is fully a *God-theology*, and that is just as characteristic for the agony of theologizing as for the agony of any life lived in critical belief. The Lutheran opening of man teaches the theologian that his very *theo*-logy brings God into theological experience on the same terms of experience as those in which the God-man lived and died.

This is not meant to be a recommendation of dolorism. Far from it. It is meant to insist on the obvious fact that human experience is not to be evacuated from the process of theologizing. The Christian life and the theological life of the Christian is an *experimental* life. This does not of course imply that in his experience of God the theologian can not be bound objectively to his subject. Thomas Torrance has seen this very well. It is a two-sided business. Objectivity is demanded by rationality. And yet in theology as in other special sciences 'man is yet free, active and spontaneous in his epistemic relations, while part of his freedom at least consists in his knowledge of his unconditional relation to the object, as well as his determination to use his knowledge of the object'.[77] This very God-given freedom to the theologian can far from being restricted also be expanded.

The Catholic theologian under Lutheran impulse can well allow in a quite fresh way that religious paradox may have its lawful place. Secondly, from Luther, *Doctor hyperbolicus*, the role of tension has something to offer. For a tension between faith and love is not only a possibility, it is a challenge demanding acceptance or rejection. It is not of course a tension between human willing and human thinking that has to be rejected outright. Thirdly the fortress tradition of Catholic theology has to learn that it has missed something vital. And that is another tension in which we live, namely the proleptic tension between the altogether *unfulfilled now* and the *eschaton*, the now of faith and the consummation of love in the end (cf. 1 Cor 13: 9ff.). A Catholic anthropology fully given to man in his actual becoming would be forced to listen to Luther as well as to Paul. Fourthly we must attend to the *theologia crucis*. I have argued something for this case in Chapter Three. Being before God is in need of a concreteness which the Tridentine anthropology cannot give it.

In live faith, presence before God is necessary to faith, and a *coram Deo* is a genuine condition of the Spirit. It is inevitable that in this opaque state of faith, the inherent paradox of God concealed and God revealed has to be lived with. There is no other way through the tension of the contraries we experience. How else is progress made through — 'love-hate'; 'free-man-slave'; 'life-death'; 'flesh-spirit'; 'letter-spirit'; 'law-gospel'; 'action-passion'; and most frequently the concrete condition, 'just sinner'? Luther is not wrong in thinking that this is where God's saving action meets us. These tensions in the *homo talis qualis nascitur* are open-ended. It is indeed true that we are here ourselves, and yet not ourselves. All this can be read off from our eucharistic liturgies. In the penitential rite of every Mass we declare ourselves *simul peccatores*.

It should be clear that both for the Catholic and the Protestant the same way of resolution is present and it is single. For Luther and indeed for the Catholic also, it is the value and accessibility of the Incarnation. That is to say that there is a death of God theology which in love pre-empts all attempts after Nietzsche to have God killed by his own death. In the death of the deathless one the words of despair on the cross are words of love. It is true that on the subject of the death on the cross Luther can be unbearable. But his subjectivity does join with and enter into his objectivity of faith. Here too there exists a unique intentionality which validates the subjective appearance of things. Why not admit that he reaches and offers a coalescence of the *fides quae* with the *fides qua*. It is not necessary to confuse the term with the procedure.

What may have to be said to Luther's disadvantage is perhaps this. His ambition to be the total Scripture reader is not necessarily fulfilled or rightly taught. He is for example weak on the Fourth Gospel. But we must find a way of looking at this weakness which is constructively ecumenical. Could we not say that there is an apprehension of divine mystery which is all-apprehension, a *totum*? It may not go all the way. It may not do so exhaustively, or let us say, *totaliter*. No more than Trent can Luther exhaust what has to be said and thought. But theology is great enough for a theologian to achieve an illumination of the whole, even in his partial apprehension.

· Why can it be said that there is a *totum* in the Lutheran apprehension? I would look for it in the reality of his Christ as his *Seelengrund* (the ground of the soul). To justify this point we would have to see how the locus of the mystical theme of the 'happy exchange' for Luther lies in the soul itself. For Luther it is by the 'happy exchange' that Christ takes on man's sin and gives his own righteousness. In an excellent study Erwin Iserloh shows how Luther in his *On the Freedom of the Christian Man* connects the 'happy exchange' 'with the mystical idea of faith as the marital embrace between the soul and Christ'.[78] For Luther as in Eckhardt and Tauler there lay the basic and graspable reality of theology.

CONVERGENCE

It is time to see whether the hierarchy of truths tells us something so that we can answer the question posed by this chapter: Should we dispense with justification? Should the 'article', justification, be entirely omitted from the Catholic-Lutheran dialogue? Regrettably the answer must be a Yes and a No. Of course the historic battle-ground should be abandoned, with, however, an abiding respect for the reasons which prompted it. But in the first years of the struggle we have an example which should still serve as a warning. Between 1520 and 1526 the flare-up of books between Erasmus and Luther was a massive dialogue of the deaf, of the deaf simply talking past each other. Minds did not meet for the basic reason I have been putting forward in this chapter. Neither could share the other's concept of man.

The phase of the ecumenism of the common ground exhibited especially by today's inter-Church dialogues is different. There has been a tacit agreement to put the question of a common or non-common concept of man in parenthesis. Outside the parentheses the search for a common ground has continued. One outstanding theological example of this process was Küng's early work, *Justification*. It is clearer now than it was on the work's first appearance, that it could only go a little way. Precisely because the question of the hierarchy of truths did not then arise, many objectives remained unattained and the resulting accumulation of pros and cons leaves unfinished and unresolved problems. Küng's book had to be left with many objectives unattained. His merit was above all to show that between Lutheran and Catholic theologies there was a genuine and common anti-Pelagian stand. He also showed that the possibility of convergent interpretations of vital Bible texts were becoming increasingly frequent. But it was quite another matter to show that when Catholic tradition distinguishes between 'objective sanctification' and justification there was the possibility of satisfying the Lutheran mind. Nor is it clear that Küng did succeed in establishing a common ground on such topics as, man *qua* man, the enslaved will, and the important question of 'assurance'.[79]

When measured against the ecumenical urgency of today the results obtained by Küng in a strenuously worked book were meagre. He was not in a position then to shift the centre of gravity of the discussion. That I think is what the hierarchy of truths bids us do. In some respects the inter-Church dialogues mentioned in the first section of this chapter are beginning to do this. But it is not looking backwards that holds out much promise. In their preoccupation with technicalities that is what ecumenically-minded authors have been tempted to do. When Otto H. Pesch insists on the difference between the sapiential and the existential styles of theologizing, a way may be opened. But it is not a clear one.

An example of a more flexible approach to boundaries would be finding a fresh treatment for the question of faith and works. Must the sixteenth-century opposition between these two continue to block any reconciling theology? There have been both Lutheran and Catholic scholars ready to maintain that the confessional boundary must remain in existence. Peter Manns thinks that above all there is a lack of a single theological foundation behind what consensus exists. Others follow Lortz and accept as a premise of history that behind the Reformation the fundamental concern was catholicity — the search for catholicity or the recovery of it. In that view one can safely deny that the confessional boundary, hidden or not, must abide for all time.[80]

Whether or not there does exist a boundary as has been described, I am not certain. However, I tend to think that, if the question of such a boundary is too energetically raised, then the necessary search for theological convergence on the basis of an open-ended anthropology will be inhibited. There will be a relapse into an ecumenism of the common ground.

On the other hand, if the thesis that the Reformation was and is basically a search for catholicity can be sustained, then another spring-board for convergence is offered us.

But we can ask why should not the technicalities be left on one side, and then further why should not newer signs of convergence be recognized? Both the Catholic and Lutheran traditions now seem to have it in them to provide such a common sign. I am thinking of the strongest piece of Christian witness they could give which would also most helpfully be of an anthropological nature. Can we not on both sides of the divide take even more seriously than we do our appreciation of the fact that Christianity is a religion of and for freedom. Of course that needs much defining. Of course both traditions have in their day failed always to exhibit this very charism which should be theirs. *Pro tanto* they have also failed the gospel of Paul in Romans.

But where both the traditions have coincided in weakness, may they not now meet in strength? If the possibility is a real one, and I believe that it is, then it can prove to be our greatest and strongest plus in any reckoning of our beliefs. The form that such a strength should take is surely the prophetic one. Are not both traditions ready for an increase in prophecy? Over social justice, liberation, peace, toleration. All these aspects of the human condition are much nearer to the significance of justification for today than is generally supposed. If one looks at Lutheranism why should it not be taken quite simply for granted that the Reformation enshrined and passed on a genuinely prophetic impulse? Ebeling asks why it was that 'the Reformation did not remain a matter of mere words, but was actually carried out'. He does not mention prophecy. But his answer points quite clearly in that direction. The reason why the Reformation was carried out was, he says, 'precisely because the Reformation was not regarded as a matter of action, but *purely as a matter of the word* (author italics).[81] There can be no doubt that preaching is meant and the Word of God which is preached. And Reformation preaching had immense authority for a prophetic reason. It set out to defend the absolute nature of God. It did this concretely and in a way that the individual knew was addressed to him. The theological name for the process was justification. As a result this prophetic word brought about a change not only in men's ways of considering God, but in their way of considering themselves. The static concept gave way to the concept in movement we have considered. It cannot be excluded that Liberation Theology will do something of the kind in Central and Latin America.

The 'angry old men' of the German Evangelical tradition are still capable of a prophetic word of protest. The prophetic value of protest lives on after death. Thomas Münzer was an inspiration to the Marxist utopian prophet Ernst Bloch.[82] Much of the latter's prophetic force came not only from Karl Marx but also from the Gospels. From a seriously theological point of view it becomes clear that, in spite of the human optimism which inspires small successes in the step-by-step approach or in the ecumenism of the common ground, a real *aggiornamento* over justification is far from being achieved. For justification is not a doctrine among others concerning God and man. It is a critical principle as well as a doctrine. It is a test of authentic response. It continues to make demands as strange as the demands of the gospel always are. I list three here as of greater importance for genuine theologizing:

(*i*) Justification asks about our 'glorying' in our Christian past. It asks if our own attitude towards our Catholic theological past is authentically Christian. Is it sufficient to preach reform and repentance according to a past idealized model of the Church in which episcopal authority, living in a technical state of perfection hands down correction in the shape of a return to the idealized model which never existed? It is not episcopal or papal authority as such which is in question. The question is a more subtle one. We have to ask whether we are not being urged towards some idealized, originally pagan, *Roma aeterna* which is being sought for? Why should the pilgrim Church, the people of God, the *respublica Christiana*, be harangued, cajoled, and even bullied along the lines of a 'return' — to what? When theology is castigated, Church discipline 'renewed', the touchstone must be real, and as justification demands, it must be about God. In reality the slogan term 'renewal' betrays itself. Should we not rather be invited to doctrinal or disciplinary 'advance', or 'progress'? The fact is, as O'Malley points out, the 'term "progress" is less frequently used to describe what is happening in the Church than are the traditional descriptions of "renewal", "renovation", and "rejuvenation" . . . These terms in themselves suggest cyclic or repetitive patterns of history rather than linear progress'.[83] Indeed terms like 'reform' or 'reformation' are practically absent, and it might be said that the word 'aggiornamento' has in practice now been abandoned, a small indication of the way the wind of officialdom has blown.

Only the adoption of an open-ended anthropology which bears some resemblance to the self-consciousness of the thinking world of today can correspond to the demands of the gospel. Justification requires that we take man seriously as he really is in his concrete existence. We must not forget that there are anonymous Catholics, Protestants as well as 'anonymous Christians'. The divide over justification has encouraged anonymity. The anonymity is ready for the gospel, but only for a gospel presented in accordance with its real demands. These cannot be met on the *Roma aeterna* principle. Nor are they met by the historic assumption that all other preaching than one's own is Pelagian. Radicalness and human realism are needed on both sides.

(*ii*) The second basic gospel demand is, I think, both theological and of the Spirit. It concerns openness and conversion. Lutheran faith-assurance is closely bound up with conversion. This is interior and on-going. A Catholic doctrine of conversion is also foundational and basic. It is not simply basic to a way of living, as common preaching often suggests. It is an existential process which enters into theological judgements and choices. It enters into man's communication with God in faith and changes man himself in the process.

The grace given in the human struggle with alienation, suffering, commitment, love and personhood, the clean *caesura* in knowing between pure subject and pure object disappear above all in the encounter with God. Lutheran faith-assurance was envisaging just this. In a post-Cartesian, post-Kantian, post-Hegelian world it affects the Catholic too. 'I believe' or 'I trust', like 'I opt for' or 'I love', is now offered a reward for its concern, an intimacy for its trust, a promise for its option and a Thou for its committed Ego. Theologians have long caught up with this, but the projected image of the *magisterium* does no such thing. It conceives its function differently and uses the term 'faith' differently. And there certainly exists a Catholic wing which would find no difficulty about obliging a modern Bautain to sign a number of propositions, just as in 1840, or in demanding even today a commitment from Church teachers to the anti-Modernist oath.[84] Such a form of social programming is easily confused with the demands of the gospel.

Yet we all know that the truths of faith are not a set of random or unconnected disclosures, and we are beginning to see better that those at the apex of a hierarchy must command those lower down. Our truths, in which I do place justification very high as to its mysterious core or heart are intimate disclosures. They are significant of and significant for my highest interest. They may demand martyrdom. They also express my desire. And desire is focused by conversion. Augustine wanted to know God and the soul. Nothing more.[85] There is the thread of ongoing salvation wholly invested with interest and desire. It may be particularized at a lesser point in the scale of gospel truth. But the aim will be encounter with God and his Christ.

The Lutheran brought a new understanding to this truth which does tie the Church back to the gospel. A *fides* which is *apprehensiva* itself enters into the object to be believed. In so doing it does breach that clean caesura between the knower and the known. On the Catholic side, since we are talking of the encounter with Christ, this process is also possible. St Thomas himself, unlike Trent, does imply an open-endedness in man especially with respect to faith and knowledge. For him the primary object of faith is the wholly personal *Prima Veritas*. It is God, not merely as guarantor, but as self-communicator especially in his incarnate Son. We should add, though Luther does not, that the self-communicating God is the God of happiness. So the Known entered into by the knower completes the knower. St Thomas sees the believer almost like a yo-yo on the end of the string returning to the hand that sent it out. This movement ranges over all that is to be believed; but the articles to be believed are inherently related in one direction, that of the return to God.

Of course it is not along the lines of a metaphysics of

symbols that Catholic and Lutheran can meet in discussing the atonement. Nevertheless in the clustering of symbols around the love of God they can meet under the eye of their common master, Augustine:

> But yet when I love thee, what is it that I love? Not the beauty of any body, not the order of time, not the clearness of this light that so gladdens our eyes, not the harmony of sweet songs of every kind, nor the fragrancy of flowers or spices of aromatical odours, not manna, nor honey, nor limbs delightful to the embrace of flesh and blood. Not these things do I love in loving my God. Yet I do love a *kind of light*, a *kind of voice*, a *kind of colour*, a *kind of food*, a *kind of* embracing, when I love my God, who is the light, the voice, the odour, the embracing of my inward man . . . That it is which I love when I love my God (Confessions X, 6, 8).

Here is a set of apperceptions which could hardly be more personal, can hardly in any way be bettered to tell us that ongoing faith leaps over that caesura between the human knower and the divine Known.

I have pleaded for a new Catholic anthropology in the sense that touches authority and the grass-roots believer. Theologians since Teilhard de Chardin, if not from De Lubac onwards, have been well aware of the need. But ecumenical openness is not for mandarins only. It must be an openness to the divine, rather than to magisterial, critique, and that exempts no one. Thus both the Catholic and Lutheran obedience to Christ and his gospel, is a shared obedience and cannot be otherwise. But it is also an obedience in faith, of which the defects are supplied for by Christ. If we unveil ourselves to something more of the reality of justification we shall find that 'the doctrine of justification is addressed to those who have recognized God's Law in all its *fullness* and *radicality* as addressed to them and meant for their lives, who have tried to live up to those demands and have experienced the depths of failure.'[86]

Doubt, failure or 'losing the faith' were not popular topics among Catholic writers. The fully-rounded man of Trent could not be expected to run the risk of defecting without fault from the perfect society, which was the Church. Following upon Vatican I majority opinion had to hold that without some fault, possibly remote, it is impossible to defect from the Catholic faith. In *Redemptor hominis* there is a section on 'the Church as Responsible for the Truth'. Thus Christ in 'transmitting' truth acts 'as a prophet and teacher' and in full fidelity to its [truth's] divine source'. In addition faith makes us 'sharers in knowledge of God', for we are sharers 'in this mission of the prophet Christ'. And there is a 'love and aspiration' to understand. The Pope sees that such a theology needs developing: 'Today we still need above all that understanding and interpretation of God's Word; we need that theology'.[87] The text then stresses that such a theology must function 'correctly' and be at the service of the *magisterium*. But no text can deny that there is an ontogenesis in the growth of the believer, and part of it seizes on Christ as prophet, and another part keeps the sharing in God's knowledge as a built-in priority.

(*iii*) In my last prerequisite I appeal rather to the spirit of the Bible. The Bible, in spite of our misunderstanding of Psalm 8, does not flatly ask the question, 'What is man?' The words, 'What is man that Thou art mindful of him, and the son of man that Thou dost care for him?' (Ps 8: 4) is not a metaphysical question but an exclamation in a song of praise. The Bible does not even ask, as Ernst Jüngel insists, 'Does God exist?', or even 'Is there a God instead of idols?'. The point is that the Bible presupposes the answer to such a question. The question it does ask about God is much nearer home. Somehow it seems to manage asking and exclaiming all in one breath, as though it were saying: 'But God, where is he?' Indeed, 'Where is the God of Israel?', it says. For in the view of the Old Testament the man who says there is no God is not so much wrong as too clever, or a fool.[88]

Let us transpose the question 'where' to man. Then we do not have to say or ask, 'Is man such and such, or has he this or that essence or quiddity?' The question that matters is put to us by Genesis 3. By being put to us it is put to man. For after the division of reality into good and evil man's own situation comes into question. Is he hiding? At any rate he is not present, he is elsewhere. Adam-man in his nakedness does not show himself. In that state the rounded anthropology of Aristotle is already shattered. There is now in him a contradiction which has prized him open. It is Lutheran. Bonhoeffer brings it out:

> Nakedness is the essence of unity and unbrokenness, of being for the other, of objectivity, of recognition of the other in his right, in his limiting me and in his creatureliness.

But the other side of the coin is also there. This man is a contradiction to himself:

> But the greatest contradiction here is that man, who has come to be without a limit, is bound to point to his limit without intending to do so. He covers himself because he feels shame. In shame man acknowledges his limit. It is the peculiar dialectic of the torn world that man lives in it without a limit, therefore as the One. Yet he always lives hating the limit and he therefore lives as one divided.[89]

It is to the man in this state, in hiding for flight, that God must call, 'Where are you?' Catholic theology is unfaithful to Augustine when it forgets to concentrate on the *where* of man. It is true that Protestants have often thought it nonsensical of Catholics to have indulged as much as they have the idea that the essence of original sin could lie in sexuality, or at least be closely tied to it with that niggling, somewhat hair-splitting doctrine of concupiscence. And the Catholic hair-splitting has gone on overtime to show that it is not such nonsense after all. The Protestant objection, as Bonhoeffer points out, is moralistic naturalism. I do not see why any post-Freudian should not give the Bible the right to say what it wants to on that matter. But the reason for the hair-splitting is what interests me here. We have to split logical hairs in theology when we are on the wrong foot, and indeed in the wrong place. So I come back to the question of where for man.

It will be answered by the theology of a *there* of man. Man, we must say is *there*: *in* faith and contradiction; *in* hope and alienation and fear; *in* love and in the struggle for *the* love beyond other loves. More biblically he is *in* God's image; *in* the dyadic state, male-female; he is *in* life and *in* death. Those metaphorical places are the rightly beamed ones. They point us back to God and to each other.

If it is asked, Is there no positive reason for my third prerequisite? Does no theology no state of man demand it? I can only reply that in addition to the ecumenical stagnation which afflicts the Churches there is the cry of man himself. It is a cry of real people not even or only for food, but for the right to survive. The post-holocaust world does not ask if men are men. It will be bound to ask, Where then are men? Where is man? The perplexity comes first. It intensifies. Where then in that world is the humanity of man? Where can the man of the Day After stand and still have meaning? The *Angst* concealed in that question cannot be satisfied by a *what*, only by a *where*. In deprivation, in life under a destiny to coming death, in and under the preposterous ideologies of power, the shift of gravity must take place from the dead-end of 'What is man?' to the open-ended 'Where is he?', so that he may still have faith, and hope, and love.

Notes

CHAPTER ONE *Why a Hierarchy of Truths?*

1. The early Church knew about a preference, namely a canon within the canon of Scripture. From Tatian to Irenaeus that was how the Fourth Gospel was viewed. See Yves Congar, *Diversity and Communion* (London, 1984), p. 129. For a bibliography on the hierarchy of truths see p. 212ff.
2. For an account see M. Hornsby-Smith, *Studies in English Catholicism* (University of Surrey, 1983).
3. Cf. P. Nichols, 'The Pope and the "Heretic"', *The Spectator*, 22 December 1979.
4. Cf. Congar, *Diversity and Communion*, p. 129.
5. Cf. *Decree on Ecumenism*, n. 4. See Bernard Leeming, *The Vatican Council and Christian Unity* (London, 1966). Text, pp. 1–18; Appendix VII, 'The Hierarchy of Truths', pp. 298–9.
6. Cf. Hornsby-Smith, *Studies in English Catholicism*, p. 34.
7. Cf. e.g. Peter Hebblethwaite, *The New Inquisition* (London, 1980), p. 93 on the signatories to an American Press Letter.
8. See Walter Goddijn, 'An Alienated Church', *The Tablet*, 28 January 1984.
9. Cf. H. Vorgrimler, *Commentary on the Documents of Vatican II*, Vol. II (London, 1968), p. 120.
10. Cf. Y. Congar, *Diversity and Communion*, p. 128.
11. AAS (1928), 13.
12. Quoted in *Konzilsreden*, edited by Y. Congar, H. Küng, D. O'Hanlon (Glen Rock, 1964).
13. Ibid.
14. See Oscar Cullmann 'Einheit in der Vielfalt im Lichte der "Hierarchie der Wahrheiten"' in *Glaube im Prozess*, edited by O. Klinger-Willstedt (Freiburg–im-Breisgau, 1984), especially pp. 356–7.
15. Cf. Vorgrimler, *Commentary*, p. 120. For New Testament examples see Cullmann, pp. 361–4.
16. *De praescriptione haereticorum*, 21, 32, 37.
17. Hermas, Mand. I, 1.
18. Cf. Hans Conzelmann, *An Outline of the Theology of the New Testament* (London, 1969), pp. 293–4.

19. This is the case in e.g. Irenaeus and Tertullian. See J. N. D. Kelly, *Early Christian Doctrines* (London, 1969), pp. 293–4.

20. Op. cit., p. 95.

21. Op. cit., p. 96.

22. Op. cit., p. 164.

23. Op. cit., p. 255.

24. Cf. Henri De Lubac, *La Foi Chrétienne, Essai sur la Structure du Symbole des Apôtres* (Paris, 1969), pp. 287–310.

25. *In Joh. Ev. Tract.* 29, 6. And cp. *In Ps.* 130, 1 (*credere in Christum, diligere Christum*); *Sermo* 144, 2 (*credit . . . qui sperat . . . et diligit*); the touching of the garment by the woman is 'with heart', *Sermo Guelferb.* 14, 2.

26. *Summa aurea*, 1. 3, tract. 2, 3, 1. This idea is to be found in Albert the Great, Bonaventure and Aquinas.

27. *In Joh. Ev. Tract.* 6, 37.

28. Cf. *De veritate* 14, 3, 10; 14, 5, ad 4. See De Lubac, *La Foi Chrétienne*, pp. 300–1; 306–7.

29. See De Lubac, op. cit., p. 101ff.

30. For Augustine see e.g. *Enchiridion*, 114, 'faith . . . summed up in the Creed . . . to carnal thought is milk for babes, but to spiritual reflection and study is meat for strong men . . .' From 1 Cor 3: 1ff. the idea began to taken on consistency, cf. e.g. Lactantius, *Institutes*, V, 4, 6.

31. A good example in Augustine is to be found in *De civ. Dei*, XXI, 26, 1, where Christ is 'foundation' in terms of love and morality. Nevertheless as the Council does not specify exactly what it had in mind by 'foundation' it may have in mind some credal expression. Rahner thinks so, cf. *Schriften zur Theologie*, Bd. XV (Einsiedeln, 1983), 'Hierarchie der Wahrheiten, Zentrale und entfernte Wahrheiten', pp. 164–5. As the Council does not specify, we may insist that it is nearer to New Testament usage to take the reference as an allusion to Christ. As to preferring *Church* before Christ as 'foundation', it should be remembered that the Church has to ask pardon for its sins (presumably not excluding errors), a point Liberation Theologians have seized upon and for which they have been criticized (cf. Robert Gelluy, 'L'Opinion du Cardinal Ratzinger', *La Nouvelle Revue*, LXXX (Juillet-Août, 1984), p. 41. (I am indebted to the Büro Karl Rahner for sending me a copy of the chapter of *Schriften* XV, which was among the author's last writings.) Cullmann notices that when we use such expressions as 'Centre', 'Foundation', 'Basic Truth' (*Grundwahrheit*) or 'Core' (*Kern*) we are still not meeting the needs of the image 'hierarchy' (c.f. 'Einheit in der Vielfalt', p. 356).

32. For an excellent summary of the imperative of love in the New

Testament see Eric Osborn, *Ethical Patterns in Early Christian Thought* (Cambridge, 1976), p. 33f.

33. Cf. Osborn, op. cit., p. 33.

34. Cf. H. von Campenhausen, *The Fathers of the Greek Church* (London, 1963), p. 99.

35. See Osborn, *Ethical Patterns*, pp. 105, 106.

36. De Trinitate, VII, 7, 10–14.

37. *De civ. Dei*, X, 3, 2.

38. *De perfectione iustitiae hominis*, V, 11.

39. See the important article by Maurice Bévenot, 'Faith and Morals in the Council of Trent and in Vatican I', *The Heythrop Journal* III (1962), pp. 15–30.

40. Cf. Thomas F. Torrance, 'Concept of Order in Theology and Science', *The Month* CCXL (December, 1983), p. 401 (author's italics).

41. Cf. AAS LXVIII (1981), pp. 101–2.

42. Cf. Karl Rahner, *Foundations of the Christian Faith* (London, 1978), p. 382.

43. Cf. Karl Rahner, 'Hierarchie der Wahrheiten', p. 164.

44. The arbitrariness would show itself in the selection of merely personal opinions. This would not be Church faith. Cf. Rahner, *Foundations*, p. 383.

45. Nevertheless a 'bit of ignorance about certain catechism questions' would be admissible, especially over some post-Tridentine developments in the R.C. Church (ibid.).

46. See Karl Rahner, 'Offizielle Glaubenslehre der Kirche und faktische Gläubigkeit des Volkes' in Karl Rahner, Heinrich Fries, *Theologie in Freiheit und Verantwortung* (Munich, 1981), p. 23.

47. Pastoral Constitution on the Church and the Modern World, n. 62.

48. Vorgrimler, *Commentary*, II, thinks it is 'the mystery of Christ which is meant', cp. *ipsum mysterium Christi et Ecclesiae*, n. 4; see also p. 120, n. 48.

49. Cf. *Pensées* (Pléiade), p. 1222, n. 481.

50. Bernard Lonergan, *Method in Theology* (London, 1975), p. 327.

51. Cornelius Ernst, *Multiple Echo* (London, 1979), p. 145.

52. Op. cit., pp. 145–6.

53. Karl Rahner, Theological Investigations, IX (London, 1972), p. 52.

54. Frag. 15 quoted by Werner Jaeger, *Aristotle* (London, 1934), p. 160.

55. DS, 3016.

56. *Dignitatis humanae*, n. 1.

57. Quoted by Theodore Davey, 'The Revised Code of Canon Law', *The Month*, CCXLV (November, 1983), p. 371.

58. Art. cit., p. 372.

59. Art. cit., p. 374.

60. Cf. Henri De Lubac, *La Foi Chrétienne*, p. 179.

61. Cf. Arthur Koestler, *The Ghost in the Machine* (London, 1976), p. 245.

62. Ibid.

63. *The Daily Telegraph*, 8 March 1980.

64. Alexander Pope, *Epistles and Satires of Horace Imitated*, IV, 1, 6, quoted by Koestler, p. 239.

65. Koestler, ibid.

66. In a judicious chapter, Avery Dulles shows how the term *magisterium* and *magisteria* may be used and considered. See Avery Dulles, *A Church to Believe In* (New York, 1983), Chapter 8, 'The Two Magisteria, an Interim Reflection', pp. 118–32. The following reminders are useful: 'nonbishops' (including laity) have 'played important roles in ecumenical councils'; canonical mission gives 'a certain temporary share' [in the magisterium]; through 'baptism and confirmation all are commissioned . . .' (cp. *Lumen gentium*, n. 33); laity should study and develop the 'sacred sciences' and with clerics possess 'a lawful freedom of inquiry and of thought' (*Gaudium et spes*, n. 62). But the emergence of what Avery Dulles calls the 'third magisterium', that of the 'untheological militant conservatives' merits special thought.

67. Cf. M. Hornsby-Smith, *Studies in English Catholicism*.

68. On Lithuania see Janice Broun, 'Religion Revives in Lithuania', *The Month*, CCLXVII (March 1984), pp. 85–8.

69. The theological evolution ran somewhat as follows: a Trinitarian formula had to be reflected upon (New Haven, 1957); as centred in Christ the biblical message must receive its Trinitarian interpretation (Heraklion, 1967); a Christological definition must be seen to be rooted in Trinitarian faith (Uppsala, 1968); the basis of the Church's unity is in the perfect unity of the Triune God (Montreal, 1964). See *The Ecumenical Advance, A History of the Ecumenical Movement, Vol. 2, 1948–1968*, edited by H. E. Fey (London, 1970), pp. 60, 136, 154, 155.

70. The good widow Rafferty's hierarchy of truths is *existentiell* and 'situational' in Rahner's thinking. It is by no means to be despised, even if it causes a theologian to despair, for it remains 'an initial and hopefully successful departure for reaching an understanding of the Christian faith' (cf. *Foundations*, pp. 452–3).

71. Cf. *New Catholic Encyclopedia* (Washington, D.C., 1966), Vol. 10, 524.

72. Cf. Karl Rahner, *Foundations*, p. 452.
73. For more extended conclusions see Edmund Schlink, 'Die Hierarchie der Wahrheiten und die Einigung der Kirchen', *Kerygma und Dogma*, 21 (1975), pp. 10–12.
74. *The Daily Telegraph*, 10 May 1980.

CHAPTER TWO   *Suffering and the Creator God*

1. See Kenneth Surin, 'Theodicy?', *Harvard Theological Review*, 76 (1983), pp. 225–47, especially, p. 230ff.
2. Cf. A. R. Peacocke, *Creation and the World of Science*, Bampton Lectures (Oxford, 1979), p. 166.
3. On positivity in origins see A. Ganoczy, *Homme Créateur, Dieu Créateur* (Paris, 1979), p. 160f.
4. A. R. Peacocke, *Creation and the World of Science*, pp. 344 and ff.
5. D. Bonhoeffer, *Creation and Temptation* (London, 1966), pp. 86–7.
6. Gorgias, 649 BC.
7. Cf. *Concluding Unscientific Postscript*, translated by Swenson and Lowrie (London, 1941), p. 446.
8. *Journals, 1853–1855*, edited and translated by Ronald Gregor Smith (London, 1968), p. 255.
9. Cf. Kenneth Surin, 'Theodicy?', p. 232.
10. On this see John Hick, *Evil and the God of Love* (London, 1968), pp. 192–3.
11. Whitehead and Hartshorne have argued that God must be the suffering Creator, and Hartshorne also argued for the possibility of God. See A. N. Whitehead, *Process and Reality* (Cambridge, 1929), p. 497; C. Hartshorne, *The Divine Relativity* (New Haven, 1948). Quoted by Peacocke, *Creation and the World of Science*, p. 200 where see note 38 for further reference to Process Theologians.
12. Cf. Ernst Käsemann, *Commentary on Romans* (London, 1980), p. 234.
13. *Sermo 213 in traditione Symboli, II*, 1, 1 (PL 38, 1060).
14. Cf. J. N. D. Kelly, *Early Christian Creeds* (London, 1972), p. 135.
15. Cf. E. R. Dodds, *Pagan and Christian in an Age of Anxiety* (Cambridge, 1968), pp. 16–17, esp. n. 3 for the 'widespread . . . view by non-Jewish Gnostics, who do not always identify the Creator God with Jehovah' and thus allow for '"whatever brute or blackguard made the world"'.
16. The importance of concrete experience in any discussion of

suffering is brought out by L.-B. Geiger, *L'Expérience Humaine du Mal* (Paris, Foi Vivante, 1969), where the account of the controversy between L. Bouyer and P. Sertillanges O.P. is still worth consulting (cf. pp. 202–9, also in *Bulletin Thomiste* VII [1943–46], pp. 528–33).

17. Voltaire, *Poème sur le Désastre de Lisbonne* (1755).

18. See Simone Weil, *Pensées sans Ordre concernant l'Amour de Dieu* (Paris, 1962), pp. 85–122.

19. The *not this but that* seems to me to correspond better with (*a*) the experiential and therefore still open side of suffering, and with (*b*) the theological area we are discussing. By contrast Kierkegaard's 'not only this but something more', and of course Nietzsche's 'Kommt nicht immerfort die Nacht und mehr Nacht?' seem to close the door on further reflection, as they are doubtless meant to do. If George Steiner is right in saying that 'in our current barbarism an extinct theology is at work' then his conclusion about the Holocaust must also be right: 'Needing hell, we have learned how to build and run it on earth . . . In locating hell above ground, we have passed out of the major order and symmetries of Western civilization' (George Steiner, *In Bluebeard's Castle*, London, 1971, especially Chapter 2, 'A Season in Hell', pp. 31–48). George Steiner's pessimism, which in the first place concerns culture nevertheless touches us: 'In the absence or recession of religious belief, close linked as it were to the primacy of language, music seems to gather, to harvest us to ourselves. Perhaps it can do this because of its special relation to the truth' (p. 94).

20. The power of sacrifice as a symbol is to some extent that of the breaking of a vicious circle. Dag Hammerskjöld wrote:

> Forgiveness breaks the chain of causality because he who 'forgives' you out of love takes upon himself the consequences of what *you* have done. Forgiveness therefore always entails sacrifice.
>
> The price you pay for your own liberation through another's sacrifice, is that you in turn must be willing to liberate in the same way, irrespective of the consequences to yourself.

Cf. Dag Hammerskjöld, *Markings*, trans. Sjöberg and Auden (London, 1966), p 163. The notion of sacrifice clearly supports the thrust of this chapter, but it is not, as in some theodicies, offered as a guideline to a resolution of our 'problem'.

21. Cf. *The Times*, 11 March 1982: on the stage version of Steiner's work on Hitler, *The Portage to San Cristobal of A.H.*

22. For Kierkegaard, 'The "cleavage" of suffering is only an expression of the change between time and eternity with fallen

man'. Cf. Louis Dupré, *Kierkegaard as Theologian* (London, 1964), p. 89.

23. See Denis Vasse, S.J., 'La Souffrance, Altération, Altérité' in *Christus*, no 111, *Souffrance Vaincue* (t. 28), June 1981, pp. 281–95. For the positive desire for life and the call to it see pp. 293, 295.

24. From a philosophical point of view it should be clear that the use of *alterity* offered here is secondary or derived. *Heterotēs, alteritas, Andersheit, Entaüsserung* and *Entfremdung* as well as alienation have a varied and wide history. For the connexion of the tradition, such as it is, with evil see, Yves Labbé, *Le Sens et le Mal, Théodicée du Samedi Saint* (Paris, 1980), especially pp. 104ff.

25. Piet Schoonenberg, *Man and Sin* (London, 1965), p. 41.

26. It is implicit in this chapter that theology in taking account of man, relates our Christian faith to man in some way as a free subject. Cf. J. Speck, *Karl Rahners Anthropologie* (Munich, 1967), p. 42.

27. I avoid writing 'alienation' here which would take us away from the subject of suffering as such.

28. Cf. Dietrich Bonhoeffer, *Creation and Temptation*, p. 53.

29. Ibid.

30. Karl Rahner, *Foundations of the Christian Faith* (London, 1978), p. 404.

31. Bonhoeffer, *Creation and Temptation*, p. 79. Cp. also: 'If the dogmatics of the Church saw the essence of original sin in sexuality, this is not such nonsense as Protestants have often said from a point of view of moralistic naturalism. The knowledge of *tob* and *ra* is originally not an abstract knowledge of ethical principles, but sexuality; i.e. a perversion of the relationship between the persons.' Bonhoeffer continues to attach the preservation of 'the dark secret of sexuality' to continuing procreation (p. 80). That sex and destruction go together is no surprise to the Freudians. For its part the Catholic tradition should have come to appreciate much sooner than it did how sin should have been much more accounted for in terms of relationships, divisions, *alterity* in various phases. Casuistry which owes more to the Stoics than to Augustine has helped to disfigure the point that Augustine echoed by Bonhoeffer made with too great literalism.

32. Bonhoeffer, *Creation and Temptation*, p. 82.

33. Schelling went behind his predecessors and placed the ultimate dualism in God himself.

34. Bonhoeffer, *Creation and Temptation*, p. 66.

35. 'If Job cries out his innocence with such an accent of despair, it

is because he himself does not succeed in believing in it. Within himself his soul takes sides with his friends. He implores the witness of God himself, because he no longer hears the witness of his own conscience. It proves to be nothing more than a remote and dead thing.' (Author translation, Simone Weil, *Pensées sans Ordre*, p. 90.)

36. See Raymond Ruyer, *La Gnose de Princeton, Des Savants à la Recherche d'une Religion* (Paris, 1974). According to the author the movement really began at Pasadena (p. 7).

37. See A. Koutsouvilis, 'Is Suffering Necessary for the Good Man?', *The Heythrop Journal*, XIII (1972), pp. 44–53.

38. Cf. W. Eichrodt, 'Faith in Providence and Theodicy in the Old Testament' in *Theodicy in the Old Testament*, edited by James L. Crenshaw (Philadelphia–London, 1983), p. 34.

39. Ibid., p. 35.

40. To this should be added the simple teleological view of suffering expounded by Epictetus. Two articles setting this against the much more sophisticated view of Simone Weil are recommended: (*a*) Diogenes Allen, 'Natural Evil and the Love of God', *Religious Studies*, 16 (1980), pp. 439–56; (*b*) Diogenes Allen in collaboration with Eric Springsted, 'Le Malheur: Une Énigme (Simone Weil et Épictète), *Cahiers Simone Weil*, Tome II, n. 4 (Décembre 1979).

41. *Zeus Elegchomenos* takes the Cynic standpoint against Stoicism and concentrates on predestination (the Fates) and free will. The subject continues more roughly in Zeus Tragōidos (see Lucian Vol. 2, Loeb edition).

42. Cf. François Varone, *Ce Dieu Censé aimer la Souffrance* (Paris, 1984), pp. 80, 236–7 and frequently.

43. See Max Scheler, Vom Umsturz der Werte, GW 3, in 'Vom Umsturz der Werte', p. 139 especially n. 1 and ff. The term is a common one in Scheler and forms an integral part of his reflections as a phenomenologist. Thus man is an *ens amans* ('Wer den *ordo amoris* eines Menschen hat, hat den Menschen'). The *ordo* contains four principal levels: (*i*) the hierarchy of values; (*ii*) the types and ordering of models of men, in whom the hierarchy of values is established; (*iii*) the activities and behaviour of these through whom the values are realized; (*iv*) the conditions under which the values can be read off.

When in 1918 Christian Socialism made an appearance in Germany, Scheler came to its support by an application of his existing theme of the 'real mutual solidarity of all for all' (GW 6, p. 264). Solidarity in short is a principle which Scheler finds in biology, ontology, the sphere of ethics, and social existence.

44. Cf. Scheler in 'Das Ressentiment im Aufbau der Moralen', GW 3, p. 140.
45. Dorothee Sölle, *Christ the Representative* (London, 1965), p. 103.
46. *Malheur* shows the meeting of extremes, for it marks 'distance' and 'contact' . . . 'between him who rules the universe and the creatures, who would be plunged into *malheur* by the cosmic order. Those afflicted by *malheur* experience his touch (*son attouchement*) through the cosmic order governed by him' (Diogenes Allen, 'Malheur', p. 190). Simone Weil indeed attaches the concept to love with the idea that in the crucifixion the infinite distance is crossed between God and God. Father and Son 'are bound by the fact that the Son accepts the mediation (*entremise*) of a world which produces *malheur*', an expression of the Father's love (cf. ibid., p. 191).
47. In *Christ* Schillebeeckx devotes a short chapter to this simple *a priori* (ET London, 1980, pp. 742–30).
48. In his effort to be concrete Schillebeeckx seeks a synthesis of 'six constants' which 'delineate man's basic form and hold one another in equipoise'. His conclusion is that the *synthesis* of this state is both an 'already now' and a 'not yet' (ibid., p. 743).
49. Sölle, p. 109 in 'The Provisionality of Christ, A Note to the Dialogue with Judaism'.
50. Ernst Käsemann, *Commentary on Romans* (London, 1980), p. 138.
51. Cf. p. 79, n. 46 above.
52. Thomas F. Torrance, *Theology in Reconstruction* (London, 1975), p. 222.
53. The key notion is that of 'his *energeia* [which] inheres in his eternal *ousia*', which it does not do in later theology (ibid., p. 224).
54. Now in the Museo delle Terme, Rome.
55. Cf. 1 Cor 1: 18. For the continuance of 'scandal' in philosophy and comparative religion see Hans Küng, *On Being a Christian* (London, 1978), pp. 396–7 and notes.
56. The difficulty is almost certainly worse than I make it appear. Thus Moltmann says: 'It is no longer the experience of their own subjectivity, which transcends the objective world: it is the experience *of their own helplessness* in an ironclad shell of objectifications, which have taken on an independent life, and the impotence in a closed society' (Jürgen Moltmann, *The Future of Creation*, London, 1977, p. 6). Moltmann's concept of 'redeeming from immobility' may parallel my 'transforming' from 'alterity' (cf. ibid., p. 13 and reff.). But Moltmann could not accept my implicit acceptance of the Neoplatonic movement of all towards the One.

57. Prosper of Aquitaine, Sent. 56, quoted by Orange II (DS, 185).

58. Fuller reflection must say that this is Trinitarian, and in Moltmann's view dialectical: 'one should think of the Trinity as a dialectical event; indeed as the event of the Cross and thus as eschatologically open history' (cf. J. Moltmann, *The Crucified One*, London, 1974, p. 255).

59. Cf. Jürgen Moltmann, *The Future of Creation* (London, 1979), p. 17.

CHAPTER THREE   *Christ Relevant*

1. Cf. my article, 'The Relevant Christ', *The Clergy Review*, LVIII (1973), p. 600.

2. Cf. Andrew Greeley, *The Jesus Myth* (London, 1972), p. 55.

3. Cf. John A. T. Robinson, *The Human Face of God* (London, 1973), p. 230.

4. Cf. Malachi Martin, *Jesus Now* (London, 1975), p. 278ff.

5. Cf. my article, 'The Relevant Christ', p. 607.

6. See for example the chapter in Edward Schillebeeckx, *Christ, The Christian Experience in the Modern World* (London, 1980), pp. 463–504.

7. Cf. ibid.

8. Rom 8: 23.

9. Heb 5: 9.

10. 2 Cor 12: 19.

11. 1 Cor 13: 3.

12. Even the supremacy of the love of God can be parodied. The Blessed Angela of Foligno begged God to rid her of her husband and her children, so that she could perfect her mystical prayer (cf. art. 'Angela of Foligno', in *New Catholic Encyclopedia*, I, 501).

13. 1 Cor 1: 28–9.

14. 1 Cor 1: 18.

15. 1 Cor 1: 30.

16. Cf. Hans Urs von Balthasar, *Love Alone, the Way of Revelation* (London, 1968), p. 110. A similar situation obtains for marriage: 'In marriage the form of agape is superimposed on sexual eros (and given the family, on private property and the free and responsible use of it)'.

17. 1 Jn 3: 2.

18. Cf. Phil 2: 6ff.

19. Jn 5: 24.

20. For the religious expression of intimacy in sacramental life, cf. Chapter Five, pp. 164–92, below.

21. Cf. John A. T. Robinson, *Exploration into God* (London, 1967), p. 145.
22. Apoc 3: 15–17.
23. On this see John A. T. Robinson (*The Human Face of God*, p. 230) who calls attention to the opposite. If we empty our churches of all stained glass, statues and the like, and concentrate all attention upon Christ as Principle of Creation, as Evolutionary Christ, or as Christ of cosmic harmonization, we end with a *Christo-sophy*, a superior wisdom not an account of our belief in Jesus Christ, the God–Man. Of course our familiar artistic triviality with statues, docetic in tendency as it is, fears the 'scandal of particularity'.
24. 1 Cor 1: 13.
25. Cf. my article, 'On Sacramental Man, III, The Socially Operational Way', in *The Heythrop Journal*, XIV (1973), p. 186 where I am much indebted to Victor W. Turner, *The Ritual Process, Structure and Anti-Structure* (London, 1967).
26. Cf. e.g. 2 Tim 4: 1: 'I charge you in the presence of God and of Christ Jesus who is to judge the living and the dead and by his appearing and his kingdom'.
27. Cf. Joseph Comblin, 'Outside Criticism of the Church', in *Perspectives of a Political Ecclesiology*, edited by J. B. Metz (New York, 1971), p. 33.
28. See Eph 6: 12 and the very sage assessment by John Bligh, 'Demonic Powers', in *The Heythrop Journal*, I (1960), pp. 314–23.
29. 1 Cor 15: 28.
30. Cf. Wolfhart Pannenberg, *Jesus, God and Man* (London, 1968), p. 369.
31. Cf. John A. T. Robinson, *The Human Face of God*, especially pp. 56ff., 63ff., 80.
32. Cf. Richard Egenter, *The Desecration of Christ*, translated by E. Quinn (London, 1967), pp. 77–8. Egenter's symptomatology of the statues of Our Lady of Lourdes is almost certainly not exhaustive. I would also see that symbol as a bright figure of light, which is (a) a diurnal symbol of ascent and thus can divide good from bad, pure from impure, healthy from diseased, and (b) as the euphemization (that is the making benign) of the otherwise dark, chthonic, threat of the feminine with which religion among its other preoccupations has to come to terms. The usual legend above the statue, *Je suis l'Immaculée Conception*, tends to confirm both these observations.
33. Egenter seems to me to be reasoning on the right lines especially in his Chapter V, 'The Breeding Ground of Kitsch

and its Moral Effects' and in Chapter VI, 'Moral Ineptitude as the Heart of Kitsch'.

34. Readers of Josefa Menéndez, *The Way of Divine Love* (Westminster, Md., 1965) will remember how such ambiguities abound there.

35. Cf. Egenter, *The Desecration of Christ*, pp. 77–8.

36. Cf. Michel Meslin, *Pour une Science des Religions* (Paris, 1973), p. 122.

37. Op. cit., p. 123.

38. Cf. John A. T. Robinson, *The Human Face of God*, p. 56. The references are to D. E. Nineham, *St Mark* (London, 1963), p. 35 and William A. Phipps, *Was Jesus Married?* (New York, 1970).

39. Cf. 1 Cor 9: 5.

40. Statements about the love of Jesus for Mary, Martha and Lazarus do not necessarily belong to my *area one*. One *could* write about Jesus in the way that Père Bruno de Jésus-Marie does about St John of the Cross: 'son energie vibrante . . . sa sexualité diraient les psychanalystes — féconde les contacts humains à l'avantage du Seigneur'. A graphologist speaks of St John's 'capacity for love', and that he 'appears to have experienced everything and to have reacted to it', also of his 'ardour without aggression'. See Père Bruno de Jésus-Marie, 'St Jean de la Croix et la Psychologie Moderne', *Études Carmélitaines* (Paris, 1951), pp. 15–16.

41. Cf. T. H. Bindley and F. W. Green, *The Oecumenical Documents of the Faith* (London, 1950), p. 196, note to line 113.

42. 'Passibilis et temporalis ex conditione assumpta', Council of Florence (DS 1337).

43. For Aquinas, Christ could not have had leprosy or a fatal disease (*Summa Theologica*, III, 14, 4).

44. On thought models in Christology see John McIntyre, *The Shape of Christology* (London, 1966).

45. Cf. C. F. D. Moule, 'The Manhood of Jesus in the New Testament' in *Christ, Faith and History* (edited by S. W. Sykes and J. P. Clayton, Cambridge, 1972), p. 102 (author italics).

46. Cf. M. Meslin, *Pour une Science des Religions*, pp. 203–4.

47. See an excellent section in Joachim Jeremias, *Jerusalem at the Time of Jesus* (London, 1969), pp. 359ff; and especially p. 356 for a summary. 'Jesus was not content with bringing women up onto a higher plane than was then the custom; but as Saviour of all (Lk 7: 36–50) he brings them before God on an equal footing with men' (Mt 21: 31–2).

48. Cf. C. H. Dodd, *The Founder of Christianity* (London, 1973), p. 58.

49. Cf. Ernst Käsemann, *Jesus Means Freedom* (London, 1969), p. 23.

50. My friend and colleague Robert Murray speaks of Christ 'who lived in celibacy but (most unusually for a rabbi of his time) in close friendship with women as well as with men . . .' Cf. R. Murray, 'Spiritual Friendship', in *Supplement to the Way, 10, Celibacy* (Summer, 1970), pp. 62–3.

51. For a powerful example of such symbolism at work in the interpretation of the Fall narrative, see Dietrich Bonhoeffer, *Creation and Temptation* (London, 1966), who wrote: 'Unrestrained sexuality, like uncreative sexuality, is therefore destruction *par excellence*. Thus it is an insane acceleration of the Fall; it is self-affirmation to the point of destruction. Passion and hate, *tob* and *ra* . . . these are the fruits of the tree of knowledge' (p. 79); and further, 'If the dogmatics of the Church saw the essence of sin in sexuality, this is not such nonsense as Protestants have often said from the point of view of moralistic naturalism. The knowledge of *tob* and *ra* is originally not an abstract knowledge of ethical principles, but sexuality; i.e. a perversion of the relationship between persons' (p. 80). See also n. 31 on p. 287 above.

52. Two chapters can be especially recommended in John Passmore, *The Perfectibility of Man* (London, 1970); Chapter 13, 'Perfection Renounced: the Dystopians' (pp. 260–85), and Chapter 15, 'The New Mysticism: Paradise Now' (pp. 304–27).

53. Cf. Norman O. Brown, *Life Against Death* (London, 1959), p. 311, quoted by Passmore, *The Perfectibility of Man*, p. 305.

54. In Hebrews, Christ is the compassionate High Priest: 'He can deal gently with the ignorant and wayward, since he is himself beset with weakness' (Heb 5: 2). 'Deal gently' is no worse than most efforts to render the much discussed *metriopathein*. It is of course especially the 'obedience' in his Passion which gave Christ's priesthood its perfection. 'He learned obedience through what he suffered' (5: 8; see also 2: 17–18, and 4: 14–16).

55. Cf. Matt 11: 30 — of the Law in the first instance.

56. Cf. Matt 12: 8.

57. Cf. T. W. Manson, *Ethics and the Gospel* (London, 1960), p. 68.

58. The classic form of the principle of affinity is that *like seeks after like* (Aristotle). In theories of knowledge *like is known by like* (Plato), and there exists a *knowledge by connaturality* (St Thomas). Almost as ancient is the principle that *contraries are cured by contraries* (Hippocrates), which sets up a dialectic with the previous principle and eventually has its place in ascetical writing. For the theological relevance see Jürgen Moltmann,

The Crucified God (London, 1974), pp. 26–7; 30–1, nn. 20–1. After a long and varied history, the principle of affinity comes down to us in astrology, which only parted company from medicine two centuries ago. Cf. P. I. H. Naylor, *Astrology, an Historical Examination* (London, 1967), p. 169.

59. Cf. Jean Lhermitte, 'Les Sentiments de Sympathie et d'Aggressivité' in *Amour et Violence, Études Carmélitaines* (1946), p. 20.

60. Rollo May, *Paulus, a Personal Portrait of Paul Tillich* (London, 1974), p. 55.

61. Beside St Bernard, William of St Thierry was a proponent of a mystical theology based upon the Song of Songs. The question is whether such a theology shows signs of a *pathos* in God. Condren for example can speak of 'Jesus Christ . . . offered . . . to the Father *also to be consummated in us*'. See Henry Bremond, *A Literary History of Religious Thought in France, III, The Triumph of Mysticism* (London, 1936), p. 316 (author italics). There was also such a notion as the intra-Trinitarian mystical kiss. Cf. *Dictionnaire de Spiritualité*, III, 888ff.

62. Cf. 1 Cor 6: 15ff.

63. See Hans Urs von Balthasar, *Love Alone, The Way of Revelation*, Chapter 6, 'Love as Revelation' sketches a *theologia crucis* for the Catholic reader which ends in the universality 'of both forms of death in Adam', and the universality of divine mercy (cf. Rom 11: 32).

64. Cf. C. F. Raven, *Jesus and the Gospel of Love* (London, 1931), p. 108.

65. See the article 'Anxiety' in *Encyclopedia of Psychology*, I, edited by H. J. Eysenk, W. Arnold, R. Meilli, London, 1972, p. 67ff.

66. See Walther Eichrodt, *Theology of the Old Testament*, translated by J. A. Baker (London, 1967) in the section 'The Fear of God', pp. 267–88. For the adoration of God in fear as the Holy One see e.g. Pss 103: 11; 110: 10.

67. Op. cit., p. 270.

68. Op. cit., pp. 273, 276.

69. Soren Kierkegaard, *The Last Years, Journals 1853–55*, edited and translated by Ronald Gregor Smith (London, 1965), p. 324.

70. Op. cit., p. 324.

71. Laeuchli continues: 'Faith becomes an idol and the powerful message of justification runs into a dead orthodoxy; the sacrament becomes *opus operatum* and the Church sets itself against the grace of God; the Law strangles the freedom of the Spirit in the legalistic narrowness of humanistic Christianity. What does all this say? The rebellion of Adam returns to the

Christian's abuse of his speech.' Cf. Samuel Laeuchli, *The Language of Faith, An Introduction to the Semantic Dilemma of the Early Church* (London, 1962). Behind the question of the Protestant theses lies that of the 'abuse of speech' by Christians under stress and anxiety. Of course there are varied types of abuse. Formerly the tendency was to over-objectify and to project evil. Now we tend to over-subjectivize or 'introject'. The demon within takes many forms today.

72. Cf. E. R. Dodds, *Pagan and Christian in an Age of Anxiety* (Cambridge, 1968), p. 135.

73. Cf. Hans Urs von Balthasar, *Man in History: A Theological Study* (London, 1968), p. 212.

74. The phrase 'on the purely natural plane' is of course only an item of theological shorthand pointing to human existence *as though* only in potentiality for religion and grace. The phrase is misleading but sometimes useful.

75. Cf. D. Krech, R. S. Crutchfield, E. L. Ballachey, *Individual in Society* (New York–London, 1962), p. 383ff.: 'All groups serve to meet the power-want of some of the members and the belongingness-want of most of the members'. The authors do not think that these purposes are unique or exclusive, nor need the 'belongingness-want' be overtly expressed or even recognized for what it is.

76. For a general account see John Richards, *But Deliver Us from Evil. An Introduction to the Demonic Dimension in Pastoral Care* (London, 1975). Some idea of the extent of the *malaise* can be gauged from the following: Richards claimed that in West Germany there were 10,000 persons engaged in witchcraft, and for this country a BBC estimate put the figure twice as high. When Alex Sanders, 'The King of the Witches' appeared on ITV screens, 'their switchboards were jammed *not with complaints, but with requests for help*' (Richards, pp. 77–8, author italics). In 1984 an Anglican bishop of an East Anglian diocese told me that on average he received one request a week for an exorcism or a similar rite.

77. Vatican I applied to ecclesiastical faith what Trent, following Augustine, had applied to justification and grace, a different matter, namely that God does not abandon unless he is himself abandoned (cf. DS, 3014, and for Trent, DS, 1537).

CHAPTER FOUR   *The Cross in Question*

1. From the cultural, as distinct from the theological, point of view our Western world (European and Russian), which has

indulged in the genocides of 1936–45, cannot be expected to recover health after such contagious insanity and crime as though nothing had ever happened. 'With the botched attempt to kill God and the very nearly successful attempt to kill those who had "invented" Him, civilization entered, precisely as Nietzsche had foretold, "on night and more night".' So George Steiner in, *In Bluebeard's Castle, Some Notes Towards the Redefinition of Culture* (London, 1974), p. 42. I thoroughly recommend these lectures of the T. S. Eliot Memorial Foundation. They are a cultural oasis after the *farouche* writings of the theologians. Chapter 2, 'A Season in Hell', is highly relevant to what I am saying. There is no doubt about what we Europeans have done: 'In locating Hell above ground, we have passed out of the major order and symmetries of Western civilization' (p. 48).

2. 1 Cor 1: 17ff; also 1: 22–4, cp. Gal 5: 11; 6: 12ff.

3. Cf. Jürgen Moltmann, *The Future of Creation* (London, 1979), p. 59.

4. Jürgen Moltmann, *The Crucified God, The Cross of Christ as the Foundation and Criticism of Christian Theology* (London, 1974). The author's later essay, 'The Theology of the Cross Today' in his The *Future of Creation*, pp. 59–79 should also be taken into account.

5. Sometimes *theologia crucis* and *theologia gloriae* are simply used to describe a strong theological emphasis on either the crucifixion or the resurrection, as, for example, in a broad difference between Western and Eastern theologies (see Karl Barth, *Dogmatics in Outline*, London, 1949, p. 114). Here the issue is rather that pin-pointed by Luther, and it concerns our way of knowing God in his redemptive mystery and our consequent idea of God.

6. The term 'de-privatization' (*Entprivatisierung*) was coined by the Catholic 'political theologian' J. B. Metz (cf. Henri de Lavalette, 'La Théologie Politique de Jean-Baptiste Metz' in Sect. II, 'La Déprivatisation', *Recherches de Science Religieuse*, 58 (1970), pp. 329–38.

7. Band V (two volumes) in the Gesamtausgabe (Frankfurt-am-Main, 1959). The work was begun during the war. The first two parts appeared in East Germany (1954, 1955). After difficulties the third appeared in both Germanies in 1959. A vast optimistic construction based on the idea that humanity is never beaten by pessimism, also a large-scale model of a dialectic between the *not-yet* and sheer *possibility*, a dream of a synergy between humanity and the world. Also a massive *credo*, and perhaps a call to a new Marxist romanticism.

8. Cf. *The Crucified God*, pp. 187–96.

9. Luther made the *theologia crucis* into a key-feature. Emphasising the 'hidden God' entailed a critical delimitation of the idea of faith. It was marked off from objective experience, and given a strongly eschatological character. This is no spectator faith. It enfolds the ambiguities of life as lived. See W. von Loevenich, *Luther's Theology of the Cross* (Belfast, 1976; A. E. McGrath, *Luther's Theology of the Cross* (Oxford, 1985).

10. Cf. Moltmann, *The Future of Creation*, p. 65.

11. Cf. *Lexikon für Theologie und Kirche*, s.v. 'Theologia Crucis' where Karl Rahner says that Catholic writing now seems to have accepted the sobriquet of *theologia gloriae* to denote the impassible existence of God when considered in the context of the drama of Christ's victory over sin and death (X, cols 60–1).

12. See DS, 401.

13. From E. Wiesel, *Night*, quoted by Moltmann, *The Crucified God*, p. 273.

14. Sydney Carter, *Friday Morning*, quoted by John A. T. Robinson, *But That I Can't Believe* (London, 1976), p. 17.

15. F. X. Durrwell, *The Resurrection*, introduction by Charles Davis, translated by Rosemary Sheed (London, 1960).

16. Edith Stein's *The Science of the Cross: a Study of St John of the Cross* (London, 1960) should not be forgotten.

17. Bernard Lonergan: 'It would seem contrary to faith to hold that it was not the only Son of God the Father that suffered but a human soul, a human body, a human consciousness, or a human subject not identical with the Son of God; again, the same is to be said of a view that maintained that, while in Christ's passion there was real human suffering, still there was no sufferer; again, the same is to be said of a view that Christ suffered unconsciously' (*Collection*, London, 1967, p. 193, n. 51). I do not suppose this author means to exclude the possibility of levels or blocks of unconsciousness in the suffering Christ, such as may occur in any suffering human being. He is not, of course, talking about the quantity or even intensity of Christ's sufferings but about the reality of the sufferings *for the one who suffered them*.

18. Cf. Karl Rahner, *Sacramentum Mundi*, II (London, 1996), 207 f., quoted by Moltmann, p. 279. That, I presume, is meant to go further than classical Thomism, though it is still true that for, e.g., St Thomas, Christ *as God* 'gave himself up to death *by the same will and act* (*voluntate et actione*) as that by which the Father gave him up' (S.T. III, 47, 3, ad 2). In that system there is no contradiction here because the divine will, both willing and accepting the death of the Son, is a contingent truth about God.

The divine simplicity is safeguarded by saying that such truths add nothing to the divine essence except a notional relation. The relation has a real created term, and the created term is really referred to the divine essence of a subsistent relation, but as a posterior reality (cf. B. Lonergan, *De Constitutione Christi Ontologica*, Rome, 1956, pp. 49–53).

19. In this connexion three of Galot's writings should be considered: J. Galot, 'Dynamisme de l'Incarnation' in *Nouvelle Revue Théologique*, 93 (1971), pp. 225–44; J. Galot, *Dieu Souffre-t-il?* (Paris, 1976); J. Galot, 'La Réalité de la Souffrance de Dieu' in *Nouvelle Revue Théologique*, 101 (1979), pp. 224–45.

20. Cf. J. Galot, 'La Réalité de la Souffrance de Dieu', p. 231. Galot also cites texts showing how God changes following upon prayer (Gen 18: 22–32; 2 Ki 20: 1 and 4–6).

21. Galot, art. cit., p. 234.

22. Galot, art. cit., p. 244.

23. Galot, art. cit., p. 245.

24. Cf. Bernard Lonergan, *Method in Theology* (London, 1971), p. 341f.

25. I take the phrase from Chapter 6 in D. W. D. Shaw, *Who is God?* (London, Centrebooks, 1968), pp. 102–18. Shaw characterizes our first (metaphysical) line of approach as follows: 'An unsympathetic observer might well see this as a sort of tailor's dummy approach: once the idea of God was arrived at, once the dummy was supplied, it seemed to be possible to deck it out in an endless variety of attributes as so many garments by devising every manner of contrast with the human condition' (p. 17).

26. Cf. Aloys Grillmeier, *Der Logos am Kreuz* (Munich, 1958), p. 129. Fr Grillmeier's solution to the problem of why a dead body should be shown open-eyed is, of course, a matter of theological interpretation and shows how strong the Logos-sarx christological framework was in popular piety.

27. Edelstein continues: 'The sage does not allow fleeting reactions to grow into passions or fixed habits, just as he is unwilling to be satisfied with merely toning them down'. That stage is negative 'and the Stoic sage aims at something more, the replacement of passions by different, sound emotions' (cf. L. Edelstein, *The Meaning of Stoicism*, Martin Classical Lectures XXI, Harvard, 1966, p. 5). Even Plotinus can be said to keep the Stoic ideal. 'There is no question of eradicating or destroying the emotions or affections of the lower self' (cf. A. H. Armstrong, 'Plotinus, Ch. 14, Man and Reality' in *The Cambridge History of Later Greek and Early Medieval Philosophy*, edited by A. H. Armstrong, Cambridge, 1970, p. 229). In his

The Crucified God, Moltmann has much to say on the *apathetic* (metaphysical) *theology* we have inherited, which he contrasts with the *pathetic theology* of Jewish writers (pp. 267–78). The tradition of the *theolgia gloriae* is an extension of the Platonic doctrine of transcendence and the Aristotelian doctrine of pure act, i.e. *energeia* without potentiality. All this became part of the Christian methodic afterthought, when it had already entered the Jewish tradition with Philo. 'Philo had no discoverable influence on later Judaism, but had a considerable impact on Christian thought' (cf. *A Dictionary of Christian Theology*, edited by Alan Richardson, London, 1969, 257, s.v.).

28. In preaching, one can assume that the congregation will automatically import the notion of three autonomous centres into the Godhead. It is therefore very important not to confine oneself to the repetition of the three persons formula. 'The general conclusion must be that the preacher will mainly speak of Father, Son and Spirit in whatever context of salvation-history and theology of grace they may occur' (Karl Rahner in *Sacramentum Mundi*, 6, 307; but see the whole article, 'Trinity in Theology').

29. Thus in the *Acts of John* (2nd–3rd c.), which the Nicene Council of 787 declared should be 'consigned to the fire', we have a section on the Revelation of the Mystery of the Cross. In it the cross becomes a great variety of things. It is sometimes Logos, or Jesus, or Christ, or Son, or Father, or Spirit as well as quite a catalogue of powers. The cross distinguishes, and unites as well. The suffering of Jesus was illusory and part of his 'dance' or 'mystery' (cf. E. Hennecke, *New Testament Apocrypha*, II, edited by Schneemelcher, translated by R. McL. Wilson, London, 1965, pp. 232–5).

30. What is 'modalistic' need by no means be 'Modalism in the heretical or Sabellian sense'. As D. M. Baillie rightly says, 'the phrase "modes of being" is part of the traditional orthodox terminology of Trinitarian doctrine, and was used in the Patristic age by the very school that was sometimes accused of leaning towards tritheism (because of their use of the analogy of three individual men) — the Cappadocian Fathers' (cf. D. M. Baillie, *God was in Christ*, London, 1968, pp. 136–7 and n. 8).

31. Cf. Moltmann, *The Crucified God*, p. 279, n. 6.

32. Since the classical kerygmatic and dogmatic statement on the Trinity ending with the Council of Florence, 'no important progress or changes have come in kerygmatic statement of religious practice' (Karl Rahner, *Sacramentum Mundi*, 6, 303–4). Moltmann holds that to interpret the cross we can presuppose

the 'metaphysical or moral concept of God' and use the 'dialectical history' of Father, Son and Spirit (p. 247).

33. Cf. Moltmann, *The Crucified God*, p. 265.

34. Ibid.

35. Moltmann quotes a fascinating passage from Origen showing the Redeemer's 'sympathy' while on the cross with the human race and the Father — from the *Hom. in Ezek* 6, 6 (GCS) — (cf. *The Future of Creation*, p. 183, n. 33).

36. Here (*The Crucified God*, pp. 270ff.) Moltmann relies upon A. Heschel, *The Prophets* (New York, 1962). For Heschel *pathos* is part of a dynamic relationship between God and men. From God's actions and attitudes in prophecy we deduce his intensely inward involvement in the lives of men. Heschel takes the biblical anthropomorphism as a serious disclosure as to what God is. His interpretation is almost Barthian. His wide learning means that though selective with Jeremiah as his best support, he is yet credible. See also Moltmann's *The Future of Creation*, pp. 69–71.

37. In one place Moltmann seems to exaggerate. It is one thing in Hebrew or in a Romantic context to say that we must allow for *pathos* in God, or even to adopt Goethe's *nemo contra Deum nisi Deus ipse*. But it is quite another to claim that a theologian like Gregory Nazianzus in his Trinitarian theogony gives colour to a theology of *stasis* in any political sense. Gregory did say that it is possible for the One (or Unity) to be at variance with itself, but he can hardly have meant that the Godhead 'was always in uproar'. In the same passage he takes pains to exclude *anarchia* and *polyarchia* in God. He also settles for an 'identity of motion and convergence' in the divine 'process', but hardly for 'true political stasiology' (cf. *The Crucified God*, p. 158, n. 4; see also Greg. Naz., *Or. Theol.* III, 2 — P.G. 36, 75).

38. Cf. Henry Bremond, *A Literary History of Religious Thought in France, III, The Triumph of Mysticism* (London, 1936), p. 316. The case for introducing Bérulle at this point is really one which should be carefully built up. A recent study shows how this could be done: Fernando Guillèn Prickler, *Bérulle Aujourd'hui*, Le Point Théologique, 25 (Paris, 1978). Thus: Christ is the *unique* point of entry for *ecstasy* and for the highest contemplation of the *Trinity* (p. 26); the *exaltation* of the Word, and the *Trinitarian* aspect of *devotion* oriented towards the divine essence and to *passivity* (p. 27); a *double annihilation* in Christ (p. 54); a *double form of the servant* (p. 61); he carries not only the *guilt* but the *state* of sin (p. 96); he suffers *at the hands* (*de la part de*) his Father . . . *putting this soul* [Christ's] in a state of suffering . . . God . . . can *lead* a soul *in suffering* (p. 97); the

dereliction on the cross is one of those sentiments *impressed by the Father* without any intervening medium (p. 98); God causes an order in suffering souls to *render homage* to his *state of the suffering* life on the cross (p. 98). Of course one cannot pin a Lutheran *theologia crucis* on Pierre de Bérulle (d. 1629) who was on the one hand an anti-Protestant polemicist and on the other influenced by the Flemish and Rhineland mystics. (Author's italics.)

39. For an outline of the intra-Trinitarian kiss in mystical theology, cf. *Dictionnaire de Spiritualité*, III, 888ff. Besides St Bernard, William of St Thierry was a proponent of this mystical theology, based of course on the Song of Songs. It is also true that some Trinitarian mystics, like St Ignatius Loyola and Mary of the Incarnation, got along very well without using any language suggestive of a divine *pathos*. The cultural milieu may have had as much to do with that as any philosophical preference. To one acquainted with courtly ways 'the divine majesty' was a phrase full of meaning. The Bérullian Fathers of the Oratory kept their distance from the various French courts of the seventeenth century. 'The Oratorians seldom visited the Court, where they were respected and feared rather than loved' (Bremond, III, p. 163).

40. The most remarkable name, not cited by Moltmann in this connexion, is that of the cobbler mystic, Jacob Böhme (1575–1624). There is a passage in the *Signatura* which, when discussing Christ's cry of dereliction on the cross, comes to a Trinitarian elaboration sealed by the Spirit . . . 'that God's Spirit might be all in all' (quoted in Hans L. Martensen, *Jacob Boehme*, edited by Stephen Hobhouse, London, 1949), pp. 160–1. Böhme was something of a Christian Gnostic and his compliance with evangelical orthodoxy is very much a matter for discussion; but several of his Christological positions can be assimilated to Luther's, though he insisted on regeneration (Catholic) rather than on justification (Lutheran) — (cf. Emanuel Hirsch, *Geschichte der neuern evangelischen Theologie*, II, Gütersloh, 1951, p. 223).

Böhme's influence on the Anglican spiritual writer, William Law (1686–1761) was considerable in the realm of Trinitarian theogony especially; but the trinitarian side of the *theologia crucis* does not seem to have got through. Böhme was also a great influence on Berdyaev. In connexion with the 'doctrines of suffering and tragedy at the heart of God', Hobhouse observes that they are such 'as the Roman Catholic Church can by no means accept', but (relying on Zernov) 'that the Church usually allows such profound questions to remain open as matters for reverent speculation and discussion' (in Martensen, *Jacob Boehme*, p. 99, Additional Note).

Approximations to the *theologia crucis* can also be found in the writings of Principal P. T. Forsyth (*d.* 1921), the so-called 'Barthian before Barth' who was influenced by Böhme and Hegel and in whom one can on occasion hear the voice of Augustine. He writes for example: 'Do not picture Christ the Intercessor as a kneeling figure beseeching God for us. It is God within God; God in self-communion; God's soliloquy on our behalf; his word to himself, which is his deed for us': cf. *P. T. Forsyth and the Cure of Souls*, edited by H. Escott (London, 1970), p. 82; see also Forsyth's *The Cruciality of the Cross* (London, 1955); John H. Rodgers, *The Theology of P. T. Forsyth* (London, 1965) and, for a short work, A. M. Hunter, *Per Crucem ad Lucem* (London, 1974).

41. On this in Luther see G. Ebeling in *Die Religion in Geschichte u. Gegenwart*, 3, VI, col. 764.

42. Cf. Moltmann, *The Crucified God*, p. 220.

43. Op. cit., p. 221.

44. Op. cit., p. 226.

45. Op. cit., p. 244.

46. Ibid.

47. Op. cit., p. 243. In this context Moltmann's afterthought that 'in Trinitarian terms' we may speak of a 'patricompassionism' seems to me quite acceptable (cf. *The Future of Creation*, p. 73).

48. In, e.g., *Sacramentum Mundi*, 6, p. 304: '. . . the economic Trinity is (already) the immanent Trinity, because the basic event of the whole economy of salvation is the self-communication of God to the world, and because all that God (the Father) is to us in Jesus Christ the Son and the Holy Spirit would really not be the *self*-communication of God to the world, if the twofold missions were not intrinsic to him, as processions, bringing with them the distinction of the three persons' (ibid. — author's italics important).

49. Cf. Manfred Köhnlein, *Was bringt das Sakrament? Disputation mit Karl Rahner* (Göttingen, 1971), p. 49.

50. Cf. Moltmann, *The Crucified God*, p. 27.

51. Op. cit., p. 161.

52. Op. cit., p. 162.

53. Op. cit., p. 163, author italics.

54. Op. cit., p. 163 and the missing ref. to note 5 on line 32.

55. Op. cit., pp. 164–5 for this argument.

56. Cf. Michel Meslin, *Pour Une Science des Religions* (Paris, 1973), pp. 123–4. See also n. 36 on p. 292 above.

57. Moltmann, *The Crucified God*, p. 292.

58. In 1973 it was thought that 'about 1 per cent of the population everywhere in the world will suffer from schizophrenia at some time in their lives' (John G. Kennedy, 'Cultural Psychology' in *Handbook of Social and Cultural Anthropology*, edited by J. J. Honigmann, Chicago, 1973, p. 1145). The evidence is mainly from 'urbanized nations'.

59. Moltmann, *The Crucified God*, p. 315.

60. *The Daily Telegraph*, 21 November 1974, p. 2.

61. See my 'Karl Barth and Justification', *Irish Theological Quarterly*, XXX, 3 (1958), pp. 274–84.

62. I think we must exclude the teaching of Jesus from any question of degree. Von Balthasar rightly speaks of 'the blazing, absolute character of the teaching [of Jesus], that shines in everything he said, promised and demanded, [and] can only be understood if the whole movement of his life is seen to be towards the Cross, so that the words and deeds are validated by the Passion which explains everything and makes everything possible'. Cf. Hans Urs von Balthasar, *Love Alone: The Way of Revelation* (London, 1968), p. 69.

63. Cf. von Balthasar, *Love Alone*, pp. 113–14. This author also takes a strongly Trinitarian view of the cross and resurrection, a revelation, the form of God's love 'as the dramatic appearance of God's trinitarian love and as the *Trinity's loving struggle* for mankind' (p. 120, author's italics).

64. Ibid., p. 114.

65. DS, 806.

66. Cf. von Balthasar, *Love Alone*, p. 71.

67. Thus, for example, in Paul, 'we who have the first fruits of the Spirit groan inwardly as we wait . . .' and 'the Spirit intercedes for us with sighs too deep for words' (Rom 8: 23 and 26).

68. Cyril of Alexandria. *In Ioann.* XI, 10 (PG 74, 544–5).

CHAPTER FIVE   *Sacramental Intimacy, the Hinge of Salvation*

1. Les sacrements sont symboles, et quels symboles! En regardant une cérémonie, que ce soit la messe ou l'un des sacrements, et ses signes (eau, onction, etc.) nous découvrons qu'un immense donné poétique — tout ce que les religions, aussi bien que les expériences psychologiques, peuvent rêver — se trouve ici récapitulé. Dieu est le maître des choses, comme des mots.' Bernard Bro, O.P., *Faut-il Encore Pratiquer?* (Paris, 1967), p. 169.

2. . . . it is very improbable that ancient man was unable to conceive of time as a linear succession of situations running in a

single direction. Rather that is the assumption, common to all mankind . . . from which they differ only later.' Norbert Lohfink, S.J., *The Christian Meaning of the Old Testament* (London, 1969), p. 124.

3. This much-used phrase has ancient antecedents. Its popularity in this century is partly due to the Oratorian tradition, with Bérulle and Thomassinus; but the best elaboration is to be found in Scheeben, who treats immediately, in this order, of the Incarnation, the Eucharist and the Church and other sacraments (cf. *Die Mysterien des Christentum*, edited by J. Höfer [Freiburg, 1958], pp. 385–504: = E.T. [St Louis, 1947], pp. 469–610 where Höfer's excellent notes have been modified and abbreviated). D. M. Baillie draws attention to some of the illogicalities that flow from the phrase, 'the extension of the Incarnation' (*The Theology of the Sacraments and Other Papers* [London, 1964], p. 61ff.), but neglects the role of the imagination. There are good reasons in psychology why experiences of the embodied self should be referred to the social body. We thus have a familiar two-way process of thinking: we pass from our own body to the mystical body of Christ, then to the body of the Lord, then to the Incarnate Lord, and in reverse order we then think down the scale again from the actions of the Lord in his body to Church and sacraments which are then seen as an 'extension of the Incarnation'.

4. See the *De resurrectione carnis*, 8 (CC II, 951). The chapter well adumbrates the role of the body (cf. E. Evans, *Tertullian's Treatise on the Resurrection* [London, 1960], p. xviii). For a summary of classical theological history on the connexion between human nature and the sacraments, cf. Bernard Leeming, *Principles of Sacramental Theology* (London, 1960), pp. 590–619.

5. I am thinking here of the successful fusion of very many factors, when the imagination of the praying community enters into the structure of ritual.

6. Cf. Odo Casel, *The Mystery of Christian Worship* (London, 1962), pp. 30, 32, 100.

7. On immediacy and distance in the symbolic imagination see Peter Homans, *Theology After Freud* (Indianapolis, 1970), Chapter 7, 'Distance and Hope', pp. 211–22.

8. Cf. *The Mystery of Christian Worship*, p. 207, n. to p. 16. Quoted by the editor from Casel's article, 'Glaube, Gnosis und Mysterium' in *Jahrbuch für Liturgiewissenschaft*, 15 (1941), p. 268.

9. 'It is a very ancient usage in cult to repeat a formula three times, sometimes in a higher tone each time', with reference to

the formula in Apuleius, *beatus et ter beatus* (*The Mystery of Christian Worship*, p. 118).

10. There is a difference between the connexions to be established between psychology and religious doctrine, and psychology and religious behaviour. Victor White, O.P., *God and the Unconscious* (London, 1952; 1967) can still be recommended, especially the fifth paper, 'The Frontiers of Theology and Psychology' which shows how 'the theologian could offer his services in a positive and constructive fashion, rather than with a suspicious resentment . . .' (p. 88).

11. Cf. F. Perls, R. F. Hefferline, P. Goodman, *Gestalt Therapy, Excitement and Growth in Human Personality* (London, 1972), p. 293.

12. C. G. Jung, 'Das Wandlungssymbol in der Messe', *Eranos Jahrbuch*, 1940/1 (Zurich, 1942), p. 134. Of special interest is the section on the symbolic content of the Mass as deeply rooted in human psychology (pp. 92–3).

13. Mary Douglas, *Natural Symbols: Explorations in Cosmology* (London, 1970).

14. Communion in the mouth is an example. Something of the intimacy of the transitional object is attached to it; and it is well known that oral attitudes are the most demanding ones (cf. Anna Freud, *Normality and Pathology in Childhood* [London, 1966], p. 40).

15. That our liturgy of praise is part of a vast cosmic whole and that it approximates to a liturgy of the angels is an ancient theme. See for example Eric Peterson, *The Angels and the Liturgy* (London, 1964) especially p. 22. For further patristic information see E. Yarnold, *The Awe-Inspiring Rites of Initiation* (Slough, 1972), p. 139, n. 54 and p. 220, n. 26.

16. Cf. F. Perls, R. F. Hefferline, P. Goodman, *Gestalt Therapy*, pp. 211, 219.

17. Cf. *The Angels and the Liturgy*, pp. 25, 37. 'The intense reality of the medieval view that the monks sang the psalms in the presence of the angels is shown by the *Regula Magistri*' which forbade spitting or clearing the nostrils in a forward direction. Doing so behind one was allowed, *angelos in ante stantes* (PL 88, 1009), quoted by Peterson, p. 37.

18. Cf. Mircea Eliade, *Myths, Dreams and Mysteries* (London, 1968), pp. 119–20. Eliade can of course be criticized, but on this point, without his own elaborations, he is following Malinowski (cf. G. S. Kirk, *Myth, Meaning and Functions* [Cambridge, 1970], p. 255 and n. 3, ibid.).

19. For a review of materials and for opinions among anthropologists cf. Roger Bastide, *Sociologie et Psychanalyse*

(Paris 1972), p. 229ff. It is interesting to note that as well as the historic interest taken in dream materials by the Chinese, we find the Jesuit missionaries after 1649 to North American Indians, such as the Iroquois, also reporting the local system of dream interpretation seriously (cf. p. 232, n. 1).

20. Theology and liturgy have many ways of referring to the paradisal 'Great Time' with each symbol bringing out another facet, e.g. Adam, the Tree of Paradise, the fruit, waters, perfumes, clothing. For Cyril of Jerusalem baptism opens the gates of 'God's Paradise', while for Chrysostom there is much greater insistence on the loss than on the restoration at baptism (cf. texts in Yarnold, *The Awe-Inspiring Rites of Initiation*, pp. 73; 159–60. See also references to Adam). Iconography brings out especially well the eschatological aspect of Paradise and its waters, a theme that was even personified in representation as far back as the sixth century (for texts and monuments cf. *Lexikon der christlichen Ikonographie*, 3, 382–4, s.v. 'Paradies-flüsse'). Ephrem in his charming Hymns on Paradise has two strophes referring the subject to baptism, IV, 4 (Adam); VI, 9 (Fall and clothing) — (SC 137, 64–5; 84–5).

21. Cf. Kirk, *Myth, Meaning and Functions*, ibid.

22. See R. W. Hepburn's criticism of Dom Illtyd Trethowan's argument in *Christianity and Paradox* (London, 1958), pp. 182–3.

23. Cf. N. Lohfink, *The Christian Meaning of the Old Testament* (London, 1969), pp. 122, 126, 134. Lohfink's Chapter VII, 'Freedom and Repetition' must be strongly recommended.

24. R. W. Hepburn, *Christianity and Paradox*, p. 183.

25. Cf. Bernard Leeming, *Principles of Sacramental Theology*, pp. 293–4, 297–8.

26. Erik H. Erikson, *Insight and Responsibility* (London, 1964), p. 26.

27. Cf. P. F. Strawson, *Individuals: an Essay in Descriptive Metaphysics* (London, 1964), pp. 15–58; 246–7. With Straw-son's approach compare an anthropologist's view by Mary Douglas, *Natural Symbols: Explorations in Cosmology*, 'that there is a strong tendency to replicate the social situation in symbolic form by drawing on bodily symbols in every possible dimension' (p. vii).

28. 'To be united with another *through blood* was to be bound within a union which no changes or chances of this mortal life could ever be allowed to destroy' — on 'the blood of the new covenant' cf. F. W. Dillistone, *Christianity and Symbolism* (London, 1955), p. 278.

29. More technically the term 'consummatory' might be expected;

but I choose *consummative* to emphasize the openness to transcendence which underlies Christian sacramental activity. The radical basis of the idea lies in pscho-physical behaviour of course. 'A "consummatory" act' is one by which 'the innate behaviour patterns are directed towards stimuli which act as rewards for the species concerned. Thus, eating, drinking, copulation are consummatory acts, whereas the learnt forms of behaviour which bring the animal into contact with food, water or sexual partner are "instrumental" responses' (cf. Jeffrey Gray, *The Psychology of Fear and Stress* (London, 1971), p. 128. It is not difficult to see here a parallel with the scholastic analysis of the act of faith which makes a distinction between an attraction which is *primary* and one which is *secondary*. A very similar finality is said to be at work in the phenomenon of *primary attraction* to the truths of faith: '*veritas prima, quae est fidei obiectum, est finis omnibus desideriorum et actionum nostrarum* (cf. 'rewards for the species concerned') . . . inde est quod *per dilectionem* operatur (Summa Theologica, II, 4, 2, ad 3).

30. On sexual life as reflecting the image of God, cf. Alfons Auer, *Open to the World, An Analysis of Lay Spirituality* (Dublin-Melbourne, 1966), p. 245ff. From the theological point of view the chapter 'Lay Spirituality in Marriage' can be recommended (pp. 235–94).

31. Cf. Victor W. Turner, *The Ritual Process* (London, 1969), p. 157, author italics.

32. Cf. Andrew M. Greeley, 'U.S. Catholics '72', *The Month*, n. s. 5, 5 (May 1972), p. 153ff. An anthropologist might of course take the view that the deviant sexual behaviour evoked by Greeley should be considered in the light of the phenomenon of desexualization. Thus among the Tongas sex is used, not for libidinous purposes, but as a rite of re-aggregation to the community after rupture. 'L'étreinte n'est plus quelque chose d'érotique, c'est un simple geste qui rappelle cette émotion de groupe et qui la signifie. Elle est devenue un rite, un symbole. Elle est bien morte comme génital pour renaître comme psyché collective' (Roger Bastide, *Sociologie et Psychanalyse* [Paris, 1972], p. 268 but for the phenomenon cf. p. 260ff.).

33. Any reader of Desmond Morris, *Intimate Behaviour* (London, 1971) will see well-documented and ample confirmation of these points from an author who observes human behaviour with all the sympathy of a zoologist or animal ethologist. Morris represents a viewpoint from which the theologian can learn.

34. Cf. Paul Tillich, *Systematic Theology*, I, 1, p. 132, n. 1. Tillich

then remarks on the Protestant distrust of such symbolizing. Catholic and Protestant outlooks on religious symbolism have of course been greatly at variance in the past. The opposition between word and sacrament, so ferociously upheld after the Reformation, now appears as quite otiose. The issue here is that both rite and word have their aspect of intimacy; in future we should study the psychodynamic attitudes we have inherited, examine how we manipulate them on our respective communities, and, when we have discovered what we are doing and criticized it by the light of the Gospel, our ecumenism will be a responsible one. When the psychologist Norman O. Brown says: 'the return to symbolism would be the end of the Protestant era, the end of Protestant literalism' (*Love's Body* [New York, 1966], p. 191), that should be an appeal to Catholic self-critical openness.

35. This is not the place to spell out the ethology of human love-making. But the comparison in my mind is this: just as in human love-making there exists a continued series of gestures (continuous not only in respect of one act of intercourse, but continuous in respect of an ongoing life of the pair) and just as that series ranges from the initial contacts of a glance, through foreplay to orgasmic satisfaction, and even further just as any point, however early in that sequence, when informed by love can be vastly precious and significant, so (my comparison goes) any point on the *symbolic* love-scale may be informed by the teleology of the divine-human love relationship. Dr Desmond Morris puts the basis of my argument with disarming straightforwardness: 'a fleeting touch on the cheek from the one they love is worth more than six hours in thirty-seven positions from someone they do not' (*Intimate Behaviour*, p. 96).

36. Cf. Summa Theologica, I, 98, 2c and ad 3.

37. Norman O. Brown in his *Life Against Death* (London, 1959) has done much to rehabilitate the role of death in Freud's thought, an often neglected factor. Death, as with Christian mortification on another level, has more to do with structure and fixation in ontogenetic development than any ontological disposition leading to a final option, as some theologians have recently held. There is no reason why the words 'mortification' and 'self-discipline' should not still be used in association, so long as we have some idea why they go together.

38. Cf. K. Ritzer, *Le mariage dans les églises chrétiennes du Ier au XIe siècle, Lex Orandi,* 45 (Paris, 1970), pp. 81–123.

39. In *The New Marriage Rite: A Study Book* (London, 1970) it is made clear how fresh is the attention to the eucharistic element, especially in the three new prefaces (pp. 46–7).

40. We thus have two-well-known contrasting doctrines: (*i*) that each individual as an object of the infinite love and election of God possesses a quasi-infinite worth; (*ii*) that each individual as a child of sin is incapable of any good work, though classical theology debated the extent and degree of the latter proposition. Theoretical speculations are all very well; but how *in practice* can the Christian live with this antinomy? My reply would be that it is in part a function of sacramental intimacy to enable him to do so, i.e. the symbolically transcendent power that can be actuated by seeing, hearing, touching, ingesting, and transposing sexual intimacy at the greatest variety of levels *in the Christian sacramental context*, is precisely for the Christian how in practice he can live with the antinomy. In so symbolizing his relationship with God and with his fellow-men, he avoids being torn between on the one hand theological gigantism (the extreme of doctrine [*i*]), and theological Lilliputianism (the extreme of doctrine [*ii*]) on the other hand. St Ignatius Loyola's 'Application of the Senses' to the 'Contemplation on the Incarnation' is a brilliant adaptation of such sacramental experience (cf. *Spiritual Exercises*, nos 247–8; 121–5). But even this technique has its debatable side (cp. the psychological manipulation on hell, nos 66–70).

41. Cf. Desmond Morris, *Intimate Behaviour*, Chapter 5, 'Specialized Intimacy'.

42. My friend and colleague Robert Murray kindly allows me to quote the following from an unpublished diary of his: 'At 7.30 began the marathon night service of four hours . . . There were crowds of the faithful all the time, standing, kneeling, prostrating themselves, kissing icons, crosses, and going in endless succession to the north door of the iconostasis with a candle and a bit of paper bearing the names of the people they wanted to commend to the monks' prayers. It being a solemn celebration with the *staret* (abbot) and several hieromonks fully vested, whenever they came out into the *naos* . . . people would grab at the vestments or at the deacon's stole and kiss them or mop their faces with them. As Donald observed to me, the Romanians' religion is a tremendously tactile and corporeal affair. Everyone behaves with enormous reverence, but also with perfect simplicity and matter-of-factness, as if they know they are at home — like children who have been brought up to know they can be cuddled whenever they feel like it, and yet retain a terrific reverence. It is remarkable to see a twentieth-century city-dweller (for many come here, as well as bare-footed peasants) performing the greater *metania* before an icon, with perfect bodily control, feet together, going down

on knees and clenched fists, bowing the head and rising, all in a
disciplined movement repeated perhaps three times, with signs
of the cross in between, all expressing quite simply the
conviction that this is suitable behaviour for man before his
God' (Robert Murray, *Diary of a Visit to Romania, 11 September
to 9 October 1971*).

43. Cf. Paul Tillich, *Systematic Theology*, III, 4, pp. 231, 233. One
must stress the phrase 'in terms of potentiality'. Tillich also
gives another argument for infant baptism based on the
difference between the 'objective' and the 'subjective' type of
church (ibid., p. 232).

44. See the *Rite of Baptism for Children* (Birmingham, 1970).
Baptism is to take place never more than one month after the
birth (p. 12). At the outset the mother symbol is used of the
Church (p. 1). Increased attention is given to the parents (p. 3),
and to the wishes of the family. Matthew 9: 13–15 is among the
readings, and, *as part of the rite*, there is a blessing for the
mother (pp. 42, 68). The intercessions are marked by an
affective tone; the exorcism has something of a protective
mother-child feeling; the anointings and blessings establish a
child-parent relationship with regard for intimacy.

45. Cf. p. 179 above.

46. Cf. Bernard Bro, *Faut-il Encore Pratiquer?*, p. 119.

47. Cf. John Macquarrie, *Principles of Christian Theology* (London,
1966), p. 455.

48. 'Knowledge by connaturality originates in the child-mother
relationship. All *knowledge by union* (author's italics) is (*a*)
knowledge by incorporation or being incorporated); and (*b*) all
knowledge through love has its natural fundament in our
primary bond with the mother . . . Faith, the most sublime
form of non-scientific knowledge is (if we consider its natural
history, independent of all questions of grace) a form of
swallowing or being received. It goes back to an infantile form
of oral union' (Karl Stern, *The Flight from Woman* [London,
1965], p. 54). Once again, *caro salutis est cardo*. This is one more
reason why full Catholicism will always be sacramental and
will retain its polarization to the Blessed Virgin. Knowledge by
connaturality does not fit into a thoroughly Protestant
theological anthropology any more than a thorough going use
of religious symbolism (cf. p. 23, n. 2 above).

49. Thus even if it were true, which it is not, that all intimacy is in
some way sexual, that would still not entail the consequence
that any sexually tinged symbol, or even piece of behaviour,
was a substitution for copulation. There is a range of sequences
in human behaviour which are intimate, but do not call for the

highly ambivalent gesture which evokes shame, guilt, fear and even a death-wish. Theological man, as well as psycho-physical man, is more than a set of experienced paradoxes. But the paradoxes are there, Freudian or other, and even in the reflection of these, man can see himself as a divine project which his very sacramentality can help to achieve. More than that, it is in his sacramental existence, and so far as I can see most normally in that way, that sacramental man can in practical living resolve the very antinomies that check his rebirth and new life.

CHAPTER SIX   *Sacramental Interiorization, the 'Yes' to Communion*

1. Yves Durand, who has made a sample survey of the incidence of water as a polyvalent symbol, finds that in the structured imagination of man water occurs 39 per cent of the time in a mystical, or enclosing context, as compared with 38.5 per cent for contexts involving separation or ascent, and only 13 per cent for contexts involving union or reunion. That makes it belong more to the *nocturnal* than to the *diurnal regime*. I shall describe both later (cf. Yves Durand, 'Symbolisation de l'Imaginaire', *Les Études Philosophiques*, Juillet-Septembre, 1971/3 [1971], p. 321).

2. Cf. Sebastian Moore, *God is a New Language* (London, 1967), p. 136. For Dom Sebastian the revitalizing of Christian images must come through living 'much more *consciously* the drama of the human community than was demanded of the preceding Christian generations . . . and this means that we must in the interim learn to live *without* symbols' (ibid., author's italics).

3. In this domain we can lay no special claims for the primacy of any one logic. 'Les syntaxes de la raison ne sont que des formulisations extrêmes d'une rhétorique baignant elle-même dans le consensus imaginaire général. Ensuite, d'une façon plus précise, il n'y a pas de coupure entre le rationnel et l'imaginaire, le rationalisme n'étant plus, parmi bien d'autres, qu'une structure polarisante particulière du champ des images' (Gilbert Durand, *L'Imagination Symbolique* [Paris, Coll. SUP, 1968], p. 84). In other words the rational thing to do is to allow for the non-rational. Durand, whose great treatise I shall rely upon later, is here saying something particularly apt for sacramental theology, where category mistakes have so often led us into dead-ends.

4. Cf. Hans Küng, *Why Priests?* (London, 1972), p. 48, author's italics.

5. On the evolution of the priestly role cf. Robert Towler, 'The Role of the Clergy', in *The Christian Priesthood*, edited by N. Lash, J. Rhymer (London, 1970), pp. 170–1.

6. Cf. Karl Rahner, 'Priestly Existence' in *Theological Investigations*, 3 (London, 1967), pp. 242, 245.

7. Cf. Albert Chapelle, *Hegel et la Religion III, La Théologie de L'Église (La Dialectique, 2ième partie)* — (Paris, 1971), p. 115. This extremely well documented work repays study, and a theologian will find there a most thoughtful conspectus of Hegel's theological speculations (cf. n. 81, pp. 136–7).

8. In passing I have distinguished between 'sacramental man' and 'mystical man'. At first sight there is a recognizable difference between the two. But, if we were to go more deeply into this, we might conclude that we were dealing with a difference in degree rather than with a difference in kind. Chapelle can speak of sacramental experience according to Hegel as in part an experience 'de la présence réalisante, et donc réelle, du Logos qui est Esprit' (p. 121). In religious terms such an experience would, I think, be called a mystical one.

9. Cf. Bernard Bro, 'Man and the Sacraments: The Anthropological Substructure of the Christian Sacraments', *Concilium* I, 4 (January 1968), p. 20, author's italics.

10. Cf. J. Le Men, 'Le Moi, L'Autre et la Symbolique Spatiale', *Les Études Philosophiques*, Juillet–Septembre, 1971/3 (1971), pp. 336–7.

11. Here at last, it seems to me, is a reason why religious authorities have maintained their stand against any watering down of the symbolism of the heart of Christ as an entirely natural and theologically necessary expression of the divine love incarnate. Cf. Pius XII, *Haurietis Aquas* (AAS 48 [1956], p. 316f.), where the heart of Christ is 'the most noble part of [his] human nature' and 'the natural sign and symbol' [*naturalis index seu symbolus*] of his infinite love' (DS, 3922). The use of the word *naturalis* should mean that there is some physiological connexion between the heart as a muscle and Jesus as a loving person. In 'high' Catholic devotion the heart of Jesus, 'hypostatically united to the Word of God', has a sacramental quality. More sense can be made of this, if it is seen as an instance of the phenomenon of interiorization with its double polarity, rather than as a specimen of folklorist physiology.

12. The question of the influence of binary opposition on formal logic *via* 'informal logic' has been studied by G. E. R. Lloyd, *Polarity and Analogy, Two Types of Argumentation in Early Greek Thought* (Cambridge, 1966). Chapter I, 'Theories Based on Opposites in Early Greek Thought', contains materials which

are very relevant to my argument here (cf. especially p. 31f.). 'Life mostly comes in pairs' is a famous saying that Aristotle attributed to Alcmaeon; and 'Parmenides probably held that the sex of the child is determined by its place on the *right* or *left* of the mother's womb (right for males, left for females)' — (cf. ibid., pp. 16 and 17). As a modern gloss I cannot resist the following: 'Even though he was a physicist he knew that important biological objects come in pairs' (James D. Watson, *The Double Helix, Being a Personal Account of the Structure of D.N.A. . . . Awarded a Nobel Prize* [London, 1968], p. 171).

13. Cf. Rodney Needham, 'The Left Hand of the Mugwe: an Analytical Note on the Structure of Meru Symbolism', *Africa*, XXX (1960), p. 21, quoting I. S. Wile, *Handedness: Right and Left* (Boston, Mass. 1934), pp. 339–40.

14. From a more accessible work, Michael Barsley, *The Left-Handed Book* (London, 1966), p. 107. See especially Chapter I, 'The Unclean Hand'; II, 'The Origins of Handedness'; XIV 'Christianity and the Left'; XV, 'Other Religions'.

15. Cf. Peter Rigby, 'Dual Symbolic Classification and the Gogo of Central Tanzania', *Africa*, XXXVI (1966), pp. 1–17; cp. also the lists and arguments in Lloyd's *Polarity and Analogy*, p. 32f.

16. Cf. Victor W. Turner, *The Ritual Process, Structure and Anti-Structure* (London, 1969), p. 40.

17. Consistency in interrelating binary opositions among the Ndembu was observed by Turner (ibid., p. 61). For further reflections, cf. the same author's 'Color in Ndembu Ritual: a Problem in Primitive Classification', Chapter III in his *The Forest of Symbols* (Ithaca, N.Y. 1967), pp. 69–72 with short bibliography.

18. Cf. Turner, *The Ritual Process*, p. 3.

19. Cf. Gilbert Durand, *Les Structures Anthropologiques de l'Imaginaire* (Paris, 1963), p. 34. See n. 29 on p. 314 below.

20. Cf. *The Ritual Process*, p. 83.

21. Cf. G. S. Kirk, *Myth, Its Meaning and Function in Ancient and Other Cultures* (Cambridge, 1970), p. 83.

22. Cf. Rodney Needham, 'The Left Hand of the Mugwe', p. 31.

23. I am delighted to see a psychologist show appreciation and understanding of the 'concreteness' with which St Teresa of Avila describes her mystical experiences. As for Bernini's *Ecstasy of St Teresa* in Santa Maria della Vittoria it cannot be too clearly said that it was 'simultaneously both a physical and a spiritual event', however much puritan behaviourists may dismiss it (cf. Liam Hudson, *The Cult of the Fact* [London, 1972], p. 173f.). Baroque, 'an art that dwelt on the

reconciliation of opposites (p. 173) is in my view very sacramentally charged. Its sociality is another matter.

24. Cf. J. J. von Allmen, *Worship, Its Theology and Practice* (London, 1965) for the section, 'The "anagnostic" proclamation of the Word of God', pp. 131–7. von Allmen finds the use of Scripture wholly for a 'preaching service' to be 'inadmissible'. He gives several reasons. Among them, 'the reading of the Bible in worship is traditionally preceded by an epiklesis, an invocation of the Holy Spirit, that the Word may really come alive for us so as to accomplish its work of salvation and judgement' (p. 133).

25. Sacramentalism as well as myth have to deal among other binary oppositions with the basic male/female opposition. We have said something about the use of sexual symbolisms in the previous chapter. It should not be forgotten that in the religious context the female element can be looked upon as a source of evil. As Lloyd points out, the idea was propagated by Hesiod and Semonides, and is to be found in Nuer and Maori belief (cf. *Polarity and Analogy*, p. 42 and n. 4). We might compare Dietrich Bonhoeffer: (*a*) 'With the creation of Woman, man's limit has now entered into the midst of the created world', and (*b*) 'Eve, the fallen wise mother of man — this is the first beginning. Mary, the innocent, unknowing mother of God — this is the second beginning' (*Creation and Temptation*, pp. 75, 88). On *féminisation* see below.

26. Cf. V. W. Turner, *The Ritual Process*, p. 25.

27. Cf. Gilbert Durand, *L'Imagination Symbolique*, p. 65 relying on Jung and Cassirer.

28. 'When we recognize the loss of a symbol we cannot say, "let's try to replace it". Symbols cannot be invented; they cannot be produced intentionally. But perhaps the mystical element may be the way in which a different sort of Protestantism, a non-moralistic and nonintellectualistic Protestantism, may return to some of the positive elements in Catholicism' (Paul Tillich, *Ultimate Concern, Dialogues with Students* [London, 1965], p. 149).

29. Gilbert Durand, *Les Structures Anthropologiques de l'Imaginaire, Introduction à l'Archétypologie Générale* (Paris, 1963) — series, Bibliothèque de Philosophie Contemporaine. I will refer to this work simply as SAI, with great regret that I can do no justice to its real scope and learning.

30. Cf. Gilbert Durand, *L'Imagination Symbolique*, p. 85.

31. If we are dealing with a myth, such as the Oedipus story, then it is clear that it is only the narrative, which effects the resolution of the opposing elements. I am not thinking of myths as 'explanations' in the sense of Lévi-Strauss. What I am

trying to convey is that from the sacramental point of view, myth and/or *descriptive-narrative* elements are part of a unity of performance (Turner's 'Gestalt'), which may or may not coincide with the unity of explanation that exists in its own right as a piece of theology, and that may or may not require myth for its specific purpose. Recital and interiorization may alone of course be effective. Mary Douglas quotes the analysis by Lévi-Strauss of a 'Cuna shaman's song which is chanted to relieve a difficult delivery in childbirth. The doctor does not touch the patient. The incantation is to have its effect by mere recital' (cf. Mary Douglas, *Purity and Danger* [Harmondsworth, 1966], pp. 88–9).

32. Cf. Gilbert Durand, *L'Imagination Symbolique*, p. 87.

33. Some reflection is needed, as Durand remarks, 'sur l'universalité et la banalité du bestiaire' (SAI, p. 63). There is no space to do that here, and we must be satisfied that there is a universality about *theriomorphism* in part from the findings of J. Piaget. The connexion between time and the dentated jaw of the beast was not obvious to me at first; but I have come to think that Durand makes out his case. We have already mentioned the anxiety induced by the distancing effect of time (cf. *Heythrop Journal* XIV [1973], p. 7). Fate and Death add their quota of aggressivity, so the great hero musicians (Marsyas, Orpheus, Dionysus) sweeten our lot by meeting their death, perhaps in a substitutionary role, in devouring jaws. In Mithraic ceremonies of initiation there were ritual bellowings, since the ceremony commemorated a sacrifice (cf. SAI, p. 80, quoting Jung).

34. 'We should begin at once to disinter the biblical themes from the ecclesiastical tombs in which they have been buried and make them available to the fantasy-hungry and ritually emasculated moderns' (Harvey Cox, *The Feast of Fools* [Cambridge, Mass., 1969], p. 80).

35. There is also of course the fascination of horror, inducing the feeling of being ground down and swallowed which is our response to sadistic voracity. Perhaps against appearances this also can be therapeutic. Ignatius of Antioch was not only coming to terms with his fate, he was also producing a sacramental, though not eucharistic, mysticism: 'I am God's wheat, and I am ground by the teeth of the beasts, so as to be the pure bread of Christ' (Rom. IV, 1). Apart from the matter of Ignatius's psychological traits it is only fair to him to remember that bread 'a single substance' from many grains is like cheese, and the many-threaded girdle a symbol of unity (cf. E. S. Drower, *Water into Wine*, [London, 1956], p. 44 and n. 1).

36. There is all the difference, as Durand points out, between the archetypal animal, and the animal we observe. Thus the pelican feeding its young with blood from its breast has served very well as an eucharistic symbol. The imagination neglects or covers up what does not suit it (SAI, p. 64).

37. The Constitution on the Liturgy (Vatican II) asks that the 'paschal character of Christian death' should be more in evidence and that there should be a change in liturgical colour. Joy in place of gloom is about interiorization indeed, but may well be going too fast. There is an intermediate stage of coming to terms with death and destiny by *theriomorphic* familiarization.

38. The blindfold Synagogue goes back to the twelfth century and was not rare in medieval art. Cf. art. 'Ecclesia u. Synagoge', in *Lexikon der christlichen Ikonographie, 1* (Freiburg, 1968), 569f., esp. 571c.

39. Cf. *Purity and Danger*, p. 187.

40. The dove, the bird of Venus, has of course sexual as well as chthonic associations, but does nonetheless represent the Holy Spirit, and, as Jung said, the word of the Mother above, Hagia Sophia (SAI, p. 134). On eucharistic tabernacles and elsewhere the dove symbolizes the eucharist as the presence of the pure fire of divine love. As such it should be taking flight upwards. It is occasionally shown as descending, thus suggesting a theophany. Cf. L. E. Keck, 'The Spirit and the Dove', NTS 17 (1970–1), pp. 41–67.

41. Moves towards *féminisation* of the priesthood are clearly well under way in the Anglican Communion. It is because we are in the realm of archetypal symbols that reactions must be strongly felt. In addition to a calm and rational discussion of the theological issues we need a comparative study of the Father symbol with reference to that of the *Magna Mater*, the *Virgo Mater* and the *Ewig-Weibliche* where there is greater symbolic polyvalency.

42. Cf. J. J. von Allmen, *Worship, its Theology and Practice* (London, 1965), p. 189, n. 1.

43. Cf. SAI, p. 150f.

44. See C. H. Dodd, *The Interpretation of the Fourth Gospel* (Cambridge, 1953), pp. 144–50; 201–12; 263–85 and in Part III where appropriate.

45. Cf. SAI, p. 161.

46. Op. cit., p. 162.

47. In exogamous societies the *word* is such a powerful institution that it is assimilated to marriage. Thus a 'bad word' *is* adultery (Cf. SAI, p. 163).

48. Cf. M. Eliade, *Myths, Dreams and Mysteries* (London, 1968), Chapter III, 'Nostalgia for Paradise', especially pp. 67–8ff.

49. Cf. SAI, p. 177f. Victor W. Turner in his *Forest of Symbols* (Ithaca, N.Y., 1967), Chapter VII, 'Mukunda: The Rite of Circumcision', pp. 151–279 says nothing to conflict with Durand. The Christian reader cannot fail to be struck by so many themes familiar to him in connexion with baptism, such as death-life and purification-life.

50. Durand sets out a 'Classification Isotopique de l'Image' (Annexe II, SAI, pp. 422–3). The scheme has a main vertical division which makes clear the separation of the *diurnal* from the *nocturnal* images.

51. Cf. H. Musurillo, *Symbolism and the Christian Imagination* (Dublin, 1962), pp. 19–20.

52. Musurillo cites: 1 Cor 3: 2; Heb 5: 12–14; 1 Pet 2: 2 where the doctrine is compared to milk because it is elementary. 1 Pet 2: 2 suggests how the rite of administering milk and honey to the newly baptized might have arisen (cf. E. G. Selwyn, *The First Epistle of St Peter* [London, 1946], pp. 154–5 for standard references).

53. Cf. Hippol. *apost. trad.* 23 (SC 57) and *elench.*, 5, 8 (GCS 94); Tert. *de cor. mil.*, III, 3. On this pair of life-symbols cf. E. S. Drower, *Water into Wine, A Study of Ritual Idiom in the Middle East* (London, 1956), pp. 7–11, 'Note on "Life-Foods"'. Lady Drower's terminology is especially convenient.

54. Cf. SAI, p. 275.

55. Durand quotes St Francis of Sales and St Teresa of Avila on the Christian souls who, like children are given the delights of the breast. St Francis of Sales sees nothing incongruous in disregarding the sex of the Saviour in order to indulge his spiritual fantasy on the symbolic oral sexuality of the lover of God (SAI, p. 226). Milk is also used as a symbol of re-birth at initiation ceremonies (Cf. E. S. Drower, *Water into Wine*, p. 9).

56. Cf. SAI, p. 274.

57. Cf. J. Le Men, 'Le Moi, l'Autre et la Symbolique Spatiale', p. 338.

58. Cf. SAI, p. 274.

59. Cf. G. S. Kirk, *Myth its Meaning and Function*, p. 269.

60. In general the ritual cup of chalice does not vary greatly between mainstream Christian communities. In Jewish ritual 'a special goblet is usually provided for drinking ritual wine' (E. S. Drower, *Water into Wine*, pp. 26–7).

61. Cf. SAI, p. 278.

CHAPTER SEVEN   *Without Justification*

1. Cf. Karl Rahner, *Foundations of the Christian Faith*, p. 382.
2. Op. cit., p. 359ff.
3. DS 3016.
4. My use of *prolepsis* would also involve the idea that the Church as Christ's body continues his history.
5. Cf. Ernst Käsemann, *Commentary on Romans* (London, 1980), p. 26.
6. But see George H. Tavard, *Justification, An Ecumenical Study* (New York–Ramsey, N.J., 1983), 1983, p. 2 who is more optimistic.
7. Hans Küng, *On Being a Christian* (London, 1978), pp. 501–2.
8. See *Salvation and the Church, ARCIC II, Agreed Statement* (London, 1987).
9. For the background to what follows see the important article, Harding Meyer, 'The Doctrines of Justification in the Lutheran Dialogue with Other Churches', *One in Christ*, XVII (1981), pp. 86–116.
10. Art. cit., p. 88.
11. Ibid., p. 89.
12. The *Malta Report* covered four previous sets of conversations (1967–1970). See Harding Meyer, 'The Joint Lutheran/Roman Catholic Study Commission on "The Gospel and the Church"' in *Lutheran World*, XVIII (1971), pp. 161–87, and for the final text see 'Report of the Joint Lutheran/Roman Catholic Study Commission on "The Gospel and the Church"' (Malta, February 1971), in *Lutheran World*, XIX (1972), pp. 259–71.
13. Cf. Harding Meyer, 'The Doctrine of Justification', p. 92.
14. See n. 10 above.
15. See *Anglican-Lutheran Dialogue, The Report of the Anglican-Lutheran European Regional Commission, Helsinki, August–September, 1982* (London, 1983).
16. Cardinal Ratzinger writes: 'Luther well understood what he meant when he indicated that justification was the genuine point of separation, which for him was identical with the opposition between "Gospel" and "Law". But justification must be taken just as radically and profoundly as Luther took it, namely as the point to which *all anthropology must be brought back* as well as all other points of doctrine on the dialectic between Law and Gospel at the same time' (author italics). In 'Luther et l'Unité des Églises, Interview du Cardinal Joseph Ratzinger', *Documentation Catholique*, no. 1866 (15 January 1984), pp. 121ff. The translation from the French is mine. I have not seen the original in *Communio — Internationale Zeitschrift* (December 1983).

17. See *A New Dictionary of Christian Theology* (London, 1983), p. 314, s.v. 'Justification'; also the handy biblical summary in Peter Toon, *Justification and Sanctification* (London, 1983), pp. 13–42.

18. Cf. Peter Brown, *Augustine of Hippo* (London, 1967), p. 392 and the *Opus imperfectum*, I, 38.

19. See e.g. *Enchiridion*, 30.

20. From the year 396 onwards the four ages, or *régimes*, of man are a feature of Augustine's anthropology. See *De diversis quaestionibus 83*, LXVI, 3 and much later *Enchiridion*, 118.

21. Cf. Summa Theologica, 110, 1.

22. 'It has to be admitted that the great theologian of grace does not teach a "Protestant" doctrine of justification' (cf. Peter Toon, *Justification and Sanctification*, p. 50).

23. See the *Prologus* to Summa Theologica, I, II.

24. Cf. Summa Theologica, I, II, 109, 5 (*Virtus altior, quae est virtus gratiae*).

25. Cf. Summa Theologica, I, II, 109, 9; also in II Sent. d. 26, q. 1; a. 4, ad 2, et 3; a. 5.

26. See Bernard Lonergan, *Grace and Freedom* (London, 1970), p. 40.

27. Op. cit., p. 103 and n. 62.

28. Cf. Summa Theologica, I, 20, 2: 'sed amor Dei est infundens, et creans bonitatem in rebus'.

29. Cf. Summa Theologica, 110, 1.

30. Cf. Summa Theologica, 109, 7.

31. Cf. Summa Theologica, I, II, 110, 3.

32. Cf. Summa Theologica, I, II, 113, 1; I, II, 113, 6, ad 2.

33. Cf. Summa Theologica, I, II, 62, 1.

34. DS, 1524.

35. Cp. Bernard Lonergan, *Grace and Freedom*, p. 42.

36. See Bernard Lonergan, *Collection* (London, 1967), Chapter 12 'Openness and Religious Experience', pp. 198–201.

37. *Contra Gentes* III, 17–25 should be read on this point, though Lonergan's warnings on the 'cosmic hierarchy' should be kept in mind (cf. *Grace and Freedom*, pp. 74–6).

38. For Trent's *tour de force* on justification and its 'causes', cf. DS, 1529.

39. Cf. R. A. Markus, *Saeculum: History and Society in the Theology of St Augustine* (Cambridge, 1970), p. 222.

40. Op. cit., p. 230.

41. Cf. Frederick C. Copleston, *A History of Philosophy*, II (London, 1964) 2nd edition, p. 416.

42. Op. cit., p. 425.

43. On the first signs of Protestantism in Italy see H. Jedin, *Papal Legate at the Council of Trent* (St Louis–London, 1947), p. 104f.

44. Hefele–Leclercq (Richard–Michel), *Histoire des Conciles*, IX, 1 (Paris), pp. 303–5.

45. See Jedin's Chapter XX, 'Justification', in *Papal Legate*, pp. 326–92. The famous Richard Hooker, without being too specific about it, came near to Seripando: 'There are two kinds of Christian righteousness, the one . . . by imputation; the other in us . . . God giveth both one justice and the other: the one by accepting us for righteousness in Christ; the other by working Christian righteousness in us'. (Richard Hooker, *The Laws of Ecclesiastical Polity*, I [London, 1954] p. 17), quoted by George Tavard, *Justification, an Ecumenical Study*, p. 68.

46. In Jedin's judgment no other theologian contributed so much to the refutation of the doctrine of twofold justice as did [the Jesuit] Laynez' (*Papal Legate*, p. 373).

47. For the free will see: DS, 1511; 1521; 1525; 1526; 1528; 1552; 1554; 1555. For the impairment of the will see: DS, 1511 (*in deterius*) 1537 (desertion of God); 1540 (the remaining power of sin).

48. See e.g. *Gaudium et Spes*, nos 2–10; 15–17.

49. Cf. Giuseppe Toffanin, *L'Umanismo al Concilio di Trento* (Bologna, 1955), p. 65.

50. DS, 1528–1531.

51. DS, 1526.

52. But Gallican and Spanish national independence over against Rome was also defended. Cf. Jean Delumeau, *Le Catholicisme entre Luther et Voltaire* (Paris, 1971), p. 62ff.

53. Best known of the new type of Cardinal were Baronius and Bellarmine.

54. Cf. Hubert Jedin, editor of *History of the Church*, V (London, 1967), p. 577.

55. Ibid., p. 579.

56. Ibid., p. 587.

57. For this metaphor see Delumeau, *Le Catholicisme*, p. 87, and Pierre Janelle, *The Catholic Reformation* (London, 1971), p. 182.

58. Romeo di Maio should be consulted, *Pittura e Controriforma a Napoli* (Rome–Bari, 1983). There is an unnumbered section of illustrations with excellent marginal comments.

59. James Brown, *Subject and Object in Modern Theology* (London, 1955), p. 172.

60. Cf. Karl Rahner, *Theological Investigations*, IX (London, 1972), p. 60.

61. Cf. Helmut Thielicke, *Glauben und Denken in der Neuzeit* (Tübingen, 1983), pp. 61–81.

62. Cf. Otto H. Pesch, O.P. in *Catholic Scholars Dialogue with Luther*, edited by Jared Wicks, S.J. (Loyola-Chicago, 1970), pp. 61–81.

63. The term is suggested by an excellent philosophical account in Théobald Süss, *Luther, Collection SUP, Philosophes* (Paris, 1969), see especially p. 34. In a happy formula Süss says that Luther is 'actualiste dans l'anthropologie' and 'ontologique dans la doctrine de Dieu' (p. 31).

64. Luther, Disputatio de homine, n. 4 (1536 — W.A., 39, 1, 174ff.).

65. 'L'anthropologie théologique de Luther présuppose une anthropologie métaphysique de nature platonicienne' and this can be especially well seen in the Lectures on the Magnificat (1521 — W.A. 7, 746–601). Cf. Süss, *Luther*, p. 59.

66. The influence of Gregory of Rimini is a probable one. See the recent short and useful survey of Ockhamism and Luther in G. Chantraine, *Erasme et Luther, Libre et Serf Arbitre* (Paris, 1981), Annexe 1, pp. 457–9; and Süss, Luther, pp. 37, 41.

67. See the *Disputatio de homine*, nos 25, 35, 40 with 1 Cor 7, 32 ('For the form of this world is passing away').

68. René Girard has drawn attention to the mythical significance of Cain's fratricide. See his *Des Choses Cachées depuis la Fondation du Monde* (Paris, 1978).

69. In the Lectures on Romans (1515–1516).

70. 'The language of Aquinas, the Scholastics and Trent does not communicate with Luther. It is simply different.' Roger Haight, *The Experience and Language of Grace* (Dublin, 1979), p. 91.

71. Cf. Gerhard Ebeling, *Luther* (Philadelphia–London, 1970), p. 156: '. . . grace does not alter something within man, but alters the situation, and alters man in respect of his standing before God, the way he is regarded from God's point of view'. The Catholic has neglected this *coram* theology to his own loss and that of ecumenism.

72. Cf. Vatican II, Decree on Ecumenism, n. 4.

73. Cf. Gerhard Ebeling, *Luther*, p. 163.

74. Gordon Rupp, 'Luther: 1483–1983, Catholics Think Again', *The Tablet*, 12 November 1983.

75. James McCue, 'The *Sitz im Leben* of the Doctrine of Justification', *Clergy Review*, LXVII, n. 8 (August 1982), p. 272.

76. Cf. Hans Walter Wolff, *An Anthropology of the Old Testament* (London, 1974), p. 93.

77. Cf. Thomas F. Torrance, *Theological Science* (London, 1969), p. 303.

78. Cf. Erwin Iserloh in *Catholic Scholars Dialogue with Luther*, p. 58.

79. Hans Küng, *Rechtfertigung, Die Lehre Karl Barths und eine Katholische Besinnung* (Einsiedeln, 1957); and E. T. *Justification, the Doctrine of Karl Barth and a Catholic Reflection* (London, 1964). See my review of the German edition in *Irish Theological Quarterly*, XXV, 3 (1958), pp. 274–84.

80. Peter Manns, 'Absolute Faith and Incarnate Faith, Luther on Justification in the Galatians Commentary of 1531–1535' in *Catholic Scholars Dialogue with Luther*, pp. 121–56; also Joseph Lortz, 'The Basic Elements of Luther's Intellectual Style', ibid., pp. 3–33.

81. Cf. Gerhard Ebeling, *Luther*, p. 65.

82. Ernst Bloch's, *Thomas Münzer* appeared in Munich, 1921 and is now to be found in the *Gesamtausgabe, Bd* I, as 'Thomas Münzer als Theologe der Revolution' (Frankfurt, 1959).

83. See John O'Malley, S.J. 'Rome and the Renaissance Studies in Culture and Religion' in *London Variorum Reprints* (London, 1981), pp. 573–601, especially 'Aggiornamento and the Historical Consciousness', p. 589ff. Also in *Theological Studies*, 32 (1971), pp. 573–601.

84. DS, 2751–2756; DS, 3537–3550.

85. *Soliloquia*, I, 2, 7. Of course this is the Augustine of 387, accepting his faith as a convert and *desiring to know now*.

86. Cf. James McCue, 'The *Sitz im Leben* . . .', p. 272.

87. *Redemptor Hominis*, 19 (AAS [1979]).

88. Eberhard Jüngel, *God as the Mystery of the World* (Edinburgh, 1983), p. 50f.

89. Dietrich Bonhoeffer, *Creation and Temptation* (London, 1966), p. 79.

Indexes

Thematic Index

Note: italicised page numbers indicate references in the Notes section (pp. 281–322)

ACT, actism, 257f, 260f
adaltereity, alterity, 64ff, 71, 73, 75, 81–84, 86, *287*
anxiety, *Angst*, 58f, 120ff, 166, 173, 201, 226, 257, 279

BAPTISM, 1, 10, 33f, 39, 175, 196, 198, 252
binary opposition, 201ff, 204, 206f, 209

CARO-CARDO, 165, 172, 176ff, 181, 191f
Christiformity, 92ff, 96, 98–100, 119, 136, 160, 191
Church, viii, 1–4, 6, 9f, 21–23, 27–38, 40–44, 99–101, 105, 118, 125, 128, 130, 191, 211, 219, 247, 254, 274f, 277, 279, *281, 283, 291, 310*
consummative element, 167ff, 185, 195, 215, *306f*
creation, re-creation, 47ff, 55, 57, 81
culture(s), 23f, 27, 61, 92, 102ff, 125, 192, 205

DESCRIPTIVE–NARRATIVE ELEMENT, 195, 199, 206, 209
dignity of man, 2, 24, 26, 45, 60, 63, 179
diurnal, nyktomorphic, 210ff, 217

ECUMENISM, 1, 4f, 8, 17, 22f, 98, 132f, 211, 220f, 223ff, 262ff, 269ff, 273, 276, 278, *321*
eschatology, end-time, 30, 48, 84f, 100–02, 134f, 147, 149, 154f, 157, 160, 165, 216, 220, 261
eucharist, 182, 186, 196, 205ff, 210, 218, 253, 269, *305*
ex nihilo, 48ff
experience, xi, 240f, 255ff, 261

FAITH, 4f, 11, 15, 18–21, 25–7, 30, 36ff, 41, 45, 99f, 176, 219, 222, 227ff, 241, 255ff, 257, 260, 264, 267, 269, 271, 274
foundation, 5, 7f, 13–15, 21, 41, 87f, *282*
freedom, unfreedom, 30, 67–69, 81, 85, 175, 188f, 232f, 238, 242, 246, 251, 254, 264, 268, 272

GOD, ix–xi, 9, 11, 15, 17, 19, 24ff, 26f, 29, 33, 38f, 41f, 44ff, 59ff, 82, 94, 122ff, 126ff, 135f, 137ff, 146ff, 162, 175, 177f, 181, 194, 197, 221, 230–33, 236, 238, 243, 246, 248, 258, 261, 265ff, 272, 274f, 277f, *294*
'godforsakeness', 131, 133, 135, 138, 149, 160

good and evil, 54ff, 70ff, 210
grace, 25, 29, 31f, 91ff, 104, 113, 119, 158, 232, 238, 240f, 246, 255–66
Great Time, paradisal state, 69, 174ff, 184, 214, 232, *306*

HISTORY, 164, 197, 234, 241f, 247f
holocaust, 53, 56, 63ff, 65, 86, 130, 223, 279, 286, 296
human, humanness, man, 22, 24, 32, 44, 68, 106, 108, 156ff, 179, 187, 232, 234ff, 238, 240f, 244, 246ff, 249f, 277, 252, 254, 257, 259, 270ff, 274, 277f

IMAGINATION, 164ff, 171ff, 176, 184f, 203, 206ff, 208ff, 213, 217
interiorization, 193ff, 198, 204f, 207, 209f, 212f, 215ff

JESUS CHRIST, ix–xi, 2, 6, 8, 13–15, 17, 20f, 23, 32, 34, 37f, 44, 88, 91ff, 98ff, 104ff, 125ff, 129ff, 133, 136, 139f, 144, 146, 149, 154, 164, 178, 188, 190–99, 214–15, 219, 231, 240, 269f, 275, 277, *291, 293, 297, 299, 303, 312*

LOVE, 11, 14–16, 21, 28f, 50–52, 54, 56–58, 63, 95–97, 116–18, 161f, 181ff, 186, 189f, 226, 233, 236f, 239, 263, 265, 268f, 276, 278f, *294, 303*

MAGISTERIUM, 2, 6, 27, 33f, 266f, 275, 277, *284*
malheur, 62f, 119, *289*
marriage, 186, 190ff, 198, *308f*
mystic life, 33, 104, 114, 183, 270

NATURE, rational nature, 232ff, 236ff, 239, 243, 246f, 250f, 253–55, 257, 259ff, 261ff
negativity, 199ff

ORDER, 4f, 8–13, 16f, 19, 21, 23, 26, 30, 32, 41, 233ff, 237–39, 248

PARTICULARITY, imparticularity, ix, 34, 54, 89–91, 101, 178
perfection, perfectibilism, 47, 95, 115, 121, 156, 187f, 241, 261, 263
pluralism, pluriformity, 5, 9, 20–24, 38, 44, 206, 257
polarization, 3, 6
prescriptive element, 168, 195, 198, 200
priest, 23f, 196ff, 250
projection, 172ff
prolepsis, proleptic, 85, 220, 229, *318*

RELATION, relativity, xi, 3, 70, 205ff, 207, 233
repetition, 169ff, 174
resurrection, 100, 132, 138, 147, 154, 158

SACRAMENT(S), 4, 8, 20, 27, 39, 164ff, 177ff, 193ff, 203ff, 211f, 217, 249f, *303, 312, 314f*
salvation (history), 3, 25
sanctification, 95, 227
secularity, 133, 155, 235
sexuality, 102ff, 106–08, 110ff, 179ff, 186, 215, 278, *287, 307f, 310f*
solidarity, 77–81, 83–85, *288*
spirit, 2, 9, 13, 33, 49, 93

THEODICY, 45, 51f, 54, 57, 73f
theologia crucis, 50, 61f, 83, 95,

127, 130ff, 136, 149ff, 156–59, 268, *290, 294, 296f, 299–302*

theology, 7, 15, 23, 25, 40, 45, 68f, 83f, 132f, 136, 149, 153, 206, 228, 241, 244, 256, 260, 266ff, 271, 273, 277f, *286*

three onlys (grace, faith, scripture), 219f, 222, 259

UNFINISHED BUSINESS, 74, 151, 168ff, 207

VIRGIN MARY, 211f, 291f, *310, 314*

WISDOM, 13, 16

woman, feminine, 111, 211f

Word of God, 2, 24, 34, 51, 146, 161, 193, 213, 272, 277

work(s), 227, 229

Index of Names

Note: italicised page numbers indicate references in the Notes section (pp. 281–322)

ADORNO, Theodor W., 156
Albert the Great, *282*
Alcmaeon, *313*
Alexamenos, 83
Alexander III, Pope, 185
Allen, Diogenes, xii, *288f*
Allmen, J. J. von, 212, *314, 316*
Angela of Foligno, Blessed, *290*
Antioch, Council of, 137
Apuleius, *305*
Aquinas, St Thomas, 12, 19, 24, 27, 38, 108, 120, 184, 234–43, 250, 258f, 262, 275, *282, 292f, 297, 321*
ARCIC II, 222
Aristotle, 23, 115, 234, 239, 245, 260, *293, 313*
Armstrong, A. H., *298*
Arnold, W., *294*
Athanasius, St, 86
Auden, W. H., *286*
Auer, Alfons, *307*
Augsburg, Confession of, 243f
Augustine of Hippo, St, ix, 8, 11f, 14f, 21, 24, 29f, 37f, 43, 52–55, 58, 60f, 71, 83, 86, 94, 221f, 227f, 230–39, 241, 245, 263, 267, 275f, *282, 287, 319, 322*

BACHELARD, Gaston, 216f
Baillie, D. M., *299, 304*
Baker, J. A., *294*

Ballachey, E. L., *295*
Balthasar, Hans Urs von, *290, 294f, 303*
Baronius, Cardinal, *320*
Barsley, Michael, *313*
Barth, Karl, 55f, 61, 79, 146, 160, 175, *296, 302f*
Basil of Caesarea (the Great), St, 14f
Bastide, Roger, *305–07*
Bautain, Louis, 275
Beaverbrook, Lord, 90
Bellarmine, Cardinal Robert, *320*
Benjamin, W., 155
Berdyaev, N., *301*
Bernard of Clairvaux, St, 150, *294, 301*
Bernini, Giovanni, *313*
Bérulle, Cardinal Pierre de, *300f, 304*
Bévenot, Maurice, *283*
Biel, Gabriel, 260
Bindley, T. H., *292*
Bligh, John, *291*
Bloch, Ernst, 134, 155, 273, *322*
Böhme, Jacob, *301f*
Bonaventure, St, 241, *282*
Bonhoeffer, Dietrich, 69–71, 277f, *285, 287, 293, 314, 322*
Bossuet, Jacques-Bénigne, 149, 246
Bouyer, Louis, *286*

Bremond, Henry, *294, 300*
British Council of Churches, 36
Bro, Bernard, 190, 199, *303, 310, 312*
Broun, Janice, *284*
Brown, James, 256, *320*
Brown, Norman O., *293, 308*
Brown, Peter, 231, *319*
Bruno de Jésus-Marie, Père, *292*

CALVIN, John, 12, 27, 193
Campenhausen, H. von, *283*
Camus, Albert, 152
Cano, Melchior, 40
Carter, Sydney, *297*
Casas, Bartolomé de las, 244, 252
Casel, Odo, 166, *304*
Cassirer, Ernst, 208, *314*
Caussade, Pierre de, 147
Celsus, 143, 155
Cervini, Cardinal, 245
Chalcedon, Council of, 42, 137, 140
Chantraine, G., *321*
Chappelle, Albert, 199, *312*
Chardon, Louis, 149
Cicero, 40
Clayton, J. P., *292*
Comblin, Joseph, 101, *291*
Condren, Charles du Bois de, 150
Congar, Yves, 8, *281*
Contarini, Cardinal, 244f
Conzelmann, Hans, *281*
Copleston, Frederick C., *319*
Costa, José da, 253
Cox, Harvey, 213
Crenshaw, James L., *288*
Crutchfield, R. S., *295*
Cullmann, Oscar, *281f*
Cyril of Alexandria, St, 89, *303*
Cyril of Jerusalem, St, *306*

DALI, Salvador, 103

Davey, Theodore, *283*
Davis, Charles, *297*
Delumeau, Jean, *320*
Descartes, René, 241, 260
Dillistone, F. W., *306*
Dionysus, *315*
Dodd, C. H., 111, 212, *292, 316*
Dodds, E. R., *285, 295*
Douglas, Mary, 171, 211, *305f, 315*
Drower, E. S., *317*
Dulles, Avery, *284*
Dupré, Louis, *287*
Durand, Gilbert, 203f, 208–10, 213, 216–18, *311, 313–17*
Durand, Yves, *311*
Durrwell, F. X., *138f, 297*

EBELING, Gerhard, 272, *302, 321f*
Eckhart, Johannes, 270
Edelstein, L., 144, *298*
Egenter, Richard, 102, 104, *291f*
Eichmann, A., 31
Eichrodt, Walter, 123, *288, 294*
Eliade, Mircea, 173f, 214, *305, 317*
Ephrem, St, *306*
Epictetus, *288*
Epicurus, 52f
Erasmus, 245f, 270
Erikson, Erik H., 177, *306*
Ernst, Cornelius, 22, *283*
Escott, H., *302*
Eutyches, 107
Evans, E., *304*
Eysenk, H. J., *294*

FEY, H. E., *284*
Florence, Council of, 20, 42, *292*
Forel, Oscar, xii
Forsyth, P. T., *302*
Francis of Sales, St, *317*
Frank, Anna, 60
Freud, Anna, *305*

Freud, Sigmund, 24, 115, 199, 208
Fries, Heinrich, *283*
Fry, Christopher, x

GALEN, 154
Galileo, 247, 253
Galot, Jean, 141f, *298*
Ganoczy, A., *285*
Geiger, L.-B., *286*
Gelluy, Robert, *282*
Giordano, 254
Girard, René, *321*
Glazik, J., 252
Goddijn, Walter, 6, *281*
Goodman, P., 169, *305*
Gray, Jeffrey, *307*
Greeley, Andrew M., 89, *290, 307*
Green, F. W., *292*
Gregory of Nazianzus, St, *300*
Gregory of Nyssa, St, 12
Gregory of Rimini, 261, *321*
Grillmeier, Aloys, *298*

HAIGHT, Roger, *321*
Hammerskjöld, Dag, *286*
Hartshorne, C., *285*
Hebblethwaite, Peter, *281*
Hefferline, R. F., 169, *305*
Hegel, G. W. F., 161, 199, 204, *312*
Hennecke, E., *299*
Hepburn, R. W., 175, *306*
Hermas, 9, *281*
Herodotus, 241
Herzog, Bert, 104
Heschel, A., *300*
Hesiod, *314*
Hick, John, *285*
Hippocrates, *293*
Hirsch, Emanuel, *301*
Hitler, Adolf, 83, *286*
Hobhouse, Stephen, *301*
Höfer, J., *304*

Homans, Peter, *304*
Honigmann, J. J., *303*
Hooker, Richard, 249, *320*
Horkheimer, M., 156
Hormisdas, Pope, 137f
Hornsby-Smith, Michael, *281, 284*
Hudson, Liam, *313*
Hunt, Holman, 103
Hunter, A. M., *302*

IGNATIUS OF ANTIOCH, St, *315*
Ignatius Loyola, St, *301, 309*
Irenaeus, St, 12, 86, *281f*
Isler, Elfriede, xii
Iserloh, Erwin, 270, *322*

JAEGER, Werner, *283*
Janelle, Pierre, *320*
Jansenius, Bishop of Ypres, 252
Jedin, Hubert, 244, *319f*
Jeremias, Joachim, *292*
John II, Pope, 137f
John Chrysostom, St, *306*
John of the Cross, St, *292*
John Paul II, Pope, 3, 17f, 20, 24, 29, 42f, 277
Julian, Pelagian bishop of Eclanum, 231
Jung, C. G., 171, 208, *305, 314*
Jüngel, Ernst, xi, 277, *322*
Justin, 14, 214

KANT, Immanuel, 72
Käsemann, Ernst, 57, 80f, 221, *285, 289, 293, 318*
Keck, L. E., *316*
Kelly, J. N. D., 10, *282, 285*
Kennedy, John G., *303*
Kierkegaard, Søren, 51f, 123f, *286, 294*
King, Martin Luther, 82
Kirk, G. S., 204, *305f, 313, 317*
Klinger-Willstedt, D., *281*
Koestler, Arthur, 31, *284*

Köhnlein, Manfred, *302*
Kolbe, Maximilian, 58, 82
Koutsouvilis, A., *288*
Krech, D., *295*
Küng, Hans, 2, 6, 160, 197, 222f, 270f, *281, 289, 311, 318, 322*

LABBÉ, Yves, *287*
Laeuchli, Samuel, *294f*
Laishley, Francis, xii
Lapide, Cornelius a, 179
Lash, Nicholas, *312*
Lateran Council, Fourth, 42, 161
Lavalette, Henri de, *296*
Law, William, *301*
Lawrence, D. H., 184
Laynez, Diego, 248, *320*
Leeming, Bernard, *281, 304, 306*
Leibnitz, Gottfried, 71f
Le Men, J., 200f, *312, 317*
Leo the Great, St, 89
Leonardo da Vinci, 248
Lévi-Strauss, Claude, 203f, *314f*
Lhermitte, Jean, 117, *294*
Lloyd, G. E. R., *312–14*
Loevenich, W. von, *297*
Lohfink, Norbert, 174, *304, 306*
Lombard, Peter, 82
Lonergan, Bernard, 21, 241, *283, 297f, 319*
Lord, Elizabeth, xii
Lorraine, Cardinal of, 244
Lortz, Joseph, 271, *322*
Lowrie, W., *286*
Lubac, Henri de, 11, 30, 276, *282, 284*
Lucian, 75
Luther, Martin, 8, 12, 24, 67, 94, 151, 193, 219, 222, 233, 241, 243, 245f, *255–70, 275, 296f, 302, 321*

MCCUE, James, 266, *321f*
McGrath, A. E., *297*

McIntyre, John, *292*
Macquarrie, John, 190, *310*
Mailer, Norman, 184
Maio, Romeo di, 254, *320*
Malinowski, B., *305*
Manns, Peter, 271, *322*
Manson, T. W., 116, *293*
Marcuse, Herbert, 157
Markus, R. A., 242, *319*
Marsyas, *315*
Martensen, Hans L., *301f*
Martin, Malachi, *290*
Marx, Karl, 204, *273*
Mary of the Incarnation, *301*
May, Rollo, 117, *294*
Meilli, R., *294*
Melanchthon, Philipp, 37f, 236
Menéndez, Josefa, *292*
Meslin, Michel, 105f, 109, *292, 302*
Metz, J.-B., 157, *291, 296*
Meyer, Harding, 224, *318*
Moltmann, Jürgen, 61, *132–35, 138, 141, 145–55, 157–62, 289f, 293f, 296f, 299–303*
Moore, Sebastian, 195, *311*
Morris, Desmond, 188, *307–09*
Moule, C. F. D., 109, *292*
Muggeridge, Malcolm, 132
Münzer, Thomas, 273
Murray, Robert, *293, 309f*
Musurillo, H., 215, *317*

NATIONAL PASTORAL CONGRESS (Liverpool), 2, 34
Naylor, P. I. H., *294*
Needham, Rodney, *313*
Nestorius, 89
Newman, John Henry, 94
Nicaea, Council of, 107, *299*
Nichols, P., *291*
Nietzsche, Friedrich, 269, *286, 296*
Nineham, Dennis, 106, *292*

OCKHAM, William of, 260
O'Hanlon, D., 281
O'Malley, John, 273f, 322
Opus Dei, 2
Orange, Second Council of, 84
Origen, 300
Orpheus, 315
Osborn, Eric, 283

PANGRAZIO, Archbishop, 8
Pannenberg, Wolfhart, 220, 291
Parmenides, 313
Psacal, Blaise, 21, 51, 252
Passmore, John, 293
Paul, St, 8f, 13f, 31, 82f, 91, 94f,
    98, 101, 114, 116, 118, 127,
    152, 221–23, 229–31, 233,
    257, 261, 267
Paul VI, Pope, 28f
Peacocke, A. R., 285
Perls, F., 169, 305
Pesch, Otto, 258f, 271, 321
Peter the Fuller, 137f
Peterson, Eric, 305
Philo, 299
Phipps, William, 292
Pius IV, Pope, 251
Pius XI, Pope, 8
Pius XII, Pope, 312
Plato, 52, 215, 293
Plotinus, 52, 64f, 298
Pole, Cardinal, 248
Pope, Alexander, 59, 144, 284
Prickler, Fernando Guillén, 300
Prosper of Aquitaine, 84, 290

RAHNER, Karl, 18f, 22f, 26, 41,
    70f, 133, 146, 153, 198, 282–
    85, 287, 297, 299, 312, 318,
    320
Ratzinger, Joseph Cardinal, 157,
    318
Raven, C. F., 121, 294
Redfearn, Tracy, xii
Regensburg, Colloquy of, 245

Renan, Ernest, 120
Rhymer, Joseph, 312
Richards, John, 295
Richardson, Alan, 299
Ricoeur, Paul, 54
Rigby, Peter, 202, 313
Ritzer, K., 308
Robinson, John A. T., x, 90,
    106, 291f, 297, 302
Rodgers, John H., 302
Romero, Oscar, 82
Rosenzweig, 155
Rousseau, Jean-Jacques, 59
Runcie, Robert, 43
Runciman, Stephen, 61
Rupp, Gordon, 266, 321
Ruyer, Raymond, 288

SANDERS, Alex, 295
Savonarola, Girolamo, 115
Scheeben, Matthias Joseph, 304
Scheler, Max, 77f, 288f
Schelling, F. W. J., 72f
Schillebeeckx, Edward, 2f, 6,
    80, 91, 289f
Schlink, Edmund, 285
Schneelmelcher, W., 299
Schoonenberg, Piet, 287
Selwyn, E. G., 317
Semionides, 314
Seripondo, Girolamo, 244–47,
    249, 264
Sertillanges, P., 286
Shaw, D. W. D., 298
Sheed, Rosemary, 297
Sixtus V, Pope, 251
Sjöberg, L., 286
Smedt, Bishop de, 7
Smith, Ronald Gregor, 294
Socrates, 52, 63, 65, 72
Sölle, Dorothee, 78, 289
Speck, J., 287
Springsted, Eric, 288
Stalin, Joseph, 83
Stein, Edith, 297

Steiner, George, *286, 296*
Stern, Karl, *310*
Strawson, P. F., *306*
Suarez, Francisco, 251
Surin, Kenneth, 54, *285*
Süss, Théobald, 258, *321*
Swenson, David F., *285*
Sykes, S. W., *292*

TANNER, Ralph, xii
Tatian, *281*
Tauler, Johannes, 270
Tavard, George H., *318, 320*
Teilhard de Chardin, Pierre, 47, 90, 186f, 276
Teresa, Mother, 60
Teresa of Avila, St, *313, 317*
Tertullian, 9f, 144, 230, *282*
Thielicke, Helmut, *320*
Thils, G., 32
Thomassinus (Louis de Or Thomassin d'Eynac), *304*
Thucydides, 241
Tillich, Paul, 117f, 182f, 189, *307f, 310, 314*
Toffanin, Giuseppe, *320*
Toon, Peter, *319*
Torrance, Thomas G., 16, 268, *283, 289, 321*
Towler, Robert, *312*
Trent, Council of, 13, 15f, 42, 222, 240, 243–55, 262, 269, 276, *283, 295, 319, 321*
Trethowan, Illtyd, *306*
Turner, Victor W., 180, 202–04, 207, 209, *291, 307, 313–15, 317*

URBAN VIII, Pope, 253

VARONE, François, 75, *288*
Vasse, Denis, 65f, *287*
Vatican Bank, 30
Vatican Council, First (Vatican I), 16, 40, 42, 220, 276f, *283, 295*
Vatican Council, Second (Vatican II), 1–7, 16–18, 20–22, 26, 32, 34, 36f, 39, 41–44, 100, 128f, 220f, 247, 250, 264, *281, 283, 316, 320f*
Verres, 231
Virgil, 241
Voltaire, F. M. Arquet de, 59f, *286*
Vorgrimler, Herbert, 7, 9, *281, 283*

WALSH, Michael, xii
Watson, James D., *313*
Weil, Simone, 62f, 81, *286, 288f*
White, Victor, 158, *305*
Whitehead, A. N., *285*
Wicks, Jared, *321*
Wiesel, E., *297*
Wile, I. S., *313*
William of Auxerre, 11
William of St Thierry, *294, 301*
Wilson, R. McL., *299*
Wolff, Hans Walter, *321*
World Council of Churches, 36

YARNOLD, E., *305f*
Young, Frances, 82

ZERNOV, W., *301*